Lecture Notes in Artificial Intelligence　　9433

Subseries of Lecture Notes in Computer Science

LNAI Series Editors

Randy Goebel
University of Alberta, Edmonton, Canada
Yuzuru Tanaka
Hokkaido University, Sapporo, Japan
Wolfgang Wahlster
DFKI and Saarland University, Saarbrücken, Germany

LNAI Founding Series Editor

Joerg Siekmann
DFKI and Saarland University, Saarbrücken, Germany

More information about this series at http://www.springer.com/series/1244

Jörg P. Müller · Wolf Ketter · Gal Kaminka
Gerd Wagner · Nils Bulling (Eds.)

Multiagent System Technologies

13th German Conference, MATES 2015
Cottbus, Germany, September 28–30, 2015
Revised Selected Papers

 Springer

Editors
Jörg P. Müller
Technische Universität Clausthal
Clausthal-Zellerfeld
Germany

Gerd Wagner
Brandenburg University of Technology
Cottbus
Germany

Wolf Ketter
Erasmus University Rotterdam
Rotterdam
The Netherlands

Nils Bulling
Delft University of Technology
Delft
The Netherlands

Gal Kaminka
Bar Ilan University
Ramat Gan
Israel

ISSN 0302-9743   ISSN 1611-3349 (electronic)
Lecture Notes in Artificial Intelligence
ISBN 978-3-319-27342-6   ISBN 978-3-319-27343-3 (eBook)
DOI 10.1007/978-3-319-27343-3

Library of Congress Control Number: 2015955909

LNCS Sublibrary: SL7 – Artificial Intelligence

This Springer imprint is published by SpringerNature
The registered company is Springer International Publishing AG Switzerland

Preface

This book contains the proceedings of the 13th German conference on Multiagent System Technologies (MATES 2015), which was held September 28–30, 2015, in Cottbus, Germany. The MATES conference series aims at the promotion of and cross-fertilization between the theory and application of intelligent agents and multiagent systems (MAS). It provides an interdisciplinary forum for researchers and members of business and industry to present and discuss the latest advances in agent-based computing with prototyped or fielded systems in various application domains.

The MATES 2015 conference was organized in cooperation with the Distributed Artificial Intelligence chapter of the German Society for Informatics (GI), and sponsored by the GI. Moreover, it was co-located with the 45th Symposium of the German Society for Informatics (INFORMATIK 2015). It also contained a joint session on "Multiagent Systems for Smart Energy" in cooperation with the GI Special Interest Group on energy information systems.

The set of regular MATES 2015 conference talks covered a broad area of topics of interest including MAS platforms and engineering, benchmarking and scalability, innovative and emerging applications, Smart Things working together (which was also the main motto of this year's MATES conference), as well as quality aspects of MAS. In keeping with its tradition, MATES 2015 also offered two excellent invited keynotes by well-known, reputed scientists in the domain, covering relevant topics of the broad area of intelligent agent technology: Tom Holvoet from Katholieke Universiteit Leuven, Belgium, addressed the support of decentralized, cooperative, anticipatory traffic management using a novel, multiagent-based concept called "Delegate MAS"; Wolf Ketter from Erasmus University, Rotterdam, gave a vivid presentation of issues of sustainability in the context of his work on the *PowerTAC* initiative.

Furthermore, the MATES doctoral consortium (DC) program, chaired by Nils Bulling, offered PhD students a platform to present and to discuss their work in an academic professional environment. Students presented their PhD projects in joint sessions receiving feedback and suggestions from their peers and experienced researchers. Moreover, each PhD student was assigned a mentor offering the student the opportunity to interact with an expert in the field on an individual basis. The mentors gave personalized feedback on the students' work and provided advice for their (academic) career development.

Overall, we received 27 submissions. Each paper was peer-reviewed by at least three members of an international Program Committee (PC). Eleven papers were accepted for long presentation, and two papers were accepted for short presentation. This volume includes selected and thoroughly revised contributions from the MATES 2015 conference, an invited paper, and extended abstracts of the best contributions to the DC. Each revised paper was reviewed again by two additional members of the MATES PC to yield the camera-ready versions contained in this book. It is our hope that the balanced set of theoretical and application-oriented contributions contained in this volume will stimulate further research in multiagent systems and technologies.

As co-chairs and on behalf of the MATES Steering Committee, we are very thankful to the authors and invited speakers for contributing to this conference, Nils Bulling for chairing the DC and editing the DC contributions for this volume, the PC members and additional reviewers for their timely and helpful reviews of the submissions, as well as the local organization team of Gerd Wagner at BTU Cottbus, who also maintained the MATES 2015 conference homepage. They all contributed in making MATES 2015 a success. We are also indebted to Alfred Hofmann and the Springer LNAI team for their very kind and excellent assistance in publishing these proceedings and for their continuing support of the MATES conference over the past 13 years.

Finally, we hope you enjoy the proceedings of MATES 2015 and draw some useful inspiration and insights from the contributions.

October 2015

Jörg P. Müller
Wolf Ketter
Gal Kaminka
Gerd Wagner
Nils Bulling

Organization

The MATES 2015 conference was organized in colocation with the 45th Symposium of the German Society for Informatics (INFORMATIK 2015), and in cooperation with KI 2015 and with the GI Special Interest Group on Energy Information Systems.

MATES 2015 Chairs

Jörg P. Müller   TU Clausthal, Germany
Wolf Ketter   Erasmus University Rotterdam, The Netherlands
Gal Kaminka   Bar-Ilan University, Israel

Local Organizing Chair

Gerd Wagner   BTU Cottbus, Germany

Doctoral Consortium Chair

Nils Bulling   TU Delft, The Netherlands

Program Committee

Vicent Botti   Universidad Politecnica de Valencia, Spain
Lars Braubach   University of Hamburg, Germany
Nils Bulling   Delft University of Technology, The Netherlands
Arthur Carvalho   Erasmus University, The Netherlands
John Collins   University of Minnesota, USA
Massimo Cossentino   National Research Council of Italy
Célia Da Costa Pereira Université Nice Sophia Anipolis, France
Mehdi Dastani   Utrecht University, The Netherlands
Paul Davidsson   Malmö University, Sweden
Yves Demazeau   CNRS - LIG, France
Joerg Denzinger   University of Calgary, Canada
Frank Dignum   Utrecht University, The Netherlands
Juergen Dix   Clausthal University of Technology, Germany
Barbara Dunin-Keplicz   University of Warsaw, Poland
Ulle Endriss   ILLC, University of Amsterdam, The Netherlands
Torsten Eymann   University of Bayreuth, Germany
Maksims Fiosins   TU Clausthal, Germany
Maria Ganzha   University of Gdańsk, Poland
Katie Genter   University of Texas at Austin, USA
Maria Gini   University of Minnesota, USA
Paolo Giorgini   University of Trento, Italy
Vladimir Gorodetsky   Russian Academy of Science, Russia

Daniel Hennes	European Space Agency, France
Axel Hessler	DAI-Labor, TU Berlin, Germany
Koen Hindriks	Delft University of Technology, The Netheralands
Benjamin Hirsch	EBTIC/Khalifa University, UAE
Max Hoffmann	RWTH Aachen University, Germany
Sabina Jeschke	RWTH Aachen University, Germany
Micha Kahlen	Erasmus University, The Netherlands
Stamatis Karnouskos	SAP, Germany
Matthias Klusch	DFKI GmbH, Germany
Franziska Klügl	Örebro University, Sweden
Andrew Koster	Samsung Research Institute, Republic of Korea
Winfried Lamersdorf	University of Hamburg, Germany
Paulo Leitao	Polythechnic Institute of Braganca, Portugal
Matteo Leonetti	The University of Texas at Austin, USA
Yixin Lu	VU Amsterdam, The Netherlands
Arndt Lüder	Otto-von-Guericke-Universität Magdeburg, Germany
Felipe Meneguzzi	Pontifical Catholic University of Rio Grande do Sul, Brazil
Ingrid Nunes	UFRGS, Brazil
Eugénio Oliveira	Universidade do Porto - LIACC, Portugal
Andrea Omicini	Alma Mater Studiorum–Università di Bologna, Italy
Sascha Ossowski	Rey Juan Carlos University, Spain
Marcin Paprzycki	Polish Academy of Sciences, Poland
Mathias Petsch	TU Ilmenau, Germany
Paolo Petta	Austrian Research Institute for AI, Austria
Alexander Pokahr	University of Hamburg, Germany
Alessandro Ricci	University of Bologna, Italy
Jörg Rothe	Universität Düsseldorf, Germany
Jordi Sabater Mir	IIIA-CSIC, Spain
René Schumann	HES-SO Western Switzerland
Onn Shehory	IBM Research, Israel
David Sislak	Czech Technical University in Prague, Czech Republic
Michael Sonnenschein	University of Oldenburg, Germany
Andreas Symeonidis	Aristotle University of Thessaloniki, Greece
Matthias Thimm	Universität Koblenz-Landau, Germany
Ingo J. Timm	University of Trier, Germany
Adelinde Uhrmacher	Universität Rostock, Germany
Rainer Unland	University of Duisburg-Essen, Germany
Leon van der Torre	University of Luxembourg, Luxembourg
Birgit Vogel-Heuser	Technical University of Munich, Germany
Gerhard Weiss	University of Maastricht, The Netherlands
Michael Weyrich	Universität Siegen, Germany
Franco Zambonelli	Università Degli Studi di Modena e Reggio Emilia, Italy
Thomas Ågotnes	University of Bergen, Norway

Additional Reviewers

Alexia Fenollar Solvay
Katie Genter
Max Hoffmann
Micha Kahlen
Julian Kalinowski

Gaurang Phadke
Thiago Rúbio
Luca Sabatucci
Daniel Castro Silva
Daniel Urieli

Doctoral Consortium PC Members

Lars Braubach
Jürgen Dix
Christian Guttmann
Wolfgang Ketter
Franziska Klügl
Brian Logan
Felipe Meneguzzi
John-Jules Meyer
Jörg P. Müller

Sascha Ossowski
Jordi Sabater Mir
Michael Thielscher
Matthias Thimm
Ingo J. Timm
Rainer Unland
Leon van der Torre
Cees Witteveen

Doctoral Consortium Mentors

Wolfgang Ketter
Jörg P. Müller
Alexander Pokahr

Ingo J. Timm
Rainer Unland

MATES Steering Committee

Matthias Klusch	DFKI GmbH, Germany
Winfried Lamersdorf	Universität Hamburg, Germany
Jörg P. Müller	TU Clausthal, Germany
Sascha Ossowski	Universidad Rey Juan Carlos, Madrid, Spain
Paolo Petta	University of Vienna, Austria
Ingo Timm	Universität Trier, Germany
Rainer Unland	Universität Duisburg-Essen, Germany

Contents

Selected Extended Abstracts of Doctoral Papers

MAS Engineering, Modeling, and Simulation

Tailoring Agent Platforms with Software Product Lines

Lars Braubach, Alexander Pokahr$^{(\boxtimes)}$, Julian Kalinowski, and Kai Jander

Distributed Systems Group, University of Hamburg, Hamburg, Germany
{braubach,pokahr,kalinowski,jander}@informatik.uni-hamburg.de

Abstract. Agent platforms have been conceived traditionally as middleware, helping to deal with various application challenges like agent programming models, remote messaging, and coordination protocols. A middleware is typically a bundle of functionalities necessary to execute multi-agent applications. In contrast to this traditional view, nowadays different use cases also for selected agent concepts have emerged requiring also different kinds of functionalities. Examples include a platform for conducting multi-agent simulations, intelligent agent behavior models for controlling non-player characters (NPCs) in games and a lightweight version suited for mobile devices. A one-size-fits-all software bundle often does not sufficiently match these requirements, because customers and developers want solutions specifically tailored to their needs, i.e. a small but focused solution is frequently preferred over bloated software with extraneous functionality. Software product lines are an approach suitable for creating a series of similar products from a common code base. In this paper we will show how software product line modeling and technology can help creating tailor-made products from multi-agent platforms. Concretely, the Jadex platform will be analyzed and a feature model as well as an implementation path will be presented.

1 Introduction

Agent platforms have traditionally been considered technical key assets for realizing agent-oriented software, because they offer technical solutions for many agent related implementation aspects like messaging, service discovery, behavior control and more. This view has been originally laid out by FIPA proposing the abstract platform architecture with its corresponding core functionalities [8,9]. In practice, agent platforms have to compete with alternative concepts and implementation technologies including, service-oriented architecture and microservices [19], components [33] as well as many focused frameworks. Based on past experiences with building research as well as commercial systems based on agent technology we noticed that many different usage scenarios for agent technology with quite diverse requirements exist. In many cases it would have been beneficial if only a subset of the agent platform could have been used fostering reduced complexity and a faster understandability of the provided software. Software product lines (SPL) [6] offer a path towards tailor-made products that

© Springer International Publishing Switzerland 2015
J.P. Müller et al. (Eds.): MATES 2015, LNAI 9433, pp. 3–21, 2015.
DOI: 10.1007/978-3-319-27343-3_1

can provide customized feature sets addressing the customer requirements better than one-size-fits-all solutions. Hence, in this paper an analysis is presented, describing steps for a transition of the Jadex agent platform to an SPL. The core contribution of the paper is a derived feature model and a systematical analysis of implementation choices leading to an adoption of three existing implementation techniques as well as the introduction of micro-features.

The remainder of the paper is structured as follows. In the next Sect. 2 motivating scenarios for the application of agent platforms are presented. Thereafter, in Sect. 3 background information on software product lines will be introduced. Section 4 tackles the domain analysis for the given scenarios as well as an asset analysis of the Jadex agent platform and presents the resulting feature models. Afterwards, in Sect. 5 implementation choices for agent platform features are discussed. Related work concerning software product lines and agent technology is presented in Sect. 6 and finally some concluding remarks and an outlook on future work is given in Sect. 7.

2 Usage Scenarios for Agent Platforms

The following sections will present different scenarios for the use of agent platforms and will explain, which features are fundamental for their realization.

2.1 Android

Android is a mobile operating system, designed to run on devices with limited resources. Most Android applications are distributed applications. Internet access is required by 68.5 % of market apps, as a study of the Android permission system indicates [31]. Common application types such as mobile commerce or social networking apps make extensive use of communication features. Those are the application types assumed in the following considerations. Whenever distribution must be handled, some common problems arise. Data serialization, communication protocols and service discovery are some of the problems that are not handled by the Android framework, but required by these applications.

Middleware agent platforms like JADE [2] or Jadex [26] provide useful abstractions for communication. E.g., Jadex, as an agent platform for distributed software development, treats distribution as first-class citizen. Remote service invocations, service discovery and an asynchronous programming model are available as platform services or in the platform API, respectively. Using Jadex for Android application development supplements the missing distribution features, but comes with two main drawbacks:

First, Jadex and Android both provide their own decomposition principles: developers divide their Android apps into Activities and Services. Jadex applications are composed of active components. Integrating or merging these design principles is not straight-forward and increases complexity of application design.

Second, to cope with the hardware limitations and performance requirements of a mobile device, a stripped-down platform variant is needed. As application

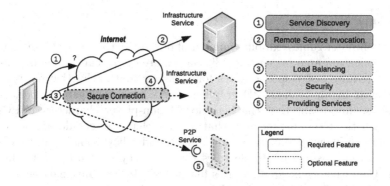

Fig. 1. Android scenario

usage times are often less than a minute, app switching time is crucial [3]. A small platform with minimal runtime components is required, because it enables faster startup times and reduces the chance of the Android system terminating the application during multi-tasking due to low memory.

This platform variant has to include communication and service discovery parts, but not decomposition or behavior logic features, as they are not required for the described application type. Assuming an existing stationary Jadex application, using the Jadex communication principles for linking-up mobile applications parts is a logical consequence, as service interfaces are most likely already defined. An ideal platform variant for this use case would *not require* a mobile app developer to learn about specification and implementation of active components. Instead, he would be able to use remote services transparently from within Android components, e.g., activities and services.

Using Jadex for handling distribution has further advantages when designing more sophisticated distributed systems, too. For example, it handles transport and service security and allows the specification and measuring of non-functional properties, such as service call execution times or current CPU load of service providers. This provides a basis for mobile cloud computing apps that have to decide between offloading a task to the infrastructure or executing it locally, using the optimal alternative at any time. Furthermore, purely distributed applications can be built that communicate in a peer-to-peer manner. Implementing such scenarios using only Android would require a lot of work.

Figure 1 shows the interaction between Android and infrastructure application parts. A basic scenario might use only one server and thus requires *service discovery* (1) and *remote service invocation* (2). A more advanced scenario might use two servers and models a mobile cloud application in which the Android part performs *load balancing* (3) by choosing the best available infrastructure service. One of the servers uses transport *security* (4) to securely transfer data. An interaction with another mobile device is also shown, using *service providing* features on the mobile device end (5).

2.2   Game

Modern computer games exhibit a number of properties that make them an interesting application area for agents [18]. Games are often real-time and dynamic and thus require fast response times for behavior control. Furthermore, games often aim at highly realistic 3D graphics. For a consistent game experience it is thus also important that the behavior of non-player characters (NPCs) is highly realistic, too. This includes that a game character should act according to incomplete knowledge of the world and should follow some consistent long-term objectives instead of simple rules that are easy to figure out for human players. Cognitive agent architectures like SOAR [16] and rational agent architectures like belief-desire-intention (BDI) [28] provide programming abstractions for these aspects. Specifically, BDI seems well suited for programming realistic NPCs, because of its reactive planning approach that fits well with dynamic environments. Despite the good conceptual match, the integration of agent technology in computer games is difficult [7]. One reason for this difficulty is the need for synchronization between the agent platform, executing the agents, and the game engine, executing the game play. For game developers it would be easier, if they could reuse just the reasoning part of an agent platform for controlling NPCs and rely on a sophisticated game engine for a better game experience.

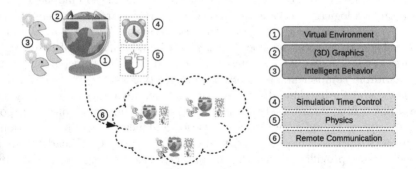

Fig. 2. Game scenario

In Fig. 2, relevant game and agent features are illustrated. The basic case requires at least a *virtual environment* (1) with a *graphics* (2) representation (2D or 3D), provided by a game engine. Furthermore, NPCs with *intelligent behavior* (3) that follows some sophisticated agent architecture would be implemented in an agent programming framework. Regarding possible extensions, e.g., a round-based strategy game might include *simulation time control* (4), which could be implemented either in the game engine or the agent platform. Some game engines also include a *physics* (5) engine that allows realistic behavior of physical objects in the virtual world. Finally, for a networked multi-player game, the *remote communication* (6) features of the agent platform could be employed.

One example of agent/game integration is Jadex-AgentKeeper[1], developed by a student of the University of Hamburg, with some help from an open developer community. In this game, a player exerts indirect control over creatures, by building an environment, e.g. a lair or a training room, to attract and support these creatures (cf. Fig. 3). The game is built using Jadex as an agent platform and the JMonkey game engine[2]. In the current integration approach, the execution is driven by the Jadex platform and JMonkey is merely used for the 3D representation. The advantage of the approach is that all Jadex features can easily be used, such as BDI reasoning for the creatures, simulation time control and remote communication. The disadvantage is a poor integration with game engine features, e.g., the JMonkey physics engine is currently not used.

Fig. 3. Jadex-AgentKeeper screenshot

2.3 Workflow

Workflows represent the automated part of a business process within an organization [34]. They coordinate labor and resources of organizations in order to achieve certain business goals such as fabrication of products, processing customer requests but also internal objectives like accounting. Workflows are generally employed within a certain environment called workflow management system which is used to communicate with internal and external service providers. Such service providers can be invoked through the issuance of work items for human participants or use of service calls in order to interact with external systems.

---

[1] https://code.google.com/p/jadex-agentkeeper/
[2] http://jmonkeyengine.org/

The reference model for workflow management systems released by the workflow management coalition provides a good summary of the functionalities that are often included in such systems [12].

Today, agility has become an increasingly important requirement for many application domains of workflows, i.e. modelling and execution of workflows should be able to adequately react to changing environments. Software agents have been perceived as promising conceptual baseline for making workflows more agile and have e.g. been used to create more stable goal-oriented workflow modeling techniques and corresponding runtimes (based on BDI) [13] as well as parts of workflow management systems [5,14,29].

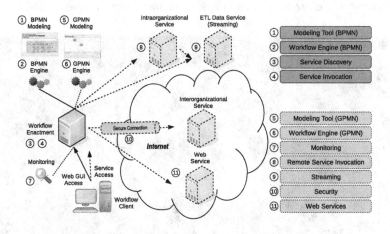

Fig. 4. Use cases and requirements for systems that employ workflows

However, while there are a number of common features that are necessary to support workflows, the exact requirements and support depend on both the business environment as well as the properties of the business processes (see Fig. 4). In order to support a minimal workflow enactment, a certain baseline feature set should be available. First, workflow models have to be produced based on previously identified business processes. This is called process definition in the reference model and requires modeling tools for targeted workflow languages (1). Following the definition of workflow models, the system must be capable of executing workflow instances and therefore requires at least one type of workflow engine such as a BPMN interpreter (2). In some scenarios, business processes have particular sets of requirements [13] which benefit from support of additional workflow engines which can process different types of workflow languages such as more agile ones like GPMN [13] (5) (6).

The third requirements for workflows are support of services, both providing them with a workflow as well as using them as part of a workflow (4). This implicitly requires the means to discover available services in order to bind them to workflow instances (3). Basic workflow management does not necessarily need support for remote communication since in some business environment a traditional centralized approach is sufficient. However, most business scenarios are

more complex. This results either from the organizations themselves being physically distributed as well as technical separation of systems such as automated
production systems and specific server system for, e.g., accounting and e-mail.

This leads to workflow systems quickly requiring the need for calling remote
services (8). While the reference model defines workflow service interfaces in
technologically neutral terms, in many cases the support of remote service calls
must also specifically include web service technology like Rest or WSDL (11).
This is particularly the case if workflows cross organizational lines where web
services are often used as a standardized common ground between organizations.

It is often worthwhile to assess the progress of workflow instances while they
are executing to derive information about the current business situation. Workflow execution data can also later be used to analyze workflow models for reengi-
neering. Thus, it is useful to include monitoring facilities in the system (7).

Finally, some workflow scenarios require additional technical support. For
example, if a workflow is cross-organizational and communicates using public
networks, support for secure service calls may be necessary to protect business
secrets and private data (10). Other workflows like those based on ETL (extraction, transformation, loading) processes need to transfer large amounts of data
in which case support for data streams are helpful (9) [4].

In conclusion, workflow systems have a small set of baseline requirements
which can quickly expand based on the particular business settings in which they
are used. As a result, closely tailoring such systems to the specific requirements
is a promising prospect.

2.4 Summary of the Scenarios

The scenarios presented in this section have been used to introduce interesting features of agent platforms. They show exemplarily, how different subsets of
these features are relevant in different scenarios. Notable differences exist with
regard to the execution environment (Android device, desktop computer, enterprise network) and regarding the distinction between local, intranet and internet
scale. The small overlap regarding the sets of minimally required features in the
different scenarios motivate the need for lean agent platforms specifically tailored
for an intended purpose. Yet, as can be seen by the extended scenarios, useful
applications for advanced features can always easily be found, thus motivating
platforms that include as many features as possible. The next section introduces
software product lines as an approach for achieving both goals simultaneously,
i.e. having lean agent platforms that include as many features as required for a
specific usage scenario.

3   Background on Software Product Lines

Historically, software engineering has always been concerned with reuse of software entities to be able to rely on sound existing solutions and avoid reinventing
the wheel in each development project. Different software concepts have been

put forward fostering reuse including e.g. libraries, components or plugins and visions about markets have been formulated, in which predefined software artifacts/services can be offered and obtained for assembling custom solutions.

In practice, even today reuse remains fairly limited and also markets for reusable software artifacts have not emerged to the envisioned degree. One key reason for low reuse is that artifact producers and consumers are decoupled and the first do not know much about the contexts in which the latter want to use the software. In this respect, software product lines can help and offer a way of enabling *strategic reuse* of software artifacts [6]. The main idea is that a set of similar software products is analyzed according to the requirements and offered features. From a comparison among the products it can be deduced which features are specific for a certain product and which ones occur in many or all of the products. From this analysis, the variability points of a set of software products can be determined and it becomes clear what the common core assets are. Software product line approaches can then help to automate the production of tailor-made products from a common code base by generating and assembling assets according to specific configurations.

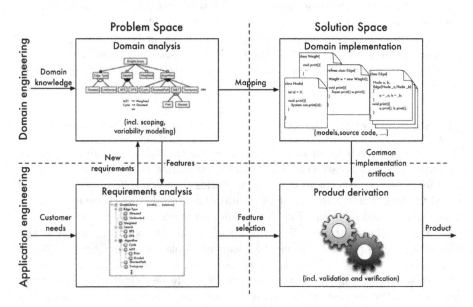

Fig. 5. Software product line overview (from [1])

The overall development activities using a product line approach are illustrated in Fig. 5. In this respect, two subprocesses are distinguished: *development for reuse* and *development with reuse* [17]. The first process is called *domain engineering* while the latter is termed *application engineering*. Domain engineering analyzes the customer requirements and intends to produce a feature model, in which the important features are listed and their domain dependencies are made explicit. A key aspect of a feature model is to identify *variability points*, i.e.

understanding which features are mandatory and which ones are optional and which choices between features exist. Based on the feature model, the implementation of features is performed leading to the core assets of the software product line. During application engineering individual products will be considered and finally produced. The idea is that customer needs for individual products can be described as configurations of the feature model. In such configurations, typically the features for a desired product are selected respecting identified domain constraints. Based on a configuration the concrete product implementation can then be generated by assembling and tying together previously created core assets. An important aim of software product lines consists in the complete automation of the product generation based on configurations.

4 Feature Modeling

The result of a domain analysis is a model of the desired features and their interrelations. Feature modeling is usually performed by identifying notable features and building up a feature tree using refinement and generalization of the identified features. Although there is currently no formal standard for feature modeling, the basic concepts are more or less agreed upon: Refinement can come in four forms - *mandatory* sub features (all of n sub features), *optional* sub features (0..n of the sub features), *or*-refinement (1..n of the sub features), and *alternative* sub features (exactly one of n sub features). The generalization can be distinguished into *concrete* features that can directly appear in a product and *abstract* features that are used to group a related set of sub features. Feature modeling is usually performed as part of the domain analysis, i.e., coming from requirements for potential products and identifying commonalities and variabilities. Another approach with a similar result is asset analysis of an existing software product. Here the focus is on identifying the variabilities with regard to the available assets. The following sub sections will show both approaches, first a domain analysis coming from requirements and second an asset analysis of an existing agent platform.

4.1 Domain Analysis

Figure 6 shows intermediary results of the domain analysis process with regard to the scenarios presented in Sect. 2.[3] The first step (Fig. 6a) is to include all the features mentioned in the different scenarios. Afterwards these features can be refined and generalized. e.g., in (Fig. 6b) the *Intelligent Behavior* and the two *Workflow Engine* features have been grouped below an abstract *Behavior* feature. An OR-decomposition is used to indicate that the abstract Behavior feature required at least one concrete sub feature, but it is also allowed to have multiple ways of behavior in the same scenario (e.g. BPMN and GPMN workflows in the same application). Additionally, all the features related to services,

---

[3] The feature model has been edited with the FeatureIDE eclipse plugin: http://wwwiti.cs.uni-magdeburg.de/iti_db/research/featureide/.

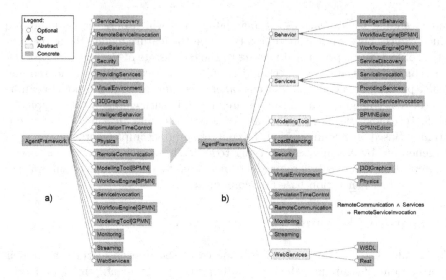

Fig. 6. Steps of the domain analysis process

as well as the modeling tools are grouped in a similar way. A different case can be seen for the *Virtual Environment*. Here, the *(3D)Graphics* and the *Physics* feature have been identified to be part of the more general virtual environment. Yet the virtual environment can be used without graphics or physics, therefore the virtual environment feature is not abstract. An exemplary refinement is shown for the *Web Services* feature. Here, it is assumed that the underlying technology is part of the requirements and thus *WSDL* and *Rest* have been modeled as separate features. Not all relationships between features can be modeled as trees. For more complex cases, constraints can be specified that further restrict, which subsets of features may form a valid selection. E.g. in Fig. 6b a constraint is included to express that when both *Remote Communication* and *Services* are used than the *Remote Service Invocation* feature should also be present ($RemoteCommunication \land Services \Rightarrow RemoteServiceInvocation$).

4.2   Asset Analysis

The general process of a bottom-up asset analysis has some similarities to the more top-down domain analysis. In both approaches, features are identified and later generalized or refined to identify their relationships. The main difference is that the domain analysis derives features by analyzing customer needs, while the asset analysis derives features from existing software modules. So the first defines a model of systems-to-be, while the latter provides a model of the current software base.

Figure 7 shows a bottom-up analysis of the features available in the Jadex agent platform (see, e.g., [26]). The diagram allows identifying the main variation points regarding *System, Behavior, Platform,* and *Tools.* Jadex currently runs

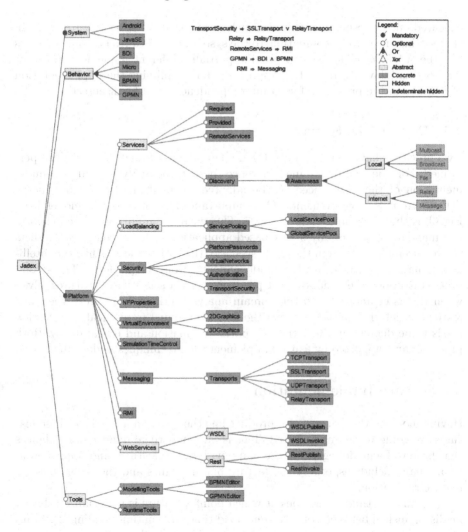

Fig. 7. Jadex features

on *Android* and *JavaSE* systems. Agents in Jadex can be implemented according to one of many *Behavior* models, including *BDI* [28] agents and *BPMN* [23] processes. The *Platform* feature is a container for many different features regarding the execution of agents in distributed environments, e.g., *Messaging*, *Security*, etc. Finally, to aid the developer during the implementation and testing of agent applications, *Tools* are provided, each of which is related to one or more platform or behavior features.

While many of the features in the diagram can be easily mapped to software modules (e.g., *SSLTransport*), it is obvious that the some features are crosscutting in that they influence the implementation of other features. E.g., the Android and JavaSE features define the possibility of the platform to be executed on the respective system, which means that all other features used in that settings need to be compatible to the system, too. As a result, some features like the *XMLEncoding* need to provide partially different implementations for Android and JavaSE. In Sect. 5, approaches for simplifying the implementation of features in the presence of such interdependencies will be discussed.

4.3 Usage of the Feature Models

Two processes have to follow after the domain and asset analysis have been performed. For one, the remaining differences need to be analyzed and the implementation of the assets needs to be adapted to finally fit the feature model derived from the requirements. One important difference to the model from Fig. 6b is the platform feature in Fig. 7. This means that currently the platform is a mandatory part of any Jadex-based application. This currently contradicts the requirement, e.g., from the game scenario, that other features like the intelligent behavior should be available independently from the platform. The second process is about the generation of products from a selection of features. Even when the asset analysis and the domain analysis ultimately produce the same feature model, the steps of deriving the finished product from a feature selection needs to be defined in a way that supports automation and repeatability. Both processes are supported by feature implementation techniques as described next.

5   Feature Implementation

Having modeled the features of a product line the question arises how these features are going to be implemented. This is far from trivial due to many choices that have to be made regarding the mapping between features and implementation. These include especially the feature binding times and the techniques for feature realization.

The binding time determines at which point a feature is materialized. It can be distinguished between compile time, load time and runtime binding [1]. Compile time binding occurs before compilation and is realized, e.g. by preprocessors. In case of load time binding, feature selection is performed at startup of the program, while with using runtime configuration also on demand feature activation is possible. On first sight this sounds as if load and runtime configuration should be preferred due to flexibility and simplicity regarding the build process which could be kept the same for all products but the problem is that deployment artifacts are an important factor, too. First, the product size is important, because also lightweight variants should be producible for resource limited devices. Second, all-in-one products contain dead code belonging to features that cannot be activated. This has drawbacks regarding security (dead code could contain security breaches) as well as compliance (there are domains in which dead code is prohibited like in avionics [22]).

5.1   Analysis of Implementation Techniques

Implementation techniques can be subdivided into language-based and tool-driven approaches [1]. The first category includes *parameters, frameworks, components* as well as *feature- (FOP)* and *aspect-oriented programming (AOP)* while especially preprocessors and build systems fall into the latter category.

Parameters are passed to the software at startup and can be used to activate or deactivate features accordingly. Frameworks typically expose specifically built-in extension points that can be exploited by plug-ins. In this respect, plug-ins can be used to realize features. Components are based on a contractual definition of what is offered to others and what is expected from the context in terms of provided and required services. This makes components also suitable for feature implementation. Finally, feature- and aspect-oriented programming have been devised for building features. Feature-oriented programming assumes a compositional approach in which feature code is combined mainly by refining core functionalities [27] whereas in aspect-oriented programming crosscutting behavior is defined in aspects and afterwards woven into the base code by using pointcuts [15].

Regarding tool-driven feature realization especially preprocessors are a simple to use technique commonly used in practice. Finally, also build systems can be used as basis for realizing product variants by integrating highly customizable build profiles. In [1] a general introduction and comparison of these approaches is available. In the following the presented implementation techniques will be discussed in light of requirements that are of specific importance to the Jadex agent platform. The main requirements are:

- The implementation technique should provide an evolutionary transition path instead of demanding a reimplementation of large facets of the system. This is especially important because the Jadex code base is large (>300.000 LOC) and the developer resources are scarce (<5 programmers).
- The code and resources structuring should not have to strictly follow the feature structure as the structure of the existing Jadex code base reflects the natural bottom up partitioning of functionalities.
- The code cleanness should not be destroyed by introducing features as implementation aspects, i.e. the code should be understandable by developers even without dedicated feature tools possibly creating product-specific views [1].
- A solution for the crosscutting feature problem [11] has to be provided by the implementation technique, i.e. it must be possible to implement features demanding code changes in a series of other features.
- The optional feature problem [1] has to be solved by the implementation technique. The key question of this problem is where glue code should be located that handles interaction with another optional feature.
- The deployment should be highly customizable. Features should be composable of various types of artifacts besides source code (e.g. documents as well as test cases) and only necessary features should be included in the resulting deployment artifacts.

	Evolutionary Transition	Flexible Structure Mapping	Code Cleanness	Crosscutting Feature Problem	Optional Feature Problem	Deployment
Parameters	+	+	- (if used on detailed level)	-	- (check every invocation)	-
Frameworks	- (if more than one framework) + (otherwise)	+	+	-	- (check if plug-in available)	+
Components	+	+	+	-	- (check if service available)	+
FOP	-	-	= (with views) - (otherwise)	-	- (where to put glue code)	+
AOP	-	-	= (looks good but hides information)	+	- (where to put glue code)	+
Preprocessors	+	+	-	=	- (check every invocation)	+
Build systems	+	-	n/a	-	-	+

Fig. 8. Technique comparison

In Fig. 8 the results of the requirements analysis for feature implementation is depicted. It can be seen that none of the techniques is perfectly suited and all have specific strength and weaknesses which is in line with previous findings supporting the idea of combining multiple implementation techniques [10].

It becomes apparent that novel languages based techniques like FOP and AOP expose many disadvantages when considering the transition of an existing code base towards features in contrast to an implementation from scratch. This fact is also supported by a refactoring case study that tried to create a feature based version of Berkley DB by using FOP and AOP [30]. The study revealed that code quality was rather reduced than improved by using aspects for creating features because many crosscutting dependencies needed to be created. Furthermore, the optional feature problem was hard to tackle because aspects had to change the implementations of all usage points of optional features.

From the comparison it can be also seen that the framework and components approach exhibit rather the same strength and weaknesses which is comprehensible due to their conceptual similarities. Both mainly have weaknesses with respect to the crosscutting and the optional feature problem but are otherwise well suited for a transition towards a feature based implementation. It has to be noted that most frameworks impose a certain program structure (inversion of control principle). For this reason a transition should avoid using more than one framework at the same time to keep the programming model comprehensible for the developers. Using preprocessors nearly all problems can be solved but at the high price of code tangled with conditional statements (cf. #ifdef hell [32]). Parameters are similar to preprocessors but operate at the runtime level so that conditional code remains within an application. Finally, it can be seen that build systems alone are not capable enough for a transition towards a product line due to weaknesses in many of the requirements.

5.2   Jadex Implementation Decisions

The aforementioned analysis led to a decision towards a combination of three different techniques: *parameters, components* and *build system*. The main idea is using a completely component-based design with service dependencies as key variability element. Following this path, most features can be directly mapped to components and each feature should be represented by a domain interface encapsulating its functionality. This allows for realizing a black-box feature view so that implementation dependencies between different features can be reduced to a very high degree due to information hiding. Furthermore, this is completely in line with the existing implementation of the Jadex platform, which has been built following the active components approach [26] so that feature decomposition remains rather non-invasive regarding the existing code base. As the core functionalities of the platform itself are encapsulated as components and the platform itself is a component as well, parameter configuration could be introduced to customize the platform at startup by activating or deactivating features. Components are a runtime feature combination technique and thus incur a slight performance penalty. For our scenarios until now this penalty was negligible. Yet, for some mobile and gaming scenarios, when peak perfomarnce is of the essence, build-time techniques such as code-weaving or preprocessors might be required.

To tackle the optional feature problem, in the spirit of microservice architectures [19] all components have to be developed in a failure tolerant way, i.e. it has to be assumed that all services may fail and that appropriate failure mitigation code is in place to handle such occurrences. The crosscutting feature problem remains tough but also does not occur very often in the Jadex platform so that we try to tackle it with custom solutions.[4] Two important features with crosscutting functionalities are the system feature and the behavior features. The system feature determines the target operating system and is crosscutting because the APIs of Java standard edition and Android differ in several places or implement functions with different semantics. This means the compilation of desktop/android variants is only possible if not supported API calls/imports are stripped out (e.g. android bluetooth api, awt/swing). Classes requiring those must be excluded from build or have to be manually refactored to not use those APIs. To avoid preprocessor usage we decided to hide sensible calls behind interfaces of abstract classes for which operating system dependent implementations are provided during the build.

The crosscutting problem within agent behavior is even more challenging because the programming model depends on features of the platform and should also work completely without a platform (for game environments). To address this issue we introduced the notion of *microfeatures* representing small cross-

---

[4] It has to be noted that the crosscutting feature means that the implementation of a feature touches multiple other features while the optional feature problem refers to the usage of another optional feature which might not be present. The latter problem seems to occur much more often than the former. Even typical crosscutting aspects like monitoring and security only lead to the optional feature problem, because they often can be implemented in one feature but need to be used from many places.

cutting behavior portions that can be activated and deactivated on a global manner for all kernels (representing agent architectures) as well as individually for each agent (e.g. to run agents with minimal memory footprint). The complete behavior is then composed of different microfeatures from which some are general for all kernels (such as provided and required services, message handling, basic lifecycle feature) and others encapsulate kernel specific functionalities such as a (BDI semantics feature). The component API reflects this by exposing a `getFeature(FeatureInterface)` method, which can be used to access microfeature specific functionalities (like `sendMessage()` on a message handling feature). The realization of this kernel architecture required a dependency resolution mechanism being developed that creates features in the intended order.

The overall mapping of features to the deployment artifacts is currently handled by a profile based build system, which creates deployment artifacts according to the predefined and not freely selectable feature set. Yet, the fully automated composition of platform features is still ongoing work and requires an explicit feature mapping being defined from the problem to the solution space. We intend to follow a transformation approach similar to that proposed in pure::variants[5].

6   Related Work

Software product lines and agent-oriented software engineering have been subject of several previous works but none has analyzed in how far agent platforms may benefit from features and variability considerations. For this reason two different topics are discussed separately in more detail. On the one hand, it will be presented how reusability and tailoring has been tackled within agent platforms and on the other hand work on combining software product lines with agents will be investigated.

In general, it can be observed by analyzing existing agent platforms like JADE [2] and LS/TS [35] that there is no special focus on extension and tailoring. Nonetheless, most platforms allow for predefined variability that is realized by parameterization as well as by shipping products for different target environments. JADE offers versions for J2ME and Android while LS/TS ships a personal, business and enterprise edition including more functionalities as well as the capability to run in an JEE environment. In addition to that, the open source platform JADE also offers predefined extension points within the platform based on a service-oriented approach. This led to the development of many third-party add-ons for JADE e.g. offering new transport mechanisms or web service integration. In LS/TS the idea of agent kernel has been identified as important extension point. LS/TS ships with kernels implementing different agent architectures like BDI and task based. Building different editions as well as tailoring is done manually for both.

Regarding the connection of software product lines with agents quite diverse proposals can be found. [24] introduces a rather general comparison of AOSE

---

with SPLs highlighting how they could conceptually benefit from each other but without presenting a concrete approach. Most other contributions tackle the problem how agent software can be used as modeling and implementation technique for product line features and how the development process differs in this respect. In [20] it has been considered how BDI agents can be used for feature implementation and how variability can be defined in terms of BDI. In addition to feature definition also MAS specific domain engineering processes have been proposed e.g. in [21,25]. The main objective in their work consists in introducing a systematic process for developing MAS based product line architectures that can be used as core assets for product generation. This is more difficult than with object-oriented technologies because it remains rather unclear what a feature should comprise on the implementation layer in agent orientation so that it can be automatically composed as part of the application engineering.

7 Conclusion

Today, numerous agent platforms exist, that often provide a multitude of features, whereas in different applications scenarios for agents often only a subset of these features is required. For developers, lean agent platforms are desirable, not only regarding a small runtime footprint, but also regarding the distribution (e.g. to avoid confusion due to irrelevant API and documentation). Moreover a lean distribution is preferred in production environments, e.g., to avoid security vulnerabilities due to dead code.

Software product lines are an approach for strategic reuse, e.g., identifying commonalities and variabilities for a set of products and developing assets (code, documentation, ...) to build many products from a set of assets. The main focus of SPL is feature modeling, i.e. describing requirements as a feature tree and mapping features to assets. Different approaches and tools exist for automatically generating software products from feature and asset models.

This paper has discussed the use of SPL technology to aid in tailoring agent platforms for specific use cases. Based on illustrative scenarios, the domain analysis process for an agent platform product line has been presented. Moreover a bottom-up feature analysis of the Jadex agent platform has been performed and next steps with regard to a Jadex SPL have been proposed. In this respect, possible approaches for feature implementation have been investigated and suitable solutions for Jadex have been identified. Furthermore, with microfeatures a novel approach for handling the crosscutting feature problem at agent kernel level has been introduced. It decomposes an agent kernel into its functionally minimal parts (lifecycle, messaging, ...) and allows for configuring kernels horizontally at a very detailed level.

The complete transition of Jadex to an SPL of agent platforms is still work in progress. As future work, we expect to develop further tools and techniques in the feature implementation area to achieve code-cleanness in the presence of crosscutting and optional feature problems. The ultimate goal is to have an easily extendable and maintainable automated build process for the current and future configurations of the Jadex platform.

References

1. Apel, S., Batory, D., Kästner, C., Saake, G.: Feature-Oriented Software Product Lines: Concepts and Implementation. Springer Publishing Company Inc., Heidelberg (2013)
2. Bellifemine, F., Bergenti, F., Caire, G., Poggi, A.: JADE - a java agent development framework. Multi-Agent Programming: Languages, Platforms and Applications. Multiagent Systems, Artificial Societies, and Simulated Organizations, vol. 15, p. 25. Springer, New York (2005)
3. Böhmer, M., Hecht, B., Schöning, J., Krüger, A., Bauer, G.: Falling asleep with angry birds, facebook and kindle: a large scale study on mobile application usage. In: Proceedings of the 13th International Conference on Human Computer Interaction with Mobile Devices and Services, pp. 47–56. ACM, New York (2011)
4. Braubach, L., Jander, K., Pokahr, A.: High-volume data streaming with agents. In: Zavoral, F., Jung, J.J., Badica, C. (eds.) IDC 2013. SCI, vol. 511, pp. 199–209. Springer, Heidelberg (2013)
5. Buhler, P.A.: A Software Architecture for Distributed Workflow Enactment with Agents and Web Services. Ph.D. thesis, Columbia, SC, USA, AAI3157120 (2014)
6. Clements, P., Northrop, L.M.: Software Product Lines: Practices and Patterns. Addison-Wesley Longman Publishing Co. Inc., Boston (2001)
7. Dignum, F., Westra, J., van Doesburg, W., Harbers, M.: Games and agents: designing intelligent gameplay. Int. J. Comput. Game Tech. 2009, 18 (2009)
8. FIPA. FIPA Abstract Architecture Specification. Foundation for Intelligent Physical Agents (FIPA), Document no. FIPA00001, December 2002
9. FIPA. FIPA Agent Management Specification. Foundation for Intelligent Physical Agents (FIPA), Document no. FIPA00023, December 2002
10. Gacek, C., Anastasopoules, M.: Implementing product line variabilities. In: Proceedings of the 2001 Symposium on Software Reusability: Putting Software Reuse in Context, SSR 2001, pp. 109–117. ACM, New York (2001)
11. Groher, I., Krueger, C., Schwanninger, C.: A tool-based approach to managing crosscutting feature implementations. In: 7th International Conference on Aspect-Oriented Software Development (AOSD). Springer (2008)
12. Hollingsworth, D.: Workflow management system reference model. In: Workflow Management Coalition (1995)
13. Jander, K., Braubach, L., Pokahr, A., Lamersdorf, W., Wack, K.-J.: Goal-oriented processes with GPMN. Int. J. Artif. Intell. Tools (IJAIT) 20(6), 1021–1041 (2011)
14. Jander, K., Lamersdorf, W.: Jadex WfMS: Distributed workflow management for private clouds. In: Networked Systems 2013 (2013)
15. Kiczales, G., Lamping, J., Mendhekar, A., Maeda, C., Lopes, C.V., Loingtier, J.-M., Irwin, J.: Aspect-oriented programming. In: Proceedings of the European Conference on Object-Oriented Programming (ECOOP 1997), pp. 220–242 (1997)
16. Lehman, J.F., Laird, J., Rosenbloom, P.: A gentle introduction to Soar, an architecture for human cognition. Invit. Cogn. Sci. 4, 212–249 (1996)
17. van der Linden, F., Schmid, K., Rommes, E.: Software Product Lines in Action: The Best Industrial Practice in Product Line Engineering. Springer-Verlag New York Inc., Secaucus (2007)
18. Nareyek, A.: Review: intelligent agents for computer games. In: Marsland, T., Frank, I. (eds.) CG 2001. LNCS, vol. 2063, p. 414. Springer, Heidelberg (2002)
19. Newman, S.: Building Microservices Designing Fine-Grained Systems. O'Reilly Media, Secaucus (2015)

20. Nunes, I., de Lucena, C.J.P., Cowan, D., Alencar, P.: Building service-oriented user agents using a software product line approach. In: Edwards, S.H., Kulczycki, G. (eds.) ICSR 2009. LNCS, vol. 5791, pp. 236–245. Springer, Heidelberg (2009)

21. Nunes, I., Lucena, C.J.P., Kulesza, U., Nunes, C.: On the development of multi-agent systems product lines: a domain engineering process. In: Gomez-Sanz, J.J. (ed.) AOSE 2009. LNCS, vol. 6038, pp. 125–139. Springer, Heidelberg (2011)

22. Special C. of RTCA. DO-178C, software considerations in airborne systems and equipment certification (2011)

23. OMG. Business Process Model and Notation (BPMN) Specification. Object Management Group (OMG), version 2.0 edition, February 2011

24. Peña, J., Hinchey, M., Ruiz-Cortés, A.: Multi-agent system product lines: challenges and benefits. Commun. ACM **49**(12), 82–84 (2006)

25. Peña, J., Hinchey, M.G., Ruiz-Cortés, A., Trinidad, P.: Building the core architecture of a NASA multiagent system product line. In: Padgham, L., Zambonelli, F. (eds.) AOSE VII / AOSE 2006. LNCS, vol. 4405, pp. 208–224. Springer, Heidelberg (2007)

26. Pokahr, A., Braubach, L.: The active components approach for distributed systems development. Int. J. Parallel, Emerg. Distrib. Syst. **28**(4), 321–369 (2013)

27. Prehofer, C.: Feature-oriented programming: a fresh look at objects. In: Akşit, M., Matsuoka, S. (eds.) ECOOP 1997. LNCS, vol. 1241. Springer, Heidelberg (1997)

28. Rao, A., Georgeff, M.: BDI Agents: From theory to practice. In: 1st International Conference on Multi-Agent Systems (ICMAS 1995), pp. 312–319. MIT Press (1995)

29. Reese, C., Ortmann, J., Moldt, D., Offermann, S., Lehmann, K., Carl, T.: Architecture for distributed agent-based workflows. In: Proceedings of the 7th International Workshop on Agent-Oriented Information Systems (AOIS-2005), pp. 42–49 (2005)

30. Rosenmüller, M., Apel, S., Leich, T., Saake, G.: Tailor-made data management for embedded systems: a case study on berkeley db. Data Knowl. Eng. **68**(12), 1493–1512 (2009)

31. Sarma, B., Li, N., Gates, C., Potharaju, R., Nita-Rotaru, C., Molloy, I.: Android permissions: a perspective combining risks and benefits. In: Proceedings of the 17th ACM Symposium on Access Control Models and Technologies, pp. 13–22. ACM (2012)

32. Spencer, H., Collyer, G.: #ifdef considered harmful, or portability experience with C News. In: USENIX Summer Technical Conference, pp. 185–197 (1992)

33. Szyperski, C., Gruntz, D., Murer, S.: Component Software: Beyond Object-Oriented Programming, 2nd edn. ACM Press and Addison-Wesley, New York (2002)

34. Weske, M.: Business Process Management Concepts, Languages, Architectures. Springer Verlag, New York (2007)

35. Whitestein Technologies. Developer Guide, LS/TS Release 2.0.0 edition (2006)

A Metrics Framework for Quantifying Autonomy in Complex Systems

Christopher-Eyk Hrabia$^{(\boxtimes)}$, Nils Masuch, and Sahin Albayrak

Faculty of Electrical Engineering and Computer Science, DAI-Labor,
Technische Universität Berlin, Ernst-Reuter-Platz 7, 10587 Berlin, Germany
{christopher-eyk.hrabia,nils.masuch,sahin.albayrak}@dai-labor.de

Abstract. Autonomous systems, often realized as multi-agent systems, are envisioned to deal with uncertain and dynamic environments. They are applied in dangerous situations, e.g. as rescue robots or to relieve humans from complex and tedious tasks like driving a car or infrastructure maintenance. But in order to further improve the technology a generic measurement and benchmarking of autonomy is required. Within this paper we present an improved understanding of autonomous systems. Based on this foundation we introduce our concept of a multi-dimensional autonomy metric framework that especially takes into account multi-system environments. Finally, our approach is illustrated by means of an example.

Keywords: Artificial intelligence · Autonomous systems · Autonomous robots · Metrics · Intelligent systems · Adaptive systems · Multi-agent systems

1 Introduction

Modern computer and robotic systems assist humans in almost every situation in workaday life. It is always the goal to simplify human life by delegating either unpleasant or dangerous tasks to artificial systems. These tasks are becoming more and more complex, facing uncertainty in their execution environment and require robust and flexible solutions. Examples range from robotic vacuum cleaners [29] to artificial personal assistants for task and time management [18] to military drones in combat.

Designing systems for uncertain environments is a challenging task. Especially because engineers are unable to foresee all conditions, interactions and influences a system will have to deal with in advance during specification and development. Sometimes there is even a general lack of information.

The term *autonomous systems* is widely used for systems that are able to deal with such situations. Many researchers are trying to improve concepts and technologies behind. As objectives of autonomous systems perfectly match to the ones of multi-agent systems the latter's paradigm is often used for realization.

In order to properly design and develop such systems we need to identify the important aspects and means to create measurable goals we can improve

© Springer International Publishing Switzerland 2015
J.P. Müller et al. (Eds.): MATES 2015, LNAI 9433, pp. 22–41, 2015.
DOI: 10.1007/978-3-319-27343-3_2

in future. For an iterative advancement it is required to benchmark and measure these systems during the development process in their application context. Furthermore, selecting an appropriate system for a required autonomy level in a particular scenario requires a quantification of autonomy, too. In our opinion there is still a lack of a widely accepted concept of autonomous systems or robots that contains a detailed definition according to different aspects and a clear distinction to other system concepts. Moreover, the consequences of bringing several different systems together are unclear.

The remainder of the paper is structured as follows. In Sect. 2, we give an overview about the variety of definitions and understandings of the term *autonomous system* and take a deeper look on metrics that are being proposed to measure such systems. Subsequently, in Sect. 3, we classify autonomous systems in relation to other system types and present our own definition of an autonomous systems. A context-specific multi-dimensional metric to control and benchmark autonomous systems is proposed in Sect. 4. In order to apply our multi-dimensional metric framework Sect. 5 highlights necessary considerations, whereas Sect. 6 illustrates the application with an artificial example. Finally, in Sect. 7, we summarize our work and outline open issues and future steps we want to work on.

2 Related Work

In order to come up with a definition of autonomous systems we will give an overview about state-of-the-art definitions and further focus on the particular metrics on which they rely.

2.1 Autonomous Systems Definitions

A review over existing literature about autonomous systems and agents reveals that there still does not exist one major agreement on definition or understanding of a concept of autonomy in computer and software systems. The developed definitions are usually depending on a specific problem or application domain and therefore are only looking on the concept from a limited perspective.

A simple and common understanding of autonomous systems derives directly from the literal translation of the word autonomy, which has ancient Greek origin and means self-government. This interpretation is used by Castelfranchi [8], often extended with a general independence from other entities [12]. In [10] the authors mention unpredictability and goal-directedness as the main aspects of autonomous systems. Moreover, they define self-directedness as the general substance of autonomy. Luck et al. [16] are also considering self-directedness or self-government, but propose the ability of goal generation based on an inner motivation or drive as the key component of an autonomous system. Further, motivation is seen as a higher-level non-derivative component that characterizes the nature of agents. The definition of autonomous systems as entities generating own goals suits also the concept of self-government.

Close to the motivation of autonomous systems that are supposed to deal with unforeseen environmental conditions is the concept of adaption. In [1] it is stated that autonomy and adaptability are interconnected and decision making requires adaption to the environment. These ideas are in accordance with the visions of the promoters of autonomic computing [15] and organic computing [25] as well. They understand self-adaptability as major property for the realization of software that can manage itself at runtime. Furthermore, self-adaptability is considered as the foundation of other envisioned self-* properties.

A different approach is presented by Barber et al. [3]. They have identified three distinct types of intervention in an autonomous agent: modification of environment, influence over beliefs and intervention in the decision-making process. In their opinion only the two last types have to be considered for autonomy-altering. Hence, they focus on independence on decision-making to pursue an agent's goal as well as independence of control over its own belief state [3,4].

One major concern of autonomy concepts is the requirement for an adjustment of the granted independence in general or a specification of a context defined by other systems or humans. As a consequence, some work is focused on the so called "adjustable autonomy" [11]. This adjustment is always seen as an outer influence on autonomous systems, though reducing the independence of systems from other entities. A common idea is the usage of policies and rules for different autonomy related properties. Scerri et al. [23] and Tambe et al. [28] focus on the aforementioned decision making capabilities. Further extensions aggregate all restrictions in role models [31]. Bradshaw et al. [5] present a formal framework for the description of action policies. They differentiate in possible, available and obligated actions that are arranged on a prescriptive and descriptive layer, representing self-directedness and self-sufficiency. Another perspective on policies is given by Myers et al. [19] as a specification for the autonomy context. This also includes possibilities of human consultation from the system's perspective. Additionally, the importance of such kind of behaviour is considered in [17], too.

Some research focusing on independence has created concepts of different areas of autonomy. An explicit external perspective of autonomous systems in a complete relational structure with classifications for user, social-dependence, norm, environment and self-autonomy is presented by Carabelea et al. [6]. Moreover, the authors mention the existence of an inner layer of autonomy focusing on the decision making process. Another work also focuses on the relational structure of independence in a hierarchical holonic agent organisation and hence classifies it into different kinds of autonomy [24]. The existing classes are skill and resource, goal, representational, deontic, planning, income, exit and processing autonomy. Verhaegen et al. [30] distinguish between natural and artificial agents, but focus as well on the aspect of independence in different areas like norms, external stimuli and motivations.

The presence of different layers of autonomy in an autonomous system is discussed by Castelfranchi et al. [9] and Maheswaran et al. [17] and was as well mentioned by Carabelea et al. [6]. In the context of adjustable autonomy there exists control from outside over a system itself and control from the perspective of the system on how or if it decides to transfer decision-making control to other entities [6]. Then again, Castelfranchi et al. [9] understand autonomy as a matter of power, with internal and external aspects. External aspects describe conditions for actions or resources, internal aspects define system abilities, skills and resources.

Further, most of the shown literature has a strong focus on single systems for their consideration of autonomy. Exceptions are made by Carabelea et al. [6], who show the concept of delegation of decision-making capabilities, as well as in the work of Scerri et al. [23] and Tambe et al. [28]. Moreover, the importance of dependence from other entities for the creation of a belief model is demonstrated [4], too.

At least, it seems there is an existing agreement, that autonomy needs to be evaluated and compared in a specific context or with respect to some goal, because a system could behave autonomously in one situation and non-autonomous in a different context [3,5,6,27].

In summary, the presented literature shows that both self-government as well as self-directedness based on an inner motivation are important aspects of an autonomy concept. Further, a general independence of the system, especially for decision making, belief management, actions and resources accessibility has to be considered. In addition, the capability of adapting to the environment is strongly interconnected with autonomy. Moreover, we see that an autonomous system seems to have different layers, usually seen as inner and outer parts. Also, an autonomous system is always related to other systems; therefore the influence from other systems, as well as the delegation of the system itself needs to be examined. However, we see that all these aspects have not yet been combined into a single concept.

2.2 Autonomous Systems Metrics

Existing publications on autonomous systems come up with a variety of properties that can affect the degree of autonomy. In the following we subsume these aspects under different metrical categories of autonomy.

Interaction: most of the publications describe the degree of necessary interaction with or observation by external entities in order to fulfil the implicit task of a system as an important category for autonomy. The authors in [7] discuss the term of autonomy for spacecrafts and deduce that it depends on the tracking intensity and the amount of communication between vehicle and ground. [32] also states that autonomy mostly represents the ability to assign the system's goals without any or with only minimal external intervention. The authors in [3] are more precise and state that they do not see the principal interaction with the environment as autonomy-altering. In their opinion it is more important to look whether there are instances that can change the environment in a way that the system changes its behaviour, which would be an indirect influence and autonomy-limiting factor.

Permissions, Norms, Obligations: these aspects are a refinement of the inter-action category. In [5] the authors state that autonomy largely depends on the attribute of self-directedness, which means that the system can decide without external influences. In general, the freedom of an autonomous system can either be limited by explicit restrictions (norms or obligations) or extended by permissions which extend a principal behavioural restriction.

Quality: the degree of quality represents a level-based scheme for defining autonomy. In [4] the authors do so by setting different levels on the system's belief autonomy, which can either be manipulated by external entities or by the quality of the system's perception.

Uncertainty: an autonomous system implicitly sets the expectation of being able to at least fulfil its intended goals. Since in most cases the environment is dynamic and sometimes also unpredictable, uncertainty is a category that autonomous systems have to deal with. As a consequence, it can be stated that the higher the level of uncertainty of the environment is the more autonomous the system (always under the assumption of fulfilling its goals) [32].

Technical Aspects: some of the publications come up with pragmatic measurements like the time of ignorance [7,20], which represents the time a system can be ignored by an external observer while still acting productively. Technical software measures are used by Alonso et al. [2]. The authors measure their determined key attributes of autonomy, which are self-control, functional independence and evolution capability, based on static and dynamic code analysis with properties like complexity of pointers and references, number of variables describing the internal state and state update frequency. For example, the functional independence of a system is being measured by using an executive message ratio $EMR = 1 - \frac{ME}{MR}$. MR defines the total number of messages the software agent receives, whereas ME represents all messages the software agent is obliged to respond or react to (e.g. because they were sent by the user the agent represents). According to this definition the system is more autonomous the less instructions the agent becomes via messages.

In conclusion, a lot of aspects have been proposed so far which play a significant role in defining the system's autonomy. However, most of the publications try to focus on very few attributes to define a metric in a particular domain, whereas a comprehensive view that is considering all different aspects together cannot be found so far.

3   Definition and Classification

As the motivation of this paper implies, autonomous systems can be quite different according to the degree of autonomy. None of the systems that exist so far are fully autonomous, so many systems fulfil only parts of existing autonomy definitions and can still be interpreted as autonomous systems. In turn, this makes it quite difficult to define exact bounds that characterize an autonomous system. For this reason, we will define different characteristics that are relevant for deciding whether we are dealing with a system that is autonomous or not.

There is not only the criteria of autonomy when talking of modern system structures. Many other aspects exist and often they overlap each other. In order to clarify our understanding of autonomous systems we will first try to set them in relation to other concepts. Afterwards, we will come up with a comprehensive discussion about autonomous systems themselves.

3.1 Classification

When talking about practical realization of Artificial Intelligence (AI) the term intelligent system is often being mentioned. Rudas et al. [21] define an intelligent system as a system that *"emulates some aspects of intelligence exhibited by nature. These include learning, adaptability, robustness across problem domains, improving efficiency (over time and/or space), information compression, extrapolated reasoning"*. So we can deduce that an intelligent system is an application of AI that is specialized to some sort of challenge and does not have to offer general intelligence. A subclass of intelligent systems are adaptive systems [22], which are able to react to changes of the environment that the developer cannot foresee completely at design time or are even able to find solutions to modified goals.

Autonomous systems in fact can also be intelligent and adaptive systems but do not necessarily have to be so. Automation systems are often classified as a subcategory of an autonomous system. An automation system realizes processes from start to end without human intervention with a clear focus on independence. However, usually the environment may not make changes, which the system developer could not foresee. An example for this would be a thermostat that fully automatically adapts the cooling or heating in order to reach a desired temperature. The state space in the system is clearly defined and it is only able to react on this range. Furthermore, the same input will lead to the same output. So we state that an automation system is autonomous but is usually not an intelligent system. Another important subcategory of autonomous systems are autonomic systems [13,15], whose focus is self-management, with the goal of configuring, healing, optimizing, and protecting itself in order to recover from failures or optimize for changed conditions.

In our opinion the real benefit and also challenge lies within autonomous systems that are simultaneously adaptive systems. In turn, adaptivity infers the necessity to learn from new experiences. These can be external motivations either to change the goals of the system or to find new or better processes to fulfil existing goals. Even more, an autonomous system, which is not considering adaptivity as a key feature of itself, is not able to solve real world problems in dynamic environments. For this reason we will focus on autonomous systems that are as well adaptive systems in the following sections.

3.2 Autonomous System

In the former sections we have argued that adaptability within dynamic environments is the main justification for autonomous systems. Further, we were able to distinguish between adaptive and autonomous systems, with the result that actually all purposeful autonomous systems are adaptive systems, too. Beyond that, an autonomous system from the engineer's point of view does only make sense, if there still exists the possibility of having some kind of influence on the system. In addition, we think that complete autonomy cannot exist at all, because at least the innermost motivation of a system needs to be defined or controlled by something else. On the other hand an autonomous system in the real world is always interacting with other systems and entities, so it is necessary to consider relational aspects in a sufficient definition of autonomous systems. Thus, our definition of autonomous systems includes two layers, an adaptive layer, including all capabilities required to adapt to changing environment and a relational layer, which specifies delegation and dependence on other systems. This corresponds with the existing concepts of self-sufficiency as the adaptive layer and self-directedness as the relational layer [16]. As a consequence we propose a definition of autonomous systems as adaptive systems extended with relational aspects. Within the relational layer there exist two different aspects, the influence from outside and the delegation of duties to other systems (see Fig. 1).

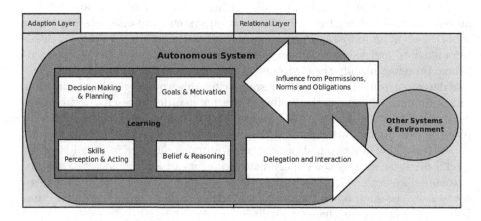

Fig. 1. Layers and capabilities of an autonomous system

The influence from outside corresponds to the popular concept of adjustable autonomy [5,17,19,23,28,31], describing influences on the system independence from another system by restricting available resources and capabilities with the usage of policies, norms or obligations. In this sense a system's autonomy is represented as a percentage of independence in the use of its available capabilities. The other relation direction is more complex, because it is not only a matter if a system delegates duties or not. It has to be considered if the system has just chosen to or if it was necessary to delegate, because it is not having the required capabilities on its own. Another question is, whether the delegation to another system is reliable or not. For example, a system would lose autonomy if it delegates to another system, which it does not fully control, saying it has a reduced reliability. If it delegates to another system which is just a simple automata having 100 % reliability in execution of the delegated task (not included in the reliability are external factors, which the other system cannot control), it would obtain its autonomy. The influence of other entities restricts the autonomy related capabilities of the system.

The inner layer of an autonomous system contains all capabilities that are required to adapt to the environment. Based on the literature, we came up with the following required capabilities: decision making, goal generation or motivation, belief generation and skills for perception and acting. In our opinion not all these capabilities sre required to achieve sufficient adaption. The very important aspect of decision making has to be extended by a more long-term consideration of planning. Belief generation depends on reasoning capabilities, thus it has to be considered as well. Finally, the capability of learning, which is mentioned in some of the discussions about autonomous systems, needs to be added, because in our opinion it is crucial for the whole system adaptability. In the following each of the capabilities is described in further detail.

The available *perception and acting skills* or actions to interact with the environment are important in terms of diversity. For example, a system with a less diverse set of moving capabilities (e.g., only walking besides crawling, driving or swimming) is probably less able to adapt to different ground surfaces, even if it does have a huge number of different leg moving styles. Thus, it is not just the quantity of available skills, in fact the diversity of skills is important.

Like already clarified from the literature, *decision making* is a core aspect of autonomy, but it is not only the resulting independence which makes it necessary. Rather it is the purpose of making the decision to adapt to the changing environment. The capability of planning is closely related, it allows the system to reach its goals factoring in environmental conditions. A system with more advanced planning and decision making features is able to consider changing conditions and as a consequence is able to adapt more quickly and appropriate.

Each system is following some *goals*. These goals are based on a motivation and are somehow entered initially from outside. The difference in the sense of autonomy and adaptability results from the level of abstraction in the goal description. The ability of creating new own goals, or to adapt existing goals is another consideration for improved adaptability.

The *belief state* of a system and its *reasoning capabilities* belong to each other. The system needs to reason from raw input information to create its beliefs. In its simplest form the system consists of reflexive mechanisms in which a rule set is triggered based on the perception. The resulting actions which modify the environment lead to a new perception and therefore a new belief state of the system. However, more complex reasoning capabilities allow for better view of the environment, which is the fundament of each adaption mechanism.

Learning was already highlighted as a crucial capability for an autonomous and therefore adaptive system. The reason for this is the superior character of this capability, enabling the system to improve all other capabilities over time. The other presented capabilities perception and acting skills, decision making, interpretation and creation of goals and reasoning and belief creation make adaption in a changing environment possible, even without learning, but learning will generate enhanced adaptability.

Combining everything our definition of an autonomous system is as follows and as well visualized in Fig. 1:

An autonomous system follows an innermost motivation in an uncertain and dynamic environment by adapting its capabilities in order to fulfil the inferred goals. It has capabilities of perception and acting, decision making and planning, interpretation and creation of goals, reasoning and belief creation for being able to adapt. Learning is superior to the other capabilities, but non mandatory. It can have relational dependence on other systems. If it is delegating its duties to them, its autonomy is depending on their reliability. Further, the relational dependence can lead to restrictions in the use of its capabilities and therefore on its autonomy.

4   Metric

In the last section an improved understanding of autonomous systems was created, which is useful to distinguish from other system concepts. Further, it clarifies the justification and the core motivation and it points out the core characteristics. These core characteristics give a direction for further improvements in making autonomous systems more autonomous in future. On the other hand, it was already shown, that it is not the actual goal to strive for an absolute 100 % autonomous system, rather it is required to create autonomous systems with a clearly defined scope of autonomy and options for external control. For this reason we have developed a multi-dimensional metric for autonomous systems that considers the core capabilities of our understanding of autonomous systems. In order to direct development efforts this metric allows for an relative estimation of the system's development progress by comparing the different states or differences to other existing systems. Further, the metric indicates which capabilities have to be considered and ultimately controlled for external adjustment of the system's autonomy. For example, it points out which characteristics of an autonomous system can be controlled in which range by a human operator in order to enable system operation in the required borders. Similar to the consensus in literature this metric and resulting ratings do only make sense in a specified context.

Our metric introduces several scales based directly on the elaborated core capabilities, namely decision making and planning, goal generation and motivation, belief and reasoning, available skills and learning. Further, it takes into account the two layer concept with external influence and delegation from inside.

As shown in Fig. 1 other systems can have influence on the autonomy of a system. If a system contains one or more subsystems it is dependent on the current scope. Other systems can restrict capabilities to some percentage based on permissions, obligations and norms. Likewise, a system can lose autonomy depending on the reliability of other systems if the system decides to delegate some of its capabilities. For example, another system could restrict the decision making capability in a way that it needs to consult another system on every decision related to its task execution order, resulting in a decreased autonomy of the system. Additionally, the system could delegate its reasoning to another system with perfect communication and 100 % reliability, resulting in no degradation of autonomy (provided that the delegating instance always remains the control to withdraw the delegation). Further, similar to Johnson et al. [14], a measure of autonomy can never describe a system's performance, it only describes the capability of independent adaption to volatile environments, while striving for its goals. Moreover, it is important to point out that it is necessary to determine the weighting between the scales of the multi-dimensional metric in the observed context of the evaluated systems based on the presented concept. This would usually be done by a domain expert.

Besides the general influence by other systems affecting specific capabilities, metrics for particular capabilities and combinations of them are presented below.

4.1 Perception and Acting Skills

The system's skill set including different perception and acting capabilities influences the autonomy by defining the outer bounds of adaptability. If a system does not have the capabilities to retain operation in a given environment or if these capabilities are restricted, it has no chance to adapt. Comparing different system adaption opportunities, the most important aspect is diversity. The quality of the capability is not important, as long as it provides a sufficient quality to achieve the system's goals in general, because we do not want to measure the performance of the system. An ideal system needs a broad range of very different capabilities. For example, a robot with ultrasonic range finders and laser range scanners is able to adapt to environments with transparent surfaces or high frequency sound noise. Having only one of these capabilities would lead to problems in one of these environmental conditions.

As a consequence of this, a dimension for diversity is required. A sufficient option is the Shannon-Index, a well known approach from information theory [26]. It is a quantitative measurement of the number of different available types in relation to the evenness of distribution. A higher number of types together with an even distribution among the skills has the highest diversity. A type refers to a group of sensors or actors providing the same kind of information or realising similar actions. The calculation is shown in Eq. 1, where p_i represents the proportion of capability belonging to the ith type of N possible capabilities in the particular context, with n_i belonging to a particular type of capabilities. H' is the diversity index, a higher number corresponds to a higher diversity.

$$H' = -\sum_{i=1}^{n} p_i \cdot ln(p_i) \quad \text{where} \quad p_i = \frac{n_i}{N} \tag{1}$$

The classification of types has to be adjusted in consideration of the context. The Shannon-Index can be applied for both the perception and the acting skills leading to the functions $H'(P_{Norm})$ and $H'(A_{Norm})$, which are normalized values based on Eq. 9. The total autonomy degree for these capabilities can then be defined as:

$$PA_{SCORE} = w_1 \cdot H'_{P_{Norm}} + w_2 \cdot H'_{A_{Norm}} \tag{2}$$

Both values are weighted according to the context by using w_1 and w_2 with $w_1 + w_2 = 1.0$.

4.2 Belief and Reasoning

The belief describes the state of the environment from the system's point of view which might be imperfect. For that reason it is critical to evaluate the environmental conditions to adapt sufficiently. In order to compare the quality of the belief and reasoning capabilities, different attributes have to be measured: the amount of information the system is able to reason from and the update rate of its belief generation.

The applied measurement methods and units have to be specified for the evaluation context, e.g. number of reasoning input sources multiplied with bandwidth, maximum storage complexity of the belief state and update rate per second.

We propose the following metric as a generic measurement to evaluate the system's belief autonomy which in turn affects the overall autonomy:

$$BR_{SCORE} = w_1 \cdot BIA_{Norm} + w_2 \cdot BUR_{Norm} \tag{3}$$

The belief and reasoning autonomy BR_{SCORE} depends on the amount of belief information BIA (amount of processed perception data) and the belief update rate BUR (frequency of refreshing the belief state) on these information. As it is necessary to normalize these values in order to combine both parameters we propose to utilize BIA_{Norm} and BUR_{Norm}, which are computed using Eq. 9. Both parameters are aggregated using weights w_1 and w_2 with $w_1 + w_2 = 1.0$.

4.3 Learning

In this context the focus of learning is the ability of long-term improvement of single capabilities with the goal of improving the system's adaptability. This is very difficult to measure, because the advantage of learning could only be determined in a direct comparison. Because learning is strongly related to reasoning the proposed measurements can be applied in a similar manner. Especially the amount of information to reason from is relevant for learning in the context of adaptability. By storing historical data the system is able to learn e.g. typical behaviour patterns of the environment. This consideration needs to be distinguished from machine learning performance metrics like precision, recall and accuracy.

$$L_{SCORE} = w_1 \cdot LIA_{Norm} + w_2 \cdot LUR_{Norm} \tag{4}$$

The L_{SCORE} for measuring the learning capability is similar to the BR_{SCORE} in Sect. 4.2. Thus, the single measurement values need to be normalized for the combination as well, see Sect. 4.5. The weights w_1 and w_2 are limited to $w_1 + w_2 = 1.0$, too. In distinction the L_{SCORE} considers the stored historic information used for learning LIA (Learning Information Amount) and the update rate of the possible temporal repeating of the learning method LUR (Learning Update Rate). A temporal repeated learning update on the updated LIA is crucial for an autonomous system for keeping track with the volatile environment.

4.4 Motivation, Goals, Planning and Decision Making

Goals, planning and decision making are fundamental attributes of intelligent systems. Without them a system would be completely static and could therefore not adapt to changing situations.

A system has more possibilities to adapt and is less influenced if it can cope with high level goal descriptions, because in this case it has more degrees of freedom on how to achieve its goals and adapt to changing environments. This is also valid for motivation, which we understand as a very general description of a goal. The ability of decomposing goals into sub-goals and atomic tasks is part of planning. Decision making is the selection of computed plans or alternatives during planning. This in turn leads to the statement that the quality of goal generation, planning and decision making affects the degree of autonomy.

Hence, from the inner perspective of the system these attributes depend heavily on each other. It is not possible to determine if a particular decision fosters adaptability on its own, as long as the system is being able to decide in general. This means, that decision making is only an on/off attribute for the adaption layer and can hardly be quantified more precisely. Thus, decision making is more important for the relational layer of our metric concept, which defines the relation to other systems in terms of independence and reliability. Due to that the adaption layer has to focus on the planning ability of creating a wide range of behaviour possibilities by using task decomposition. Therefore, the aim is to measure the ability of decomposing tasks or goals in as many atomic actions as possible or measuring the level of abstraction in goal descriptions the system is able to understand.

A sufficient measure could determine the mean number of atomic system actions resulting from a given goal. For example, a less adaptable system like a 100 % remote controlled robot has already atomic actions, like "move forward" and "turn right", in its goal description. On the contrary a robot that receives the destination position as a goal can decompose the goal in different ways, enabling the choice of e.g. way points, velocity and locomotion style.

Formally, a goal G can be decomposed into a set of predicates $Pred$ and Tasks T as shown in Eq. 5. A predicate, which is in fact a subgoal, again consists of a set of elements that are either predicates or tasks (Eq. 6).

$$G = \{Pred \cup T\} \tag{5}$$

$$Pred = \{x_1...x_n \mid x_i \in Pred \cup T\} \tag{6}$$

Because of its recursive structure, each goal G can finally be decomposed into a set of atomic tasks. Therefore, $t \in T$ is defined as a task which is atomic and consequently not decomposable. T_G is defined as the amount of all atomic tasks that – in some combination – help fulfilling G.

$$T_G = |\{t \mid t \in T, t \underset{partiallyFulfills}{\longrightarrow} G\}| \tag{7}$$

Equation 8 shows our suggestion of defining the goal and planning autonomy GP_{SCORE}.

The term describes the average fraction between the tasks the system was able to decompose out of the goal (DT_G) and all possible tasks related to a goal for each potential step i. If DT_G contains the same tasks as T_G, then the system has a complete view on the possible task sets for reaching G. In consequence this part reflects the decomposing and planning ability of the system.

$$GP_{SCORE} = \frac{\overline{DT_{G_i}}}{T_{G_i}} \tag{8}$$

In some cases the goal of a system might change over time. The GP_{SCORE} will then be dynamic, which would have to be considered in the evaluation of the system. For instance this can be achieved by aggregating measurements at each state where the system's goal changed at runtime.

4.5 Scaling and Aggregation of the Capabilities

The capability scores together with relational characteristics result in a set of measurements. C_i represents one of the capability scores. In order to interpret and evaluate the results the capability scores have to be scaled and aggregated. Therefore it is required that for particular measurements a greater value corresponds to extended autonomy support and all values are greater than 0. If necessary the measurements have to be quantified and rescaled.

Further, all measurements need to be normalized for being able to compare them with each other, as well as with other systems. We applied unity normalization, shown in Eq. 9. The same normalization approach is used for the normalization of the multiple measurements as part of the capability scores of perception and acting, belief and reasoning and learning. All normalizations are applied before the weighting.

$$C_{\mathrm{Norm}_i} = \frac{C_i - \min(C_i)}{\max(C_i) - \min(C_i)} \tag{9}$$

with C_i as a single capability measurement, $C_i > 0$ and a higher value corresponding to extended autonomy support.

One important aspect is the definition of the maximum and minimum values for these measurements. If several systems or system states are compared in a given context, maximum and minimum are at least defined by the measurement result range of the evaluated systems. If only a single system is evaluated the bounds have to be defined based on domain and system knowledge, planned development roadmaps or envisioned future upgrades. These definitions can also be used to extend the range given by different system measurements in case of a system comparison in order to extend the considered context.

In a next step each capability score C_i is combined with its delegation reliability R_i and restriction influence I_i, as well as a general weighting factor w_i, see Eq. 10. R_i and I_i express the dependence on a percentage basis. If there is no information about restricting influences, we define $R_i = 1.0$ and $I_i = 0.0$ corresponding to neutral values. If the situation is unknown or too complex to estimate an approximation should be used. The weighting factor w_i can be adjusted according to the context and problem domain, but needs to be the same for a comparison amongst several systems. The default configuration weights all capabilities equally within a score, as well as between the scores.

$$C_{\text{Score}_i} = C_{\text{Norm}_i} \cdot w_i \cdot R_i \cdot (1 - I_i) \qquad (10)$$

with $0 < C_i, w_i, R_i, I_i < 1$ and $\sum_{i=1}^{n} w_i = 1.0$

At the end all capability scores C_{Score_i} can be aggregated into a single autonomy score A_{Score}, shown in Eq. 11. This autonomy score with a range from 0..1 allows for an absolute context specific comparison of the considered systems or system configurations. Nevertheless, a detailed comparison considering all capability scores should be preferred most of the time.

$$A_{\text{Score}} = \sum_{i=1}^{n} C_{\text{Score}_i} \qquad (11)$$

5   Metric Application

In the following we discuss required decisions to be made and points to consider when utilizing our metric framework approach.

Context Selection. First, the context of the evaluation has to be defined. This includes the application of the systems, the corresponding environment and the bounds of the studied systems, if they are taken out of a larger context.

Even though the metric framework would support context independent comparisons amongst several systems because of applied normalizations, we do not recommend it. The reason is that some measurements of single capabilities are strongly dependent on the context, like the set of possible tasks belonging to the mission goal or the set of available sensors and actors.

Weight and Capability Selection. Next, the domain expert has to define weights for the relation between capabilities as well as amongst the measurement of single capabilities. This can be used to express priority or importance of a capability in a given context. Induced by the normalization an equal weighting provides a reasonable starting point. Here it would also be possible to omit or extend capabilities and their corresponding measures in correspondence to special requirements, as long as the general concepts of the metric, like normalization, weighting and focusing on adaption, are not violated. It should always be revised, that this metric framework does not try to evaluate the performance of systems, but rather possibilities and capabilities valuable for adaption to uncertain environments.

Adaption Layer: In case of the adaption layer the following important aspects of each capability have to be considered.

Perception and Acting: Available sensors and actors need to be grouped to types. An actor or sensor belongs to one type if it is addressing similar means.

Planning and Goals: T_G and DT_G are abstracted values for a given context, if an abstraction is not possible they can be determined by measuring and averaging during execution in reality or simulation.

Belief and Reasoning: Defining suitable units for information amount and update rate. For instance using the size of the state space or the amount of processed bytes for the BIA and frequency in relation to global time or relative to the refresh frequency of the sensory input for the BUR.

Learning: The learning measures are based on the belief and reasoning, for this reason the same considerations are required. The difference is just the consideration of historic data and the capability of repeated learning on it.

Decision Making: Since decision making can not be evaluated in connection with adaptability, it is only necessary to determine if it is available or not.

All measurements have in common that a greater value corresponds to an extended autonomy support. If necessary the measurements have to be quantified and rescaled for all systems in the same manner. If it is only the intention to evaluate the progress of a single system it is necessary to envision possible future extensions defining the range of single measurements.

Relational Layer. For the relational layer it is necessary to examine if the system's capabilities are influenced by others or if it is known to delegate its duties to other systems. Furthermore, the amount of this relations has to be estimated and discretised to a percentage value. These estimations can be based on averaged frequencies of influence or length of time periods for I_i and error rates or confidence measures for R_i. If there are no restrictions known or can not be determined from historical data external influence is $0\,\%$ ($I_i = 0.0$) and reliability is $100\,\%$ ($R_i = 1.0$).

6   Example

In this section we illustrate the application of our multi-dimensional metric with an artificial example. It was the intention to keep it simple and comprehensible.

The example scenario is represented by different robots that are crawling through a garbage dump in an autonomous multi-robot recycling system. They pursue the goal of recycling as much material as possible. Therefore the robots need to detect valuable and recyclable materials and need to plan collection and transport to the disassembly unit.

In this simple example we have two different types of robotic systems. System A is a wheeled robot with one arm and one gripper. It has a standard 2D-vision, a thermal camera vision and a medium sized multi-purpose computing architecture. Further, it delegates object recognition to a remote web-service with $80\,\%$ accuracy. Moreover, it supports to learn object recognition from the 100 last recognized items. Learning is performed every $60\,\text{s}$. System B is a wheeled robot with two arms and two grippers. It has a standard 2D-vision and small size multi-purpose competing architecture. Furthermore, it is obligated to validate its self-made recognitions by a human $20\,\%$ of the time.

Table 1 shows the domain and scenario specific application of our metric with quantified, adjusted scales and units. For clarification, we have assumed that a less powerful computing architecture results in degraded belief, reasoning and planning capabilities. Hence, a small computing architecture can process smaller information amounts with a lower update rate, as well as less average decomposed subtasks for a given goal. This also illustrates the application of a capability score if not enough information for a full evaluation is available. Here, medium and small are directly taken from the computing architecture description and quantified in the range of 0–4 (extra small, small, medium, large). This exposes further the definition of a custom measurement range. Perception and acting are calculated with the Shannon-Index, see Eq. 1. Because both systems are capable of decision making ($1 = capable, 0 = not\ capable$) the capability is set for both to $C_{\text{Decision Making}} = 1$. This ensures also a valid calculation for the relational component of the capability score C_{Score_i}. For the relational layer we have only the two mentioned statements, highlighted in red, all other cases are either $100\,\%$ $= 1.0$ reliable or have $0\,\% = 0.0$ influence by restriction.

The normalized measurements, the applied default weights for the main capabilities and the measurements as part of their scores and the calculated results for the capability and autonomy score are presented in Table 2. The measurements "Learning Update Rate" and "Belief Update Rate" were rescaled with Update Rate $= 1/$Update Rate. It has to be highlighted that C_{norm_i} of perception and acting are 0 for one of each configurations because of unity normalisation and the used minimal value range.

Table 1. Autonomy metric values of the presented example for both systems

Capabilities		Adaption-Layer		Relational-Layer			
		C_i		Reliability of Delegation R_i		Influence by Restriction I_i	
		System A	System B	System A	System B	System A	System B
Perception and Acting	PA_{Score}						
Perception Diversity		0.35	0.69	1.0	1.0	0.0	0.0
Acting Diversity		0.69	0.35	1.0	1.0	0.0	0.0
Belief and Reasoning	BR_{Score}						
Belief Information Amount		2.0 (Medium)	1.0 (Small)	1.0	1.0	0.0	0.0
Belief Update Rate		2.0 (Medium)	1.0 (Small)	1.0	1.0	0.0	0.0
Decision Making		1 (available)	1 (available)	0.8	1.0	0.0	0.2
Goals and Planning	GP_{Score}	2.0 (Medium)	1.0 (Small)	1.0	1.0	0.0	0.0
Learning	L_{Score}						
Learning Information Amount		100 items	0 items	1.0	1.0	0.0	0.0
Learning Update Rate		1/60 s	∞	1.0	1.0	0.0	0.0

Based on such an evaluation result a system designer can compare two systems in a specific scenario or evaluate which capabilities can be improved in order to increase its autonomy. In the presented example with overall equal weights system A achieves a higher autonomy score as system B, because it has higher or equal capability scores for all capabilities except "perception". This result is even more obvious in the visual representation of the multi-dimensional metric in Fig. 2, where the larger covered area corresponds with a higher autonomy score. In consequence it is possible to select a system with appropriate autonomy based on the score for a scenario or to determine if a planned or implemented extension gives the intended enhancement on capability level or in aggregation.

The presented example has illustrated the process of applying our generic multi-dimensional autonomy metric framework. This, as well as the proposed capability measurements, can be used as a guideline to evaluate and compare autonomous systems in a particular context. Indeed it can be sufficient to adjust

Table 2. Normalized autonomy metric values with default weights, calculated results and aggregation

Capabilities		Weight	Adaption-Layer C_{norm_i}		Relational-Layer				C_{Score_i}	
					Reliability of Delegation R_i		Influence by Restriction I_i			
		w_i	A	B	A	B	A	B	A	B
Perception and Acting	PA_{Score}	0.2	0.50	0.50	1.00	1.00	0.00	0.00	0.10	0.10
		0.5	0.00	1.00	1.00	1.00	0.00	0.00		
		0.5	1.00	0.00	1.00	1.00	0.00	0.00		
Belief and Reasoning	BR_{Score}	0.2	0.50	0.25	1.00	1.00	0.00	0.00	0.10	0.05
Belief Information Amount		0.5	0.50	0.25	1.00	1.00	0.00	0.00		
Belief Update Rate		0.5	0.50	0.25	1.00	1.00	0.00	0.00		
Decision Making		0.2	1.00	1.00	0.80	1.00	0.00	0.20	0.16	0.16
Goals and Planning	GP_{Score}	0.2	0.50	0.25	1.00	1.00	0.00	0.00	0.10	0.05
Learning	L_{Score}	0.2	1.00	0.00	1.00	1.00	0.00	0.00	0.20	0.00
Learning Information Amount		0.5	1.00	0.00	1.00	1.00	0.00	0.00		
Learning Update Rate		0.5	1.00	0.00	1.00	1.00	0.00	0.00		
Autonomy Score	A_{Score}								0.66	0.36

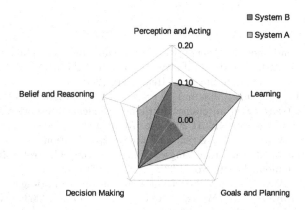

Fig. 2. Multi-dimensional autonomy system comparison with a spider chart

certain capability measurements to the context and the available information, while still respecting all main capabilities and the developed relational concept. Moreover, it has to be incorporated that autonomy values for just one system are not meaningful. They have always to be considered in comparison to other systems or with itself during the development process.

7   Conclusion

In this work we presented an extended understanding of autonomous systems. Moreover, we have differentiated our concept from other system concepts like adaptive systems and automation systems. The core of our autonomy concept is that an autonomous system is always striving for its innermost goal or motivation while it is adapting to the uncertain and dynamic environment. Further, important capabilities were exposed and specified, namely perception and acting, decision making and planning, interpretation and creation of goals, reasoning and believe creation and learning in general. Furthermore, we have introduced a layer concept that contains an adaptation and relational layer. The adaption layer consists of mentioned capabilities and the relational layer models the interaction with other systems. The explicit integration of reliability and independence for modelling the multi-system interaction is an important contribution and clarifies the role of autonomous systems in the context of multi-agent systems.

Based on the definition a generic multi-dimensional metric framework for classification and benchmarking of autonomous systems in a specified evaluation context or domain was developed. This metric allows for a quantified inter-system comparison, controlling and goal specification during the development process.

In the future we are looking for options of defining valid presets of scale combination weightings that can be used as a base for domain experts. Further, we are planning a comprehensive evaluation of the whole concept in several robotic research and development projects within different application domains.

References

1. Alonso, E., Mondragón, E.: Agency, learning and animal-based reinforcement learning. In: Nickles, M., Rovatsos, M., Weiss, G. (eds.) AUTONOMY 2003. LNCS (LNAI), vol. 2969, pp. 1–6. Springer, Heidelberg (2004)
2. Alonso, F., Fuertes, J.L., Martínez, L., Soza, H.: Towards a set of measures for evaluating software agent autonomy. In:Eighth Mexican International Conference on Artificial Intelligence, MICAI 2009, pp. 73–78. IEEE (2009)
3. Barber, K.S., Martin, C.E.: Agent autonomy: specification, measurement, and dynamic adjustment. In: Proceedings of the Autonomy Control Software Workshop at Autonomous Agents, vol. 1999, pp. 8–15. Citeseer (1999)
4. Barber, K.S., Park, J.: Agent belief autonomy in open multi-agent systems. In: Nickles, M., Rovatsos, M., Weiss, G. (eds.) AUTONOMY 2003. LNCS (LNAI), vol. 2969, pp. 7–16. Springer, Heidelberg (2004)
5. Bradshaw, J.M., Feltovich, P.J., Jung, H., Kulkarni, S., Taysom, W., Uszok, A.: Dimensions of adjustable autonomy and mixed-initiative interaction. In: Nickles, M., Rovatsos, M., Weiss, G. (eds.) AUTONOMY 2003. LNCS (LNAI), vol. 2969, pp. 17–39. Springer, Heidelberg (2004)
6. Carabelea, C., Boissier, O., Florea, A.: Autonomy in multi-agent systems: a classification attempt. In: Nickles, M., Rovatsos, M., Weiss, G. (eds.) AUTONOMY 2003. LNCS (LNAI), vol. 2969, pp. 103–113. Springer, Heidelberg (2004)
7. Carraway, G.F., Squibb, J.B.: Autonomy metrics. In: Proceedings of 4th International Symposium on Space Mission Operations and Ground Data Systems, vol. 2, Munich (1996)
8. Castelfranchi, C.: Guarantees for autonomy in cognitive agent architecture. In: Wooldridge, M.J., Jennings, N.R. (eds.) Intelligent Agents. Lecture Notes in Computer Science, vol. 890, pp. 56–70. Springer, Heidelberg (1995)
9. Castelfranchi, C., Falcone, R.: From automaticity to autonomy: the frontier of artificial agents. In: Hexmoor, H., Castelfranchi, C., Falcone, R. (eds.) Agent Autonomy. Multiagent Systems, Artificial Societies, and Simulated Organizations, vol. 7, pp. 103–136. Springer, US (2003)
10. Delaroche, L., Fogel, D.F.L., Freeman, W., Grossbcrg, S., Lee, S., Lima, P., Pouchard, L., Schultz, A.: Measuring performance of systems with autonomy: metrics for intelligence of constructed systems. In: Measuring the Performance and Intelligence of Systems: Proceedings of the 2000 PerMIS Workshop, 14–16 August 2000, vol. 970, p. 4. The Institute (2001)
11. Dorais, G., Bonasso, R.P., Kortenkamp, D., Pell, B., Schreckenghost, D.: Adjustable autonomy for human-centered autonomous systems. In: Working notes ofthe Sixteenth International Joint Conference on Artificial Intelligence Workshopon Adjustable Autonomy Systems, pp. 16–35 (1999)
12. Gouaich, A.: Requirements for achieving software agents autonomy and definingtheir responsibility. In: Proceedings of Autonomy Workshop at AAMAS 2003, vol. 236 (2003)
13. Hinchey, M.G., Sterritt, R.: Self-managing software. Computer **39**(2), 107–109 (2006)
14. Johnson, M., Bradshaw, J., Feltovich, P., Jonker, C., van Riemsdijk, B., Sierhuis, M.: Autonomy and interdependence in human-agent-robot teams. IEEE Intell. Syst. **27**(2), 43–51 (2012)
15. Kephart, J.O., Chess, D.M.: The vision of autonomic computing. Computer **36**(1), 41–50 (2003)

16. Luck, M., D'Inverno, M., Munroe, S.: Autonomy: variable and generative. In: Hexmoor, H., Castelfranchi, C., Falcone, R. (eds.) AUTONOMY 2003. Multiagent Systems, Artificial Societies, and Simulated Organizations, vol. 7, pp. 11–28. Springer, Heidelberg (2003)

17. Maheswaran, R.T., Tambe, M., Varakantham, P., Myers, K.: Adjustable autonomy challenges in personal assistant agents: a position paper. In: Nickles, M., Rovatsos, M., Weiss, G. (eds.) AUTONOMY 2003. LNCS (LNAI), vol. 2969, pp. 187–194. Springer, Heidelberg (2004)

18. Myers, K., Berry, P., Blythe, J., Conley, K., Gervasio, M., McGuinness, D., Morley, D., Pfeffer, A., Pollack, M., Tambe, M.: An intelligent personal assistant for task and time management. AI Mag. **28**(2), 47–61 (2007)

19. Myers, K.L., Morley, D.N.: Policy-based agent directability. In: Hexmoor, H., Castelfranchi, C., Falcone, R. (eds.) Agent Autonomy. Multiagent Systems, Artificial Societies, and Simulated Organizations, vol. 7, pp. 185–209. Springer, Heidelberg (2003)

20. Olsen, D.R., Goodrich, M.A.: Metrics for evaluating human-robot interactions. In: Proceedings of PERMIS, vol. 2003, p. 4 (2003)

21. Rudas, I.J., Fodor, J.: Intelligent systems. Int. J. Comput. Commun. Control **3**(3), 132–138 (2008)

22. Salehie, M., Tahvildari, L.: Self-adaptive software: landscape and research challenges. ACM Trans. Auton. Adapt. Syst. **4**(2), 1–42 (2009)

23. Scerri, P., Pynadath, D., Tambe, M.: Adjustable autonomy in real-world multiagent environments. In: Proceedings of the Fifth International Conference on Autonomous Agents, AGENTS 2001, pp. 300–307. ACM, New York (2001)

24. Schillo, M., Fischer, K.: A taxonomy of autonomy in multiagent organisation. In: Nickles, M., Rovatsos, M., Weiss, G. (eds.) AUTONOMY 2003. LNCS (LNAI), vol. 2969, pp. 68–82. Springer, Heidelberg (2004)

25. Schmeck, H.: Organic computing - a new vision for distributed embedded systems. In: 8th IEEE International Symposium on Object-Oriented Real-Time Distributed Computing (ISORC), pp. 201–203, May 2005

26. Shannon, C.: A mathematical theory of communication. Bell Syst. Tech. J., **27**, 379–423, 623–656, July, October 1948

27. Sierhuis, M., Bradshaw, J.M., Acquisti, A., Van Hoof, R., Jeffers, R., Uszok, A.: Human-agent teamwork and adjustable autonomy in practice. In: Proceedings of the Seventh International Symposium on Artificial Intelligence, Robotics and Automation in Space (I-SAIRAS) (2003)

28. Tambe, M., Scerri, P., Pynadath, D.V.: Adjustable autonomy for the real world. J. Artif. Intell. Res. **17**(1), 171–228 (2002)

29. Ulrich, I.R., Mondada, F., Nicoud, J.D.: Autonomous vacuum cleaner. Robot. Auton. Syst. **19**, 4–233 (1997)

30. Verhagen, H.: Autonomy and reasoning for natural and artificial agents. In: Nickles, M., Rovatsos, M., Weiss, G. (eds.) AUTONOMY 2003. LNCS (LNAI), vol. 2969, pp. 83–94. Springer, Heidelberg (2004)

31. Weiß, G., Rovatsos, M., Nickles, M.: Capturing agent autonomy in roles and xml. In: Proceedings of the Second International Joint Conference on Autonomous Agents and Multiagent Systems, AAMAS 2003, pp. 105–112. ACM, New York (2003)

32. Yavnai, A.: Entropy-based criteria for intelligent autonomous systems. In: Proceedings of the 1991 IEEE International Symposium on Intelligent Control, pp. 55–60, August 1991

Measuring and Comparing Scalability
of Agent-Based Simulation Frameworks

Fabian Lorig$^{(\boxtimes)}$, Nils Dammenhayn,
David-Johannes Müller, and Ingo J. Timm

Business Informatics I, University of Trier, 54296 Trier, Germany
{fabian.lorig,s4nidamm,s4dsmuel,ingo.timm}@uni-trier.de
http://wi1.uni-trier.de

Abstract. While computer simulation gained importance as a technique for generating knowledge in various research disciplines, the size of simulation models representing real world scenarios is growing, too. In Social Simulation, e.g., there is a need to simulate a large number of humans using individual software agents for generating and analyzing human-like behavior in artificial societies. Nowadays, a variety of toolkits and frameworks exists providing functionalities for supporting implementation and execution of simulation experiments. Yet, the choice of a suitable framework is difficult as unforeseen scalability issues may arise when extending agent models. Therefore, this paper aims at providing a method for analyzing and comparing agent-based simulation frameworks regarding their ability to scale simulation models and experiments. Based on performance metrics, standardized experiments are conducted while altering internal and external scaling parameters. As part of the study, four Java-based agent frameworks are analyzed and compared: Aimpulse Spectrum, JADE, MASON, and Repast.

1 Introduction

Computer simulation has been established as a standard means for analyzing, understanding, and developing systems as part of the research process in information systems research. By transferring real world scenarios into executable models, artificial systems representing real processes can be created and analyzed. Doing so provides various advantages regarding further examination and consideration of the system. For one thing there are physical advantages as the real world system is not exposed to any risk during the study, e.g., instability or damage due to experiments, and access restrictions, e.g., in companies, do not apply in simulations. For another thing creating artificial systems using computer simulation provides practical advantages, too. In terms of time and expense, the costs of conducting computer simulation experiments are lower compared to real world experiments. Changes of the experiment setup can be implemented easily and experiments can be repeated any number of times, with the artificial environment staying the same. Furthermore, simulation experiments can be delayed or accelerated, depending on whether detailed observations or fast results are required [1].

© Springer International Publishing Switzerland 2015
J.P. Müller et al. (Eds.): MATES 2015, LNAI 9433, pp. 42–60, 2015.
DOI: 10.1007/978-3-319-27343-3_3

Nowadays, various non-technical research disciplines have added computer simulation to their spectrum of methods, too. Especially in the liberal arts, e.g., economics and the social sciences, the simulation of social phenomena gains in importance for exploring human behavior. Due to the high availability of information and communication technology and the resulting interconnectedness of people, the identification of small and isolated groups to be observed during field studies became more difficult. Hence, larger groups of humans became the focus of empirical observations and studies, e.g., when considering the spread of information in social online networks [8]. Social simulation provides methods for dealing with difficulties resulting from these conditions. By integrating theories and approaches from psychology, sociology or economics, "human-like" behavior can be imitated and simulated. Artificial societies resulting from simulating human behavior can then be used for analyzing group and decision dynamics without observing or surveying humans in the real world [7].

Emergent effects, caused by local interactions between actors within a society which result in a superior meta-behavior of the group, are of special interests for researchers. Thus, when simulating human behavior and group dynamics, these effects need to be generated as well. Instead of using stochastic approaches or sets of differential equations for modeling and simulation resulting in "average behavior", actor-oriented simulation approaches can to be used for modeling of individual human behavior and resulting complex interaction dynamics [9].

When implementing autonomous behavior and decision-making in computer systems, *intelligent software agents* have been established as suitable technique. By defining actions for achieving individual objectives, software agents autonomously reason which goal to pursue and which actions to perform, considering the current and expected future states of their environment [35]. Agent-based social simulation (ABSS), as a special type of social simulation, employs agent-based modeling for performing social simulation experiments [2,4]. Each person involved in scenarios being analyzed using ABSS is modeled as an individual software agent, including behaviors and attitudes as well as opportunities for actions and overarching goals. However, the growing range of humans to be considered during empirical studies is causing the number of software agents required for ABSS to increase, too.

1.1 Challenges in Agent-Based Social Simulation

Nowadays, some ABSS scenarios consist of several hundred thousand up to several million software agents [8,28]. Hence, when executing simulation experiments, the optimal use of available hardware for providing results within an appropriate period of time is a key challenge for simulation engineers. In order to facilitate handling of simulation experiments, numerous toolkits and frameworks providing assistance functionalities for modeling, performing, and evaluating computer simulation have been developed [16]. But this results in a challenge for simulation engineers: *Which toolkit or framework is best suited for a certain simulation experiment?*

When considering small and unsophisticated simulation models, the choice of a suitable simulation toolkit mostly depends on technical and structural aspects of the underlying model. Functions provided by the toolkit for simplifying implementation (e.g., preimplemented FIPA performatives or consoles for controlling experiments) and evaluation (e.g., visualization of results) of simulation experiments are crucial for the decision. In this regard, surveys have compared agent-based simulation platforms highlighting advantages and disadvantages. These comparisons have been mostly done on a descriptive level, gathering features of different frameworks or by rating selected aspects of the frameworks using differing sets of criteria [25, 30].

But as ABSS has to deal with highly sophisticated and extensive models, performance-based features of simulation toolkits are in focus, too. Therefore, *scalability*, describing an increasing performance of a system as a result of increasing hardware, is a major requirement when choosing a framework [34]. For the last 20 years, researchers have been facing scalability issues when simulating real world scenarios, e.g., when simulating communication networks [10] or electric power management [31], especially when using distributed systems [26]. At the same time, a need for developing scalable simulation frameworks has been identified and existing frameworks have been analyzed regarding their ability to scale simulation experiments [6]. Furthermore, in terms of agent-based simulation, scalability has been of particular interest [17, 24, 32] and scalable architectures and frameworks have been developed [11, 14]. But also the decision of whether to execute a simulation experiment distributed over multiple CPU cores or to execute multiple instances of the same simulation experiment using less cores has gained in importance [22, 29].

1.2 Scalable Simulation Frameworks

Even tough the execution and extension of simulation experiments has been considered by some of the framework surveys, the results are mostly limited with regard to the author's perception and experience when implementing certain models using different frameworks. Railsback et al. [23], e.g., have implemented a simple scenario with 100 agents randomly moving on a small grid (100x100 cells) for measuring the performance of simulation frameworks. During their studies, the models has been extended by implementing more sophisticated agent behavior and by adding real-time statistical evaluations, yet, the number of agents has not been greater than 1.700 and the execution time of most of the simulation experiments has not exceeded 5 min.

Comparing popular agent-based simulation frameworks and toolkits reveals that crucial information regarding scalability parameters, e.g., maximum amount of software agents supported or the maximum number of CPU cores supported by the framework, are rarely provided. Yet, such information is most relevant for an informed selection of a framework for a certain task and for determining how simulation experiments need to be designed. Therefore, this work aims at proposing a method for dynamically comparing simulation frameworks regarding their ability to scale simulation experiments. As a first step, parameters influencing a framework's ability to scale experiments are determined. Additionally, performance metrics for measuring these parameters are defined and a five-step-method for comparing frameworks based on these metrics is proposed. Finally, this method is applied to four agent-based simulation frameworks: Aimpulse Spectrum, JADE, MASON, and Repast.

2   Measuring Scalability

The approach for comparing simulation frameworks proposed in this paper is based on different parameters being measured using performance metrics. In this chapter, relevant scalability parameters are introduced and a brief technical overview on the simulation frameworks considered in this paper is given.

2.1   Dimensions of Scalability

Scalability is considered to be "the ability [of a system] to handle increased workload" [34]. In the context of distributed systems, providing and improving scalability has been an important factor challenging developers for years [21]. While performance is defined as how quickly and efficiently a software can accomplish a certain task, scalability describes the change of performance when increasing a system's load.

In case of a dramatical performance decrease resulting from increased load, a system is considered "not scalable" [18]. Song and Korba identified *load* and *complexity* as two main factors influencing the scalability of agent-based systems. The load is derived from the amount of memory and CPU threads used by the multiagent system. Complexity, in contrast, describes the computational effort of an agent-based system [27].

Scalability can be considered from two different perspectives: *vertically* and *horizontally*, also referred to as *scale-up* and *scale-out*. Vertical scalability describes the deployment of one large server providing many CPU cores and sufficient RAM. Horizontal scalability, in contrast, integrates a number of smaller servers into one unit to distribute a system's load [19].

This work focuses on vertical scalability because of the fact that vertical scalability can be examined in every framework whereas the distribution of simulation experiments across multiple servers has to be provided by the frameworks as an additional functionality.

2.2   Parameters

Many contributions present parameters for scaling simulation [3,5,24,32]. With respect to the dimensions of scalability, a differentiation by external and internal parameters needs to be made. External scaling parameters refer to the context, respectively the environment, of the simulation: The processor, its clock rate in MHz and the number of processor cores, the available RAM or the operating system.

Internal parameters refer to the simulation model itself and have to be adjusted on the software side: The number of simultaneously active agents, the volume of messages send between the agents or the complexity of the problem to be solved by the agents.

Summarizing, a variety of different experiment scenarios can be derived from the parameters listed above. But in the context of ABSS, the number of agents being active simultaneously seems to be most relevant.

2.3 Performance Metrics

For measuring a system's degree of scalability, performance metrics have to be defined. The central measurement unit of the method proposed in this paper is the execution time of simulation experiments. It takes all scalability parameters into account and changes of the performance can be detected immediately [17].

Based on the execution time, the *speedup* can be calculated when distributing a simulation experiment across multiple CPU cores. This value describes the ratio between serial and parallel execution time and expresses the increase in speed by the use of parallelization [13]. The ideal case would be a full linear speedup. However, in practice this ideal case is unrealizable due to additional effort caused by distributing and coordinating simulation runs. The *efficiency*, as second metric, results from the ratio between speedup and the number of CPU cores used. It describes the utilization of available CPU cores. As the execution of simulation experiments can even be slowed down due to parallelization, values may be negative.

Our focus on the ratio between resources used by the simulation experiment and the time required for executing the experiment enables a straightforward assessment of the simulation frameworks [5].

2.4 Frameworks

In this section, the considered frameworks are introduced and discussed briefly. As numerous toolkits, libraries, and frameworks to support agent-based modeling exist, a selection needs to be made. In order to provide comparability, only frameworks using the same programming language have been chosen. Even though several well-known frameworks use C++, C, Objective-C, or Python, e.g., Repast HPC[1], this paper focuses Java-based frameworks, as Java is a widespread, simple, and architecture-neutral programming language. Hence, even though using GPUs as execution platform for high performance computing when simulating complex problems has gained popularity, GPU-based frameworks, e.g., FLAME GPU[2], were not considered. These frameworks mostly rely on efficient and machine-oriented programming languages like C [15]. Furthermore, mainly educational modeling environments such as NetLogo as well as platform-dependent toolkits

---

[1] http://repast.sourceforge.net/repast_hpc.php (last visited Oct. 3, 2015).

[2] http://www.flamegpu.com (last visited Oct. 3, 2015).

like AnyLogic[3] were not considered in this paper. In Table 1, an overview of the characteristics of the selected frameworks can be found.

Table 1. Comparison of selected multiagent frameworks

	Aimpulse Sp.	JADE	MASON	Repast
Version	1.3.1	4.3.3	18	3.1
Description	Runtime environment for simulation of many agents	Software framework for developing multiagent systems	Library for large discrete-event multiagent simulations	Toolkit for modeling agents, organizations, and institutions
Focus	Highly scalable parallel execution of large scenarios	Integrated components for distribution across multiple systems	High execution speed of lightweight simulation experiments	Flexible modeling of social agents
Scheduling	Execution within a thread-pool	One thread per agent	Step-based	Event-based
FIPA	FIPA compliant	FIPA compliant	Not FIPA compliant	Not FIPA compliant
License	Proprietary software	Open source, under "GNU Lesser General Public License" (LGPL)	Open source, under "Academic Free License"	Free software, under "new BSD License"

Aimpulse Spectrum[4] is a commercial runtime environment for large multiagent systems. Based on experiences collected when developing PlaSMA [33], an event-driven simulation system originally developed for evaluating logistical scenarios, Aimpulse Spectrum has been developed as a general purpose platform with regard to simulating large systems and providing scalability. The framework focuses on the parallel execution of agents, even in very large simulation scenarios with more than one million agents. For this purpose, a thread pool is used and a custom scheduling method has been developed. Aimpulse Spectrum supports the development of agents by providing agent behaviors and interaction templates. Furthermore, communication between agents follows the FIPA messaging standards.

---

[3] http://www.anylogic.com (last visited Oct. 3, 2015).
[4] http://www.aimpulse.com (last visited Oct. 3, 2015).

JADE[5] is a software framework for the development of multiagent systems. Even though JADE primarily aims at supporting the implementation of multi-agent systems, it can be used for executing simulation experiments, too. Due to the high relevance of JADE in practice, e.g., when modeling workflows as large networks of agents in organizations, and as scalability issues are not only related to simulating but also to modeling of multiagent systems, JADE is included in the comparison [20]. As the only one of the considered frameworks, JADE provides integrated components for distributing a simulation. It can run on different, even mobile, platforms, and is FIPA-compliant. JADE works thread-based, each agent of a simulation is implemented as a separate CPU thread. In addition, graphical tools for administration and debugging of software agents are included.

MASON[6] is a multiagent simulation toolkit which has been developed at George Mason University, Virginia, USA. It is distributed under the Academic Free License, making it open source. The toolkit mainly focuses on the execution speed as well as configurable large simulations with many agents. MASON implements discrete stepwise simulation and distribution of simulation experiments across multiple machines is not provided. But, simulation runs can be paused, transferred to other computers and continued there. Another feature are extensive libraries for the visualization of simulations in 2D and 3D.

Repast[7] is part of the Repast Suite, a collection of free and open source platforms for agent-based modeling and simulation. Currently, *Repast Simphony* and *Repast HPC* are the main toolkits provided by the Repast Suite. However, Repast Simphony is firmly integrated into a powerful graphical user interface and was designed for the use on workstations. Therefore, it is unsuitable to be compared to other frameworks being executed without GUI, as the results may be unrepresentative due to additional computational effort. Repast HPC does not provide a GUI for configuring and visualizing the simulation experiments, since it is a high performance system for supercomputers, developed in C++. As we focus on Java-based frameworks, we used Repast 3, a more lightweight, Java-based implementation.

3   Comparing Agent-Based Simulation Frameworks

For comparing the agent-based simulation frameworks introduced in the previous section, a coherent and sound method needs to be applied. Only if the results are replicable, but still individually represent the simulation framework being analyzed, comparability can be achieved. Therefore, the framework-specific implementation and execution of a reference scenario, as well as the configuration of the parameters used for evaluating the frameworks need to be defined properly.

---

[5] http://jade.tilab.com (last visited Oct. 3, 2015).

[6] http://cs.gmu.edu/~eclab/projects/mason (last visited Oct. 3, 2015).

[7] http://repast.sourceforge.net/repast_3 (last visited Oct. 3, 2015).

We propose a five-step approach for analyzing agent-based simulation frameworks starting from the specification of an reference experiment up to the evaluation of the results being generated.

1. **Specification of Experiment**: First, a reference experiment needs to be specified for all frameworks to be investigated. When doing so, the case-specific requirements of the frameworks need to be considered carefully (e.g., agent count, communication bandwidth, etc.) and monitoring points for measuring the metrics have to be determined.
2. **Implementation of a Simulation Model**: Following this, the reference experiment must be implemented individually for each single framework using the standards defined by the developers of the framework. Only necessary and suitable functions for the implementation of the problem should be used to benefit from the opportunities provided by the framework. Additionally, a straightforward adjustment of the internal scaling parameters should be provided, e.g., by using configuration files, and a consistent output of the simulation results for further comparison is needed.
3. **Configuration of Parameters**: The parameters need to be defined in detail. External scaling parameters can be adjusted by the use and configuration of a virtual machine[8] serving as a basis for the experiments. By choosing a light-weight operating system for running simulation experiments, a distortion of the results caused by irrelevant processes can be minimized. Internal parameters, in contrast, need to be defined according to the implementation specified in step 2. This results in the relations shown in Fig. 1.
4. **Execution of Experiments**: After the experiments have been successfully implemented, validated, and verified, and after the parameters have been configured, the simulation experiments need to be conducted. For generating reliable results, multiple runs should be performed for each scenario. While doing so, statistical dispersion of the results needs to be measured in order to verify a sufficient number of samples have been taken.
5. **Evaluation of Results**: The execution times measured in the previous step can be used to determine speedup and efficiency of a particular simulation framework. Finally, the interpretation of the obtained results and a comparison of the examined frameworks can be accomplished. As a result of this, simulation engineers are provided with information for choosing a well-suited simulation framework for simulating a particular scenario.

In the following sections, the five-step approach presented above will be applied to the frameworks. In order to do so, a comparison of the four Java-based agent frameworks introduced in Sect. 2.4 will be performed and described step by step.

3.1 Experiment Specification

In order to measure the execution time of simulation frameworks, consistent experiments are required. Besides the quantity of generated software agents,

---

[8] A virtual machine (VM) emulates a real computer system. Doing so, hardware configurations can be adjusted easily and without physically modifying the system.

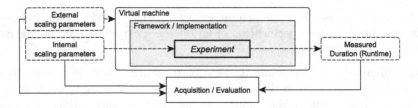

Fig. 1. Relations between scaling parameters and the experiment using a particular simulation framework.

the actions performed by the agents are part of the scalability challenges, too. Here, we have chosen the calculation of prime numbers as a simple and reproducible, yet CPU-intensive task. At this point, other agent actions causing a high processor load can be chosen as well, e.g., sophisticated reasoning processes. Furthermore, communication between the agents for information exchange or coordination purposes is an inherent part of multiagent systems, too. Yet, as the scalability of the frameworks regarding the increasing number of agents is a mandatory precondition for communication and as the communications behavior very much depends on the specific scenario being modeled and simulated, communication will not be considered at first.

The reference experiment consists of a master agent and a variable amount of calculation agents. The master agent is in charge of coordinating the calculation agents and the time measurement of a single simulation run. Here, a simulation run consists of the one-time calculation of a certain amount of prime numbers per agent up to a limit given by the master agent. When this limit is reached by an agent, the number of primes found is sent back to the master agent. The model is completely static, without any dynamic adding or removing of agents. Furthermore, the initialization and calculation phase of the simulation are strictly separated. The master agent will not start the calculation phase until all calculation agents have been initiated.

For altering the simulation conditions (external scaling parameters), virtual machines equipped with three different CPU configurations are used, only differing in the number of processors and amount of RAM. The internal scaling parameter, the number of agents, is increased stepwise after each simulation run. The execution time is considered as a performance metric. For each run the total execution time, including the initialization effort, is measured as well as the execution time for the calculation of each individual agent.

3.2 Implementation of Simulation Model

Next, the simulation model is implemented in each framework, focusing on the composition to ensure comparability. The model implementation needs to focus on the indispensable components of the model and be limited to the use of appropriate functions provided by the framework. Optional components, e.g., visualization or extended logging of the simulation runs, are not applied, in order to limit the processor load caused by the simulation experiment to the execution of the agents. Figure 2 displays the sequence flow of a simulation experiment.

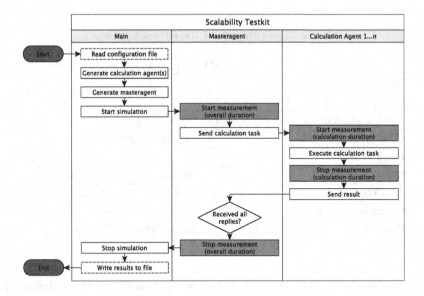

Fig. 2. Sequence flow of a simulation experiment

For entering and adjusting different internal scaling parameters, including the amount of calculation agents, and for managing further settings of the simulation model, a configuration file can be imported at the beginning of each simulation run. The master agent's output containing the execution times of the calculation agents is saved for further processing. It is essential that management overhead is not included in the time measurement.

The result is a parameterizable testkit that runs without any further user intervention after being started.

3.3 Configuration of Parameters

The external scaling parameters are adjusted via the virtual machines. The configurations we have selected for the experiments are shown in Table 2. Furthermore, the following internal scaling parameters and settings need to be altered for the experiments:

- Parameter `framework`: Specifies the framework being used for the simulations experiments, i.e., Aimpulse Spectrum, JADE, MASON or Repast.
- Parameter `agentCount`: Defines the number of calculation agents to be instanced. It is increasing stepwise from run to run, starting with 1.000 agents.
- Parameter `limit`: Sets the upper limit to which the prime numbers shall be calculated. For this experiment it is set to `limit = 50`. In ABSS the high number of agents causes performance issues, rather than the complexity of

individual actions or resulting computations. Therefore, the limit for calculating prime numbers can be set low.

Table 2. Configurations of the virtual machines

	VM1	VM2	VM3
No. of CPU sockets	1	2	2
No. of cores per socket	1	1	8
Total amount of CPU cores	1	2	16
CPU type	AMD Opteron 6380		
Clock rate	2,5 GHz		
RAM	16GB		64GB
Java version	8u25 64bit (1.8.0_25-b18)		
Operating system	Debian 7, 64bit		
Hypervisor	VMware vSphere (ESXi)		

Besides the execution time the system utilization is examined during the simulation runs as well to observe trends in hardware utilization. Furthermore, it provides information about possible characteristics or features of the simulation frameworks.

4   Results

For each of the four simulation frameworks mentioned, Aimpulse Spectrum, JADE, MASON, and Repast, the process presented in Sect. 3 has been conducted. In this section, the results obtained from the experiments are presented and discussed. Furthermore, a distinction is made between the computation time each agent needed and the overall time for executing the entire simulation experiment. Finally, a concluding comparison of the presented frameworks is given.

Aimpulse Spectrum: As a first important observation we can remark that Aimpulse Spectrum can handle a very high number of agents. Experiments comprising of more than 10 million agents can be performed within less than 15 min using current standard hardware. Due to limitations of the other frameworks and for achieving comparability between the frameworks, experiments exceeding 1 million agents were not conducted. Therefore, the suitability of these frameworks for simulating a higher number of agents cannot be evaluated using the method presented in this paper. Figure 3 presents the durations of the experiment runs depending on the number of agents.

For both, the overall time as well as the calculation time per agent, a linear increase relative to the number of agents can be observed for all three VMs.

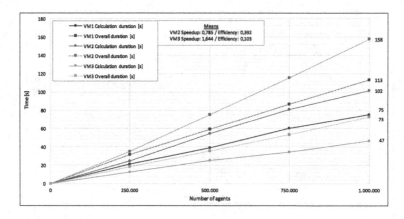

Fig. 3. Results of analyzing aimpulse spectrum, 20 simulation runs

This leads us to the conclusion that Aimpulse Spectrum scales in the considered scenarios, even when handling a high number of software agents.

Considering the use of one CPU core (VM1) compared to the use two CPU cores (VM2), the simulation's speed decreases even though the number of provided CPU cores increases. Most likely this is caused by an increased scheduling overhead. The extra effort needed for managing the distribution of the simulation is higher than the benefit of parallelizing the simulation experiment. When looking at the results of VM3 (16 CPU cores), the benefit of using multiple CPU cores is apparent, as the distribution overhead is more than compensated by the increase of utilized processing power. 16 CPU cores lead to a speedup of a factor of 1.6, meaning the simulation experiment was executed 60 % faster compared to the use of a single core. However, the efficiency of VM3 is very low (0.103). The 16 processor cores can only be utilized at about 10 % while on VM2, even tough the simulation experiment did not run faster, available hardware resources were used with an efficiency of 40 %.

The observation of the system load during the experiments shows that Aimpulse Spectrum utilizes all of the RAM allocated by the Java Virtual Machine as well as all available processors. The framework's execution speed benefits from its own scheduling mechanism and the use of a thread pool instead of dedicated threads. By implementing sequential agents following the *actor model* [12], CPU as well as RAM of the executing computer can be used more efficiently by enabling asynchronous communication. Furthermore, the Java construct *Future* is used for representing the results of the agents' executions, increasing the performance of Aimpulse Spectrum.

JADE: JADE was only analyzed up to an agent count of 100.000. When implementing more agents framework-specific exceptions occurred and the system crashed.

It is conspicuous that JADE's initialization causes up 50 % of the total runtime on all of the three VMs. JADE's approach is to create dedicated CPU

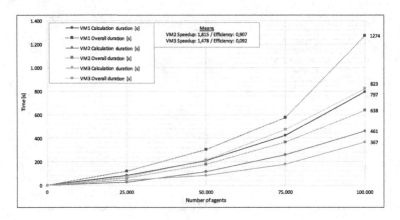

Fig. 4. Results of analyzing JADE, 20 simulation runs

thread for each agent at startup, and after generating all threads, the simulation is started. Observations of the system load during the simulation suggest that JADE, although every core is heavily loaded during the creation of threads, mostly uses only one core during simulation experiments (Fig. 4).

Even though the calculation time decreased when using two CPUs and more RAM, a desirable linear increase of the execution time when adding further agents could not be observed on any of the VMs. Instead, the duration times rise exponentially implying that JADE gets less performant with increasing the amount of agents. This can especially be noticed at about 75,000 agents: an addition of one-third of the agents results in approximately a doubling of execution and total time.

VM2 shows a speedup of about 1.8, almost halving the overall time, the efficiency (approximately 90 %) is satisfying, too. Interestingly, with increasing number of cores (VM3), JADE shows a strong decline in efficiency (about 10 %). It is also remarkable, that at 16 cores the calculation time indeed decreases compared to only 2 CPU cores, but the total time is higher. This could be explained by the increased amount of communication when using more CPU cores or by the non-optimal utilization of the hardware in this respect. However, when interpreting these results it should be considered that JADE focuses on implementing multiagent system, rather than running simulations.

MASON: The results of analyzing MASON are shown in Fig. 5. Similar to Aimpulse Spectrum and Repast, experiments with up to 1 million individual agents could be executed.

Regarding the execution times of each VM it can be observed that MASON slows down with increasing the number of CPU cores. This phenomenon occurs due to the design of MASON, causing each simulation step to be executed individually and therefore not in parallel. MASON, in contrast to Aimpulse Spectrum, JADE, and Repast, focuses on the stepwise execution of simulation experiments executing agents one after another. This results in the use of just

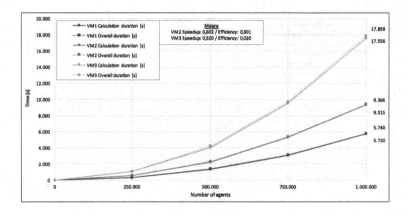

Fig. 5. Results of analyzing MASON, 20 simulation runs

a single CPU core even if more cores are available for the framework. In case of multiple processors being available, the core used for executing MASON is altered from time to time by scheduling mechanisms of the operating system. These time-consuming context switches do not occur on a single core architecture. The speedup on both VMs with multiple processor cores is smaller compared to the reference VM with only one core and the efficiency of utilizing the cores is rather low.

When considering the execution time and the number of agents it can be noted that no linear correlation exists. An experiment with 1 million agents takes 1.5 h, even on the single core machine. It is an asset that MASON hardly needs any initialization time, the simulation starts nearly immediately and thus MASON is fast when simulating less than 10.000 agents. It also does not allocate much RAM, the limit of two gigabytes has not been exceeded in any of the experiments.

Repast: Figure 6 shows the results of the simulation experiments conducted using Repast. The simulation of up to 1 million agents is possible, yet, when exceeding 100.000 agents the duration of the simulation experiments increases exponentially.

While the differences between the times measured on VM1 (one core) and VM2 (two cores) can be neglected when simulating a low number of agents, adding further CPU cores results in an increased computation time for simulating the same amount of agents. Analogous to MASON, Repast only utilizes a single CPU core for its computations. Compared to Aimpulse Spectrum, simulation runs conducted with Repast are considerably slower. Still, Repast outperforms MASON when comparing the results (speedup) achieved on virtual machines with an increased number of CPU cores.

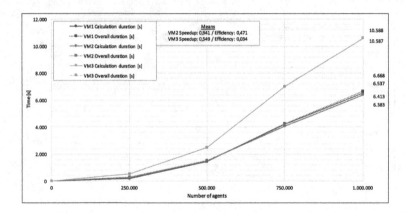

Fig. 6. Results of analyzing Repast, 20 simulation runs

4.1 Advantages and Disadvantages of the Frameworks

Summarizing, as shown in Fig. 7, it can be said that Aimpulse Spectrum is the most performant framework regarding the different VM settings considered in this research. When instantiating 100.000 agents using 16 CPU cores, Aimpulse Spectrum is 100 times faster than JADE and about 15 times faster than MASON or Repast. While the execution time of Aimpulse Spectrum has not even doubled when increasing the amount of agents from 50.000 to 100.000, it has quadrupled for the other frameworks.

In all of the experiments, JADE takes the third place, which is mainly due to the high initialization overhead. Although it can be argued that JADE

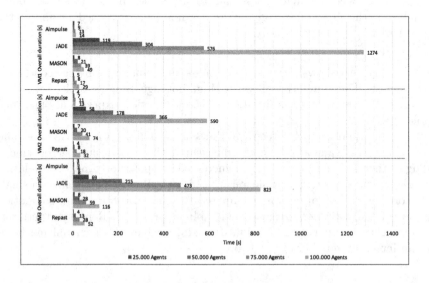

Fig. 7. Comparison of the simulation frameworks

simulations can be distributed across several computers, which would reduce these times in total, the results shown in Fig. 6 indicate that even MASON is much faster than JADE in each run. In addition, a distribution would create further organization overhead and network communication is rather slow. Hence, distributing JADE simulation experiments over five machines would still result in the last place. Despite everything, on the dual-core machine (VM2) JADE obtained the highest results for speedup and efficiency.

MASON and Repast prove to be the fastest frameworks when considering the pure computation time of each agent, but the strict limitation to only one CPU core leads to a slowdown in case more resources are available. In addition, the performance on very large simulations decreases considerably. Compared to JADE, they are faster up to 100.000 agents, but the execution times rose exponentially in other test runs with up to 1 million agents, in contrast to Aimpulse Spectrum showing a linear growth.

In summary it can be said that Aimpulse Spectrum, as the only one of the four framework tested, scales better when increasing the number of agents and shows a linear growth of the execution time on both, single- and multicore machines. It is the best performing framework, too, but still has only a low efficiency when running on a larger number of CPU cores.

5   Conclusions

Due to simulation models continuously growing in size, e.g., in social sciences (ABSS), and the increasing number of simulation frameworks for implementing and executing simulation experiments, the choice of the framework which is best suited for a certain task is challenging. For one thing, the number of software agents to be simulated can overwhelm simulation frameworks. ABSS models easily consist of more than one million individual software agents. For another thing, modern computer systems provide a high number of CPU cores for distributing computations and thus increase the performance of the computations. Hence, the decision of using many cores for distributing the simulation in contrast to using single CPU cores running a larger number of experiments parallel is a forced one.

In this paper we proposed a five-step approach for analyzing and comparing agent-based simulation frameworks regarding these scalability questions. By designing standardized experiments being implemented individually for each simulation framework, comparable experiments can be executed while altering scalability parameters. Here, we modified the virtual machine used for executing the simulation experiments and added CPU cores. Thus, advantages and disadvantages of four exemplary, popular simulation frameworks, Aimpulse Spectrum, JADE, MASON, and Repast, could be identified.

Considering the results presented in this paper, only one of the frameworks, Aimpulse Spectrum, was scalable when simulating a large amount of agents. Furthermore, it was the only framework to fully utilize the hardware being provided by the virtual machines even if with a lack of efficiency. JADE, in contrast, only was able to handle a small fraction of the agents Aimpulse Spectrum or Repast could handle. The number of agents MASON and Repast can simulate was satisfying with regard to current ABSS scenarios, yet, only a single CPU core was used for computations.

It could be shown that there are considerable differences in how modern agent-based modeling and simulation frameworks handle scalability of simulation models. Therefore, an objective method for comparing simulation frameworks is needed in this regard. However, this is only a first step towards a holistic comparison of agent-based simulation frameworks. As a next step, the exchange of messages between agents needs to be addressed as well to extend the complexity of the simulation. Additionally, further simulation frameworks need to be identified and analyzed for gaining more insights. Finally, it needs to be noted that scalability of software systems remains a current topic of interest, as resources provided by computer hardware are still not used optimally.

References

1. Banks, J.: Handbook of Simulation. Wiley Online Library (1998). http://onlinelibrary.wiley.com/doi/10.1002/9780470172445.fmatter/summary
2. Conte, R., Gilbert, N., Sichman, J.S.: MAS and social simulation: a suitable commitment. In: Gilbert, N., Sichman, J.S., Conte, R. (eds.) MABS 1998. LNCS (LNAI), vol. 1534, pp. 1–9. Springer, Heidelberg (1998)
3. Cortese, E., Quarta, F., Vitaglione, G., Vrba, P.: Scalability and performance of jade message transport system. In: AAMAS Workshop on AgentCities, Bologna, vol. 16 (2002)
4. Davidsson, P.: Agent based social simulation: a computer science view. J. Artif. Soc. Soc. Simul. **5**(1), 7 (2002)
5. Deters, R.: Scalability & multi-agent systems. In: 2nd International Workshop Infrastructure for Agents, MAS and Scalable MAS, 5th International Conference on Autonomous Agents (2001)
6. Di Caro, G.A.: Analysis of simulation environments for mobile ad hoc networks. Technical Report, Dalle Molle Institute for Artificial Intelligence (2003)
7. Doran, J., Gilbert, N.: Simulating societies: an introduction. In: Simulating Societies: The Computer Simulation of Social Phenomena, pp. 1–18 (1994)
8. Gatti, M., Cavalin, P., Neto, S.B., Pinhanez, C., dos Santos, C., Gribel, D., Appel, A.P.: Large-scale multi-agent-based modeling and simulation of microblogging-based online social network. In: Alam, S.J., Van Dyke Parunak, H. (eds.) MABS 2013. LNCS, vol. 8235, pp. 17–33. Springer, Heidelberg (2014)
9. Goldstein, J.: Emergence as a construct: History and issues. Emergence **1**(1), 49–72 (1999)
10. Hamida, E.B., Chelius, G., Gorce, J.M.: Impact of the physical layer modeling on the accuracy and scalability of wireless network simulation. Simulation **85**, 574–588 (2009)
11. Helsinger, A., Thome, M., Wright, T.: Cougaar: a scalable, distributed multi-agent architecture. In: 2004 IEEE International Conference on Systems, Man and Cybernetics, vol. 2, pp. 1910–1917. IEEE (2004)
12. Hewitt, C., Bishop, P., Steiger, R.: A universal modular actor formalism for artificial intelligence. In: Proceedings of the 3rd International Joint Conference on Artificial Intelligence, pp. 235–245. Morgan Kaufmann Publishers Inc. (1973)

13. Hill, M.D.: What is scalability? ACM SIGARCH Comput. Archit. News **18**(4), 18–21 (1990)
14. Horling, B., Mailler, R., Lesser, V.: Farm: a scalable environment for multi-agent development and evaluation. In: Lucena, C., Garcia, A., Romanovsky, A., Castro, J., Alencar, P.S.C. (eds.) SELMAS 2003. LNCS, vol. 2940, pp. 225–242. Springer, Heidelberg (2004)
15. Kiran, M., Richmond, P., Holcombe, M., Chin, L.S., Worth, D., Greenough, C.: Flame: simulating large populations of agents on parallel hardware architectures. In: Proceedings of the 9th International Conference on Autonomous Agents and Multiagent Systems, vol. 1, pp. 1633–1636, International Foundation for Autonomous Agents and Multiagent Systems (2010)
16. Kravari, K., Bassiliades, N.: A survey of agent platforms. J. Artif. Soc. Soc. Simul. **18**(1), 11 (2015)
17. Lee, L.C., Nwana, H.S., Ndumu, D.T., De Wilde, P.: The stability, scalability and performance of multi-agent systems. BT Tech. J. **16**(3), 94–103 (1998)
18. Liu, H.H.: Software Performance and Scalability: A Quantitative Approach, vol. 7. Wiley, New York (2011)
19. Michael, M., Moreira, J.E., Shiloach, D., Wisniewski, R.W.: Scale-up x scale-out: a case study using nutch/lucene. In: Parallel and Distributed Processing Symposium, IPDPS 2007. IEEE International, pp. 1–8. IEEE (2007)
20. Müller, J.P., Fischer, K.: Application impact of multi-agent systems and technologies: a survey. In: Shehory, O., Sturm, A. (eds.) Agent-Oriented Software Engineering, pp. 27–53. Springer, Heidelberg (2014)
21. Neuman, B.C.: Scale in distributed systems. ISI/USC (1994)
22. Pawlaszczyk, D., Strassburger, S.: Scalability in distributed simulations of agent-based models. In: Proceedings of the 2009 Winter Simulation Conference, pp. 1189–1200. IEEE (2009)
23. Railsback, S.F., Lytinen, S.L., Jackson, S.K.: Agent-based simulation platforms: review and development recommendations. Simulation **82**(9), 609–623 (2006)
24. Rana, O.F., Stout, K.: What is scalability in multi-agent systems? In: Proceedings of the Fourth International Conference on Autonomous Agents, pp. 56–63. ACM (2000)
25. Allan, R.: Survey of agent based modelling and simulation tools (v1.1) (2011). http://www.grids.ac.uk/Complex/ABMS/
26. Singhal, S.K., Cheriton, D.R.: Using projection aggregations to support scalability in distributed simulation. In: Proceedings of the 16th International Conference on Distributed Computing Systems, pp. 196–206. IEEE (1996)
27. Song, R., Korba, L.: Modeling and simulating the scalability of a multi-agent application system. NRC/ERB-1097 (2002)
28. Squazzoni, F., Jager, W., Edmonds, B.: Social simulation in the social sciences a brief overview. Soc. Sci. Comput. Rev. **32**(3), 279–294 (2014)
29. Timm, I.J., Pawlaszczyk, D.: Large scale multiagent simulation on the grid. In: IEEE International Symposium on Cluster Computing and the Grid, CCGrid 2005, vol. 1, pp. 334–341. IEEE (2005)
30. Tobias, R., Hofmann, C.: Evaluation of free java-libraries for social-scientific agent based simulation. J. Artif. Soc. Soc. Simul. **7**(1), 6 (2004)
31. Tolbert, L.M., Qi, H., Peng, F.Z.: Scalable multi-agent system for real-time electric power management. In: Power Engineering Society Summer Meeting, vol. 3, pp. 1676–1679. IEEE (2001)

32. Turner, P.J., Jennings, N.R.: Improving the scalability of multi-agent systems. In: Wagner, T.A., Rana, O.F. (eds.) AA-WS 2000. LNCS (LNAI), vol. 1887, pp. 246–262. Springer, Heidelberg (2001)

33. Warden, T., Porzel, R., Gehrke, J.D., Herzog, O., Langer, H., Malaka, R.: Towards ontology-based multiagent simulations: the plasma approach. In: ECMS, pp. 50–56 (2010)

34. Weinstock, C.B., Goodenough, J.B.: On system scalability. Technical report, DTIC Document Technical Note CMU/SEI-2006-TN-012 (2006)

35. Wooldridge, M., Jennings, N.R.: Intelligent agents: theory and practice. Knowl. Eng. Rev. **10**(02), 115–152 (1995)

Integrating Agent Actions and Workflow Operations

Thomas Wagner[(✉)] and Daniel Moldt

Informatics and Natural Sciences, Department of Informatics,
Faculty of Mathematics, University of Hamburg, Hamburg, Germany
wagner@informatik.uni-hamburg.de
http://www.informatik.uni-hamburg.de/TGI/

Abstract. This paper presents the AGENT ACTIVITY, a Petri net construct combining workflow tasks with the abilities of software agents. AGENT ACTIVITIES are at the core of our new approach, in which they are used by novel modelling entities. These entities provide integrated workflow **and** agent functionality. This supports a modelling perspective incorporating the strengths of both multi-agent systems and workflow management systems to allow for e.g. better support of inter-organisational modelling. The paper focuses on the role, function and construction of the AGENT ACTIVITY in the approach.

Keywords: Workflows · Agents · Modelling · Integration · High-level Petri nets

1 Introduction

Modelling a system requires choosing adequate primary concepts and associated techniques for the task at hand. These concepts imply a certain perspective on the system. Usually, each perspective has some distinct strengths associated with it, which are reflected in a superior capability to represent, express and model aspects related to that perspective.

For our research we are particularly interested in multi-agent systems and workflow systems. Multi-agent systems (MAS) associate as the main, but of course not only, perspective a structural perspective on a system, while workflow systems associate a behaviour-centric one. Consequently, multi-agent systems are especially good at representing and modelling the structure within the system. Workflow systems excel at representing and modelling behaviour.

Our research goal is to combine the strengths of both of these perspectives by creating one unified, integrated modelling technique, which features the structural strengths of agents and the behavioural strengths of workflows. Using the two technologies to improve one another has been done before, e.g. [5,9,19]. However, we aim for a more comprehensive integration of the two. Basing both agent and workflow concepts on Petri net technology we are able to integrate them quite naturally.

© Springer International Publishing Switzerland 2015
J.P. Müller et al. (Eds.): MATES 2015, LNAI 9433, pp. 61–78, 2015.
DOI: 10.1007/978-3-319-27343-3_4

In this paper we introduce the central foundation for the proposed integration, the AGENT ACTIVITY (AGAC). An AGAC is a Petri net structure, which combines the most basic facilities of agents (internal actions, sending and receiving messages) and workflows (requesting, completing and aborting tasks). It is used as the main building block in process-protocols, a combination of agent behaviour and workflows, which are executed by novel modelling entities. The paper also introduces the overall system architecture for the integrated technique, which provides the context of the AGAC.

This paper is structured as follows. Following this introduction the background is presented in Sect. 2. The main contribution is presented in Sects. 3–5, which describe the modelling context, the AGENT ACTIVITY-system and the core net structure respectively. This is followed by a practical example showcasing the prototype in Sect. 6. Section 7 highlights and compares related work to our approach. The paper is concluded with a discussion in Sect. 8 and a summary and outlook in Sect. 9.

2   Background

The technological and formal basis for our work is the reference net formalism [17]. It allows tokens in nets to be references to other net instances or arbitrary Java objects. Our development and runtime environment is RENEW[1] [18].

The utilised agent and workflow implementations are realised as reference net systems in RENEW. Agents follow the MULAN (**Mul**ti **A**gent **N**ets) reference architecture [22]. MULAN describes multi-agent systems in four layers: system; platform; agent; agent protocols. CAPA (**C**oncurrent **A**gent **P**latform **A**rchitecture) [10] is an implementation of MULAN. The majority of the executable code in CAPA is implemented in reference nets annotated with Java inscriptions. The MULAN architecture serves as the conceptual basis for the agent aspects utilised within the context of this paper. CAPA serves as the basis for practical agent aspects.

Workflows follow the workflow net principles [23], with a specialised implementation of tasks for RENEW [13]. A task is represented as a single task transition, which hides a powerful, complex, standardised net structure for improved readability of the nets.

The idea of integrating agents and workflows is based on [21,25]. These publications are discussed as related work in Sect. 7. The approach to realise the idea through a construct like the AGENT ACTIVITY is based on general observations and discussions described in [24].

3   Modelling Context

3.1   Agents and Workflows in General

In agent-orientation, the main abstraction for modelling is the agent. Agents are entities, which are logically located (and usually also physically executed)

---

[1] **Reference net** workshop. Available at www.renew.de

on agent platforms, communicate through asynchronous messages and have a set of proactive and reactive behaviours, called protocols (in MULAN/CAPA). An agent protocol describes the agent's part in an interaction between multiple agents, i.e. which messages to expect, send and which internal actions to execute. This means that the agent is always the centre of consideration.

The corresponding modelling perspective is, consequently, very structure-centric. The structure of the system, which includes its infrastructure, architecture, distribution, etc., is easy to model and easy to inspect at runtime since it is directly mapped onto the agents. The behaviour on the other hand is described *directly* only in the protocols, which take just one agent into account. Indirectly the behaviour is also described in the interactions, which take a limited set of agents into consideration and are not directly executed (as opposed to the protocols). This can lead to some difficulties when modelling the behaviour. In small scales the approach works without problems. But, with an increasing number of agents, interactions, branching protocols, etc., to take into consideration a view on the system's global behaviour quickly becomes challenging.

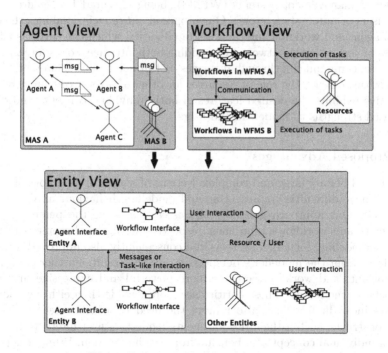

Fig. 1. Perspectives on a software system

When modelling a system with workflows, the main abstraction is the titular workflow. Workflows describe a set of processes, including the order of tasks, the eligible resources for task execution and the data flow between tasks. This is a behaviour-centric modelling perspective. The behaviour of a large number of resources, as well as the dependencies between individual tasks and considerations to data flow, are easy to model and represent. However, the structure of the system is mostly hidden within the executing resources. This means that global behaviour of a system can be expressed easily, while the structure is constrained to inspecting individual resources. Similar to agent orientation, this leads to difficulties when modelling very large systems. For workflows, however, this affects the structure of the system, which becomes increasingly challenging to manipulate and administrate.

For both technologies this does **not** mean that they are not capable or suited to model large and complex systems. It simply means that both technologies have strengths in some areas. The strengths of agents and workflows complement each other quite naturally. One excels at structure, the other at behaviour. Integrating them combines the structural strengths of agents with the behavioural strengths of workflows. Our integrated system features *entities*, which can either act as agents, workflows or both, depending on the current needs at runtime.

Figure 1 illustrates our motivation w.r.t. perspectives. The agent view is centred on agents in different multi-agent systems (MAS) communicating via asynchronous messages. The workflow view is centred on different workflows in workflow management systems (WFMS), being executed by resources (i.e. human users or automated actors). Our proposed *entity view* combines the concepts of agent and workflow into an integrated entity, which can serve as agent, workflow or something in between by providing both interfaces to resources/users. Entities can communicate through messages *or* through task-like interactions, in which entities take on the role of resources for other entities. Consequently, this perspective exhibits the desired features of both individual concepts and offers the related strengths to modellers and users.

3.2 Proposed Advantages

As motivated before, large and complex systems of agents or workflows individually *can* have difficulties representing and modelling behaviour and structure respectively. Our approach generally addresses this, since the perspectives of both agents and workflows (and their respective strengths) become available. Improved modelling for larger systems and consequently also improved scalability, at least from the modeller's perspective, are the result. Furthermore, integrating agents and workflows creates more powerful and expressive first-class constructs for modelling. These entities are more flexible than either workflows or agents individually. They also remove the need for complicated, inefficient helper-constructs, such as facilities for agents requesting user interaction.

Each individual concept also benefits from the integration. While it is possible to realise process management, related user interaction, task atomicity and rollback in agent systems it is not an easy task and can be quite cumbersome. The same is true for enabling intelligent decision making mechanisms, simple communicative facilities or distribution in workflow systems. For a detailed look at the advantages workflows can gain from the integration with agents see [25]. By opening up the structural perspective to workflows and the behavioural one for agents we can realise these advantages and more in a natural way.

There are a few settings, in which the proposed integration and its features are very useful. One such setting is the inter-organisational context. From a technical perspective, inter-organisational workflows are workflows executed by multiple organisations. The proposed approach offers functionality desirable in this context. Processes communicating like agents, encapsulation and protection of critical data, and an agent-like distributed system architecture are just some of the possibilities. Furthermore, modelling inter-organisational *systems* in our integrated approach is closer to reality and more natural then modelling in classical agents or workflows. Exclusively considering an organisation as either structural actor or behavioural process does not completely capture reality. An organisation needs to be able to behave as an actor at some times and as a process at others. It shares aspects of classical agents **and** workflows alike and is thus a good example for our proposed integrated entities.

From a more abstract perspective inter-organisational processes are social processes as they involve multiple actors working together. Social software and infrastructures that directly support such processes and activities are very desirable. While workflows can be seen as a support from the more technical side, agents are also well suited for an (applied) social perspective. They can incorporate social aspects of systems with a focus on the structural perspective. For models of social systems, like multi-organisations, both perspectives are essential in order to cover all requirements completely.

4   The Agent Activity-System

4.1   An Informal View on the Agent Activity

Our stated goal is to provide an integrated perspective of structure and behaviour for modelling software systems. We want to combine the concepts of agents and workflows into a novel entity, which features the strengths of both classical concepts. On a technical level, the integration is realised by the AGENT ACTIVITY. An AGAC combines agent actions with workflow tasks. This is the most basic technical level and was consequently chosen as the starting point for the integration. It enables building the integration from the ground up, instead of having to deal with technical encumbrances and overhead from lower levels. For a more detailed description and discussion of this topic see [24].

An AGAC consists of the fundamental actions of agents and the different operations within a workflow task. The fundamental agent actions (for MULAN and CAPA agents) are sending a message, receiving a message and performing an internal action (e.g. accessing the knowledge base, operating on data). The operations within a workflow task are accepting a workitem and subsequently completing the activity or aborting it. This is illustrated in Fig. 2. The AGAC combines these agent actions and workflow operations into a new complex construct. The basic granularity of actions and operations allows us to model any behaviour of agents or workflow tasks with AGACS.

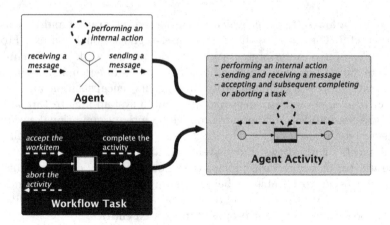

Fig. 2. An informal view of the AGENT ACTIVITY

Within the context of this paper we examine reference Petri net-based agents and workflows. Hence, the AGAC is also realised and presented here as a complex reference net structure. This structure, like the workflow task transition in RENEW, is represented as one specialised transition in models. The conceptual idea behind the AGAC can, however, easily be applied to other agent and workflow implementations. This is outside of the scope of this paper.

AGACs are the basic building blocks for the behaviour of entities. Each AGAC represents one abstract task for its executing entity. This abstract task can contain multiple sub-actions and -operations. It is up to the modeller to define the granularity of the AGACs. Conceptually they can represent tasks ranging from individual actions/operations (e.g. sending a message to another entity) to complex processes (e.g. a full workflow with document control and database access). Of course, modellers need to take care to define the scope and granularity of their AGACs clearly, without sacrificing readability and manageability.

Note that AGACs only *define* the behaviour of entities. The actions and operations are actually *executed* directly by the entity. In order to read, manage and execute the different AGACs entities possess an internal technical backend.

4.2   The Agent Activity-System Architecture

This section describes the overall system architecture, in which the AGAC is deployed. The architecture is inspired by and based on the MULAN reference architecture but enhances and combines it in many areas with workflow components. We especially retained the four layers of the MULAN architecture. The resulting system provides the integrated modelling possibilities we seek.

The resulting architecture is outlined in Fig. 3. The boxes within the layers represent important responsibilities and functionality between the different layers. Each layer is nested within the layer directly above it.

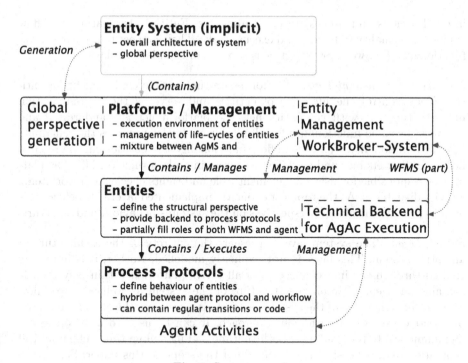

Fig. 3. System overview

Process-Protocols. Process-protocols describe the behaviour of an entity. They connect and combine a set of AGACS and thus share similarities to agent protocols and workflow processes (hence their name). A process-protocol is implemented as a workflow-like net consisting of AGACS connected through arcs and places. They can also feature regular Petri net structures with possible Java-calls for data-handling and manipulations that do not require an AGAC. The process-protocol nets are created, initiated and executed directly in their entities. During execution the process-protocol is available to and managed by the technical backend of the entity. When the process-protocol has been completed it is also terminated within the entity.

Entities. Entities are the executing constructs of the approach, which define the structure of a system, similar to agents. Generally, entities share many similarities to agents and feature their properties such as encapsulation, mobility, etc. In contrast to process-protocols the entity net is standardised. Each entity uses the same net structure but possesses different knowledge and behaviour. Entities manage and execute their process-protocols and provide the technical backend for the execution of AGACS. The backend manages the execution of the AGAC, updates the AGAC's state throughout its execution and, most importantly, actually executes the actions which the AGAC defines. Consequently the backend has the capabilities to execute the fundamental agent actions and workflow operations (see Sect. 4.1). It can (make the entity) send messages, execute internal actions and process received messages. Entities also feature workflow engine functionality to handle and execute tasks. They connect to further WFMS functionality (i.e. workflow enactment service) in the platform layer.

Platform/Management Layer. Platforms are the runtime environment for entities. They control the life-cycle of entities and serve as the communication infrastructure. As with the entity net, the platform net is standardised and provides the same functionality for all platforms. It also provides the remaining WFMS functionality. W.r.t. workflow functionality the entities can be seen as both workflow engines and workflow resources in a platform's WFMS. The platform is responsible for user management, role and rights checks, and workitem/ activity dispatches. As the topmost explicitly implemented layer (see below), it is used to provide the global perspectives on the system's behaviour and structure.

System-Layer. The system layer represents the entirety of the architecture of an entity system. This layer is **not** explicitly modelled. Rather, it is implicitly created through the interconnection of all active platforms within a system. It contains an agent view on the structure of the system as well as a workflow view on the behaviour of the system. As such, it represents the global integrated perspective we motivated for our approach. It can be used to monitor, assess and administrate the system at both runtime and modelling time. The practical generation of this perspective is outside of the scope of this paper. See Sect. 8 for a short discussion and outlook.

Modelling is mostly restricted to process-protocols and the knowledge of entities. Modelling the knowledge includes defining the roles an entity inhabits in the system, the process-protocols it is to execute, as well as any necessary internal data (e.g. identifiers of other entities). Modelling the process-protocols is similar to workflow modelling and twofold. On the one hand, the process-protocol net structure needs to be defined as the overall workflow-like process. Then the individual AGACs need to be defined, similarly to workflow tasks.

Platforms serve as the execution environments of the entities. These environments must be established and defined, but since the nets for them are standardised modelling is relatively simple here. The same is true for entities. Except for small, application-specific details modellers can focus their attention on the above-mentioned knowledge and process-protocols.

5   The Agent Activity Net Structure

The core of the AGENT ACTIVITY is the net structure shown in Fig. 4. This net structure implements the main functionality required to provide an integrated agent and workflow action. It communicates at various points of its life-cycle with the technical backend of its entity (see Sect. 4.2). The communication is handled through synchronous channels.

When used in a process-protocol, every AGAC is represented by just **one** transition with thick horizontal bars (see Fig. 2). This transition is an abstract

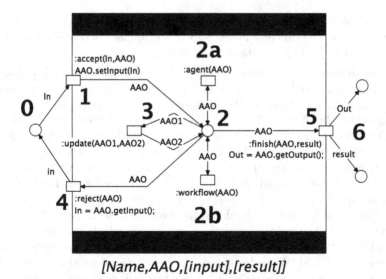

[Name,AAO,[input],[result]]

Fig. 4. AGENT ACTIVITY net structure

representation of the net structure of Fig. 4. The complete net structure is hidden in the technical layer of RENEW. As indicated by the figure, incoming and outgoing arcs of the (entire) net structure correspond to pre- and postconditions of the single transition Firing atomicity is retained for these transitions through an additional, internal rollback option.

As the net structure of the AGAC is standardised, it requires the instance data to be handled by a data object. This is called the AGENT ACTIVITY Object (AAO). The AAO is created by the technical backend of the entity when an AGAC is started. It contains all data relevant to executing the particular instance of the AGAC. Each entity stores the information about its AGACs and the related AAOs in its knowledge base.

The AAO contains the information about the sub-actions and -operations within the AGAC. This information is represented as a reference net as well. The net is similar to a workflow net featuring CAPA actions and workflow tasks. Since it is possible for different instances of an AGAC to require slightly different implementation or handling, different AAOs might be required. Which AAO is used for a specific AGAC is defined in its inscription. The AAO also stores and processes runtime data like input, output and result for its instance of the AGAC.

Each AGAC requires specific data for execution, which is inscribed to the abstract transition (see Figs. 4 and 5). This inscription is a RENEW tuple containing four elements. Except for the AGAC name, all of these elements are *optional*. If an element is not set for a specific AGAC an empty tuple ([] in RENEW) is set in its place. The elements are the (unique) AGAC name used to determine which AGAC to instantiate, the name of the AAO used for this particular instance of the AGAC[2], the optional input data objects to be processed by the AGAC and the optional result objects.

---

[2] If this element is left empty, a predefined standard AAO for the AGAC is loaded.

An example of how AGACs are used and inscribed in a process-protocol can be seen in Fig. 5. The different AGACs in this example are described in Sect. 6. The net structure in Fig. 4 contains the following parts:

0: Preconditions. The (arbitrary number of) preconditions of an AGAc are all the places connected to it via incoming arcs to the abstract AGAc transition. Input data for the AGAc is also contained in the incoming arcs.

1: Triggering the Agent Activity. When the preconditions are satisfied the AGAc can be triggered. In the abstract view considered as one transition the firing begins at this point. There are three different possibilities to trigger: direct, reactive and proactive. Direct triggering does not require any further control from the backend. Reactive triggering waits for an incoming message or signal from outside the entity. Proactive triggering is controlled by the entity and is used to e.g. delay the execution of AGACs. Triggering is managed by the technical backend in each entity, which only allows triggering when both the preconditions of the AGAc and the preconditions of the trigger are fulfilled. When the triggering begins the definition of the AGAc is read from the knowledge base. From that definition and the input data the initial AAO is created, transmitted to the AGAc and put on the central place **2**. The input data is set as one of the parameters of the AAO.

2: Executing an Action. The central place holds the AAO during the main part of the execution of the AGAc. From this place the AAO can trigger the individual sub-actions and operations. Depending on the state of the AAO it can trigger all currently enabled actions/operations. Agent actions fire the transition **2a**, workflow tasks fire the transition **2b**. The individual actions are then executed by the backend. This firing process is fire-and-forget, since the sub-tasks might take a while to be completed.

3: Updating the AAO. At some points during the execution of the AGAc it may become necessary to update the AAO to adapt to changed circumstances. This is handled by the transition connected to the *:update (AAO1,AAO2)* channel. It removes the old AAO (AAO1) from the central place **2** and puts an updated AAO (AAO2) back. Reasons for a required update of the AAO are changed pre- or postconditions (for the sub-actions), relevant state-changes, etc. The backend listens for these changes and triggers the updates to the AAO. This mechanism enables the support of adaptive processes that can change at runtime to adjust to changes during execution. It is possible to extend this mechanism to involve completely replacing the AAO with a new definition. This would enhance modelling possibilities w.r.t. on-the-fly adaptability but is considered future work.

4: Aborting the Agent Activity. If at any point of the execution of the AGAc a problem occurs or the entity decides to cancel the execution, this part of the net is fired and a local rollback initiated. The transition connected to the *:reject(AAO)* channel is fired by the technical backend. It removes the AAO from the central place **2** and cancels the execution of the AGAc in the backend by removing and resetting the administrative data. The original input data is read from the AAO and the different tokens put back onto their respective precondition places. The AGAc can then fire again.

5: Finishing the Agent Activity. Once the AAO has successfully completed its main functions by executing all sub-actions and -operations, the backend can trigger the finalisation of the AGAC. The transition connected to the channel: *finish(AAO,Result)*, removes the AAO from the net-structure and generates the result token(s) from it. The output tokens carried through the AGAC from the input unchanged are also read from the AAO at this point. The backend finishes the AGAC administratively and the execution of the process-protocol can continue.

Parts **4** and **5** realise the only ways to end the execution of an AGAC. This leads to a type of atomicity, as an AGAC can only be successfully completed in part **5** or cancelled with a local rollback in part **4**. This atomicity is not affected by the (possibly large amount of) actions and firings performed during the course of the AGAC.

6: Postconditions. The postconditions are the places connected to the AGAC transition by outgoing arcs. As with the preconditions there can be an arbitrary number of them.

6   Practical Example

This section presents a small system example to exhibit the modelling properties of the AGENT ACTIVITY-system. The example runs on an early prototype of the overall system. The core of the example is the process-protocol shown in Fig. 5.

The system is an information gathering game played by a number of users. Each user is represented in the system by one entity. That entity proactively

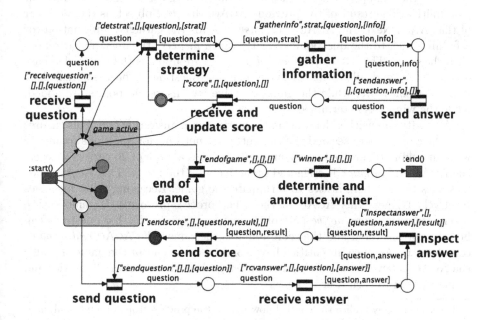

Fig. 5. Example process-protocol

executes the process-protocol of Fig. 5. The process-protocol net is *identical* in each entity. Each entity knows the addresses of all other entities and the predefined questions but only has a subset of the answers. The single requirement on the platform and system layers is that the entities are able to communicate.

While the game is active, each entity must ask another entity questions (lower branch) and answer incoming questions from other entities (upper branch). The game ends, when an entity gets 20 questions correct. The game initialises by putting empty tokens[3] on the places in the *game active* part of the net. The two middle places correspond to virtual places in the other branches and are used to initialise these branches.

Each entity can only ask one question at a time. The AGAC *send question* randomly chooses another known entity and sends a question to it. Then it waits for an answer from that entity. When it receives an answer through the AGAC *receive answer*, it proceeds to inspect it in the AGAC *inspect answer*. It first checks its own knowledge for the answer. If it already knows the answer it can proceed to the next AGAC. If it does not know the answer it asks its user to determine, whether the answer was correct or wrong. Finally, the AGAC *send score* sends the result back to the questioned entity, which increments its score if the answer was correct.

While the game is active an entity can receive an arbitrary amount of questions at any time through the AGAC *receive question*. First, the entity determines its strategy (AGAC *determine strategy*) by asking its user. It can either look up the answer in its own knowledge base, ask another entity or ask its own user. The AGAC *gather information* executes the chosen strategy. This is the only AGAC in the example, which makes use of different AAOs for the three different possibilities. The result of the previous AGAC, the *strat* object, is the identifier of that AAO. Next, the AGAC *send answer* sends the gathered information (or a failure) back to the questioning entity, which inspects the answer and replies with the score. The AGAC *receive and update score* updates the knowledge base of the entity and allows for the next pending question to be answered. This AGAC can only fire, while the game is active (to ensure, no points are added, while the winner is determined).

An entity can neither delay asking a question, nor answering one. This ensures that the game progresses and that an entity cannot wait for questions to answer without asking them itself. Once an entity reaches a score of 20 correct answers the AGAC *end of game* is triggered proactively by the entity. This AGAC sends messages to all other entities to terminate the game. Receiving these messages reactively triggers this AGAC in the other process-protocols. It removes the tokens from the *game active* part of the net to ensure no further questions can be asked or answered and the score remains the same. The AGAC *end of game* completes firing, once all entities have confirmed the end of the game. Finally, the AGAC *determine and announce winner* gathers the scores of all entities and displays them to each user.

---

[3] Tokens generally realise the control flow within the process-protocol. Optional, non-empty content encapsulates data that is required for future AGACs.

The AGACS in the example feature some pure agent actions (e.g. the *receive question* and *send score* AGACS), a pure workflow task (the *determine strategy* AGAC) and a number of hybrid AGACS, which can exhibit agent or workflow behaviour depending on the current state. For example, the *gather information* AGAC combines functionality in one transition, which would otherwise require a series of agent and workflow actions with multiple branches. Depending on the AGAC it executes at any moment an entity can be (at that moment) regarded as either an agent, a workflow or both. The example also makes use of different AAOs as already discussed. Through the use of AGACS modelling is simplified, since the series of actions is defined within the construct of the AGAC and the AAO. In this way, using AGACS simplifies complex actions by breaking them down into smaller, more manageable and also re-usable constructs.

The example also features different possibilities of triggering an AGAC. Most of the AGACS trigger directly, e.g. *send question, gather information*. These are only dependant on their preconditions and can be executed as soon as those are fulfilled. The reactive AGACS in this example all react to incoming messages, e.g. *receive question, receive and update score*. The *end of game* AGAC is the only proactive AGAC in the example. It can fire as soon as the entity determines it has reached the score limit. However, it also triggers reactively, if it receives a message from another entity that has reached the score limit. The example shows, how easy it is to model, use and combine the different triggering mechanisms in a process-protocol. Since they are incorporated into the AGACS they do not clutter the net but still retain their expressiveness.

The example showcases one of the scenarios the AGAC-system is aimed for: interconnected, communicating processes. The core process-protocol of the game features two classical workflow-like processes: asking questions and gathering information. These processes include user interactions in some parts and more-or-less automated agent actions in others. The overall process-protocol also needs its entity to behave like an agent, when communicating with other entities and deciding upon strategies. The principles here can be easily translated to inter-organisational systems. With AGACS each organisation can act as a structural entity or as the process it represents. Both options are necessary at times. Organisations need to act as entities, e.g. when they want to communicate with other organisations or negotiate with them. They also need to act as processes, e.g. when work is to be allocated to and executed by their resources. While it is possible to realise this kind of behaviour in classical agent or workflow systems, it is at the very least cumbersome and requires complex constructs. Our approach can model both options in a unified and natural way, which is demonstrated by this section's example.

7   Related Work

As mentioned in Sect. 2 our work is directly related to [21, 25]. These works realised a **partial** integration of agents into a workflow management system. This partial integration allows for workflows to exhibit agent properties (e.g. mobility, intelligence), though modelling was restricted to workflows. The resulting outlook was the idea of a **full** integration, which we now adopted. However, the AGENT ACTIVITY-system is a completely new approach, which bypasses the technical and conceptual obstacles introduced by the partial integration. A related approach is featured in e.g. [16], though it focuses on self-organisation of organisations and not on modelling.

Agents have been used to improve workflow management in numerous contributions e.g. [8,26]. An area heavily focused on is the improvement of adaptability and flexibility using an agent's reasoning mechanisms and intelligence e.g. [5,9]. In [1,4] web service composition, instead of "classic" workflow management, is integrated with agents. This changes the technology behind the behavioural view but does not affect our conceptual view on structure *and* behaviour. To a lesser degree workflows have been used to improve agents e.g. [19]. The work in [11,20] aims to improve agent behaviour representation and modelling but largely avoids workflow management aspects.

These works do not offer the degree of integration our approach adopts. They still offer only agents **or** workflows as modelling constructs and do not combine the concepts on the modeller's level. They do, however, use the respective other concept in the background, which allows some properties to be translated. These kinds of *partial* integrations are also possible and encouraged in our approach.

There is some research that shows a larger degree of integration. The WADE platform [3] follows a similar approach to ours. WADE agents are capable of executing workflow tasks, however, the focus of WADE still lies on providing workflow management functionality. Other approaches with a larger degree of integration can be found in e.g. [12,27]. These approaches rely heavily on agents and their capabilities but still focus on workflows. Our approach does not have such a focus as workflows and agents are conceptually merged into the entities.

[6,14,15] examine combinations of BDI agents with workflow management. The research presented in these papers focuses on the workflow management side and follows a goal-oriented description of the agent behaviour, while we follow a more procedural approach to allow for possible formal verification via Petri nets in our future work.

8   General Discussion

We set out to provide system modellers an integrated agent and workflow perspective. AGENT ACTIVITIES provide a basis for this perspective on a local level. W.r.t. the explicit layers of the system architecture this affects the process-protocol layer. On this layer there is a strong dynamic in the modelling perspective, as switching between viewing (parts of) the system as agent, workflow or something in between is easy and quite natural. Each AGAC provides its own categorisation as agent, workflow or hybrid to this dynamic of the perspective. This eliminates the rigid perspective of either structure *or* behaviour. The effect of the AGACS pervades to a lesser degree through the higher layers of architecture. There it is supported by the incorporation of agent and workflow management aspects. The dynamic of the modelling perspective becomes more abstract in these layers.

Providing this integrated perspective to the implicit top system layer of the architecture is the next step. This will consolidate the local views from process-protocols, entities and platforms into one complete global view of the system. The generation of this perspective involves the aggregation of the individual process-protocols into a behavioural view, as well as the aggregation of all entities into a structural view. The connections between these views are defined in the lower level, local views, which are already available. This will help to improve the difficulties w.r.t. the representation of global aspects motivated for classical agent and workflow perspectives. At this point, tool support becomes crucial, since the individual views and their connections need to be provided to a modeller in a reasonable, intelligent and useful way. The incorporation of the approach and the related perspectives into a full software development process like PAOSE (PETRI NET-BASED, AGENT- AND ORGANIZATION-ORIENTED SOFTWARE ENGINEERING [7]) is also quite interesting.

In general, the integration provided by the AGENT ACTIVITY-system allows an *intelligent* combination of behavioural and structural modelling. This simplifies several implementation issues of systems, as the AGAC construct incorporates a wide range of predefined mechanisms, e.g. triggering, data handling and flexibility. Furthermore, it provides a powerful abstraction mechanism which incorporates changes of individual perspectives during the abstraction processes of the modellers (see above). Due to the agent concepts, intelligent and flexible decisions can be smoothly integrated into the design of processes. Similarly, task concepts can be integrated into the design of agent interactions due to the incorporation of workflows. The problem of just having (more abstract) processes, being derived from underlying processes, is overcome and active and dynamic model parts within the abstraction hierarchy can be supported.

By integrating agents and workflows the resulting entities are, in themselves, more expressive. Modelling with entities allows for shortcuts in functionality that are unavailable in classical agents or workflows. Dealing with this expressiveness, though, can be difficult. Effectively utilising all the possibilities provided by the approach can be difficult for modellers. Due to the fact that two larger, well-engineered areas have been integrated, a considerable effort must be put into tool development. Some constraints on the modelling options may also be useful, although the right balance has to be found. Our current prototypes are highly promising in this regard.

An issue relates to the increased management overhead introduced by the integration. Management functionality needs to handle and differentiate both agent and workflow aspects of execution. This requires a clear separation of the concepts on all development levels. Our conceptual model provides the basis for this. Another issue is also the introduction of some centralised WFMS aspects (i.e. workflow management in the platform level). These are implementation issues for which the prototypes need to provide adequate, practical solutions, which can be found in established distributed technology. Currently our group addresses this topic via cloud computing [2].

Limitations of the AGAC are also a concern. In general, we assume that any agent-internal action can be incorporated into the AGAC. Even complex behaviour like inference or deliberation can be captured. It is an open question though, how AGACs and process-protocols should incorporate these mostly internal behaviours. MULAN and CAPA feature so-called decision components for such internal behaviour. Introducing a comparable mechanism for entities is currently being examined.

Looking back at the proposed advantages of the overall integration, one important point is the flexibility in modelling. Using the AGAC we can model both agent **and** workflow actions in one unified construct. We can use this construct to create combined functionality, which benefits the individual concepts greatly. As proposed, the entities and process-protocols can serve as workflows with agent properties. They can also provide agent functionality with user interactions through tasks. The AGAC supports these kinds of hybrid results with inherent and natural mechanisms.

9   Summary and Conclusion

This paper introduced the AGENT ACTIVITY. It provides the mechanisms to design agent actions and workflow tasks in one unified modelling construct. It is nested within a novel entity system architecture, which makes full use of its capabilities and complements the remaining management aspects of agents and workflows. The AGAC is realised through a Petri net structure, which is managed in its execution by communicating with a technical backend within the entity. AGACs allow modelling the behaviour of our entities in a consistent way and thus provide the very core for the integration of agents and workflows we seek.

As immediate future work we will continue working on improved prototypes to support the current modelling functionality with better and easy-to-use tools. Furthermore, we will address the points we discussed throughout this paper and improve the overall integration. Especially the global, integrated perspective on the system-layer is a major research focus. Larger and more complex case-studies will also be examined to better understand the advantages and disadvantages of the new approach. Scalability and usability of the approach, as well as the comparison to other modelling approaches, will be an important focus.

In conclusion, the AGENT ACTIVITY is the core of our Petri net-based integration of agents and workflows. It combines the two concepts on the lowest level, which pervades throughout the entire system. Agents, workflows and their respective managements are consolidated into one architecture with a shared infrastructure. This infrastructure exhibits the combined strengths of their individual parts, which allows designing systems with a novel consideration of behaviour and structure on the *same* level of abstraction. This, in turn, provides a distinct, natural and improved way of modelling each aspect of the system.

References

1. Bansal, A., Kona, S., Blake, M.B., Gupta, G.: An agent-based approach for composition of semantic web services. In: Workshop on Enabling Technologies: Infrastructure for Collaborative Enterprises. WETICE 2008. IEEE 17th, June 2008
2. Bendoukha, S., Wagner, T.: Improving performance of complex workflows: Investigating moving net execution to the cloud. In: Moldt, D., Rölke, H., Störrle, H. (eds.) Petri Nets and Software Engineering. International Workshop, PNSE 2015, Brussels, Belgium, June 22–23, 2015 Proceedings, vol. 1372 of CEUR Workshop Proceedings. CEUR-WS.org (2015)
3. Bergenti, F., Caire, G., Gotta, D.: Interactive workflows with wade. In: IEEE 21st International Workshop on Enabling Technologies: Infrastructure for Collaborative Enterprises (WETICE 2012). IEEE (2012)
4. Blake, M.B., Gomaa, H.: Agent-oriented compositional approaches to services-based cross-organizational workflow. Decis. Support Syst. - Special issue: Web services and process management, 40(1), 31–50 (2005)
5. Both, F., Hoogendoorn, M., van der Mee, A., Treur, J., de Vos, M.: An intelligent agent model with awareness of workflow progress. Appl. Intel. 36(2), 498–510 (2012)
6. Burmeister, B., Arnold, M., Copaciu, F., Rimassa, G.: BDI-agents for agile goal-oriented business processes. In: Proceedings of the 7th International Joint Conference on Autonomous Agents and Multiagent Systems: Industrial Track, AAMAS 2008, Richland, SC (2008). International Foundation for Autonomous Agents and Multiagent Systems
7. Cabac, L.: Multi-agent system: a guiding metaphor for the organization of software development projects. In: Petta, P., Müller, J.P., Klusch, M., Georgeff, M. (eds.) MATES 2007. LNCS (LNAI), vol. 4687, pp. 1–12. Springer, Heidelberg (2007)
8. Czarnul, P., Matuszek, M., Wójcik, M., Zalewski, K.: BeesyBees - efficient and reliable execution of service-based workflow applications for BeesyCluster using distributed agents. In: Proceedings of IMCSIT 2010 (2010)
9. Delias, P., Tsafarakis, S., Doulamis, A.: Manual intervention and statefulness in agent-involved workflow management systems. In: Casillas, J., Martínez-López, F.J., Corchado, J.M. (eds.) Management of Intelligent Systems. AISC, vol. 171, pp. 239–249. Springer, Heidelberg (2012)
10. Duvigneau, M., Moldt, D., Rölke, H.: Concurrent architecture for a multi-agent platform. In: Giunchiglia, F., Odell, J.J., Weiss, G. (eds.) AOSE 2002. LNCS, vol. 2585, pp. 59–72. Springer, Heidelberg (2003)
11. Ebadi, T., Purvis, M., Purvis, M.K.: A colored petri net model to represent the interactions between a set of cooperative agents. In: Beventano, D., Despotovic, Z., Guerra, F., Joseph, S., Moro, G., de Pinninck, A.P. (eds.) AP2PC 2008/2009. LNCS, vol. 6573, pp. 141–152. Springer, Heidelberg (2012)
12. Hsieh, F.-S.: Collaborative workflow management in holonic multi-agent systems. In: O'Shea, J., Nguyen, N.T., Crockett, K., Howlett, R.J., Jain, L.C. (eds.) KES-AMSTA 2011. LNCS, vol. 6682, pp. 383–393. Springer, Heidelberg (2011)
13. Jacob, T.: Implementierung einer sicheren und rollenbasierten Workflowmanagement-Komponente für ein Petrinetzwerkzeug. Diploma thesis, University of Hamburg, Department of Computer Science (2002)
14. Jander, K., Braubach, L., Pokahr, A., Lamersdorf, W., Wack, K.: Goal-oriented processes with GPMN. Int. J. Artif. Intel. Tools 20(06), 1021–1041 (2011)

15. Jander, K., Lamersdorf, W.: Jadex WfMS: Distributed workflow management for private clouds. In: Conference on Networked Systems, NetSys 2013, Stuttgart, Germany, March 11–15, 2013 (2013)
16. Köhler-Bußmeier, M., Wester-Ebbinghaus, M., Moldt, D.: A formal model for organisational structures behind process-aware information systems. In: Jensen, K., Aalst, W.M.P. (eds.) Transactions on Petri Nets and Other Models of Concurrency II. LNCS, vol. 5460, pp. 98–114. Springer, Heidelberg (2009)
17. Kummer, O.: Referenznetze. Logos Verlag, Berlin (2002)
18. Kummer, O., Wienberg, F., Duvigneau, M., Köhler, M., Moldt, D., Rölke, H.: Renew - the reference net workshop. In: Veerbeek, E. (ed.) Tool Demonstrations. 24th International Conference on Application and Theory of Petri Nets (ATPN 2003). International Conference on Business Process Management (BPM 2003), June 2003
19. Mislevics, A., Grundspenkis, J.: Workflow based approach for designing and executing mobile agents. In: Second International Conference on Digital Information Processing and Communications (ICDIPC), July 2012
20. Purvis, M., Savarimuthu, S., de Oliveira, M.: Mechanisms for cooperative behaviour in agent institutions. In: IEEE/WIC/ACM International Conference on Intelligent Agent Technology. IAT 2006, December 2006
21. Reese, C.: Prozess-Infrastruktur für Agentenanwendungen. Agent Technology - Theory and Applications, vol. 3. Logos Verlag, Berlin (2010)
22. Rölke, H.: Modellierung von Agenten und Multiagentensystemen - Grundlagen und Anwendungen. Agent Technology - Theory and Applications, vol. 2. Logos Verlag, Berlin (2004)
23. van der Aalst, W.M.P.: Verification of workflow nets. In: Azéma, P., Balbo, G. (eds.) ICATPN 1997. LNCS, vol. 1248, pp. 407–426. Springer, Heidelberg (1997)
24. Wagner, T., Moldt, D.: Approaching the integration of agents and workflows. In: Bergenthum, R., Desel, J. (eds.) 18. Workshop AWPN, Tagungsband, Hagen, September 2011
25. Wagner, T., Quenum, J., Moldt, D., Reese, C.: Providing an agent flavored integration for workflow management. In: Jensen, K., Donatelli, S., Kleijn, J. (eds.) Transactions on Petri Nets and Other Models of Concurrency V. LNCS, vol. 6900, pp. 243–264. Springer, Heidelberg (2012)
26. Liu, Y.-H., Li, C.-L.: A workflow engine model based on multi-agent. In International Conference on Computer Application and System Modeling (ICCASM), vol. 14, October 2010
27. Zhaohui, L., Jia, C., Rui, G., Bin, X.: A reconfigurable platform of manufacturing execution system based on workflow and agent. In: WRI World Congress on Software Engineering. WCSE 2009, vol. 1, May 2009

A Spatio-Temporal Multiagent Simulation Framework for Reusing Agents in Different Kinds of Scenarios

Daan Apeldoorn[✉]

Information Engineering Group, Technische Universität Dortmund,
Dortmund, Germany
daan.apeldoorn@tu-dortmund.de

Abstract. In this paper a spatio-temporal simulation framework for multiagent systems is introduced. Its fundamental idea consists in the possibility to develop agents that can be easily deployed in different kinds of scenarios without adapting the agents' percepts, actions or communication model to a specific scenario. This can be useful to observe and evaluate agents in the context of various scenarios, e.g. to measure their generality and adaptivity against different kinds of problems. To demonstrate the framework, two different example scenarios are considered that are both simulated with the same simple agent implementation.

Keywords: Multiagent simulation · Reusable agents · Graphical modeling

1 Introduction

This paper considers the possibility to easily use and evaluate cooperative problem-solving agents in the context of different scenarios. For this purpose, a simulation framework for spatio-temporal multiagent scenarios is presented, which is based on the ABSTRACTSWARM modeling language [1]. Unlike other approaches, the presented framework strictly separates the description of a scenario (the environment and the agents' tasks) from the modeling of the agents (their percepts, actions and communication model). This results in two major benefits: (i) Modelers can quickly create and run multiagent simulations by only considering the description of the scenario (without modeling the agent behavior) and (ii) agents can be implemented in a generic way, such that they can be reused in any modeled scenario (i.e. agents that are implemented using the framework's programming interface can be deployed in any scenario created with the modeling language). The presented framework can also be used as a multiagent planning tool for practical problems similar to the *problem of spatio-temporally constrained motion planning for cooperative vehicles* (STCMP), which was proposed as a challenging problem to the planning community by Scheuren et al. [17].

© Springer International Publishing Switzerland 2015
J.P. Müller et al. (Eds.): MATES 2015, LNAI 9433, pp. 79–97, 2015.
DOI: 10.1007/978-3-319-27343-3_5

Considering related work of the last decades, a wide range of systems have been developed for creating and running multiagent simulations, which can be roughly divided into two groups:[1]

- Domain specific systems, e. g. for transport chain scenarios (TAPAS [6]) or public transport networks [5], trading simulations (DMARKS II [9]), crowd simulations (SIMTREAD [7]), biological simulations (BIOMASS [16]), etc.
- General platforms, languages, libraries or architechtures which can be used to develop agents and multiagent scenarios in multiple domains (e. g. SESAM [8], NETLOGO [18], REPAST [12], JASON [2], MULAN [3], MASON [10], SWARM [11]).

Systems of the first group can be configured (e. g. by modifying parameters) to quickly create and run different simulation scenarios. Agents of these systems can usually perform in any of the created scenarios (e. g. agents of a traffic simulation are still able to drive, if the overall speed limit is changed). But being related to a specific domain, these systems are not very flexible and can only be used for a small family of similar problems. In contrast, systems of the second group are very flexible. But creating and running a simulation scenario requires both the environment *and* the agents (e. g. their percepts and actions within the environment) to be modeled. As a consequence, agents are reliant on the environment and cannot be used in any other scenario (e. g. to evaluate their behavior in the context of different applications).

The framework presented in this paper tries to combine the advantages of both groups: On the one hand, scenarios can be quickly created using the provided graphical modeling language. On the other hand it is very flexible and can be used to model scenarios of various domains (e. g. in the broad field of Logistics). In addition, agents can be deployed directly in different scenarios without changing their implementation.

The remainder of the paper is organized as follows: First, the underlying graphical modeling language will be briefly introduced, which serves as an interface between the scenario descriptions and the implementation of agents (Sect. 2). After that, the simulation system and the agent programming interface will be explained, which both operate on the abstract concepts provided by the modeling language (Sect. 3). To demonstrate the idea of using agents in different kinds of problems, two scenarios will be considered as examples (Sect. 4) and finally a conclusion will be given (Sect. 5).

2   Graphical Modeling Language

The graphical modeling language serves as a meta-model for multiagent scenarios and allows to quickly set up scenarios in a spatio-temporal context. Furthermore, it helps the modeler to decompose more complex scenarios using a special concept called *perspectives*, which will be defined later in Sect. 2.4. Since the language

---

[1] Only a small selection will be mentioned here as a brief overview over recent and earlier related approaches.

itself is a preliminary work to the simulation framework, this section only focuses on the basic ideas of the language and the modeling elements needed for the use case examples shown in Sect. 4 (for a more detailed introduction see [1]).

The fundamental idea of the modeling approach is to describe multiagent scenarios using the two basic components *agents* and *stations*. Agents are used to model the mobile or active components of a scenario (like vehicles, humans, products, etc.), whereas stations represent the immobile or passive components (like rooms, buildings, machines, etc.). Agents can visit stations and thereby trigger so-called *visit events*: Every time an agent visits a station, a visit event is triggered on both components.

A scenario is modeled as a graph, which is defined as the triple[2]:

$$G := (V, E, \Psi) \tag{1}$$

The set $V := S_{T_C} = S_{T_A} \cup S_{T_S}$ consists of two different kinds of nodes, representing the two basic *component types*: S_{T_A} is a set of *agent types* and S_{T_S} is a set of *station types*. The set $E := E_V \cup E_T \cup E_P$ consists if three different kinds of edges to model visiting, temporal and spatial relations among the component types. Ψ is a set of perspectives, which divide the graph into subgraphs. Every perspective $\psi \in \Psi$ consists of a name and a subset of the nodes $V_\psi \subseteq V$. Every component type (and therefore every node) must belong to exactly one perspective, such that for each $\psi_i, \psi_j \in \Psi$ with $i \neq j$ it holds that $V_{\psi_i} \cap V_{\psi_j} = \emptyset$ and $\bigcup_{\psi \in \Psi} V_\psi = V$. Every agent type $T_A \in S_{T_A}$ contains a set A of agents and every station type $T_S \in S_{T_S}$ contains a set S of stations. In the following, for any $a \in A$, we say that a is of type T_A and, for any $s \in S$, we say that s is of type T_S.

To illustrate the different language concepts, Fig. 1 will be used as a running example, where a simple school timetabling scenario is considered (an extended version of this example will be given in Sect. 4.1).

2.1   Agents and Stations

As described in Sect. 2, component types are the nodes of a scenario graph and are used to model agents and stations. In this section, both agent and station types are explained.

Agent Types. An agent type $T_A \in S_{T_A}$ is defined as a triple:

$$T_A := (t_A, A, P_A) \tag{2}$$

where t_A is the type name, $A \neq \emptyset$ is the set of agents that belong to the type and P_A is a set of attributes that are applied to every agent $a \in A$ (see Sect. 2.3).

Agent types are represented as circles, which are annotated with the type name t_A and the cardinality $c_A := |A|$ (see Fig. 1, e.g. "Class").

---

[2] Note that this definition slightly differs from [1] to outline the concept of perspectives more clearly.

Station Types. A station type $T_S \in S_{T_S}$ is defined as a triple:

$$T_S := (t_S, S, P_S) \tag{3}$$

where t_S is the type name, $S \neq \emptyset$ is the set of stations that belong to the type and P_S is a set of attributes that are applied to every station $s \in S$ (see Sect. 2.3).

Station types are represented by squares, which are annotated with the type name t_S and the cardinality $c_S := |S|$ (see Fig. 1, e. g. "Mathematics").

2.2   Relations

The graphical modeling language provides three different kinds of edges to model visiting, spatial and temporal dependencies among the component types.

«visit» Edges. A «visit» edge $e_V \in E_V$ is an undirected unweighted edge between an agent type T_A and a station type T_S. It is defined as:

$$e_V := (\{T_A, T_S\}, b) \tag{4}$$

where $b \in \mathbb{B} := \{\text{True}, \text{False}\}$ is a boolean value.

A «visit» edge states that agents of type T_A have to visit stations of type T_S. In case $b = \text{True}$, it also determines that the agents have to be located at one of the connected stations at the beginning of a simulation (see Fig. 1, e. g. between "Class" and "Mathematics").

«place» Edges. A «place» edge $e_P \in E_P$ is an undirected or directed weighted edge between two station type $T_{S_1}, T_{S_2} \in S_{T_S}$. It is defined as:

$$e_P := (\{T_{S_1}, T_{S_2}\}, D_P, w_P) \tag{5}$$

where $D_P \in \{\{T_{S_1}\}, \{T_{S_2}\}, \emptyset\}$ is a set containing the station type to which the edge is directed (with $D_P = \emptyset$ in case e_P is undirected) and $w_P \in \mathbb{N} \cup \{0\}$ is the weight.[3]

A «place» edge models a route of length w_P between every station of type T_{S_1} and every station of type T_{S_2}. Thus, agents can reach a station of type T_{S_2} from a station of type T_{S_1} in w_P time units (and vice-versa). In case e_P is directed, it additionally states that the stations of the connected types must be visited in the order given by the edge's direction (see Fig. 1, between "Mathematics" and "Literature", as an example of an undirected «place» edge).

«time» Edges. A «time» edge $e_T \in E_T$ is an undirected or directed weighted edge between any two component types $T_{C_1}, T_{C_2} \in S_{T_C}$. It is defined as:

$$e_T := (\{T_{C_1}, T_{C_2}\}, D_T, L, w_T) \tag{6}$$

where $D_T \in \{\{T_{C_1}\}, \{T_{C_2}\}, \emptyset\}$ is a set containing the component type to which the edge is directed (with $D_T = \emptyset$ in case e_T is undirected). The set $L \in \{\{T_{C_1}\}, \{T_{C_2}\}, \{T_{C_1}, T_{C_2}\}, \emptyset\}$ contains the component type(s) to which e_T is connected with a logical conjunction (in case more than one temporal dependencies are declared to a component type). If $L \neq \emptyset$ then either e_T must be undirected or $D_T = L$. The weight of the edge is defined as $w_T \in \mathbb{N} \cup \{0\}$.[3]

A «time» edge defines a temporal synchronization between the components of type T_{C_1} and the components of type T_{C_2}: The weight w_T determines how many time units have to elapse between a visit event triggered on a component of type T_{C_1} and a visit event triggered on a component of type T_{C_2}. In case the edge is directed, it additionally states that the visit events must be triggered in the order given by the edge's direction. Graphically, a double line is used to distinguish «time» edges from «place» edges (see Fig. 1, e. g. between "Mathematics" and "Course", as an example of an undirected «time» edge).

2.3 Attributes

To refine a model, attributes can be annotated to agent types and station types, which are then applied to every agent/station of the respective type. Some attributes can be assigned to any kind of component type, others can be assigned to agent types or station types only.

An attribute is defined as a tuple:

$$p := (n, v) \tag{7}$$

where n is the attribute's name and $v \in \mathbb{N} \setminus \{0\}$ is the attribute's value.[4]

The current implementation of the modeling language comprises ten different attributes, e. g. *Necessity* (Nec.) to determine how often agents must visit connected stations or *Time* to determine the duration of a visit event. These attributes cover common use cases for spatio-temporal scenarios (further attributes could be part of future extensions). The example in Fig. 1 demonstrates how attributes can be used to create more detailed models (e. g. the Nec. attributes with a value of 1 determine for every station to be visited exactly one time).

2.4 Perspectives

Perspectives are structural modeling elements, that do not contribute any semantics to a simulation. Perspectives support the decomposition of complex scenarios by enforcing the modeler to consider a scenario from different point of views. The resulting perspectives each represent a simplified aspect of the modeled scenario.

A perspective $\psi \in \Psi$ is defined as a tuple:

$$\psi := (f, V_\psi) \tag{8}$$

---

[3] The edge's weight is restricted to $\mathbb{N}$, since the current implementation of the framework is based on both discrete time and space units. For alternative implementations the weight could also be extended to $\mathbb{R}$.

[4] Some attributes are semantically restricted to $\mathbb{N}$ by nature (e. g. attributes for limiting the number of visit events). Other attributes could also be extended to $\mathbb{R}$ in alternative implementations of the framework.

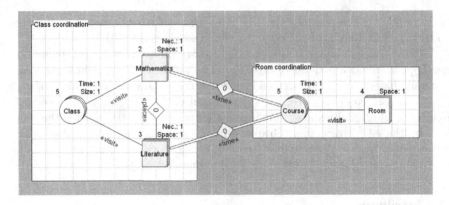

Fig. 1. A small timetabling scenario where classes have to be assigned to courses and courses have to be assigned to rooms. The scenario can be easily decomposed by separately considering the problem from the classes and the rooms points of view.

where f is a name, that describes the aspect on which the perspective is focused and $V_\psi \subseteq V$ is a set of component types belonging to the perspective.

Perspectives can be easily connected using «time» edges between their component types. Figure 1 shows an example on how perspectives can be used to decompose a problem (here, a small timetabling problem is first considered from two different perspectives, which are then synchronized using «time» edges).

3   Simulation Framework

This section introduces the simulation framework.[5] First, Sect. 3.1 provides detailed semantics of the graphical modeling language by describing the basic state transition mechanism of the framework according to the relations among the component types. In Sect. 3.2, the basic idea of the simulation algorithm is outlined. Section 3.3 explains the generic visualization scheme and in Sect. 3.4 the agent programming interface is introduced.

3.1   Formal Semantics

The transition mechanism of the framework is based on the sets A_G and S_G, where A_G is the set of all agents and S_G is the set of all stations in a scenario graph G.

The semantics are formalized using rules with a $\frac{premises}{conclusion}$ notation based on operational semantics [14] (where premises represent a state and the conclusion represents the resulting subsequent state), with a special focus on temporal

---

[5] The project can be downloaded from GITHUB: https://github.com/dapel/Abstract Swarm.

aspects:[6] Premises are described using one or more conjunctive expressions of the form $\langle expr, \sigma_t^a \rangle$, yielding the value of $expr$ in state σ of agent a at time t (where $t = 0$ is the time of the initial state of the simulation before the simulation starts). A conclusion is given by the expression $\sigma_t^a \triangleright \sigma_t'^a$, describing the transition of agent a from state σ to the subsequent state σ' at time $t > 0$. A state σ_t^a is defined as a tuple $\sigma_t^a := (a.target, a.distance, a.visiting)$ containing the state variables of agent a at time t, which will be described in the following:

- $a.target \in S_G \cup \{Null\}$: the current target station selected by a (Null if a currently has no target)
- $a.distance \in \mathbb{N} \cup \{0\}$: the current distance of a to its target station $a.target$
- $a.visiting \in \mathbb{B} := \{True, False\}$: a Boolean value that specifies whether a is currently visiting a station

To be able to create compact representations of the semantics, the following shorthands are defined for agent $a \in A_G$ and station $s \in S_G$:

- $a \,@\, s := (a.distance = 0) \wedge \neg a.visiting$
  (a is located at s but not visiting s)
- $a \odot s := (a.target = s)$
  (a has selected s as next target)
- $a \rightarrow s := (a.target = s) \wedge \neg a.visiting \wedge (a.distance > 0)$
  (a is on the way to s)
- $a \odot s := (a.target = s) \wedge (a.distance = 0) \wedge a.visiting$
  (a is visiting s)

Using these preliminaries, the semantics can be formalized as follows.[7]

Semantics of «visit» Edges. Given a «visit» edge $e_V = (\{T_A, T_S\}, b) \in E_V$, an agent a being of type T_A and a station s being of type T_S, the semantics of e_V is defined by the following rule:

$$sem^{e_V}: \quad \frac{\langle a \odot s, \sigma_t^a \rangle \quad \langle a \,@\, s, \sigma_t^a \rangle}{\sigma_t^a \triangleright \sigma_t'^a} \tag{9}$$

with $\sigma_t'^a = (s, 0, True)$.

The rule states that e_V allows a to visit s, given that a is located at s and a decided to enter s. Note that there is no temporal change from σ_t^a to $\sigma_t'^a$, since the simulation time progresses not until *all* agents have been handled (see "Global State Transition" at the end of Sect. 3.1).

---

[6] Note that only the simulation semantics of the graphical modeling language are formalized here, and not the action selection or the communication mechanism of the agents, which will be explained separately in Sects. 3.2 and 3.4.

[7] Note that the semantic formalism may appear complicated to the reader, in contrast to the claims made in the beginning about the framework being easy to use. But users usually use the graphical modeling interface and therefore don't have to deal with the formalism, which serves as a foundation of the simulation algorithm here.

Semantics of «place» Edges. Given a «place» edge $e_P = (\{T_{S_1}, T_{S_2}\}, D_P,$ $w_P) \in E_P$, a station s_1 being of type T_{S_1}, a station s_2 being of type T_{S_2} and an agent a of type T_A being connected to T_{S_1}, T_{S_2} by «visit» edges, the semantics of e_P is defined by the following rules:

$$sem_1^{e_P}: \quad \frac{\langle a @ s_1, \sigma_t^a \rangle \quad \langle a \odot s_2, \sigma_t^a \rangle}{\sigma_t^a \triangleright \sigma_t'^a} \tag{10}$$

with $\sigma_t'^a = (s_2, w_P, \text{False})$ and

$$sem_2^{e_P}: \quad \frac{\langle a \rightarrow s, \sigma_t^a \rangle}{\sigma_t^a \triangleright \sigma_t'^a} \tag{11}$$

with $\sigma_t'^a = (s, \langle a.distance, \sigma_t^a \rangle - 1, \text{False})$.

The first rule states that e_P allows a to go from s_1 to s_2, given that a is located at s_1 and a wants to visit s_2. The second rule states that a can continue going from s_1 to s_2 (until s_2 is reached), given that a is already on its way to s_2.

In case e_P is directed such that $D_P = \{s_2\}$, the following additional rule is provided:

$$sem_{D_P \neq \emptyset}^{e_P}: \quad \frac{\langle a @ s_2, \sigma_t^a \rangle \quad \langle a \odot s_2, \sigma_t^a \rangle \quad \langle a \odot s_1, \sigma_{t_0 < t - w_P}^a \rangle}{\sigma_t^a \triangleright \sigma_t'^a} \tag{12}$$

with $\sigma_t'^a = (s_2, 0, \text{True})$.

This rule states that a is allowed to visit s_2 given that s_1 was visited by a at least w_P time units before.

Semantics of «time» Edges. Since «time» edges can be defined between any two component types T_{C_1} and T_{C_2}, we consider two agent types T_{A_1}, T_{A_2} and two station types T_{S_1}, T_{S_2}, with T_{A_1} being connected to T_{S_1} and T_{A_2} being connected to T_{S_2} by «visit» edges. A «time» edge $e_T = (\{T_{C_1}, T_{C_2}\}, D_T, L, w_T) \in E_T$ can then be defined between either T_{A_1} and T_{A_2}, T_{A_1} and T_{S_2}, T_{S_1} and T_{S_2} or T_{S_1} and T_{A_2}, resulting in the same semantics. Given two agents a_1, a_2 being of type T_{A_1}, T_{A_2} and two stations s_1, s_2 being of type T_{S_1}, T_{S_2} respectively, the semantics of e_T, is defined by the following rules:

$$sem^{e_T}: \quad \frac{\langle a_1 @ s_1, \sigma_t^{a_1} \rangle \quad \langle a_1 \odot s_1, \sigma_t^{a_1} \rangle \quad \bigwedge_{t=t-w_T}^{t} \langle \neg (a_2 \odot s_2), \sigma_t^{a_2} \rangle}{\sigma_t^{a_1} \triangleright \sigma_t'^{a_1}} \tag{13}$$

with $\sigma_t'^{a_1} = (s_1, 0, \text{True})$.

The rule states that e_T allows a_1 to enter s_1 if there are at least w_T time units elapsed after a_2 visited s_2.

In case e_T is directed such that either $D_T = \{T_{A_2}\}$ or $D_T = \{T_{S_2}\}$ (depending on which component types are connected by the edge), instead the following (simpler) rule is provided:

$$sem_{D_T \neq \emptyset}^{e_T}: \quad \frac{\langle a_1 @ s_1, \sigma_t^{a_1} \rangle \quad \langle a_1 \odot s_1, \sigma_t^{a_1} \rangle \quad \langle a_2 \odot s_2, \sigma_{t_0 < t - w_T}^{a_2} \rangle}{\sigma_t^{a_1} \triangleright \sigma_t'^{a_1}} \tag{14}$$

with $\sigma_t'^{a_1} = (s_1, 0, \text{True})$.

This rule states that a_1 is allowed to visit s_1 given that a_2 visited s_2 at least w_T time units before. Note that this automatically fulfills the premises of rule sem^{e_T} as well.

The special case that e_T is both undirected and having a weight of 0 (thus $D_T = \emptyset$ and $w_T = 0$), leads to the additional rule:

$$sem^{e_T}_{D_T=\emptyset,w_T=0}: \quad \frac{\langle a_1 @ s_1, \sigma_t^{a_1} \rangle \ \langle a_1 \odot s_1, \sigma_t^{a_1} \rangle \ \langle a_2 \odot s_2, \sigma_t^{a_2} \rangle}{\sigma_t^{a_1} \rhd \sigma_t'^{a_1}} \qquad (15)$$

with $\sigma_t'^{a_1} = (s_1, 0, \text{True})$, which states that a_1 and a_2 must visit s_1 and s_2 simultaneously.

Global State Transition. Having the semantics of the relations to describe the state changes of agents during a single time unit, in this section, the transition of a global simulation state $\Sigma_t = (\{\sigma_t^{a_1}, ..., \sigma_t^{a_n}\}, t)$ at time t to its consecutive state Σ_{t+1} will be defined.

Since it is not always possible to apply one of the transition rules to an agent (e. g. some rules depend on the decision of other agents or attributes may prevent a station from being visited, etc.), a default rule is introduced, which is applied to every agent a to which no other rule can be applied at time t:

$$default: \quad \frac{}{\sigma_t^a \rhd \sigma_t'^a} \qquad (16)$$

with $\sigma_t'^a = \sigma_t^a$.

This rule simply allows the transition of agent a from state σ_t^a to state $\sigma_t'^a$ without changing any state variables.

Given all transition rules, a global simulation step can be defined as follows:

$$simstep: \quad \frac{\bigwedge_{a \in A_G} \langle \sigma_t^a \rhd \sigma_t'^a, \Sigma_t \rangle}{\Sigma_t \rhd \Sigma_{t+1}} \qquad (17)$$

with $\Sigma_{t+1} = (\{\sigma_t'^{a_1}, ..., \sigma_t'^{a_n}\}, \langle t, \Sigma_t \rangle + 1)$.

According to this rule, the simulation progresses to the next time unit by applying the transition rules to every single agent.

3.2 Simulation Algorithm

The discrete simulation algorithm operates on the two sets A_G and S_G (where A_G is the set of all agents and S_G is the set of all stations of a graph G as introduced in Sect. 3.1). In every time step t all (active) components are processed sequentially in random order (as proposed e. g. in [11]).

A *single step* for an agent $a \in A_G$ is calculated according to Algorithm 1, which makes use of the following variables/function: $a.visiting \in \mathbb{B} := \{\text{True}, \text{False}\}$ determines whether a is currently visiting a station, $a.target \in S_G \cup \{\text{Null}\}$ is the current target station of a (Null in case a currently has no target), $a.distance \in \mathbb{N} \cup \{0\}$ is the current distance of a to its target station $a.target$, and

Algorithm 1. Single Agent Step

```
01  if ¬a.visiting:
02      Ask a for next target station s
03      a.target := s
04  if ¬a.visiting ∧ a.target ≠ Null ∧ a.distance > 0:
05      Move a towards its target station a.target
06  else:
07      if a.distance = 0 ∧ visitingOk(a, a.target):
08          Trigger visit event on a and s
09          a.visiting := True
10      if a.visiting:
11          Progress visit time of a
12  Allow a to communicate to other agents
```

$visitingOk : A_G \times S_G \to \mathbb{B}$ is a function, which returns whether a is currently allowed to visit its target station (according to the constraints of the modeled scenario).

A special problem of this approach arises when dealing with «time» edges having a weight of 0: These «time» edges require visit events to be triggered *simultaneously* on the connected agents/stations (see Sect. 2.2). But since the single steps of all agents are computed *consecutively*, this cannot be checked within the calculation of an agent's single step (in function $visitingOk$).

Since «time» edges are essential modeling elements and are usually used extensively (e. g. for synchronizing perspectives), solving this problem is crucial. To achieve this, the simulation system makes use of a "relax and repair" approach (as more generally described e. g. in [4]): An entire simulation step (including the single steps of all agents) is first calculated without considering any «time» edges (*relaxation*). If this results in an inconsistent simulation state containing violated «time» edges, the inconsistency is *repaired* by successively removing all illegally visiting agents.

3.3   Simulation Visualization

The simulation visualization follows a generic approach: It allows to observe a running simulation without the need to define a specific visualization scheme for a modeled scenario.

This is achieved by making use of a concept known from Petri nets (e. g. [15]): Since a scenario is represented as a graph, the graph itself can be used to visualize the simulation process, by varying the size of the nodes over time.

The size of an agent type decreases the more agents of that type are currently vising a station and the size of a station types increases, the more agents are having one of its stations as target.

The visualization of the simulation results also follows a generic approach: By simply logging whenever an agent visits a station, the outcome of a simulation can be intuitively visualized as a Gantt chart (e. g. [13]).

3.4   Agent Programming Interface

The agent programming interface is designed to be light-weight with a focus on the simple implementation of agent behavior. By making use of the abstract concepts of the graphical modeling language (according to Sect. 2), it allows to implement agents independently from a specific scenario (i. e. agents basically have to deal with stations and with other agents in any case). Thus, the resulting agents can be deployed in any modeled scenario.

The agent interface consists of three functions, which can be implemented using the PYTHON programming language. The functions serve to determine the action selection, the communication behavior and the treatment of the reward gained by the agents. All of them will be explained in the following.

Evaluation Function. An action of an agent $a \in A_G$ consists of (i) moving to a target station and (ii) visiting that station. An agent initiates such an action by selecting its next target station s_{next}. The selection is determined by the evaluation of every *potential* target station through the evaluation function. Potential stations are all stations $S_a \subseteq S_G$ to which a is connected with «visit» edges (and which are still relevant for the running simulation according to their attributes).

The evaluation function is called by the simulation system at time t_{act}, when the agent a has to choose its next action (see line 2 in Algorithm 1) and it is called subsequently for every potential station $s \in S_a$.

The evaluation function has the following signature:

$$evaluation(a, A, S, t_{act}, s) \tag{18}$$

where a is the agent itself, A is an associative data structure containing all other agents of a scenario with their recently communicated data, S is the set of all stations of the scenario, $t_{act} > 0$ is the current simulation time and s is the station to be evaluated by a as potential next target.

The return value of the function determines which station will be selected: The station for which the highest value is returned will be selected as the next target station of a. Note that implementing the agent's decision making through the evaluation function can also comprise complex behavior like planning, learning, etc. since further data structures can be created and attached to a, and external processes can be called here (e. g. for integrating external inference or other modules).

Communication Function. The communication function can be used to implement the communication behavior of agents by determining the information that are sent from one agent to the others for coordinating their actions.

It is called in every time unit t_{com} for every agent $a \in A_G$ at the end of its single step (see line 12 in Algorithm 1).

The communication function has the following signature:

$$communication(a, A, S, t_{com}, C) \tag{19}$$

where a, A, S are defined analogously to the evaluation function, $t_{com} > 0$ is the current simulation time and C is a tuple with predefined basic communication information (consisting of a's target station, the time unit when the station will be reached and the corresponding evaluation value).

The return value of the function consists of the information sent by a to all other agents. The most basic form of communication can be implemented by simply returning the basic communication tuple C: In this case, agents are only able to coordinate their immediate next action. In general, it is possible to return any kind of information (e. g. a list of actions representing a plan), which then must be considered accordingly by other agents in the evaluation function.

The communicated information can be received by other agents by accessing the parameter A. Agents can then consider these information in their decision making process (e. g. when evaluating a station as potential next target).

Reward Function. The reward function allows to implement how agents treat the rewards they gain for their actions during the simulation.

The function is called for every agent $a \in A_G$ at the end of time unit $t_{rwd} \geq t_{act}$, where t_{act} is the time unit in which a selected a target station (see Evaluation Function) and t_{rwd} is the time unit in which a finished visiting the previously selected target station.

The reward function has the following signature:

$$reward(a, A, S, t_{rwd}, r) \qquad (20)$$

where a, A, S are defined analogously to the evaluation function, t_{rwd} is the current simulation time and $r \in [0, 1]$ is the reward of a for its most recently selected target station.

Since the framework serves as a meta-model for spatio-temporal scenarios, the reward value r is defined independently from a specific scenario. To achieve this, the current implementation of the framework acts on the assumption, that good decisions are those leading to advantages for *all* agents $a \in A_G$ (and not only for the one making the decision). Following this idea, r is defined as follows:

$$r := \frac{1}{t_{rwd} - t_{act} + 1} \sum_{t=t_{act}}^{t_{rwd}} \left(\frac{1}{|A_G|} \sum_{a \in A_G} w(\sigma_t^a) \right) \qquad (21)$$

with function

$$w(\sigma_t^a) := \begin{cases} 1, & \text{if } \langle a.visiting, \sigma_t^a \rangle = \text{True} \\ 0, & \text{otherwise.} \end{cases}$$

Note that usually not all agents A_G have to be considered in the inner sum, e. g. some agents could not be relevant anymore for the simulation due to attributes limiting the number of visit events (like Freq. or Nec.).

According to this, a decision of an agent is higher rewarded the more agents are able to visit stations simultaneously and lower rewarded the more agents are constrained in visiting stations.

4   Use Case Examples

To evaluate the framework's fundamental idea of reusing and evaluating agents in different kinds of scenarios, this section introduces a use case study with two example scenarios represented by the graphs G_{school} and G_{prod} and a simple agent model that will be deployed in both cases. The scenarios stem from two different domains (school vs. industry) and although the scenarios are both related to scheduling, the underlying problems cover different aspects (as will be shown in Sect. 4.3).

The two scenarios are introduced in Sects. 4.1 and 4.2. Section 4.3 outlines the dissimilarity of the underlying problems. Section 4.4 introduces an example of a simple agent model and Sect. 4.5 presents the simulation results with the simple agent model being used to simulate both scenarios.

4.1   School Timetabling

This scenario extends the example given in Fig. 1 to a more realistic scenario: A small fictive school is considered, where timetables have to be created for teachers, pupils and rooms. The school comprises:

- 2 math teachers, 2 English teachers and 1 music teacher
- 5 classes (every class has to get 2 math lessons, 2 English lessons, 1 music lesson)
- 4 rooms (3 normal class rooms, 1 special music room)

Perspectives are implied by considering the scenario separately from the teachers, the classes and the rooms points of view. The perspectives (each containing a simplified view on the scenario) then are synchronized using «time» edges.

Figure 2 shows the corresponding scenario graph G_{school}.

4.2   Production Simulation

In this scenario, a small factory is considered, where workers are producing different products. As part of the quality assurance process, the products have to be analyzed using different machines. The factory comprises:

- 8 workers
- 2 kinds of products (5 of each kind, one kind having the need to be analyzed at higher priority)
- 3 machines (2 of which being able to analyze on their own, 1 needing a worker to monitor the analysis)

The scenario is modeled by separately considering it from the workers and the products perspective. Figure 3 show the corresponding scenario graph G_{prod}.

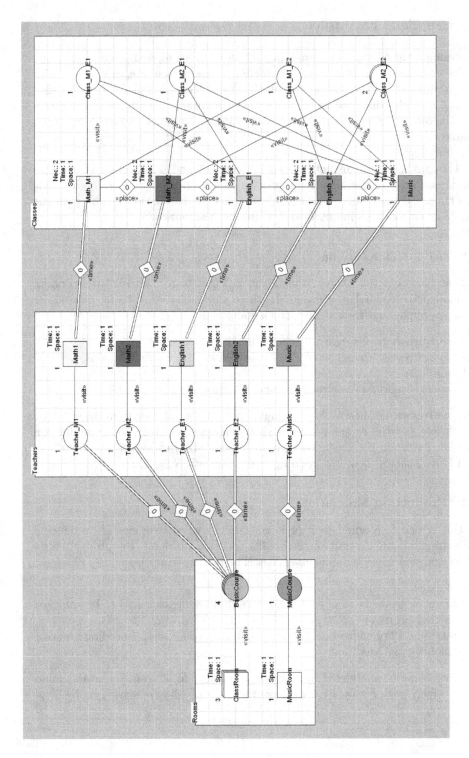

Fig. 2. The scenario graph G_{school} of the school timetabling example.

4.3 Dissimilarity of the Scenarios

Although the two scenarios represented by the graphs G_{school} and G_{prod} are both related to scheduling, the underlying problems are different in several aspects:

- G_{school} only comprises synchronizing time dependencies, whereas most of the «time» edges used in G_{prod} are directed with a weight > 0 and therefore contain sequential time relations.
- No Priority attributes are used in G_{school}, whereas priorities play an essential role in the scenario described by G_{prod}.
- All visit events of the scenario described by G_{school} take exactly one time unit, whereas in case of G_{prod} visit events are of different durations.
- Space is not important in the scenario described by G_{school} (since all station types have the same space attributes), whereas in case of G_{prod}, some stations can be distinguished by their maximum available space (see "Analysis2" in Fig. 3).

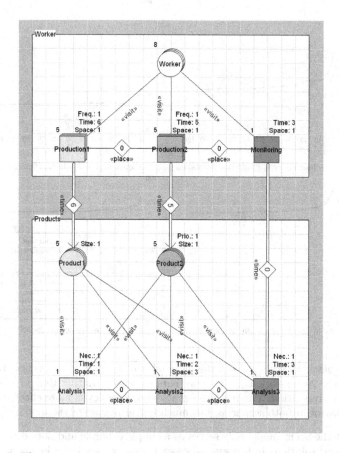

Fig. 3. The scenario graph G_{prod} of the production simulation example.

These differences lead to different percepts and actions on the agent level (e.g. agents have to deal with different kinds of spatio-temporal constraints). In addition, the state-action spaces of agents are of different dimensions and shapes. However, due to the abstract representation of the scenarios as graphs and due to the generic agent interface, percepts are generalized by the graphical modeling elements and the agent behavior can be implemented independently from a specific scenario by only determining the selection of stations as a function of time. This will be demonstrated by the agent model in the following.

4.4 A Simple Agent Model

To simulate the two use case scenarios, a simple reactive agent model will be implemented as an example in this section.[8]

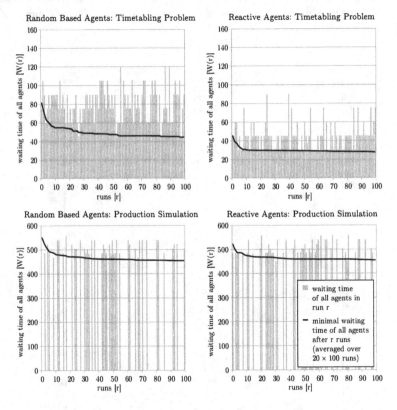

Fig. 4. The black curves represent the minimal waiting time of all agents after r runs (averaged over 20 repetitions). The gray bars show the waiting time of one selected representative repetition. The reactive agents' simple policy is more effective than the random behavior in both scenarios, but much better in case of the first scenario.

---

[8] Note that the agent model only serves as a simple example and does not necessarily lead to good solutions in the general case. More complex behaviors (e.g. adaptive, learning, knowledge-based or BDI-like agents) could be also implemented using the agent programming interface.

The agent behaves according to the following simple rule:

"If station s is the one with the most free space, then select s as next target."

The rule can be implemented easily using the agent programming interface (see Sect. 3.4) by simply returning the current free space of station s in the evaluation function (also considering the next decision of the other agents by making use of the communication function).

This rule seems to be intuitive to produce a reasonable behavior in several situations, since it prevents agents from queuing at the same station (however, it is obvious that this may not lead to optimal behavior in the general case).

4.5 Simulation Results

To demonstrate how agents can be evaluated in the context of different problems, this section provides the simulation results of the scenarios introduced in Sects. 4.1 and 4.2 by using the agent model from Sect. 4.4 in both cases.

The total waiting time of all agents during a simulation run is considered and compared against a random base line (i. e. agents selecting their target stations randomly). Figure 4 shows the simulation results for both scenarios.

5 Conclusion and Future Work

This paper presented a framework for the modeling and simulation of spatio-temporal multiagent scenarios, where agents can be easily deployed and observed in the context of different scenarios.

The first part introduced the graphical modeling language ABSTRACTSWARM according to [1], which allows to quickly setup multiagent scenarios by only considering the scenario description (without modeling the agent behavior). In addition, it was explained how the concept of *perspectives* can contribute to the decomposition of more complex problems.

Based on the modeling language, a simulation system was developed comprising a generic visualization scheme and a light-weight agent programming interface, which allows to implement agents in a generic way, such that they can be immediately reused in any other scenario without adapting their percepts, actions or communication.

To demonstrate the idea of deploying and monitoring agents in the context of different scenarios, two use case scenarios were considered and it was shown that agents can be implemented in a generic way to be studied across scenarios with different underlying problems.

Besides continuing the developement of the framework itself, future work should comprise further evaluation of the framework by applying it to existing real world problems, like the STCMP [17] mentioned in Sect. 1.

Acknowledgements. The author would like to thank Matthias Thimm for constant feedback on this paper. The research leading to these results has received funding from the European Community's Seventh Framework Programme (FP7/2007-2013), REVEAL (Grant agree number 610928).

References

1. Apeldoorn, D.: AbstractSwarm – a generic graphical modeling language for multi-agent systems. In: Klusch, M., Thimm, M., Paprzycki, M. (eds.) MATES 2013. LNCS, vol. 8076, pp. 180–192. Springer, Heidelberg (2013)
2. Bordini, R.H., Hübner, J.F.: BDI agent programming in agentspeak using *jason* (Tutorial Paper). In: Toni, F., Torroni, P. (eds.) CLIMA 2005. LNCS (LNAI), vol. 3900, pp. 143–164. Springer, Heidelberg (2006)
3. Cabac, L., Dörges, T., Duvigneau, M., Reese, C., Wester-Ebbinghaus, M.: Models and tools for mulan applications. In: Burkhard, H.-D., Lindemann, G., Verbrugge, R., Varga, L.Z. (eds.) CEEMAS 2007. LNCS (LNAI), vol. 4696, pp. 328–330. Springer, Heidelberg (2007)
4. Domschke, W., Scholl, A.: Logistik: Rundreisen und Touren. Oldenbourg Wissenschaftsverlag, München (2010)
5. Greulich, C., Edelkamp, S., Gath, M.: Agent-based multimodal transport planning in dynamic environments. In: Timm, I.J., Thimm, M. (eds.) KI 2013. LNCS, vol. 8077, pp. 74–85. Springer, Heidelberg (2013)
6. Holmgren, J., Davidsson, P., Persson, J.A., Ramstedt, L.: Tapas: a multi-agent-based model for simulation of transport chains. Simul. Model. Pract. Theory **23**, 1–18 (2012)
7. Kimura, T., Sano, T., Hayashida, K., Takeichi, N., Minegishi, Y., Yoshida, Y., Watanabe, H.: Representing crowds with a mulit-agent model. Architectural Plann. Res. **74**(636), 371–377 (2009)
8. Klügl, F.: Sesam: visual programming and participatory simulation for agent-based models. In: Weyns, H., Uhrmacher, A. (eds.) Multi-Agent Systems: Simulation and Applications, pp. 477–508. CRC Press, Boca Raton (2009)
9. Kutschinski, E., Polani, D., Uthmann, T.: Dmarks ii: An agent-based platform for automated trade and its simulation. In: 14. ASIM Workshop Simulation and Artificial Intelligence on Multi-Agent Systems and Individual-Based Simulation. Würzburg, Germany (2000)
10. Luke, S., Cioffi-Revilla, C., Panait, L., Sullivan, K., Balan, G.: Mason: a multi-agent simulation environment. Simul. Trans. Soc. Model. Simul. Int. **81**(7), 517–527 (2005)
11. Minar, N., Burkhart, R., Langton, C., Askenazi, M.: The swarm simulation system: a toolkit for building multi-agent simulations. Working paper 96–06-042, Santa Fe Institute (1996)
12. North, M., Collier, N., Ozik, J., Tatara, E., Altaweel, M., Macal, C., Bragen, M., Sydelko, P.: Complex adaptive systems modeling with repast simphony. Complex Adapt. Syst. **1**, 3 (2013)
13. Pinedo, M.: Scheduling: Theory, Algorithms, and Systems. Springer, New York (2012)
14. Plotkin, G.D.: A structural approach to operational semantics. J. Logic Algebraic Program. **60–61**, 17–139 (2004)
15. Reisig, W.: Petrinetze: Modellierungstechnik, Analysemethoden. Fallstudien. Vieweg+Teubner, Wiesbaden (2010)

16. Sansores, C.E., Reyes, F., Gómez, H.F., Pavón, J., Calderón-Aguilera, L.E.: Biomass: a biological multi-agent simulation system. In: 2011 Federated Conference on Computer Science and Information Systems (FedCSIS 2011), pp. 675–682. IEEE, Szczecin (2012)

17. Scheuren, S., Stiene, S., Hertzberg, J., Hartanto, R., Reinecke, M.: The problem of spatio-temporally constrained motion planning for cooperative vehicles. In: Proceedings of the 26th Workshop "Planen, Scheduling und Konfigurieren, Entwerfen" (PuK 2011) (2011)

18. Tisue, S., Wilensky, U.: Netlogo: A simple environment for modeling complexity. In: Proceedings of the Fifth International Conference on Complex Systems (ICCS 2004). Boston (2004)

Smart Things Working Together

A Multiagent Systems Perspective on Industry 4.0 Supply Networks

Marc Premm[⊠] and Stefan Kirn

Information Systems 2, University of Hohenheim, Stuttgart, Germany
{marc.premm, stefan.kirn}@uni-hohenheim.de

Abstract. Industry 4.0 scenarios involve Cyber-Physical-Systems to achieve a higher degree of individualization. Multiagent systems show the main characteristics to reach the goal of increased individualization possibilities by flexible interactions of agents. However, the organizational complexity of individualized manufacturing processes and thus the complexity of current supply networks require the extension of current multiagent system models. Enabling interaction between various multiagent systems representing autonomous actors of a supply network is necessary to cope with the increased complexity. This paper presents ongoing research and adds to the literature by modelling multiagent systems as fractals of a supply network using logistics modelling approaches. We present three examples for applying the multiagent perspective to such Industry 4.0 supply networks.

Keywords: Multiagent systems · Supply networks · Organizations

1 Introduction

The Industry 4.0 paradigm describes the forth industrial revolution with the vision of "everything connected with everything else". In particular, the focus is set on companies that build up cooperative networks of unique specialists [1]. These networks facilitate the step from single plants to supply networks, but require substantial information exchange between the actors for a seamless inter-organizational process flow. The demand for highly customized products and services is continuously increasing. Hence, processes in supply networks have to be constantly adapted to changing conditions that, due to the high and further increasing complexity, cannot be handled with current planning and control methods [2]. An important new element of these networks are Cyber-Physical-Systems (CPS). Due to their IP-based communication capabilities, they offer new options to bridge the gap between physical manufacturing processes, human employees, and information technology supporting monitoring, coordination, and controlling of the operations, and the local processes themselves [3].

New organizational forms are required to manage Industry 4.0 operations in emerging hybrid organizational settings, where humans and CPS cooperate in well-organized, small teams to produce and deliver their local output to the overall supply network. In such supply networks, the competitiveness of each of its parts is directly related to the competitiveness of the overall supply network. The key factor for

J.P. Müller et al. (Eds.): MATES 2015, LNAI 9433, pp. 101–118, 2015.
DOI: 10.1007/978-3-319-27343-3_6

competitive success of these networks is their ability to react appropriately to changing market demands. These factors include (i) a faster reaction with less costs and of higher quality to individual customer demands, and (ii) the creation of new products and services for customers.

The concept of intelligent, cooperative software agents and multiagent systems (MAS) offers a well-suited approach to model, analyze and design such systems. Research in Distributed Artificial Intelligence (DAI) has identified appropriate organizational concepts for problem solving systems. However, they mainly focus on the flexibility of distributed and cooperative search algorithms, neglecting the stability of the organizational structure such as stable resource and task allocation within enterprises.

Existing approaches in multiagent technology often neglect the fact that autonomous software agents generally cooperate in a loosely coupled MAS, which dissolve after the objectives have been achieved. For industrial applications, however, it is mandatory for MAS to guarantee a certain degree of economically required stability concerning their existence and structure, while preserving their problem solving flexibility. Further, supply networks are built on a set of flexibly cooperating organizational units. They are capable to immediately adapt their network structure to the changing demands of suppliers, customers and their environments.

A number of Industry 4.0 scenarios exhibit the complexity of MAS. For instance, the application of autonomous agents in the automotive manufacturing industry has gained significant attention. However, these manufacturing companies are generally situated in a supply network and thus depend on multiple suppliers. This further increases the complexity of the system and raises the question, whether and how the concept of MAS can be extended to meet these network-related requirements.

The aim of this paper is twofold: First, we survey extant literature from DAI and management science with respect to organization theory. Second, we develop a model for cooperation between different MAS, which is suitable for Industry 4.0 scenarios. The proposed artifact is based on (i) logistics (the right material in the right quantity, at the right time and the right place) and on the (ii) paradigm of fractal companies introduced by Warnecke [4].

The remainder is structured as follows. Section 2 discusses related work on multiagent organizations. Section 3 introduces models used in logistics. Section 4 presents the extension to multi-multiagent systems with corresponding examples in Sect. 5. Section 6 concludes.

2   State of the Art

This section surveys the state of the art on DAI, management science and their interrelations. First, literature on multiagent organization from the perspective of DAI is presented. Then, we compare the findings to approaches in management science, followed by reviewing the paradigm of fractal enterprises.

2.1 Multiagent-Organization Models Revisited

Organization as a Social Metaphor. Researchers in the field of MAS/DAI with backgrounds in management science have noted that "organization" is a metaphor that can be useful to describe, study, and design distributed software systems [5, 6]. As compared to organizational theories in management, however, MAS/DAI still lacks similar fine-grained concepts and instruments for describing, analyzing, understanding and designing organizational phenomena within agent-based systems [7]. It is very difficult to find out how an organization made up of people will change if software agents are joining this organization. This is a significant barrier for collaborative DAI innovations. However, first approaches consider the formation of teams within organizations, which may involve both software and human agents [8].

Organization has often been thought of as a top-down concept: starting from a given task, and, through iterative processes of task/sub-task decomposition, fine-grained task trees (top-down) and sub-solution synthesizing procedures (bottom-up) are designed. This approach leads to a top-down design of distributed problem solving systems. However, there exist many problems, in which large parts of the problem space are unknown. In such cases agent systems need to be configured bottom-up such that the relevant method is self-organization [9–12].

Organization as a Pool of Resources. The concept of cooperative problem solving (CDPS) approaches the integration of existing single problem solving experts (intelligent agents) into an overall framework [13]. The aim is to make synergetic use of their individual abilities. Otherwise, these abilities can only be used locally. This bottom-up perspective of building up a CDP system is accompanied by a top-down perspective on coordinating global processes of problem solving.

This approach can be compared to the perspective of management science, in which organizations are systems that pool individual resources in order to gain additional benefits for all of their members. However, so far in contrast to organizational theory, MAS/DAI research does not adequately address the question why an agent may join and contribute to a system.

Organization as Partitioning of Problem Spaces. From an organizational perspective, distributed problem solving implements the concept of dividing labor among a set of individuals, each possessing a particular capabilities profile. The idea is to assign to each agent the competence to solve a particular task type. For instance, Gasser states that "Organization is a precise way of dividing the problem space without specifying particular problem subtrees. Instead, agents are associated with problem types, and problem instances circulate to the agents which are responsible for instances of that type" [14].

As an immediate consequence, distributed problem solving leads to role concepts such as the role concept of the C-Net system [15]. However, the definition of roles in DAI is quite different to organization theories in management science. The latter refers to a role as to a precise definition of the expected behavior a particular organization member will exhibit. Role definitions are created by formal organizational procedures. Whenever a new individual joins an enterprise it has to formally commit itself to a particular set of organizational roles.

Computational and Mathematical Organization Theory. Besides models for solely human organizations this field of research does also comprise organizational models that involve software agents and consider distributed artificial intelligence. For instance, Kaufer and Carley model IT components as artificial agents that have different levels of information processing capacities. One major part of the model is the communication capabilities of agents: (i) how agents find communication partners, (ii) how information is communicated to the selected communication partner, and (iii) the consequences for the organization resulting from the communication [16]. This approach analyzes the effects of adding or removing agents from the organization by observing additional communication channels between the organizations' participants [17]. Literature on computational and mathematical organization theory mainly focuses on two ways of conceptualizing the design of an organization: (i) as a set of attributes or (ii) as a set of matrices [18]. Both ways can be used to structure parts of the overall design including resource access, authority/communication, or requirements.

OperA. Organizations per Agents (OperA) is a framework that enables the representation of organizational structures [19]. It incorporates an organization modelling language to define organizations and strictly distinguishes between the organizational structure and the instantiated agents populating the organization [20]. The modelling language uses three interrelated models: (i) The Organization Model describes the organizational structure including objectives, norms, roles, interactions, and ontologies, (ii) the Social Model mapping previously defined organizational roles to specific agents including contracts about role enactment, and (iii) the Interaction Model specifies the interaction among agents enacting organizational roles at run-time [20]. The OperettA toolset can be used for graphically supported modelling in OperA [21]. In the context of OperA the term organization describes a "specific solution created by more or less autonomous actors to achieve common objectives" [19]. The restriction to common goals is widespread in literature. However, in social organizations it is not necessary for all participant to share a common goal but they have to be motivated to contribute to the goal of the organization. Of course an incentive system might lead to the adaption of organizational goals for single agents but this cannot be generalized.

2.2   Comparison with Organizational Theory in Management Science

The concept of cooperating intelligent agents incorporates several important advantages with respect to the challenges of more and more human-like robots, of self-contained autonomic systems, of (so-called) autonomous cars and drones, and of Industrial 4.0 systems. However, in all these cases two conceptually different types of actors are involved. Thus, two completely different bodies of organizational theories have emerged.

On one hand, management science mainly considers organizations from a social science perspective. They build on the basic assumption that humans form an enterprise in order to fulfill a concrete market demand (e.g., production of autonomous cars). Organizational rules and definitions (e.g., definition of positions) are required to coordinate the division of labor, the behavior of employees, and all operational processes to produce, sell, and maintain goods and services. It is well understood, that enterprises need stability with respect to their suppliers and customers, to their employees, and to their infrastructural, technical and financial production factors. Indeed, the increased dynamics of their environments (e.g., changing consumer behaviors, changing market demand, changing market structures, changing market coordination, etc.) does also require an increase of organizational flexibility.

On the other hand, DAI has developed organizational theories that build on the assumption that artificial intelligent software agents form a "well-organized" problem solving system. DAI distinguishes so-called distributed problem solvers from cooperative distributed problem solvers and MAS. In any of these cases aims and success factors are given by technical criteria, based on methods and definitions of artificial intelligence. The main tasks include to conceptualize, implement and run an AI system, which is capable to efficiently deal with distributed knowledge and with knowledge requests. "Organization" thus refers to the "organization of symbolic knowledge within one knowledge base", to the division of overall knowledge into a well-"organized" set of sub knowledge bases, or to the "organization of search processes". "Organization" is understood as a tool to facilitate the search for symbolically represented formal knowledge within a set of knowledge bases. It enables agents to achieve their aims even in previously unknown environments and to pursue their goals even in hostile environments or, if necessary, also in collaboration with antagonistic agents. These include either antagonistic technical systems (e.g., several autonomous cars approaching a crossing, where each car has been implemented as a selfish agent with the overall aim to drive as fast as possible) – or humans aiming to stop their robots[1], which exhibit a behavior that is unacceptable for their owners (or human organizations).

2.3   Fractal Enterprises and Fractal Enterprise Processes

In order to meet the challenges of the increasing complexity and the dynamics of world-wide competition, it has been argued that the enterprise of the future will be radically decentralized. Decentralization involves the allocation of autonomy, resources, and responsibilities to deeper levels of the organizational hierarchy (for instance, see work of Tapscott and Caston [23] or Warnecke [4]). This requires enterprises to replace hierarchical planning by more decentralized concepts of coordination. In turn, autonomous organizational subunits need to exhibit a much greater degree of intelligence and self-referencing skills than they do today. This has given rise to the notion of organizational fractals [4]. Organizational fractals are characterized by the following major criteria [4]:

- **Self-similarity.** The criterion of self-similarity describes the structural characteristics of the organization and the modalities of generating added value. The self-similarity between different fractals enables resource sharing especially for informational resources.

---

[1] In this paper robots are cyber-physical systems controlled by agent-based software (see the concept of mouth-head-body architectures suggested by Steiner, Mahling & Haugeneder [22]).

- **Self-organization and Self-optimization.** Self-organization and self-optimization require autonomy to apply individual solutions to the corresponding tasks, and thus addresses the strategic, the tactical as well as the operational level. This decentralized approach aims at processes that require highly dynamic adaptation.
- **Goal-orientation.** This paradigm assumes that the overall goal system results from the individual goal systems of the fractals and is designed in a way that prevents conflicts between different goal systems. Thus, the performance of each fractal can be measured continuously.
- **Dynamic.** In contrast to traditional manufacturing islands, fractals show a higher degree of autonomy and thus of dynamic behavior. Different fractals are connected by an information and communication system and enable flexible adaptations to dynamic environmental requirements.

Organizational fractals involve a maximum degree of local autonomy, self-control, and self-organization skills. Organizational fractals aim to maximize their local utility (for instance, in terms of profit). They make decisions on their own whether they are willing to cooperate or collaborate with other organizational units. There is no direct means by which fractals can be compelled to behave in a certain manner. The only acceptable way to control the behavior of an organizational fractal or a group of cooperating fractals is the design of a globally consistent system of aims and objectives [4]. However, due to bounded rationality, organizations are generally not able to establish consistent goal hierarchies. Instead, the different goals that exist within an organization are more or less inconsistent, the knowledge about goals and relationships between them remains necessarily incomplete, uncertain, fuzzy, and sometimes even false. Additional goal conflicts may arise between the goals of an organization and the preferences of its customers, between different organizations that wish to cooperate, and between the customers of distinct organizations that wish to pursue their aims in close cooperation.

Organizational fractals form organizationally stable parts of an enterprise. They have well-defined interfaces to their environments. They execute locally well-defined production functions (transformations) and they are supposed to guarantee a maximum

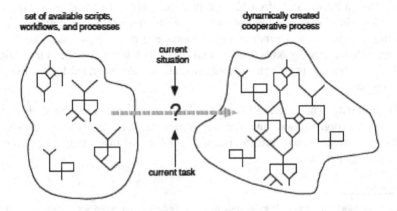

Fig. 1. Integration of business processes

of internal stability in terms of their operations and processes, their requests for resources, their availability, and their responsiveness. Their flexibility results from their capability to cooperate and even merge with other fractals in order to create a more complex fractal. This is depicted in Fig. 1, where four different fractals described by their individual process landscapes (left hand side of the picture) decide to establish a close cooperation (right hand side of the picture) in order to jointly fulfill an external demand.

3   Models for Logistics

The flow of goods and its optimization have always been a major concern in logistics research. The term "organization of logistics" in literature is mainly used in the context of structural enterprise organization. However, a strict focus on structural organization does not sufficiently consider the increasing influence of process organization especially in a logistics context [24]. The following sections introduce some of the existing models for logistics and highlight necessary extensions for the use of multiagent technology.

3.1   Systematic of Logistics Tasks

The task of logistics is that some requesting entity is supplied with the right good (quantity and quality), at the right time and the right place at minimal costs. A general model of logistics processes uses a graph to visualize temporal storage points of objects as vertices and the possibilities of the objects travelling through the logistics network as edges [25]. Figure 2 shows the three different basic structures of logistics systems: (i) single-tier systems with direct flow from source to sink, (ii) multi-tier systems with break-bulk and consolidation points in between, and (iii) combined systems that have direct and indirect flow of goods.

As stated above, the basic functionality of logistics systems is the spatiotemporal transformation goods. The optimization of these transformations are fulfilled by the following processes [25]: (i) Core processes of goods flow (transport, transshipment and storage processes), (ii) supporting processes, e.g. packaging processes and (iii) order transmission and processing processes.

The core processes of logistics together with the production processes can be modularly assembled to form a supply chain and are independent of a certain domain. A generic example from the manufacturing industry would be the storage of a resource (temporal transformation) that has to be prepared for pickup (transshipment), transported to the targeted destination (spatial transformation), prepared for further processing (transshipment), physically adapted (production), again prepared for pickup (transshipment) and so on. This short example shows that the core logistics processes occur continually. Even for information goods that are not physically transformed, the schema can be applied: An information is stored in a database (temporal transformation), made available by some database accessing protocol (transshipment), transported via a network connection to another destination (spatial transformation), handled by the

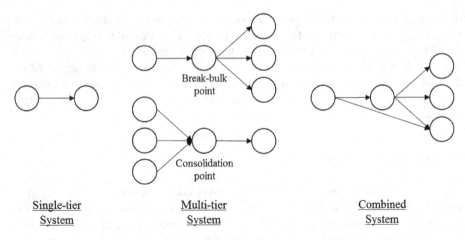

Single-tier
System

Multi-tier
System

Combined
System

Fig. 2. Basic structures of logistics systems [25]

local network layer (transshipment) and processed by the IT system. The single processes are characterized as independent and modular fractals that individually optimize their processes to obtain an overall process flow.

These processes are independent of a certain domain and also independent whether the processed object is a physical good or an information. The widespread visualization as a graph is also domain-independent and enables also logistics networks as an extension of a logistics supply chain [26].

3.2   Approaches for Formalizing Logistics Tasks

Dependent on the specific modelling goal, there are numerous approaches for formalizing logistics tasks. This section will provide a short excerpt of available methods that are used to model intra- and inter-organizational problems. Besides business driven approaches like the Architecture of Integrated Information Systems (ARIS) that provides general means for business process modelling [27] and the Supply Chain Operation Reference (SCOR) Model that is an industry-independent framework for evaluation and improvement of supply-chains [28] a huge range of quantitative decision models exist in literature.

For models that go beyond sole descriptive analysis and that are used for planning and decision making, at least particular aspects have to be represented in quantitatively parameterized mathematical models [29]. The problem is often modelled as a deterministic single or multi criterial optimization model, either as a linear (mixed integer) or non-linear optimization model. In that way, numerous variants of supply chain optimization problems can be addressed. In general, these models assume some central designer that is able to enforce an optimized production plan to all instances of the supply chain. However, in real-world scenarios this is usually not the case as even in supply chains with one dominant company the other companies remain autonomous and follow their own interests.

Hence, these models are used to describe and optimize single fractals by aiming for an increased stability of the subsystem. The following classes of quantitative decision models are representative for this kind of logistics task formalization [29]:

- *Deterministic single-criteria optimization models* show only one single objective function that has to be maximized or minimized. The correlations between different parameters are known and, thus, the solution is not uniquely defined. Dependent on the structure of the objective or restrictive functions linear and non-linear as well as integer or mixed-integer optimization may be distinguished.
- *Multi-criteria optimization models* have multiple objective functions or criteria that have to be considered simultaneously. This allows even for competitive objective functions, which however hinders unambiguous optima. In this case, optima can only be determined per objective and overall solutions may only be distinguished by the dominance of other solutions.
- *Stochastic optimization models* assume that the available data is not complete and, thus, multiple environmental states are possibly occurring with a certain probability. Like for multi-critera models, there is no unambiguous solution as even the feasibility of the solution cannot be clearly determined, in case of stochastic elements appearing in side conditions.

3.3   Logistics in the Perspective of a Fractal Supply Network

Logistics is about the transportation of goods and the systematics mentioned in Sect. 3.1 are independent of a certain domain and the types of processes presented show similar characteristics: Goods have to be transported, handled and stored. In general, this is even independent of the fact, whether the good in question is physical or informational. For information goods the border between these core processes and the order transmission or processing might diminish as no physical good is present. In this case, the core process is an information flow just like the order processes.

Independent of the physical presence of a good, it can be observed that supply chains are in many cases divided into different fractals. These fractals are autonomous and cannot be fully controlled from a macro perspective. Depending on the context, these fractals might be whole enterprises (e.g. in a manufacturing supply chain) or different departments (e.g. in a hospital) that show a certain amount of autonomy. Hence, the overall process cannot be planned in detail against the motivation of the single fractals.

4   Multi-multiagent Systems

Logistics fractals in a supply network are autonomous and are organized to maximize internal stability as well as efficacy and, thus, show high potential for the representation by MAS. However, the formation of supply network requires the different MAS to communicate and cooperate with each other to fulfil their goals. This section addresses problems arising when different MAS are involved in the formation process including the dynamic reconfiguration as presented by Hannebauer [30].

4.1 Basic Approach

Since the emergence of the multiagent paradigm numerous MAS have been developed for various domains, e.g. manufacturing and logistics, and in most cases the design is focused on specific issues [31]. Although developed independently, the different MAS cannot be viewed as separated autarkic systems as they interrelate with each other in many ways. The coupling of these MAS imply new questions: (i) How should interfaces be designed between different MAS? (ii) How should the information exchange and service delivery between these separated systems be organized? The first question may be addressed by standardization of communication protocols, like the FIPA-standards (Foundation for Intelligent Physical Agents). The standard is widespread, but still not all MAS under development pursue the specification with the corresponding overhead, so communication between different systems is still an issue. The second question, however, cannot be solely solved on a technical level: The organizational structure between two or more independently developed MAS usually involves the relations between the represented real world organizations. The technical as well as the organizational question has been addressed by the platform Agent. Enterprise in a logistic scenario [32]. Agent.Enterprise is not restricted to intra-organizational value chains already represented by MAS, but integrates multiple instances of these into inter-organizational supply chains. This combination of multiple MAS is called a multi-multiagent system (MMAS) and works cross-organizational. Each MAS remains locally controlled, but obtains features of inter-organizational communication and cooperation to further increase flexibility and decrease costs. In Agent.Enterprise each MAS plans and optimizes its logistic and production processes individually, but informs other systems of unforeseen and potentially disturbing events. On the basis of this information exchange, plans of other MAS may be adapted or inter-organizational contracts may be renegotiated [32]. Figure 3 shows the Gateway-Agent concept used to structure the communication between two FIPA-compliant MAS [31].

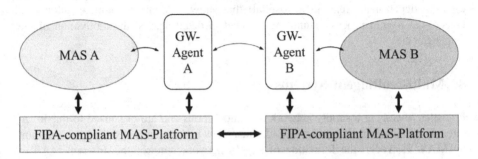

Fig. 3. The gateway-agent concept [31]

4.2 Abstractions

Already in 1966, Grochla raised the question in organizational theory, whether machines are getting intelligent enough that the task they are carrying out can be placed on the same level like those of humans [33]. One main argument is the increasing autonomy of technical systems and this thesis has been controversially discussed in organizational theory literature. Since then, the technical development has made substantial progress and also multiagent literature states autonomy as the key feature of actors in MAS enabling the consideration of unpredictable environmental effects. The agents gain autonomy by learning from experience and thus are able to compensate incorrect or incomplete built-in knowledge making the agents themselves independent from the developer [34].

Hence, different MAS show differing characteristics. Each MAS exhibits its own identity by defining interfaces to its environment and by developing an individual internal organization. This organization might be structured top-down or bottom-up depending on the learning capabilities and includes appropriate coordination mechanisms and responsibility rules. In logistics supply chains, one can find different levels of organizational structure, e.g. in a manufacturing supply chain, there are usually different companies that work together for one final good. Thus, we can distinguish between intra- and inter-organizational structures, e.g. the intra-organization structure of a company is embedded into the inter-organizational structure of the supply chain that involves various other companies whose behavior is not controllable, but has to be motivated. However, this structure is also present in other domains: Processes in hospitals are characterized by highly autonomous departments that can only be limitedly controlled by the central hospital process management. This leads to fractal processes within the hospital where each department again can be represented by a single MAS.

Table 1. Meta-model of fractal modelling

Label	Symbol	Description
Process Fractal	⌒	A self-contained and self-organized series of activities with a permanent nature that involves a certain number of actors and is available via interfaces
Actor	◯	Smallest organizational entity in a process fractal that has the competency to make decisions with a given scope
Interface	▯	Coupling point of a process fractal that allows for incoming or outgoing products, services or humans from or to another process fractal
Interaction Path	╲	Bidirectional communication link between two actors of a process fractal
Transshipment	╲	Transition of a product, service or human from one process fractal to another one

Independent of a certain domain, network-wide processes consist of flexibly coordinated process fractals being under local control of complex agents, e.g. a single MAS. Table 1 presents the meta-model for modelling fractal supply chains that is used in Fig. 4 to show an abstract example of a supply chain consisting of multiple MAS that represent autonomous fractals. The figure shows that two dependent organizational problems evolve: (i) the intra-organizational structure of each MAS that may differ significantly and (ii) the overall inter-organizational structure that aims at a final product and that is not able to fully control the single process fractals.

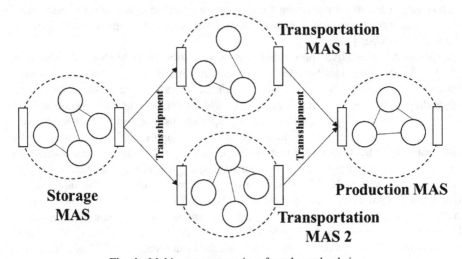

Fig. 4. Multiagent systems in a fractal supply chain

Each fractal has a logistics task based on domain independent types: (i) spatial transformation in form of a transportation process, (ii) temporal transformation in form of storage as well as (iii) physical transformation in form of a production process. The single fractals are each represented by a MAS that has input and output interface to form a supply chain and to follow the objective of the MMAS. The interfaces are connected by a transshipment function that allows the output of one MAS to be used as an input for another one.

5   Examples

This section presents three examples of research projects that used the flexibility of MAS for the supply chain networks. The examples are further analyzed in Sect. 5.4 with respect to principle of fractal enterprises.

5.1   Example 1: Agent.Hospital

Agent.Hospital is a virtual clinic that consists of various sections representing the different parts of the healthcare domain in Germany [35]. With unpredictable courses of

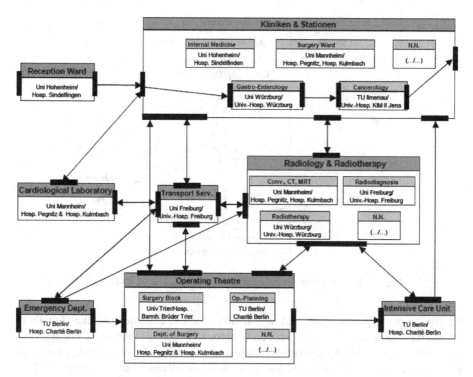

Fig. 5. Organizational structure of agent.hospital with selected supply chains [36]

treatment, highly situational dynamic and the consideration of emergency cases, planning in the healthcare domain requires high flexibility considering numerous priorities, preferences and goals. The variety of available resources and significant time consumption of each case further contribute to the complexity of the decision problem. The research project ADAPT as part of Agent.Hospital addressed this problem with an agent-based approach in which the goal system of each participant has been implemented as a BDI-agent [37]. Figure 5 shows the organizational structure of Agent. Hospital with the supply chain of a selected scenario.

5.2   Example 2: BREIN

The research project BREIN funded by the European Commission had the goal to open grid technologies for the appliance in companies. BREIN considered the supply chain optimization with the involvement of multiple companies at an airport. The considered ground handling scenario of airline service providers shown in Fig. 6 is highly dynamic and short-term orientated: Local disturbances at the airport apron and the aircraft ground handling require rapid adaption to increase the number of slots and therewith revenue. Here, only the customer of the supply chain, the airline, is fixed and resources, e.g. busses, baggage, staff, have to be assigned to the ground handling. An agent-based approach ensures that the individual interests of all participants are considered and that

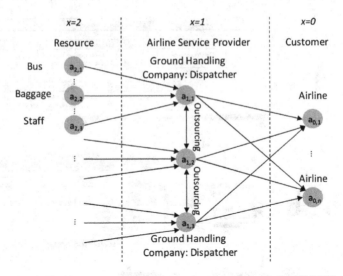

Fig. 6. Service networks for airport ground handling in BREIN [39]

the service network can be adapted in a flexible manner. This intra-organizational n:m market is characterized by n resources and m ground handling companies. The resource allocation is performed by a reverse auction and is specified in an allocation protocol, which prevents overcommitments and guarantees socially optimal allocations [38].

5.3   Example 3: EwoMacs

The research project EwoMacs addressed the coordination complexity and the ability to supply in customizable supply chains. The supply chain is viewed as a problem solving network that has been analyzed in a shoe manufacturing scenario. Shoes are produced according to individual requirements and, thus, the customer has been modelled as the first software agent. The contributions of each participant of the supply chain are coordinated using the principal agent theory. The organizational roles of customer and supplier have been specified according to the individual situation. The coordination was optimized by identifying, analyzing and designing transaction costs of the whole supply chain (see Fig. 7).

5.4   Lessons Learned

The examples presented in the previous sections show only a short excerpt of the variety for domain specific instantiations of MAS for supply networks. The overall MMAS, however, reveal significant correlation concerning their structure. Table 2 gives an overview on the presented research projects and their individual challenges by showing the organizational structure on the macro level as well as the appearance of

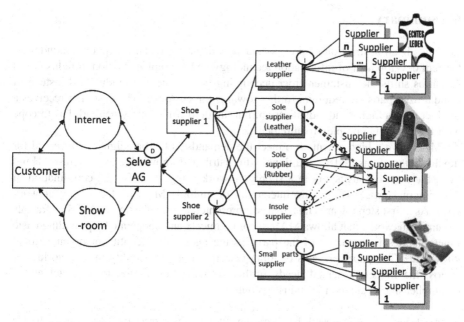

Fig. 7. Supply chain of shoe production in EwoMacs [40]

Table 2. Overview on research projects

	Agent.Hospital	BREIN	EwoMacs
Problem/ Challenge	Unpredictability of demand and resource capacities	Coordination of adaptive business grids	Complexity of co-ordination and ability to supply
Organizational Structure	Hierarchical Structure of an hospital with autonomous departments	Supply chain with different autonomous companies that have individual organizational structures	
Fractals/MAS	Different departments of a hospital	Ground handling companies at airports	Supplying companies for individual shoe producer

fractals that are represented by single MAS. The examples exhibit that the presented formalization of MAS as fractals of a supply network has potential to provide a structure that addresses the balance between organizational stability for reliability issues and flexibility to achieve an efficient inter-MAS process on the macro level.

6 Summary

Logistics is an abstraction of processes across departments and corporate boundaries. Current development of information technology and its implementation in industry 4.0 scenarios shifts the customer order decoupling point, where individualized instead of standardized parts are required, further towards the customer. The customer receives a product with a higher individualization, but the delivering supply network has to cope with the resulting complex requirements.

MAS have a high potential to meet the demands as the paradigm is conceived for flexible interactions under conditions with distributed knowledge and interests. However, the autonomous actors in a supply network using MAS for the coordination of their internal processes, require interaction of multiple MAS on the supply network level. As a first step towards this goal, we presented a formalization of MAS as fractals of supply networks that allows MAS to communicate and cooperate by providing basic functionalities independent of the participating agents like identity or organizational knowledge. The paper presents ongoing research. For applicability in real-world scenarios, the model presented needs further formalization of the meta-model and a comprehensive evaluation in industry context.

Acknowledgements. This work has been supported by the project InnOPlan, funded by the German Federal Ministry for Economic Affairs and Energy (BMWi, FKZ 01MD15002).

References

1. Brettel, M., Friederichsen, N., Keller, M., Rosenberg, M.: How virtualization, decentralization and network building change the manufacturing landscape: an industry 4.0 perspective. Int. J. Mech. Aerosp. Indus. Mechatron. Eng. **8**(1), 37–44 (2014)
2. Scholz-Reiter, B., Görges, M., Keller, M., Philipp, T.: Autonomously controlled production systems – Influence of autonomous control level on logistic performance. CIRP Ann. – Manufact. Technol. **58**, 395–398 (2009)
3. Rajkumar, R., Lee, I., Sha, L., Stankovic, J.: Cyber-physical systems: the next computing revolution. In: Proceeding of the Design Automation Conference, Anaheim, USA (2010)
4. Warnecke, H.J.: Revolution der Unternehmenskultur – Das Fraktale Unternehmen. Springer, Heidelberg (1993)
5. Malone, T.: Modeling coordination in organizations and markets. Manage. Sci. **33**(10), 1317–1332 (1987)
6. Fox, M.: An organizational view of distributed systems. IEEE Trans. Syst. Man Cybern. **11**(1), 70–80 (1981)
7. Hübner, J.F., Boissier, O., Kitio, R., Ricci, A.: Instrumenting multi-agent organisations with organisational artifacts and agents. Auton. Agents Multi-Agent Syst. **20**, 369–400 (2010)
8. Dunin-Keplicz, B., Verbrugge, R.: Teamwork in Multi-Agent Systems – A Formal Approach. John Wiley & Sons, Chichester (2010)
9. Conte, R., Castelfranchi, C.: Cognitive and Social Action. UCL Press, London (1995)
10. Ishida, T., Gasser, L., Yokoo, M.: Organization self-design of distributed production systems. IEEE Trans. Knowl. Data Eng. **4**(2), 123–134 (1992)

11. Jennings, N.R.: Joint Intentions as a Model of Multi-Agent Co-operation. Ph.D. thesis, University of London, United Kingdom (1992)
12. Bond, A., Gasser, L.: An analysis of problems and research in DAI. In: Bond, A., Gasser, L. (eds.) Readings in Distributed Artificial Intelligence, pp. 3–35. Morgan Kaufman Publishers, San Mateo (1988)
13. Durfee, E., Lesser, V., Corkill, D.: Trends in co-operative distributed problem solving. IEEE Trans. Knowl. Data Eng. 1(1), 63–83 (1989)
14. Gasser, L.: DAI approaches to coordination. In: Avouris, N.M., Gasser, L. (eds.) Distributed artificial intelligence: theory and practice. Comput. Inf. Sci., vol. 5, pp. 31–51. Kluwer Academic Publishers, Boston (1992)
15. Davis, R., Smith, R.G.: Negotiation as a metaphor for distributed problem solving. Artif. Intell. 20, 63–109 (1983)
16. Kaufer, D., Carley, K.M.: Communication at a Distance: The Effect of Print on Socio-Cultural Organization and Change. Lawrence Erlbaum, Hillsdale (1993)
17. Carley, K.M.: Computational and mathematical organization theory: perspective and directions. Comput. Math. Organ. Theor. 1(1), 39–56 (1995)
18. Carley, K.M., Gasser, L.: Computational organization theory. In: Weiss, G. (ed.) Multiagent Systems – A Modern Approach to Distributed Artificial Intelligence, 1st edn. MIT Press, Cambridge (2001)
19. Dignum, V.: A Model for Organizational Interaction: Based on Agents, Founded in Logic. Dissertation, Utrecht University (2004)
20. Dignum, V., Padget, J.: Multiagent Organizations. In: Weiss, G. (ed.) Multiagent Systems, 2nd edn. MIT Press, Cambridge (2013)
21. Aldewereld, H., Dignum, V.: OperettA: organization-oriented development environment. In: Dastani, M., El Fallah Seghrouchni, A., Hübner, J., Leite, J. (eds.) LADS 2010. LNCS, vol. 6822, pp. 1–19. Springer, Heidelberg (2011)
22. Steiner, D.D., Mahling, D.E., Haugeneder, H.: Human computer cooperative work. In: Proceedings of the 10th DAI Workshop, Bandera, Texas (1990)
23. Tapscott, D., Caston, A.: Paradigm Shift: The New Promise of Information Technology. McGraw-Hill, New York (1993)
24. Klaas-Wissing, T.: Logistikorganisation. In: Arnold, D., Isermann, H., Kuhn, A., Tempelmeier, H., Furmans, K. (eds.) Handbuch Logistik, 3rd edn. Springer, Heidelberg (2008)
25. Pfohl, H.-C.: Logistiksysteme – Betriebswirtschaftliche Grundlagen, 7th edn. Springer, Heidelberg (2004)
26. Domschke, W., Scholl, A.: Grundlagen der Betriebswirtschaftslehre – Eine Einführung aus entscheidungsorientierter Sicht, 4th edn. Springer, Heidelberg (2008)
27. Scheer, A.-W., Nüttgens, M.: ARIS architecture and reference models for business process management. In: van der Aalst, W.M., Desel, J., Oberweis, A. (eds.) Business Process Management. Models, Techniques, and Empirical Studies. LNCS, vol. 1806, pp. 376–389. Springer, Heidelberg (2000)
28. Stewart, G.: Supply-chain operations reference model (SCOR): the first cross-industry framework for integrated supply-chain management. Logist. Inf. Manage. 10(2), 62–67 (1997)
29. Scholl, A.: Grundlagen der modellgestützten Planung. In: Arnold, D., Isermann, H., Kuhn, A., Tempelmeier, H., Furmans, K. (eds.) Handbuch Logistik, 3rd edn. Springer, Heidelberg (2008)
30. Hannebauer, M.: Autonomous Dynamic Reconfiguration in Collaborative Problem Solving. Ph.D. thesis, Technische Universität Berlin (2001)

31. Stockheim, T., Nimis, J., Scholz, T., Stehli, M.: How to build a multi-multi-agent system – The Agent.Enterprise Approach. In: Proceedings of the 6th International Conference on Enterprise Information Systems, Porto, Portugal (2004)
32. Woelk, P.-O., Rudzio, H., Zimmermann, R., Nimis, J.: Agent. enterprise in a nutshell. In: Kirn, S., Herzog, O., Lockemann, P., Spaniol, O. (eds.) Multiagent Engineering – Theory and Applications in Enterprises. Springer, Heidelberg (2006)
33. Grochla, E.: Automation und Organisation – Die technische Entwicklung und ihre betriebswirtschaftlich-organisatorischen Konsequenzen. Gabler, Wiesbaden (1966)
34. Russel, S., Norvig, P.: Artificial Intelligence – A Modern Approach, 3rd edn. Pearson, London (2009)
35. Kirn, S., Anhalt, C., Krcmar, H., Schweiger, A.: Agent. hospital – health care applications of intelligent agents. In: Kirn, S., Herzog, O., Lockemann, P., Spaniol, O. (eds.) Multiagent Engineering – Theory and Applications in Enterprises. Springer, Heidelberg (2006)
36. Heine, C., Herrler, R., Petsch, M., Anhalt, C.: ADAPT – adaptive multi agent process planning & coordination of clinical trials. In: Proceedings of 9th Americas Conference on Information Systems, Tampa, USA (2003)
37. Heine, C., Herrler, R., Kirn, S.: ADAPT@ agent.hospital: agent-based optimization & management of clinical processes. Int. J. Intell. Inf. Technol. (IJIIT) 1(1), 30–48 (2005)
38. Karaenke, P.: Multiagent resource allocation in service networks. Ph.D. thesis, University of Hohenheim (2014)
39. Karaenke, P., Schuele, M., Micsik, A., Kipp, A.: Inter-organizational interoperability through integration of multiagent, web service, and semantic web technologies. In: Fischer, K., Müller, J.P., Levy, R. (eds.) ATOP 2009 and ATOP 2010. LNBIP, vol. 98, pp. 55–75. Springer, Heidelberg (2012)
40. Dietrich, A.J., Kirn, S., Sugumaran, V.: A service-oriented architecture for mass customization – a shoe industry case study. IEEE Trans. Eng. Manage. 54(1), 190–204 (2007)

Cyber-Physical Multiagent-Simulation in Production Logistics

Christoph Greulich[✉], Stefan Edelkamp, and Niels Eicke

Institute for Artificial Intelligence, University of Bremen, Bremen, Germany
{greulich,edelkamp,neicke}@tzi.de

Abstract. A growing network of technical systems, embedded and autonomous, influence our daily work. Among them, cyber-physical systems establish a close connection between the virtual and the real world. In this paper we show how an existing multiagent system that controls the physical production of goods on a monorail is virtualized by extracting the agents as black boxes and by integrating them into a multiagent simulation system. As a result, the exact same agents run in physical and cyber world. Towards this end, the physical environment has been mapped and visualized. Experiments show that the modeling and simulation error is small, such that scenarios can be varied, tested, debugged, and scaled, saving huge amounts of labor.

1 Introduction

Production logistics has undergone a significant transformation in recent years. While in the past, mechanization and automation were clearly marked, nowadays there is a rising interest in autonomous and interconnected software solutions. The political and economic significance of this development has been associated with the name *Industry 4.0* [14].

Cyber physical systems (CPS) have been identified as transformative technologies for managing interconnected systems between its physical assets and computational capabilities [3]. In our setting, the CPS maps the digital into a real factory. Therefore, we aim at integrated planning, evaluation and continuous improvement of the essential structures, processes and resources in a real factory. We observe an increasing complexity of such systems and an increasing number of time-consuming tasks in their practical evaluation. Analytical methods are only partly sufficient for the study of such systems. Instead, *simulations* are preferred, because they often show a better mapping of the real behavior of the systems.

Even though no unified definition of *agents* exists in the literature, most authors agree that agents are autonomous software programs with certain social abilities [7]: agents can use sensors to perceive the world around them, control actuators to manipulate their environment and are able to communicate with other agents or even human users if necessary [28]. Agents use the perceived information to make decisions on their own and change the world around them

© Springer International Publishing Switzerland 2015
J.P. Müller et al. (Eds.): MATES 2015, LNAI 9433, pp. 119–136, 2015.
DOI: 10.1007/978-3-319-27343-3_7

to their advantage. The degree of autonomy an agent has is only restrained by its software program. The biggest advantage of agent technology in comparison to equation-based modeling is the capability of *multiagent systems* (MAS) to solve problems locally and react dynamically to occurring events [19].

Despite the growing body of research in Industry 4.0 applications, accessible MAS that run on real hardware for in-door production are rare. One of the few successful real-world implementations of a MAS is the so called Z2 production floor unit that has been developed at BIBA[1]. As individual production steps are performed at different stations, the stations are interconnected by a monorail transport system. The structure of the transport system is shown in Fig. 2. The transported goods are autonomous, which means that each product decides on its own which variant it aims at and which station to visit. This way, a decentralized control of the production system is possible [25].

At the University of Bremen, the Platform for Simulation with Multiple Agents (PlaSMA) has been developed [24]. It has mainly been applied to the simulation of macro-logistical processes. PlaSMA expands the functionality of the Java Agent Development toolkit (JADE) to a discrete-event simulation. Due to the need for simulation for CPS in production logistics, in this work we investigate, whether PlaSMA is able is accurately simulate existing production logistics scenarios by providing a model of the physical environment and by extracting existing agents without any change.

In this paper we provide a mapping of the Z2 monorail production unit to PlaSMA, leading to a cyber-physical system scenario of already existing agents and new ones; and an experimental study that shows how much executing the simulated and the real-world systems differ. The main contribution is the successful mix of existing agents as black boxes that operate seamlessly together with additional ones, substituting the hardware units by agents in the simulated world. Aspects of the agent models are detailed.

The text is structured as follows. First, we give insights to the architecture of the system and analyze the components of the real, the virtual system, as well as the agent model. We analyze the properties of the available agents from the existing physical system and introduce agents which represent the products, the stations, as well as the readers and the plant management. For the technical transformation we first explain how PlaSMA and JADE had to be adapted, and the communication unit had to be integrated. Then, we adapt the model into simulation and implement and visualize the according agents. For the validation of our approach we test the implementation in terms of concept adequateness and operational consistency. Both the physical and the simulated systems are ran and the according results are compared. Finally, we conclude and provide a brief outlook to possible future research avenues.

---

[1] Bremer Institut für Produktion und Logistik GmbH.

2   Multiagent System

The JADE-based agent model of the Z2 monorail production unit was designed and implemented within *Collaborative Research Center 637* [11,17]. Unlike most MAS representations of in-house logistics, the Z2 software was developed to control a real-world hardware implementation as a decentralized, heterarchical approach to achieve *positive emergence* and adaptability to changes in the environment and the goals of various stakeholders. During the development of Z2, the authors identified similarities between the *Internet of Things*[6], *Intelligent Products*[16] and MAS.

Z2 is a monorail-based assembly network for automotive tail-lights. The modular system consists of six different workstations, each is operated manually by a human worker and dedicated to one specific production step. At production steps III and V, different parts can be used to assemble different variants of the tail-lights as illustrated in Fig. 1.

At the first station, the basic metal cast parts enter the monorail on a dedicated shuttle. The monorail connects all stations, each station is assigned to one specific task, such as adding bulbs or diffusers. Each tail-light is transported from station to station until it is assembled completely. The scenario is illustrated in Fig. 2.

Low frequency RFID tags are embedded into the metal cast parts in order to identify and locate every tail light automatically. Morales-Kluge et al. [17] emphasize the dedicated *Hardware Abstraction Layer* of their implementation, which provides interfaces to various hardware machines of the scenario, including the transport shuttles.

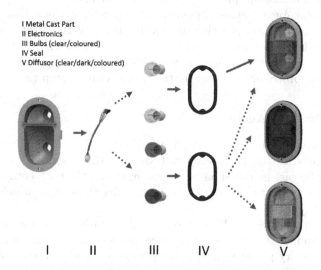

I Metal Cast Part
II Electronics
III Bulbs (clear/coloured)
IV Seal
V Diffusor (clear/dark/coloured)

I   II   III   IV   V

Fig. 1. Assembly states of tail lights [11].

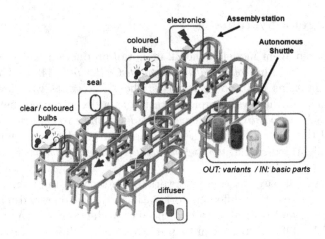

Fig. 2. Assembly scenario for tail-lights [17].

To add autonomy to this scenario, agents are applied to represent the individual stakeholders of the assembly line. A number of simple reflex agents [22] represent entities such as RFID readers which keep track of the traffic and each product's current location, information providers and even a Graphic User Interface (GUI) to supervise the agents' activities and to manually manipulate the current order status of each tail-light type variant. However, two particular agent types stick out, as they are the most relevant for the system's overall performance. The *Station Agent*, which provides an interface between the MAS and the individual worker at the respective station and the *Product Agent* which represents each individual product on the assembly line.

Each Station Agent represents one of the six workstations. The agent provides information regarding estimated waiting time for the service provided at its station and handles reservation requests by product agents. Furthermore, each Station Agent autonomously negotiates entrance and departure of product agents into the processing area where the manufacturing step takes place.

2.1 The Product Agent

The most interesting agent, however, is the Product Agent. The Product Agent is directly linked to the RFID chip embedded in the metal cast part of a tail light. When the cast is placed on an autonomous shuttle, both entities establish a connection, so that the Product Agent can order the shuttle which station to approach next.

Based on the current utilization of assembly stations and the overall order status, the Product Agent chooses the next production step and targets a type variant. After every production step, the plan is reconsidered to ensure that the current plan is still the optimal choice.

The Product Agent is a Finite State Machine (FSM) as illustrated in Fig. 3. Its behavior strongly depends on its current state. While transferring between

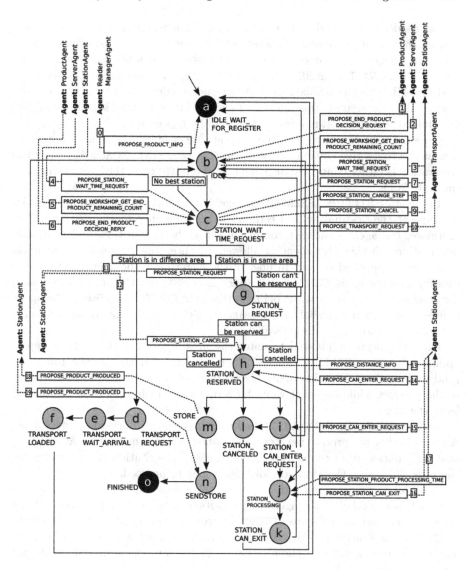

Fig. 3. Architecture of the product agent.

stations, the agent is in the state IDLE_WAIT_OF_REGISTER, listening for messages from RFID readers until the destination is arrived. The navigation is executed by the shuttle itself, the Product Agent only registers at RFID readers to keep track of its own location.

In the state IDLE, the Product Agent acquires all necessary information to decide which production step to take next. First, the agent decides which tail-light variant its product should become. The decision is based on the current order status for each type variant and on the previously applied production steps which may limit the amount of possible choices.

Once a decision is made, the agent decides which production step to take next and which station to approach. Therefore, the agent requests the current waiting time and queue length at each considered station and waits for replies in the state STATION_WAIT_TIME_REQUEST. Once the response messages were received, a MATLAB server is invoked by a direct socket connection to determine the next production step for this individual agent. If no satisfying solution could be determined, the decision-making process will be repeated.

Once a destination is chosen, the Product Agent attempts to make a reservation at the respective station and waits in the state STATION_REQUEST until the reservation is either confirmed or denied. In the latter case, the agent returns to the state IDLE.

In the state STATION_RESERVED, the agent constantly keeps track of the waiting time at the destination and estimates the remaining spatial distance. Furthermore, the agent handles incoming messages by the station, which provide information whether the agent is allowed to enter the processing area upon arrival or is supposed to wait in line. In the latter case, the agent continues to wait for the message in STATION_CAN_ENTER_REQUEST after the product arrived at the station. Furthermore, while being in the state STATION_RESERVED, the agent handles reservation cancellations messages, which may be sent by the station if the service cannot longer be provided.

Once the agent is allowed to enter the area where the production step is applied, the state STATION_PROCESSING is reached and the shuttle takes the product into the production area. The worker now applies the production step to the product while its agent waits for a message which allows the product to leave the area.

In the state STATION_CAN_EXIT, the Product Agent is informed by the Station Agent, whether the production step was applied or not. The Station Agent gains that information from the worker. In both cases, the Station Agent returns to the state IDLE and, therefore, decides again how to proceed.

After all parts are assembled, only storage stations can be chosen for reservation. In this special case, the agent registers its final tail-light type variant at the respective storage in the state STORED. Afterwards, the agent waits in the state SENDSTORE for a message which confirms that the product was removed from the assembly line by a worker. The agent then switches to the state FINISHED and terminates permanently.

2.2   Decision Making

The research presented in this paper was partly motivated by our interest in the application of alternative decision-making and optimization methods for this particular setup, since we consider it an interesting testbed for real-world application of AI methods. However, because of time and personnel required to run the hardware, the need for a simulation model compatible to the hardware was indispensable.

Currently, the decision-making process in this agent model is based on *hierarchical aggregation* as presented in [20]. During the process, the agent splits his overall goal into sub-goals and evaluates the effect of every possible action on each sub-goal. Depending on the current context, different sub-goals may have a different weight for the overall utility function. The overall utility value is calculated by solving a *multi-criteria evaluation problem*, where each criterion corresponds to the effect the action will have on one specific sub-goal.

In this model, knowledge is represented by a set of rules. As *decision support systems* like *analytic hierarchy process* and *weighted average* lack the ability to handle linguistic variables, *fuzzy logic* is used to express information.

Fuzzy sets and fuzzy logic are a solid research branch of computational intelligence, allowing to draw reliable inferences about vague concepts that are inherent in linguistic terms. The main idea is to have a partial membership of elements in the set, or propositions that are only partially true. In difference to probabilities, where truth is only uncertain, in such a possibilistic world, truth itself is a fractional term.

There are many applications of *fuzzy decision-making*. E.g., in Robotics, such reasoning can be used to trade conflicting behaviors like wall-following and obstacle avoidance. Fuzzy decision-making goes back to work of Bellmann and Zadeh [1]. As surveyed by Carlsson and Fuller [5], after some first doubts on the impact of fuzzy decision-making by French [8], it has shown considerable impact in the improved working of rational agents, as predicted by Gaines et al. [10].

Interestingly, in the Z2 MAS, the decision-making process based on fuzzy reasoning is completely separated from all other agents' programs and made available via a dedicated MATLAB server through a TCP/IP socket connection. The Product Agents communicate their individual perception of the environment and their respective product's states to this MATLAB server. Furthermore, the agents provide a set of available decision options to the server and receive an answer on what to do next.

3   From Reality to Simulation

The original implementation of the Z2 monorail system consists of three layers, as illustrated in Fig. 4. On top of the architecture lies the agent model layer which contains the MAS including all its agents. The agent layer is set upon a virtual model of the hardware system. The lowest level consists of the hardware itself. Since the MAS and the hardware have already been described in detail in the previous sections, we now focus on the virtual model layer.

The virtual model is a simplified model of the real-world hardware system. From the agent's perspective, the virtual model is its environment, since the agent only percepts and manipulates the virtual model and does not directly interact with the hardware layer. The virtual model encapsulates all dynamic and static features of the system in data structures accessible by the MAS.

The static features, which cannot be modified at runtime, describe the infrastructure of the system as well as its purpose. The infrastructure of the system consists of Radio Frequency Identification (RFID) reader entities, Intelligent Routing Module (IRM) sensor entities, and RFID/IRM sensor types, the various assembly stations and areas of the monorail system, the shuttles and their

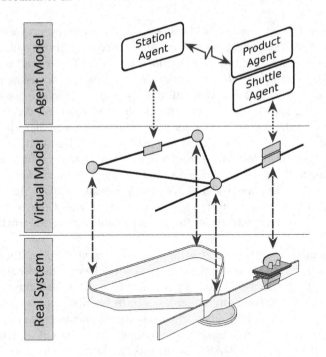

Fig. 4. The different abstraction layers.

respective IDs. Some of the IRM sensors, which are referred to as *stop modules*, require the shuttles to stop on arrival. Stop modules are interconnected by railways, which are referred to as *edges*. Furthermore, fixed routes are defined between all stop modules, given that the shuttles are not capable of executing any shortest-path search algorithms.

Since the purpose of the system is the manufacturing of tail-lights, the virtual model additionally contains information about the different parts and production steps, the interdependencies between production steps, possible part combinations (type variants) and variant groups. Furthermore, the virtual model stores information regarding the initial order status of each type variant and the interface towards the MATLAB decision-making server. The static features of the system are stored in an Extensible Markup Language (XML) file, which is made available to each agent at the beginning of its lifecycle.

Far more interesting, however, are the dynamic features of the system, which encourage application of agents and decentralized control. The dynamic features are the current order status of the different variants, the varying product states, waiting times at the various stations, and the position of products and shuttles.

While shuttles are located by the IRM system, products are located by the RFID system. Both systems update the virtual model but do not depend on each other. Hence, if a worker decides to manually remove one product from its shuttle and attach it to another one, the product will determine its new location and continue its work from the new position. Respectively, shuttles adapt to

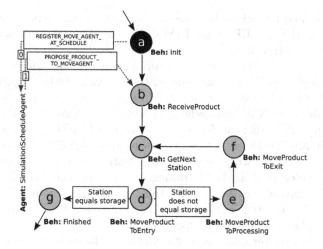

Fig. 5. Architecture of the move agent.

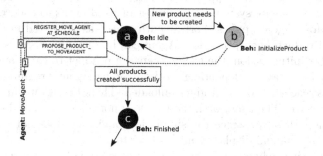

Fig. 6. Architecture of the simulation scheduling agent.

a change of carriage and establish a connection with the new product. It is worth mentioning, that the positions of products and shuttles are not constantly tracked. Instead, the discrete model is updated whenever a shuttle or a product registers or deregisters at a reader.

Since dynamic reactions on changing order situations are considered one of the major advantages of digital factories [2], the order situation within the system can be manipulated by a human operator at runtime. A dedicated agent provides a GUI for the operator and updates the virtual model when the situation changes. The GUI allows to increase or decrease the amount of orders for each tail-light variant separately. The information is used by the Product Agents during their decision-making processes.

3.1   Supporting Simulation Agents

To run this MAS in a simulation environment, the underlying hardware layer has to be replaced by a software system, which adapts the interfaces between hardware layer and virtual model. The data exchange between both layers covers discrete time updates of RFID and IRM data. Therefore, a simulation model of the monorail infrastructure is of particular interest.

We adapted the hardware infrastructure into a PlaSMA-compatible graph, where nodes represent IRM sensors and RFID readers and edges represent direct railway connections between the nodes. More precisely, we derive the required information from the XML data scheme used in the original system to generate our own graph infrastructure. Each edge is weighted by the physical length of the corresponding hardware railway. Nodes representing RFID readers or railway switches are tagged with additional information regarding the waiting time per shuttle. The original hardware routing treats every connection between two nodes as a one-way railway. We adapted this behavior by defining the infrastructure graph to be directed. Furthermore, we model shuttles as virtual physical objects to be placed on nodes or edges.

Since shuttles are autonomous entities in the hardware layer, we implemented a new Move Agent type to represent one unique shuttle. The agent controls movement and speed of the virtual physical object. While pathfinding is only mocked in the original hardware system by a number of fixed paths to choose from, the simulation Move Agent applies shortest path search as presented in [13].

Like the Product Agent, the Move Agent can be seen as a FSM as illustrated in Fig. 5: After initialization, the agent receives a product to carry and moves it around to various stations depending on the Product Agent's requirements until a storage was reached and the product unloaded. Then, the agent waits for a new product to receive. The agent architecture does not allow manual displacement of the product. However, since the simulation obviously does not contain any human workers, manual displacement is obsolete.

The Simulation Scheduling Agent instantiates virtual shuttles and the corresponding Move Agents as well as Product Agents according to the simulation configuration. While shuttles are created immediately when the simulation starts, batches of new products can be created at regular intervals. The Simulation Scheduling Agent is illustrated in Fig. 6.

In order to simulate the behavior of the various RFID/IRM units, a third agent is applied, which keeps track of all sensors within the system. The agent maintains the order of waiting shuttles (first-in-first-out (FIFO)) and simulates waiting times at railway switches if the switch needs to change its routing direction.

4   Multiagent Simulation Model

As in other types of concurrent systems, issues like dead- and livelocks are often met while analyzing MAS. Concurrent process models enable reasoning the support for dynamic change and parallel execution.

There have been different formalizations of an MAS that are available in the literature. Burkhard [4] uses a formal language approach to represent a MAS M as a quadruple (A, T, τ, L), where A is a set of agents, T is a set of actions, and τ is a mapping from A to 2^T, so that for all a in A we have that

$T_a = \{t \in T \mid t \in \tau(a)\}$ is the set of actions executable in a. The set of actions sequences (solutions, plans) is denoted as $L \subseteq T^*$.

Recall that by definition for a homomorphism h we have $h(x \circ y) = h(x) \circ h(y)$. For strings $x, y \in \Sigma^*$ a homomorphism $\circ$ is the concatenation $x \circ y = xy$. The identity for this homomorphism is $\epsilon \in \Sigma^*$, the empty string.

In the formalization, homomorphisms are used as selection operators. In the overall plan each agents applies a homomorphism to select its own actions. Additionally, another string denotes which turn it is.

The *behavior* of each agent $a \in A$ is described by a homomorphism $h_a(L)$ with $h_a(l) = t$, if $t \in T_a$, and ϵ otherwise. $h_A(L) \subseteq A^*$ and *the behavior of a MAS* is characterized by a homomorphism h_A acting on the set L.

We exemplify the formalization for the Z2 demonstrator. Let $P = \{P_1, \ldots, P_k\}$ be the set of RFID locations for the shuttles, and $\mathtt{move}(P_i, P_j)$ the action for moving the vehicle via the shortest path from $\langle P_i = P_{\pi(1)}, P_{\pi(2)}, \ldots, P_{\pi(n)} = P_j \rangle$ from P_i to P_j. Action $\mathtt{move}(P_i, P_j)$ decomposes into $\mathtt{step}(P_l, P_k)$, with P_l and P_k being adjacent.

Assume that we have two shuttle agents a_1 and a_1 and a global plan that consists of steps $S_{l,k} = \mathtt{step}(P_l, P_k)$ from P_l to P_k. The empty string ϵ correspond to an action wait. We may assume, that each agent is asked in turn to resume, and answers ϵ if there is nothing to do.

Let $L = S_{1,2}, S_{1,2}, S_{2,3}, S_{3,4}, S_{2,5}, \ldots$ be the observed overall plan. The MAS behavior $h_A(L) = a_1 a_2 a_1 a_1 a_2 \ldots$ is sequence of agents defining the order to execute the actions. Hence $h_{a_1}(L) = S_{1,2}, S_{2,3}, S_{3,4}, \ldots$ is the behavior of agent a_1, and $h_{a_2}(L) = S_{1,2}, S_{2,5}, \ldots$ is the behavior of agent a_2.

It is also possible to add communication to the model. A (rendezvous) communication activity is a pair of actions (often a reading and a writing event), so that the entire communication is a string of the communication activities, modeled as a homomorphism $h_k(L)$ into $A \times A$. Communication activities can also be thought of mandatory synchronization points. While so far the order of actions is inherited by L it may be that there are several interleavings of agent executions in form of MAS behaviors that lead to the same result. For example, $L' = S_{1,2}, S_{1,2}, S_{2,3}, S_{2,5}, S_{3,4}, \ldots$ together with $h_A(L') = a_2 a_1 a_1 a_2 a_1$ yields the same outcome as $L = S_{1,2}, S_{1,2}, S_{2,3}, S_{3,4}, S_{2,5}, \ldots$ together with $h_A(L) = a_1 a_2 a_1 a_1 a_2 \ldots$.

Usually, the interpretation is unit time, so that each action takes one time step. However, this is not necessary, since we may associate a time stamp with each plan step, such that time extend and concurrency of actions can be modeled.

The $\mathcal{LORA}$ MAS formalization provided by Wooldridge [26,27] origins in model checking, with labeled transition and Kripke systems characterizing the behavior of the agents (their belief, their desire and their intention), and temporal logics expressing their required interplay, as well as the progression of knowledge. Alternatives consider an MAS as a game, in which agents –either in separation or cooperatively– optimize their individual outcome [23]. Communication between the agents is available via writing to and reading from channels, or via common access to shared variables. Other formalization approaches include work in the context of the MCMAS tool by Lomuscio[2]. Recently, there has been some approaches by Nissim and Brafman to formulize MAS as planning problems [18].

In the present paper, we define a multiagent system as an arbitrary complex concurrent computer program (that can be best thought of an ensemble of C or Java program threads). By the virtue of the Theorem of Rice [21], every non-trivial condition in such MAS (even while considering only one agent) is, therefore, already undecidable, so that essentially, we are bound to simulate MAS to get definite insights to their working. Such simulation leads to the concept of *simulation time*, which is measured in *ticks* or *cycles*, sometimes mapped to a more realistic time scale.

As in our case, quite often birth-giver agents create other agents according to some random process. We have one initial agent running: the environment agent (which can be thought as the main thread in the execution of a computer program), but as agents can be created or deleted in the course of the simulation, the number k of currently acting agents is not known in advance and has to be adapted dynamically.

Every agent (program) is further partitioned into *finite state machines* (FSM) of subprograms, whose states are called *behaviors*. Edges taken depend on the outcome of evaluating these behaviors. To ease the implementation, we assume that agents are parameterized, such that one FSM can be instantiated to many different individual agents. In object-oriented terms, each agent schema is a class, and each agent is a class object.

Together with a discrete event queue Q an MAS may now be exploited to simulate the evolution of time. The data structure Q offers the traditional set of priority queue operation of inserting, finding, and (minimum) deletion of events. Ordered wrt. timestamps it can be implemented in form of a heap. An element in Q is a triple of $(key, agent, state)$ where the key is the current timestamp of the simulation, and $(agent, state)$ is the information about where a particular agent's execution has to be resumed.

After extracting the event with minimum timestamp, we know the agent's behavior to be resumed. There might be several agents that have to execute code at the same point in time. Physically, all those agents run in different threads.

Each resumed agent knows its FSM state, where it was suspended and first looks into his inbox for messages that have arrived. After committing to all incoming messages, by calling the *action* method of the behavior, the agent tries progressing his individual task unless he reaches a point where it suspends (with each suspension a time interval is fixed, where no resuming is foreseen). While each action execution takes physical time, its simulation time is zero, so that each individual progression from a resume to a point in time for suspension requires no tick. Under certain assumptions the event-based simulation will progress, and with an upper bound on the maximum number of ticks eventually terminate.

In *multiagent simulation*, we distinguish the following three notions of time [9]: *physical time* (alias *real time*) refers to the time in the real world, i.e., at which

---

[2] http://vas.doc.ic.ac.uk/software/mcmas/

simulated events would happen in reality; *simulation time* models physical time in the simulation; and *wallclock time* that is consumed by the simulation system in order to execute the simulation. While physical time is continuous in multiagent-based simulation [15] simulation time is discrete, so that simulated events are mapped to timestamps. In *multiagent communication*, for the flow of information between agents, effective message handling is essential [12]. To ensure quality criteria for message handling we require

Time Model Adequacy. It is important to choose an appropriate granularity of time progression.

Causality. Due to the autonomy in accessing the message inbox, agents may process messages early. To ensure causality, message visibility has to be controlled: processing earlier messages is deferred, until local time has progressed.

Reproducibility. The ordering of messages may still depend on the system scheduling of the respective senders. For the sake of traceability, additional orderings (besides message arrival time) like the *agent's ID* are imposed.

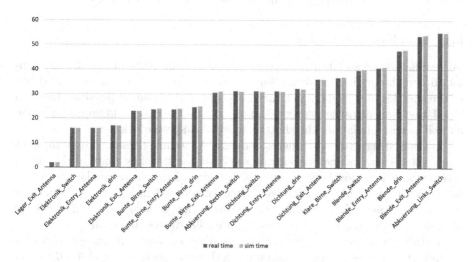

Fig. 7. Time distance between start position departure and arrival at nodes without waiting times.

5   Evaluation

The original hardware implementation runs on the Z2 demonstrator, for which the timing results are measured manually. All simulations are executed with the latest release of the PlaSMA software on a laptop computer, equipped with an Intel Pentium i7 processor and 16 GB RAM. Each agent is a Java thread, and can be profiled individually using appropriate tools. Performance indicators of

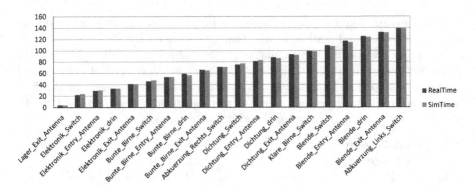

Fig. 8. Time distance between start position departure and arrival at nodes with waiting times.

the simulation have been selected and stored in a database. A virtual machine[3] contains the MATLAB server. The PlaSMA software includes a graphical user interface, where the progress of the simulation can be visualized.

5.1 Simulation Accuracy

We evaluated the simulation layer by comparing the performance of the simulation and the original hardware implementation. In both cases, we traced one of the shuttles in various target variant setups and measured physical time and simulation time distance at every stop module. In the real world implementation as well as the simulation, the shuttles move at a speed of 3 km/h.

In the first series of experiments, we neglect the time consumed by waiting at readers and switches and concentrate solely on the traveling times of the agent. The average deviation between real world physical time and simulation time is 0.216 s with a peak of 0.4 s. However, since some routes have positive and others have negative deviation, the difference between the physical and simulation time of arrival at the final station is 0.8 s. Figure 7 illustrates the results.

To validate the correct waiting behavior at sensors and switches, we conduct a second series of experiments. When waiting times are included, the total duration increases to 2.3 times the duration of the first experiment series on average. However, the deviation between simulation and the real hardware system is exactly the same as in the first series. The results lead us to believe that the deviation emerges during the acceleration of the shuttle, which is not considered in the simulation model. Figure 8 illustrates the deviation in one example setup.

In a third series of experiments, we evaluated planning and routing behavior of the Product Agents, which lead to the same results in hardware and simulation environments, given the same requirements and the same target variant. We set up check points at every hardware station and measured the physical time distance between the start of a shuttle and the arrival time at the respective check

---

[3] http://www.virtualbox.org

point. We repeated this experiment for every type variant and compared the results with results from simulation runs. Since we could not install a hardware measurement system in the simulation software, we recorded entering and exiting times of the product at the given station's first and last sensor. Table 1 shows an excerpt from our experiment results, indicating minor deviations, which are caused by the hardware itself. In simulation, results are deterministic, as shown in Table 2. Results show, that in any case, the check point within a station in the real world is reached at a physical time instant which lies between the simulation time instants of arrival at the entrance node and arrival at the exit node of the corresponding station in simulation. Consequently, we conclude that even though we have minor modeling errors in our simulation, they are insignificant to the simulation outcome.

Table 1. Real-world results for one single product agent per target variant.

	Target variant	Electronics	L1 (Colored Lamps)	L2 (Clear Lamps)	Seal	Cover
Exp. 1	Colored Lamps	0:32	1:00	-	1:31	2:09
Exp. 2	Colored Lamps	0:33	1:01	-	1:33	2:15
Exp. 3	Colored Lamps	0:32	1:01	-	1:33	2:12
Exp. 4	Colored Lamps	0:33	1:00	-	1:31	2:11
			⋮			
Exp. 1	Clear Lamps	0:33	-	1:47	1:15	2:19
Exp. 2	Clear Lamps	0:32	-	1:44	1:13	2:17
Exp. 3	Clear Lamps	0:32	-	1:46	1:13	2:18
Exp. 4	Clear Lamps	0:33	-	1:45	1:14	2:19
			⋮			

Table 2. Simulation results for one single product agent per target variant.

Target variant	Electronics		L1 (Col. Lamps)		L2 (Cl. Lamps)		Seal		Cover	
	Enter	Exit	Enter	Exit	Enter	Exit	Enter	Exit	Enter	Exit
Colored Lamps	00:31	00:45	00:57	01:11	-	-	01:29	01:41	02:03	02:23
Clear Lamps	00:31	00:45	-	-	01:33	01:48	01:10	01:22	02:03	02:23
				⋮						

5.2   System Performance

As mentioned before, this research was partly motivated by our interest in evaluation of other planning, decision making and optimization methods in the given manufacturing scenario. Additionally, hardware resources in the real-world setup are limited to a certain amount of shuttles and product parts. In simulation, however, the number of physical entities is only limited by the computer's physical limitations regarding RAM and CPU. Therefore, the whole manufacturing system can be simulated, tested and improved on one single machine with each component still being an individual agent program.

We conducted a series of experiments over a limited simulation time of 30 min to explore the performance of the simulation system. With each experiment, we increased the number of shuttles and/or available products to investigate the wallclock time of the simulation as well as the changes in capacity utilization of station agents and the production duration of each tail light.

Table 3. Simulation performance with increasing agent numbers (Rail and Idle refer to time spent on the rail and in idle mode, respectively, Lifecycle is averaged over the products, WC is wallclock time and TP is throughput).

Agents		MAT	Sim	Time spent processing						Lifecycle		Performance	
Shuttles	Prod.	LAB	Time	Electr.	L1	Seal	L2	Cover	Avg.	Rail	Idle	WC	TP
1	1	2	30:00	0:12	0:12	0:10	0:00	0:18	0:13	2:42	0:19	0:40	1
1	30	2.7	30:00	1:39	1:14	1:22	0:25	2:09	1:22	3:52	0:21	3:05	7
2	30	3.5	30:00	3:18	1:14	2:43	2:16	4:54	2:53	3:30	0:21	3:45	15
4	30	3.3	30:00	4:58	1:52	4:25	3:18	6:08	4:08	3:55	0:21	5:59	28
6	30	3.1	30:00	4:45	3:06	4:25	1:54	6:29	4:08	4:10	0:21	6:01	30
8	40	3	30:00	6:17	4:20	5:30	2:16	6:00	4:53	4:44	0:21	10:18	34
10	50	3	30:00	7:40	5:10	6:13	3:09	8:48	6:12	4:53	0:21	12:58	43
15	70	3.1	30:00	7:58	5:10	7:13	4:20	8:45	6:41	5:28	0:21	24:32	54
20	100	3	30:00	8:52	7:14	7:55	4:50	9:11	7:36	6:03	0:22	43:32	61
30	110	3	30:00	9:17	5:36	7:20	6:12	9:57	7:40	6:38	0:22	57:22	64

Table 3 presents an excerpt of our simulation results. The numbers show, that with an increasing number of shuttles, the various stations spend more time processing and, therefore, less time in idle mode. Furthermore, the average production time of each product increases as the products have to wait in front of the stations. Interestingly, the average number of MATLAB invocations per agent hardly increases and the maximum never exceeded 5.

With an increasing number of agents, the wallclock time of our experiments also increases. Consequently, with a certain amount of agents acting in parallel, the wallclock time actually exceeds the simulation time and, therefore, the physical time. However, since the number of available shuttles in the real world environment is limited to 12, physical time is only exceeded in experiments which could not be conducted on the hardware system. Furthermore, the time required to set up the system (30 min. approx.) and the number of human operators required to conduct experiments on the hardware system indicate that a slightly exceeding simulation time is insignificant to the overall advantage of the simulation.

6 Conclusion

In this paper we have presented a multiagent simulation of a production unit that integrates already existing agents as black boxes with a few additional virtual agents that drive the simulation. We showed that the implementation of intelligent products as agents in such cyber-physical system design is a viable option for controlling and simulating smart factories.

The decision-making process is done by frequently calling an external software server that applies advanced fuzzy reasoning methods. The obtained close match between the real and the simulated system is remarkable, given that, e.g., shortest paths are computed differently.

During the implementation process, we fixed a number of bugs both in the real and the simulated system, showing that running a simulation is also a means to improve multiagent software quality. We provided experiments showing that the implementation scales (to a rising number of shuttles and products).

In future work, we are interested in exploring distributed decision making and optimization strategies suitable for similar production units. We consider the given system as a testbed for further research in simulation and real world application and the performance of the original Z2 system as an interesting benchmarking baseline.

Acknowledgement. This research was partly funded by the International Graduate School for Dynamics in Logistics, University of Bremen, Germany.

References

1. Bellmann, R.E., Zadeh, L.A.: Decision-making in a fuzzy environment. Manage. Sci. **17**(4), 141–164 (1970)
2. Bracht, U., Geckler, D., Wenzel, S.: Digitale Fabrik: Methoden und Praxisbeispiele. Springer, Heidelberg (2011)
3. Broy, M.: Cyber-physical systems. In: Broy, M. (ed.) acatech DISKUTIERT. Springer, Heidelberg (2010)
4. Burkhard, H.D.: Liveness and fairness properties in multi-agent systems, pp. 325–330, August 1993
5. Carlsson, C., Fullér, R.: Fuzzy multiple criteria decision making: Recent developments. Fuzzy Sets Syst. **78**, 139–153 (1996)
6. Fleisch, E., Mattern, F. (eds.): Das Internet der Dinge - Ubiquitous Computing und RFID in der Praxis. Springer, Heidelberg (2005)
7. Franklin, S., Graesser, A.: Is it an agent, or just a program?: a taxonomy for autonomous agents. In: Müller, J.P., Wooldridge, M.J., Jennings, N.R. (eds.) Intelligent Agents III Agent Theories, Architectures, and Languages. Lecture Notes in Computer Science, vol. 1193, pp. 21–35. Springer, Heidelberg (1997)
8. French, S.: Fuzzy decision analysis: some criticisms. In: Zimmermann, H.J. (ed.) TIMS/Studies in the Management Sciences, vol. 20, pp. 29–44. Elsevier Science Publishers, Amsterdam (1984)
9. Fujimoto, R.: Parallel and Distributed Simulation Systems. Wiley, New York (2000)

10. Gaines, B., Zadeh, L.A., Zimmermann, H.J.: Fuzzy sets and decison analysis - a perspective. In: Zimmermann, H.-J. (ed.) TIMS/Studies in the Management Sciences, vol. 20, pp. 3–8. Elsevier Sciences Publishers, Amsterdam (1984)
11. Ganji, F., Morales-Kluge, E., Scholz-Reiter, B.: Bringing agents into application: intelligent products in autonomous logistics. In: Schill, K., Scholz-Reiter, B., Frommberger, L. (eds.) Artificial Intelligence and Logistics (AiLog) - Workshop at ECAI 2010, pp. 37–42 (2010)
12. Gehrke, J., Schuldt, A.: Incorporating knowledge about interacting for uniform agent design for simulation and operation. In: AAMAS, pp. 1175–1176 (2009)
13. Greulich, C., Edelkamp, S., Gath, M., Warden, T., Humann, M., Herzog, O., Sitharam, T.G.: Enhanced shortest path computation for multiagent-based intermodal transport planning in dynamic environments. In: Filipe, J., Fred, A. (eds.) ICAART 2013, vol. 2, pp. 324–329. SciTePress, Barcelona (2013)
14. Kagermann, H., Wahlster, W., Helbig, J.: Umsetzungsempfehlungen für das Zukunftsprojekt Industrie 4.0. Abschlussbericht des Arbeitskreises Industrie (2013)
15. Klügl, F.: Multiagentensimulation - Konzepte, Werkzeuge. Addison-Wesley, Munich (2001). Anwendung
16. McFarlane, D., Sarma, S., Chirn, J.L., Wong, C., Ashton, K.: Auto ID systems and intelligent manufacturing control. Eng. Appl. Artif. Intell. 16(4), 365–376 (2003)
17. Morales Kluge, E., Ganji, F., Scholz-Reiter, B.: Intelligent products - towards autonomous logistic processes - a work in progress paper. In: 7th International Product Lifecycle Management Conference PLM 2010, Bremen (2010)
18. Nissim, R., Brafman, R.I.: Cost-optimal planning by self-interested agents. In: Proceedings of the Twenty-Seventh AAAI Conference on Artificial Intelligence, July 14–18, 2013, Bellevue, Washington, USA (2013)
19. Van Dyke Parunak, H., Savit, R., Riolo, R.L.: Agent-based modeling vs. equation-based modeling: a case study and users' guide. In: Sichman, J.S., Conte, R., Gilbert, N. (eds.) MABS 1998. LNCS (LNAI), vol. 1534, pp. 10–25. Springer, Heidelberg (1998)
20. Rekersbrink, H., Ludwig, B., Scholz-Reiter, B.: Entscheidungen selbststeuernder logistischer objekte. Industrie Manage. 23(4), 25–30 (2007)
21. Rogers, H.: Theory of Recursive Functions and Effective Computability. McGraw-Hill, New York (1967)
22. Russell, S.J., Norvig, P.: Artificial Intelligence - A Modern Approach, 3rd edn. Pearson Education, New Jersey (2010)
23. Saffidine, A.: Solving Games and All That. Ph.D. thesis, University Paris-Dauphine (2014)
24. Warden, T., Porzel, R., Gehrke, J.D., Herzog, O., Langer, H., Malaka, R.: Towards ontology-based multiagent simulations: the plasma approach. In: Bargiela, A., Azam Ali, S., Crowley, D., Kerckhoffs, E.J.H. (eds.) European Council for Modelling and Simulation ECMS 2010, pp. 50–56 (2010)
25. Windt, K., Böse, F., Philipp, T.: Autonomy in production logistics: Identification, characterisation and application. Robot. Comput. Integr. Manuf. 24(4), 572–578 (2008)
26. Wooldridge, M.: Reasoning about Rational Agents. The MIT Press, Cambridge (2000)
27. Wooldridge, M.: An Introduction to Multi-Agent Systems. Wiley, Chichester (2002)
28. Wooldridge, M., Jennings, N.R.: Intelligent agents: theory and practice. Knowl. Eng. Rev. 10(02), 115–152 (1995)

Modeling and Simulation of Web-of-Things Systems as Multi-Agent Systems

Ion Mircea Diaconescu[1]([✉]) and Gerd Wagner[1,2]

[1] Brandenburg University of Technology, Cottbus, Germany
{M.Diaconescu,G.Wagner}@b-tu.de
[2] Old Dominion University, Norfolk, USA

Abstract. In the Web of Things (WoT), special communication networks composed of sensor nodes, actuator nodes and service nodes form the basis for new types of web application systems, which are directly connected to the real world via sensors and actuators. We propose a conceptual framework for simulating WoT systems as multi-agent systems where both sensor nodes, actuator nodes and service nodes, as well as other systems in their environment interacting with them (such as other web applications, web services and human users), are modeled and simulated as agents. Our conceptual framework includes an ontology of WoT systems as sensor/actuator systems, and a meta-model for defining an agent-based WoT system simulation language.

Keywords: Web of things · Sensor-actuator systems · Agent-based modeling · Simulation

1 Introduction

In the Web of Things (WoT), special communication networks composed of sensor nodes, actuator nodes and service nodes form the basis for new types of web applications, which are directly connected to the real world via sensors and actuators, and can be private, such as smart home apps, personal robotics apps and factory control applications, or public, such as air pollution monitoring systems and city parking management apps. We propose a conceptual framework for simulating WoT systems as multi-agent systems where both sensor nodes, actuator nodes and service nodes, as well as other systems in their environment interacting with them (such as other web applications, web services and human users), are modeled and simulated as agents.

We consider systems of purposeful interacting systems (with some degree of autonomy) as *multi-agent systems.* Our conceptual framework includes an ontology of WoT systems (WoTS) as sensor/actuator systems, and a meta-model for defining an agent-based WoT system simulation language. Our approach supports "hardware in the loop", "software in the loop" and "humans in the loop", where "hardware" refers to sensor or actuator nodes, "software" refers to web applications and web services, and "humans" refers to human users, which can

© Springer International Publishing Switzerland 2015
J.P. Müller et al. (Eds.): MATES 2015, LNAI 9433, pp. 137–153, 2015.
DOI: 10.1007/978-3-319-27343-3_8

interact with a WoTS simulation via the user interface of a web application or via a user interface of a sensor or actuator node.

Our proposed simulation framework is not concerned with low-level networking issues in WoTS, e.g., resulting from specific network topologies. Rather, the goal is to develop a WoTS simulation approach including and above the application layer, with a focus on simulating the sensor, actuator and service nodes as parts of a WoTS, and the WoTS as a whole.

2 Related Work

In [4], an approach to agent-based simulation of a network of web-service-enabled devices is proposed. The authors argue that the *Service-Oriented Architecture* (SOA) paradigm can be used for achieving interoperability between the nodes of a WoT system and between such a system and modern enterprise networks. When devices expose their data and operations as web services, this provides an integration of devices with enterprise applications, allowing new innovative solutions to enterprise automation problems. The authors choose the open standard protocol *Devices Profile for Web Services* (DPWS) as the interaction protocol for web-service-enabled devices [5]. However, this protocol is based on a protocol stack that is too complex for constrained resource devices as needed, for instance, in battery-operated WoT networks, while it may work well in non-constrained office or factory environments. A Java-based multi-agent platform is used to create the agents that simulate DPWS devices. These agents are connected to the enterprise network in the same way as real DPWS devices. The resulting system can be used for evaluating the impact of a large number of networked devices on the running enterprise applications, without the need to set up a real device network, which would be quite expensive and more difficult.

In [6] is proposed a decentralized architecture where agents providing atomic system services run inside IoT devices. The authors argue that it is possible, by using their approach, to dynamically distribute system load and move the data processing tasks into the IoT devices in the edges of the network. HTTP and CoAP (for low resource devices) are used as communication protocols, and a proxy translates messages between these protocols. The assumption is that IoT devices exist in a physical form (they are not software simulated), and the discussion is rather generic, not making clear how such a system, composed of various IoT devices (software and hardware platforms) can be practically implemented.

A language and platform independent composition for mobile agents-based smart objects is proposed in [7]. Using this approach, communication and data sharing between agents is possible over disparate networks. The information infrastructure is realized with the IETF CoRE framework [8]. The REST principles are utilized in agent creation, migration, control, smart object communication and resources exposal to the internet. The authors discuss a system reference architecture as well as an application programming interface which allows basic HTTP and CoAP communication, content negotiation and authorization methods. Some of the principles presented in this work are also used in the implementation of our JavaScript simulation framework, allowing agents to share information among heterogeneous networks and provide access to resources with the help of web interfaces.

3   IoT and WoT Systems

An *Internet-of-Things (IoT) system* is a communication network consisting of sensor nodes, actuator nodes and service nodes, such that at least one node is connected to the Internet. A sensor node consists of a controller to which one or more sensors and a communication unit are attached. An actuator node consists of a controller to which one or more actuators, zero or more sensors and a communication unit are attached.

A *WoT system (WoTS)* is an IoT system that is built with Web technologies. These technologies do not only include the classical Web technologies HTTP(S), HTML, CSS and JavaScript, but also the more recent Web technologies *Server-Sent Events, Web Sockets*, and the *Constrained Application Protocol (CoAP)* proposed in [9]. We distinguish between the following three cases:

1. WoT systems that do not have the limitations implied by constrained resource devices. These systems can use ordinary networking and web technologies such as IEEE 802.11 for wireless networking, HTTPS and SOAP for application-level messaging, and SOAP-based co-ordination and security techniques, as proposed in [4].
2. WoT systems based on constrained resource devices having unlimited power supply (not using batteries), such that power consumption is not a concern. These systems need an alternative software/technology stack that is adapted to the limited main memory, storage and processor speed of the constrained resource devices. Ethernet (or IEEE 802.11) can still be used for (wireless) networking, but only CoAP or an HTTP subset, and no HTTPS, can be used for application-level messaging.
3. WoT systems based on constrained resource devices that are battery-powered, requiring low-energy wireless networking technologies, such as *IEEE 802.15.4*, and small footprint software technologies, such as CoAP for application-level messaging. These systems often have higher packet error rates and a lower throughput (say, of only tens of kbit/s).

Unlike many other authors, such as [2,4], we consider the issue of using the new Internet Protocol (IP) version 6 (IPv6) instead of the established version 4 (IPv4) as orthogonal to the WoT. The main issue solved by IPv6, allowing a greater address space than IPv4, is not necessarily an issue for WoT systems, which can, in many cases, be built with either of them. Of course, the increasing use of IoT apps will contribute to the increasing demand for IP addresses. But since most IoT/WoT devices will not have to be reachable via an IP address, the expected explosive growth of the IoT/WoT will not imply a similar explosion of the IP address space.

The following are considered to be desirable features of a WoTS:

- self-configuration: the dynamic composition of WoTS by nodes joining and leaving the network at any time
- self-diagnosis: automatic discovery of failures and faults
- self-optimization of constrained energy (battery-based) WoTS: automatic monitoring and on/off-time control of resources

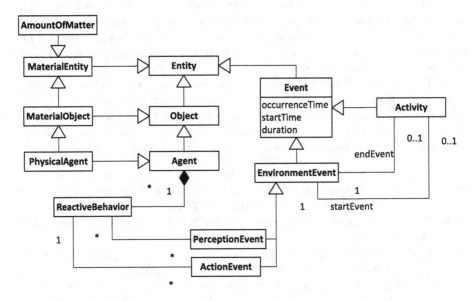

Fig. 1. A fragment of the AOES ontology.

Further, we discuss an approach for modeling sensor and actuator nodes as agents. The AOES ontology fragment shown in Fig. 1 is the basis of our proposal. PhysicalAgent represents the core of a WoTS model, and it consists of a set of built-in properties representing the physical characteristics of the agent (e.g., spatial position) and zero or more (built-in or custom defined) reaction rules defining its behavior. When needed, additional custom properties can be defined for specific agent types derived from PhysicalAgent.

3.1   Sensor Nodes

As described in the UML class diagram shown in Fig. 2, a sensor node represents a PhysicalAgent. It consists of a controller, a communication unit and one or more sensors. A sensor consists of one or more detectors, which represents simple (non-composite) sensors. A sensor is a measurement device that is attached to a controller within a sensor node. As shown in Fig. 3, we distinguish between three types of detectors:

1. quality detectors with an analog interface,
2. quality detectors with a digital interface,
3. event detectors.

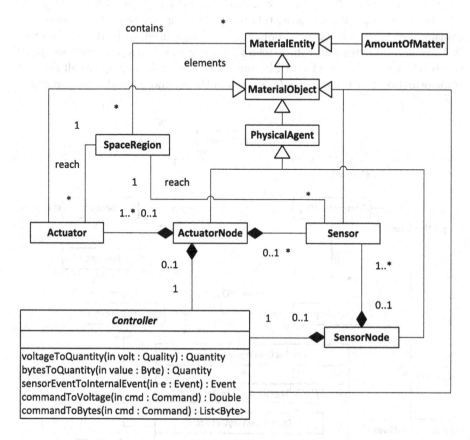

Fig. 2. An overview of the sensor and actuator nodes model.

Quality detectors and event detectors are simple (non-composite) sensors. A *quality detector* is a device that allows measuring a physical quality of its environment (or *reach*). An *event detector* allows detecting events occurring in its reach. Notice that the concept of physical qualities has been defined in the philosophical discipline of *ontology* (or *metaphysics*). A quality is an entity, and not a data value, but it can be approximately represented by a data value (namely the value of an attribute that captures the type of quality). For instance, the voltage level of a wire of a particular detector at some moment in time is a quality, which can be approximately represented by the value of an attribute `outputVoltage` used for expressing statements about, and measurements of, the detector.

Figure 3 shows how the sensing operation of an analog quality detector can be conceptualized as a transformation, which converts a quality to be measured in the detector's reach to an internal quality of the detector device (typically, to a voltage level) that can be read and transformed to a measurement quantity by the controller. In our WoTS sensor ontology, we call the first transformation function *quality-to-voltage*, and the second one *voltage-to-quantity*.

The sensing operation of a digital quality detector can be conceptualized as a transformation, which converts a quality to be measured in the detector's reach to a sequence of bytes that can be read and transformed to a measurement quantity by the controller (see Fig. 3). In our WoTS sensor ontology, we call the first transformation function *quality-to-bytes*, and the second one *bytes-to-quantity*.

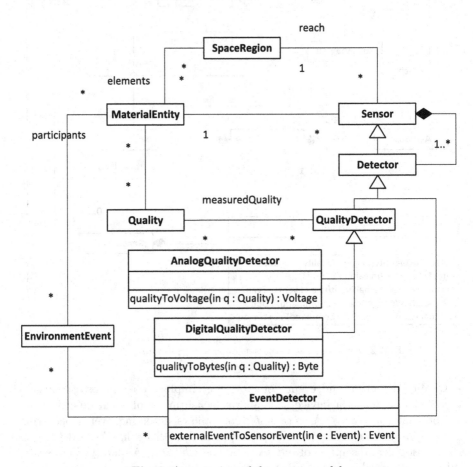

Fig. 3. An overview of the sensor model.

The sensing operation of an event sensor can be conceptualized as a transformation, which turns the occurrence of an event of a certain type in its reach to an internal event of the sensor device itself (typically corresponding to digital voltage signals) that can be detected and transformed to a control event by the controller. In our WoTS sensor ontology, we call the first transformation *externalEvent-to-sensorEvent*, and the second one *sensorEvent-to-internalEvent*.

3.2 Actuator Nodes

As shown in the UML class diagram in Fig. 2, an actuator node represents a `PhysicalAgent`. It consists of a controller, a communication unit, one or more actuators and zero or more sensors.

As a component of an actuator node, an actuator is an enactment device that is attached to a controller within an actuator node. Common types of actuators are electro-mechanical devices that are controlled with the help of a (voltage or digital interface) signal. Examples are motors, water pumps and relays.

Based on the interaction with the environment, we distinguish between two types of actuators: *event actuators* and *activity actuators*.

As shown in Fig. 4, the effect of an *event actuator* is an event which directly or indirectly affects qualities of its reach. A direct effect is when the resulting event produces immediate state changes in the environment (reach) quality. For example, a relay actuator which turns on a light, produces an immediate change in the light intensity value of the actuator reach. An indirect effect is when the resulting event produces a set of actions which later can result in reach state changes.

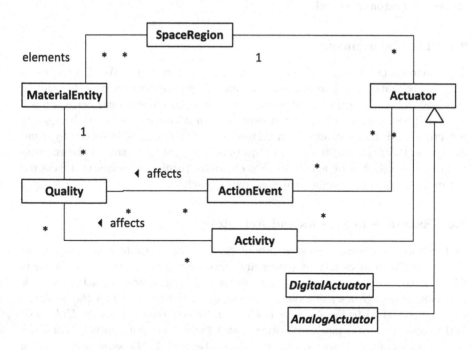

Fig. 4. An overview of the actuator model.

An *activity actuator* produces environment (reach) state changes over a time period. It has a start and an end triggering event. For example, a watering activity is started when the soil moisture is below a threshold and is ended when the soil moisture reaches the required level. During the watering activity time, the soil moisture increases as a result of the water flow, and a soil moisture sensor reads the changes of this quality.

We distinguish between two main types of actuators (see Fig. 4), with respect to their communication interface: digital and analog. Digital actuators are either controlled with a simple high/low signal or by using a specific digital communication protocol, such as I2C, SPI or UART.

Analog actuators are controlled by voltage levels, and their effect is represented by one or more functions, sometimes provided in the actuator datasheet. While for a vaste majority of actuators this information is not available, a linear, exponential or logarithmic function can be used to simulate the output of an actuator. Controlling an analog actuator requires to use a DAC (digital to analog convertor) capable controller, such as Arduino DUE [1].

Some *digital actuators* are controlled with a simple high/low signal. They can be in one of the two states: open or closed. Examples of such actuators are relays and electro-valves. Other digital actuators accept as input a set of bits which describes the command to be executed. For example, some PWM actuators expect a 64 bits encoded duty cycle and frequency values. In general, standard digital communication protocols (e.g. I2C, SPI or UART) are used to communicate with digital actuators, but for some, the datasheet may also describe a custom protocol.

3.3 The Environment

The environment (reach) of the sensors and actuators of a WoTS consists of amounts of matter (such as soil and air) and of discrete material objects (such as cars and animals). Amounts of matter and material objects bear certain physical qualities (such as color or temperature) that can be measured by quality detectors, and may participate in certain events that can be detected by event detectors. Physical qualities of the objects or amounts of matter in the environment can be affected by actuators. For example, turning on a heater affects the temperature of that specific heater actuator reach.

3.4 Examples of Sensors and Actuators

In the above sections we discuss about sensors and actuators as components of a node. A large variety of sensor and actuators, such as the ones shown in Fig. 5, exists for being used in WoT projects. For instance, an actuator node may consist of a *Grove* soil moisture analog quality detector and a *Pump* digital actuator attached to an *Arduino UNO* [1] micro-controller, plus an *ESP8266*[1] WiFi communication module. Notice that a Pump represents an actuator type, the instances of which are individual *Pump* actuators. In the same way, a sensor node may consist of a *DHT22*[2] (itself consisting of a temperature and humidity detectors) sensor, an *Arduino UNO* micro-controller, and an *ESP8266* WiFi communication module.

---

[1] ESP8266 WiFi module - http://www.esp8266.com/.

[2] DHT22 Sensor - https://www.adafruit.com/datasheets/DigitalhumidityandtemperaturesensorAM2302.pdf.

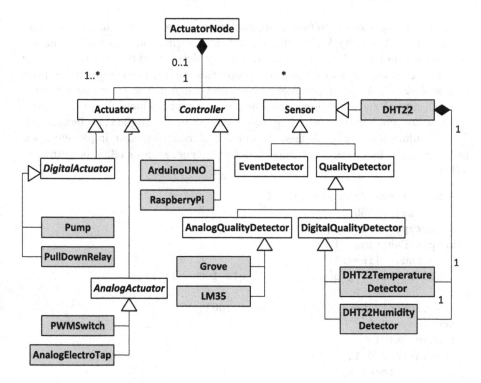

Fig. 5. Examples of sensor and actuator types.

4 The AOE Simulation Framework

Our AOES framework includes a simulation language and a simulator implementation, with support for various built-in sensor (e.g., LM35) and actuator types (e.g., PullDownRelay).

The simulation language is based on AORML [10] (Agent-Object-Relationship Modeling Language), and provides the language elements used to define WoTS simulations. In AORML, an entity is either an agent, an event, an action, a claim, a commitment, or an ordinary object. Agent and object form, respectively, the active and passive entities, while actions and events are the dynamic entities of the system model. Commitments and claims establish a special type of relationship between agents. These concepts are fundamental components of social interaction processes and can explicitly help to achieve coherent behavior when these processes are semi or fully automated. Only agents can communicate, perceive, act, make commitments and satisfy claims. Ordinary objects are passive entities with no such capabilities.

We extend the AOE Simulation Language with support for the new types required in a WoT simulation. The basic elements used to define a sensor node are shown in Fig. 6. Interfaces are used to describe operations (functionality), such as the *attribute-to-voltage* mapping function needed for the analog quality detectors. Concrete WoT component types, such as ArduinoUNO (a microcontroller type) and LM35 (an analog quality detector type) are instances of MaterialObject, from which physical properties are inherited (e.g., spatial position and sizes). A set of parameters are used when a new component type is created, one of the most important being supertype which allows to classify the new component (e.g., as a DigitalActuator or AnalogQualityDetector). This simulation language is used by our JavaScript simulator implementation prototype. For instance, a new analog detector type, such as LM35, is defined as follows:

```
var LM35 = new MaterialObject( {
  typename: "LM35",
  supertype: "AnalogQualityDetector",
  mappingFunction: {
    method: "linear",
    initialData: { q0: 0, v0: 0, q1: 100, v1: 1},
  },
  measurementRange: { min: 0, max: 100},
  accuracy: 0.5,
  precision: 1,
  resolution: 0.1,
  supplyVoltage: 5,
  properties: {
    "outputVoltage": { range: "Decimal"}
  }
});
```

Notice that in the class diagram of Fig. 6, the ArduinoUNO class represents, like a product type, a controller type, the instances of which are individual *ArduinoUNO* micro-controllers. Likewise, the LM35 class represents a detector type, the instances of which are individual *LM35* detectors.

5   Modeling and Simulation of WoT Systems

A *WoTS simulation* consists of one or more simulated WoTS nodes, an environment simulator, and zero or more real WoTS nodes, satisfying certain conditions as defined below. The environment simulator is in charge of managing the state of the simulated environment, including the reaches of all simulated sensor and actuator nodes, and of simulating environment events, which may change the state of the simulated environment, e.g., by changing certain property values in certain simulated sensor reaches, and may affect event detectors if a simulated environment event of the right type occurs in the reach of a simulated event detector.

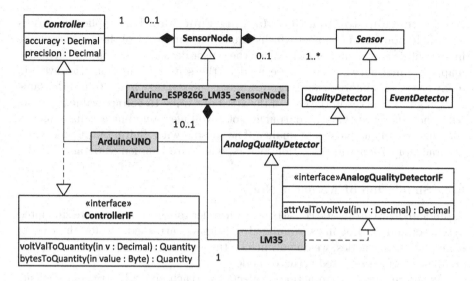

Fig. 6. AOES sensor node example.

5.1 Simulation of Sensor Nodes

A simulated sensor node consists of a controller to which one or more simulated sensors are attached. Since our simulation framework is not concerned with low-level communication issues, we do not include the communication unit as an explicit component of a simulated sensor node. A detailed discussion about how a simulated sensor reads a quality of the environment and produces a result representing the measured quantity was presented in [3]. We provide a summary of the mapping functions used to simulate the sensor output.

The Attribute-Value-to-Voltage-Value Function. In a measurement simulation, the value of a reach attribute is read by the simulated analog quality detector and transformed to a voltage value. The sensor resolution is used to compute the "detected" input value, then, using a mapping function, a voltage output value is obtained. The mapping function is either provided in the sensor datasheet, or approximated by a linear, logarithmic or exponential function, as shown in [3]. Considering the sensor characteristics, such as accuracy and precision, the final voltage output of the sensor is computed.

The Voltage-Value-to-Quantity Mapping Function. This function is used to provide a quantity for the measured quality when analog detectors are used. Using ADC (analog to digital converted) enabled controllers (such as Arduino UNO), the sensor analog output is mapped to a value representing the measured quantity of the environment quality. The ADC unit has accuracy and precision, like a sensor, since it is a voltage sensor with a digital output, which are reflected in the ADC output.

Attribute-Value-to-Quantity Mapping Function. This applies to sensors with digital output, no matter which communication protocol they use, since the final result is a decimal number. When the sensor datasheet specifies a particular mapping function, then it can be used in the sensor simulation. However, in many cases, this information is not available, the strategy being to use the same mapping functions as in the case of the attribute-value-to-voltage-value function, with the difference that the output is not a voltage value but a value which is the quantity of the measured quality. The sensors with digital output have also accuracy, precision and resolution factors, which are handled as detailed in [3].

5.2   Simulation of Actuator Nodes

A simulated actuator node consists of a controller to which one or more simulated actuators and zero or more simulated sensors are attached. As for the case of simulated sensor nodes, we do not include the communication unit as an explicit component of a simulated actuator node.

As shown in Fig. 4, an actuator affects the reach either by triggering events with direct or indirect effect, as discussed earlier in this paper, or by producing an activity. For the simulation of the environment state changes produced by actuators, *uniform* and *radial* mapping functions are used. Whenever needed, custom mapping functions may also be implemented, e.g., when a simulation scenario has custom requirements.

The Unform Mapping Function. This mapping function is used whenever a quality of the reach is affected in a uniform manner in the environment (or reach), no matter the physical coordinates. For example, a relay which turns on a set of lights may produce uniform light (considering an ideal environment) over the reach.

The Radial Mapping Function. Using this mapping type, the effects of the actuator are reduced (or amplified) with the increase of the distance between the actuator spatial position and the coordinates within the affected reach. For example, a water pump actuator produces a radial effect with respect to the soil moisture environment quality. In other words, the soil moisture level decreases along with the increase of the distance between the water pump, considered the origin of the water flow, and the spatial coordinates in the reach where the soil moisture quality measurement is performed. Concrete formulas used to compute the radial effects depends on the affected physical properties. One example is provided at the end of this paper, when a "Green House" simulation scenario is discussed.

5.3   Simulation of the Environment

The simulated environment (simulation world) consists of simulated actuator and sensor reaches, which overlap partially or totally. The physical space of the simulated environment is divided in cells, which represent the atomic space units. A simulated reach is composed of a set of such neighbor cells. In a real world WoTS, a sensor or actuator can have a irregular physically shaped reach, i.e., a mesh shape. For simplicity reasons, in the case of simulated sensors and actuators, the corresponding reach spaces are described by using regular shapes, such as cuboids or approximated spheres. A simulated actuator actions have effects only on that specific actuator reach, while a simulated sensor is able to read (sense) only from its reach.

Actuator actions create environment events which activates environment reaction rules. As result, state changes of the physical qualities of the objects or matter within the simulated actuator reach may occur or activities are started or ended, as shown in Fig. 4. Simulated quality detectors (or sensors) detect quality state changes, while simulated event detectors (or sensors) receive perception events. For example, a simulated *LM35* analog quality temperature detector senses changes of the temperature quality within its reach, and a *PIR* (passive infrared sensor) detects the presence of an infrared emitting object within its reach.

For simulations with sensor hardware in the loop, it is important to notice that while simulated sensors have a simulated reach, real sensors are situated in a real-world environment. A simulated environment does not affect any real sensor node and a real-world environment does not affect any simulated sensor node, but the two can be part of the same sensor network, share the same gateway and provide data to the same services.

5.4 Modeling and Simulation of a WoT System as a Whole

A *WoTS simulation* consists of one or more simulated WoTS nodes, an environment simulator, and zero or more real WoTS nodes, such that

1. All simulated quality detectors (on simulated sensor and actuator nodes) can sense/read as their input the value of an attribute of their simulated reach corresponding to the quality to be measured. A simulated analog quality detector first maps the attribute value to a voltage value with the help of an attribute-value-to-voltage-value function, such that the simulated sensor node can then map it to the simulated measurement result with the help of a voltage-value-to-quantity function. A simulated digital quality detector directly maps the property value to the simulated measurement result with the help of a attribute-value -to-quantity function.
2. All simulated event detectors can detect simulated external perception events as inputs from the environment simulator
3. All simulated actuators on simulated actuator nodes create simulated action events as outputs to the environment simulator, which maps them to simulated physical signals as inputs to simulated sensors in the reach of the simulated actuator.
4. Simulated sensor nodes are not "coupled" with real actuator nodes: the reach of any real actuator node does not overlap with the reach of any simulated

sensor node. The reach of an actuator node is its local environment, in which real state changes can be caused by it. The reach of a simulated sensor node is the spatial region corresponding to its sensing radius in the simulated local environment of the simulated sensor node.

This definition of a WoTS simulation includes the special case where all nodes are simulated.

Notice that while there is a crisp boundary between real and simulated sensor and actuator nodes, the boundary between real and simulated service nodes is more fuzzy, since service nodes are not connected to the "real world", but only to digital network signals, which may represent real or simulated signals.

6   A Green House Test Case

Our Green House scenario considers a closed environment with three important parameters: soil moisture, air temperature and relative humidity. It has an area of $1250 \ m^2$ $(50 \times 25m)$ and a volume of $3750m^3$ $(50 \times 25 \times 3m)$.

We consider a plant type, for which the optimal values corresponding to the three qualities and the quantity of water consumption per unit of time are known. The temperature variable (producing water vaporization) but also the water consumed by the plant affects both, the soil moisture and the relative air humidity.

6.1   Simulated Hardware Configuration

Two sensor types (three quality detectors) are used in our simulation, measuring the important environment qualities:

- DHT22/AM2302 digital temperature and humidity sensor with a custom 1-Wire digital interface (two quality detectors on the same physical package, with a common data interface). It allows measurements of air humidity in the range from $[0, 99]\%$ with a typical accuracy of 2% and precision of 1%, as well as temperature measurements in the range from $[-40, 80]°C$ with a typical accuracy of $0.5°C$ and precision of $0.2°C$.
- GROVE analog soil moisture detector, with a range of $[0, 100]\%$ and a typical accuracy of 10%. The datasheet does not provide information about the sensor's precision, but our research on the web has shown that typically a value of 5% is to be expected for this sensor type. This sensor has an analog quality detector.

Two actuator types are used to control the three monitored environment qualities, i.e., soil moisture, air temperature and relative humidity:

- Heaters, activated or deactivated by PullDownRelay digital actuators, are used to increase the temperature when needed. Each heater is able to increase the temperature with $5°C$ per hour, for $750m^3$ volume of air. Cooling is not considered in this scenario. The pull down relays are directly connected to heaters, and the composition of the two components represents the actuator.

- Ventilators, activated or deactivated by `PullDownRelay` digital actuators, are used to provide air flow to and from outside the green house space, thus providing some degree of control for this quality. The ventilators can rotate either forward or backward and can be on or off, without speed control. Each ventilator is able to provide a volume of $1250m^3$ air per hour. The pull down relays are directly connected to ventilators, and the composition of the two represents the actuator.
- A `Pump` digital actuator is used to increase the soil moisture when required. It can be on (provides water flow) or off (no water flows). The pump is able to provide $9\,dm^3$ water per minute.

A simulated sensor node consists of an Arduino Mini [1] controller (a cheap variation of Arduino UNO, much lower in size and with half the power consumption), an WiFi communication module and a DHT22 or a Grove sensor (or both). Because the temperature and humidity are considered uniform over the entire green house space, only one node contains a DHT22 sensor.

A simulated actuator node consist of an Arduino Mini controller, an WiFi communication module and a pull down relay or a water pump actuator (or both). Some of the actuator nodes contains also Grove sensors, depending on their spatial position.

In general, the goal is to allow using real devices in combination with simulated devices. Technically, this is possible by using a virtual router, a piece of software, which allows the simulated sensor and actuator nodes to behave in the network same as real hardware: connects to a Wi-Fi or Wired network, acquire IP from DHCP and use standard communication protocols, e.g., CoAP over UDP, for data transmission.

6.2   Environment Simulation

In this scenarion, the simulated sensor and actuator nodes exist in a simulated environment. The variation of the environment qualities, such as air temperature and humidity, is sensed by the simulated sensors and transformed to quantities by the controller, e.g., soil moisture level (in percent), for soil moisture quality. The environment physical space is discrete and it is composed of cubic cells with a size of $1 \times 1 \times 1m$. A cell represents the atomic space unit. A sensor or actuator reach (a region in the environment space) consists of a neighborhood set of such cells. Sensor reaches and actuator reaches share environment space (one or more cells), but a complete overlap is not required. The environment simulator takes into consideration the following qualities:

- *Temperature*: the variation from day to night is considered linear. The variation interval is set for 24 hours. The temperature starts to increase after sunrise until a specified daytime, e.g., 5:00 PM for summer time, then decreases until the next sunrise. Close to reality events, such as clouds, are simulated by introducing small random variations. In this scenario, we consider a uniform temperature distribution over the simulated environment (the temperature value is the same on each space cell). The heaters are activated if the temperature goes below 22°C, and deactivated when the temperature reaches 25°C or more.

- *Air humidity*: the variation depends on the environment temperature and water dew point. Water dew point is the temperature at which the air can no longer hold all of the water vapor which is mixed with it, and some of the water vapor must condense into liquid water. In this scenario, air flow to and from outside allows to increase or decrease the air humidity. The minimum and maximum values for this quality are dependent on the values from the space outside the green house. The formula used to compute the relative air humidity is: $RH = 10^{m\left(\frac{T_d}{T_d+T_n} - \frac{T_a}{T_a+T_n}\right)} * 100\,\%$, where T_d is the water dew point temperature, T_a is the temperature in the environment, while m and T_n are constants which depend on temperature ranges and are provided in constant tables. In this scenario, we consider a uniform air humidity distribution over the simulated green house environment (the value of this quality is the same on each space cell).
- *Soil moisture*: the variation depends on both, the temperature which affects the water vaporization, and the quantity of water known to be consumed by the plant. When watering is required, because the soil moisture is below a threshold, the water pump is started. The water distribution in soil is computed by using the following formula: $\frac{d\theta}{dt} = \frac{d}{dr}\left(D\frac{d\theta}{dr}\right) - S$, where θ is the volumetric water content, t is the time, D is the soil water diffusivity, r is the radius, and S is the water uptake by the plant(s) root. In this scenario, for simplicty reasons, we do not consider the gravitational force when computing the water distribution in the soil, therefore the soil moisture is the same no matter the depth in the soil at which it is measured.

During the simulation runtime, various activities are possible. For example, when the measured soil moisture goes under a specified level, a *watering activity* is started. A *water pump* is then activated in the specific reach. A known quantity of water per unit of time starts to flow and the soil moisture in the actuator reach starts to increase (according with the above presented formula). The soil moisture sensor reads the value of this quality, and when it reaches an optimum level, the water pump is deactivated.

7   Conclusions

We have presented a proposal for modeling and simulating certain types of sensor-actuator systems and WoT systems consisting of simple sensors based on quality detectors and event detectors, such as LM35 analog temperature sensors and Proximity Infra-Red (PIR) sensors. Although our approach is more general than the approaches discussed in the section on related work, it does not provide a completely general model of sensors and actuators, since it does, for instance, not account for more advanced types of sensors such as LIDAR devices and video cameras. We work on a JavaScript implementation of the proposed simulation framework and expect to be able to present evaluation results, of the simulator and the presented test case, in a follow-up paper.

References

1. Arduino Foundation: Arduino Platform (2005). http://arduino.cc
2. Brambilla, G., Picone, M., Cirani, S., Amoretti, M., Zanichelli, F.: A simulation platform for large-scale internet of things scenarios in urban environments. In: Proceeding of the of the First International Conference on IoT in Urban Space (Urb-IoT 2014), Rome, Italy, pp. 50–55 (2014). Institute for Computer Sciences, Social Informatics and Telecommunications Engineering (ICST)
3. Diaconescu, M., Wagner, G.: Modeling and simulation of web-of-things systems Part 1: sensor nodes. In: Winter Simulation Conference (WSC 2015), Huntington Beach, CA (To appear)
4. Karnouskos S., Tariq, M.M.J.: An agent-based simulation of SOA-ready devices. In: Proceedings of the Tenth International Conference on Computer Modeling and Simulation, pp. 330–335 (2008). IEEE Computer Society
5. Microsoft Corporation: Devices profile for web services. http://specs.xmlsoap.org/ws/2006/02/devprof/devicesprofile.pdf (2006). Accessed 23 May 2015
6. Leppnen, T., Riekki, J.: A lightweight agent-based architecture for the Internet of Things. IEICE Technical Report
7. Leppnen, T., Riekki, J., Liu, M., Harjula, E., Ojala, T.: Mobile agents-based smart objects for the internet of things. In: Fortino, G., Trunfio, P. (eds.) Internet of Things Based on Smart Objects, pp. 29–48. Springer, Heidelberg (2014)
8. Shelby, Z.: Embedded web services. IEEE Wirel. Commun. 17(6), 52–57 (2010)
9. Shelby, Z., Hartke, K., Bormann, C.: Constrained Application Protocol (CoAP) RFC 7252, June 2014. Internet Engineering Task Force (IETF)
10. Wagner, G.: The agent-object-relationship meta-model: towards a unified view of state and behavior. Inf. Syst. 28(5), 475–504 (2003)

A Conceptual Approach to Place Security in Systems of Mobile Agents

Héla Hachicha[1(✉)], Donies Samet[2], and Khaled Ghedira[3]

[1] Institut Supérieur d'Informarique, Université El Manar, Tunis, Tunisia
hachichahela@yahoo.fr
[2] Faculté des Sciences Economiques et de Gestion,
Université de Sfax, Sfax, Tunisia
donies.samet@yahoo.com
[3] Institut Supérieur de Gestion, Université de Tunis, Tunis, Tunisia
khaled.ghedira@isg.rnu.tn

Abstract. Mobile agents' security is a major challenge for the expansion of their use. Actually, most research works have been interested in integrating mobile agents' security requirements in the implementation stage. However, the integration of security requirements in the design stage could help towards the development of more secure systems based on mobile agents. In this paper, we are interested to model the security requirements of mobile agents in the design stage in order to protect places from malicious visitor agents. An example from a teleexpertise system is used to illustrate the proposed approach.

Keywords: Mobile agents · Security requirements · MA-UML profile · Agent-Oriented software engineering

1 Introduction

Mobile agent technology is gaining wide acceptance for their ability to deal with complex systems. Mobile agents are a particular type of software agents whose predominant feature is their ability to move throughout networks from an execution environment to another. This environment is called "place". A place represents a "context" where mobile agents run, meet and communicate with other agents, and handle some local resources [1]. Among the advantages of using mobile agents we quote: reducing network traffic, reducing bandwidth usage, improving network latency, robustness and fault tolerance [2]. However, the mobile agents' security issue is an obstacle to the effective use of this technology and it is not yet fully resolved.

Generally the definition of mobile agents' security requirements is considered in the implementation stage of the development process. However, the integration of security requirements during the design stage could help towards the development of more secure systems based on mobile agents [3].

In this context and in order to contribute to solve this problem, the aim of our research is to integrate mobile agents' security requirements into a mobile agent-oriented methodology. In this work, we are interested essentially in ensuring the security of places in systems of mobile agents by introducing new security properties in the

© Springer International Publishing Switzerland 2015
J.P. Müller et al. (Eds.): MATES 2015, LNAI 9433, pp. 154–170, 2015.
DOI: 10.1007/978-3-319-27343-3_9

design stage. These new security properties represent new extensions of the MA-UML profile (Mobile Agent UML) [4] in order to define the "Secure MA-UML profile".

This paper is structured as follows. In Sect. 2, first we briefly describe the security requirements and we discuss the security issues of mobile agents based systems. Section 3 describes the main approaches towards designing security requirements. In Sect. 4, we present our proposed extensions in order to secure places in systems of mobile agents. Section 5 describes two scenarios implementations to show the useful of the introduced extensions. Finally, Sect. 6 summarizes the paper and offers directions for future work.

2 Mobile Agent and Security

2.1 Security Requirements

In the following points, we provide a brief overview of the security requirements [5]:

- *Confidentiality*: guaranteeing that information is only accessible to authorized entities and inaccessible to others.
- *Authentication*: proving the identity of an entity.
- *Integrity*: assuring that the information remains unmodified from source entity to destination entity.
- *Access Control*: identifying the access rights an entity has over system resources.
- *Non-repudiation*: confirming the involvement of an entity in certain communication.
- *Availability*: guaranteeing the accessibility and usability of information and resources to authorized entities.

2.2 Security Issues in Systems of Mobile Agents

According to the literature [5, 6], four classes of attacks can be identified in systems of mobile agents, which are:

- *An Agent to Another Agent*: this class spread the attacks that an agent may suffer from another agent. There are basically four types of risks: attacks against authentication, attacks against confidentiality, attacks against availability and attacks against non-repudiation.
- *A Place to a Mobile Agent*: an agent that runs on a place is exposed to security threats which are: attacks against authentication, attacks against confidentiality, attacks against availability and attacks against integrity.
- *A Mobile Agent to a Place*: in this class the problems include masquerading, denial of service, unauthorized access and repudiation.
- *External Entities to Mobile Agent*: to migrate to another place, an agent must pass through a communications network on which the agent may suffer different types of attacks such as listening, alteration of its content or even its destruction.

In this paper, we are interested only in the attacks caused by a mobile agent to a place. These attacks are discussed in detail in the following subsection. The others classes of attacks will be treated in our future research.

2.3   Attacks Caused by a Mobile Agent to a Place

In this class, the mobile agent exploits the vulnerabilities of a place or launches attacks against a place. The set of attacks are described in the following points [5, 6]:

Attack Against the Authentication. Masquerade: A mobile agent masks its identity to present itself as an authorized agent to access the services and resources that it does not have the right.

Attack Against the Availability. Denial of service: Mobile agent can launch denial of service attacks by consuming the resources of the visited place excessively, by cloning or migrating indefinitely without end. Denial of service can be launched to exploit system vulnerabilities, to disrupt the services offered by the place or to degrade its performance. As a consequence, this attack has an effect on other agents because it can disrupt their access to the place or their use of resources.

Attack Against Access Control. Unauthorized access: Each agent visiting a place must be subject to the security policy of this platform. To implement appropriate mechanisms for access control, a mobile agent must authenticate itself before it is instantiated on the place. A mobile agent who has access to a place and its services without proper authorization can affect the place. Depending on the access level, the agent may be able to switch off or reside the place. A platform that accepts agents, representing the various users and organizations, must ensure that agents do not have access to data for which they have no authorization.

Attack Against Non-repudiation. Repudiation: The repudiation occurs when an agent can deny having performed an action. For example, a mobile agent belies the fact that it visited a platform and used its resources. If a platform cannot prevent malicious agents to repudiate a transaction, it must be able to resolve disagreements arising.

3   Related Work

Security plays an important role in the development of mobile agent technology. As a result, some works on security for systems of mobile agents have been interested to include the security requirements when the system is being deployed or is already in use, or in the best case they are considered only during the final stage of software development (i.e. implementation). Among these approaches, we mention: an efficient approach for mobile agent security [9], the formal modeling and analysis of a secure mobile-agent system [8], and d'Agents: Security in a multiple-language, mobile-agent system [17] and others approaches [19, 20, 21, 22].

These kinds of approaches have been considered by the field of security engineering which focuses essentially on providing advances in security models, techniques, mechanisms and protocols. However, they so far have not considered the design stage of the development process and they so far have not integrated security concerns into software engineering techniques; models and processes, in order to build up more secure mobile agents based systems.

In our work, we are interested essentially in the secure software engineering (conceptual approaches) which consists of integrating the security requirements at the design stage of software development process. This research discipline has emerged relatively recently and only little works have been proposed. Among the approaches which have been interested to mobile agents, we mention: the conceptual model for systems based on secure mobile agents [7], Modeling Secure Mobile Agent Systems [18]. These approaches are useful and interesting contributions. However, several limitations have been identified: First, the specification of the security requirements is limited only to the implementation stage and the security properties have not specified in the design stage of software development process. Second, not all the security requirements of mobile agent have covered by these works.

Other approaches have been interested to offer their own agent-oriented methodologies to specify the security concepts related to multi-agent systems, such as SecureTROPOS [23] and NEMO [24]. Some other works have been proposed to extend the UML language to deal with the security requirements of objects and agents, such as: UMLSec [10] and SecureUML [11] (object-oriented approaches) and Adaptive security model for MAS [12] and the extension of FAML [14] (agent-oriented approaches).

In our work, we are interested only to the conceptual approaches which integrate the security requirements in UML language at the design stage. In the following subsections, we present an overview of those works, highlighting their strengths and limitations.

3.1   The UMLSec Profile

The UMLSec profile [10] is an extension of UML for the specification of object's security requirements. This profile extends UML diagrams (class, object, sequence, etc.) in order to describe aspects of security, either by simple annotations in graphs (a data confidentiality, non-repudiation action) or by dedicated functions (e.g. for hashing, encrypting, or decrypting, used in security protocols). Moreover, UMLsec includes tools for verifying the security constraints placed on diagrams. The information security is guaranteed by:

- the hypotheses of security in the physical level (e.g. the stereotype "Internet");
- the security requirements in the logical structure of the system (e.g. the stereotype "secrecy") or on data values (e.g. the stereotype "critical");
- the security policies which subsystems are supposed to obey (e.g. stereotypes "fair exchange", "secure links", "data security" or "no down-flow."

Some stereotypes on subsystems refer to stereotypes on elements of the model contained in the subsystems. For example, the constraint of the stereotype "data security" refers to objects in the subsystem stereotyped "critical" (which have the tags {secrecy}). The UMLsec follows the standard security modeling method.

The UMLSec profile is a modeling language that allows the specification of security requirements, which are: confidentiality, integrity, access control, non-repudiation, and secret stream. However, it does not address the other security requirements such as: authentication, availability and confinement.

3.2   The SecureUML Profile

The SecureUML profile [11] is a modeling language that defines a vocabulary for annotating UML-based models with relevant information for access control. It is based on the RBAC model (Role based Access Control) [13] and specifying authorization constraints. The SecureUML defines a vocabulary to express different aspects of object's access control such as roles, permissions and role assignments user-role.

The SecureUML meta-model is defined as an extension of the UML metamodel. RBAC concepts are represented directly as elements of the meta-model.

The SecureUML profile is an object-oriented language which deals only with the security requirement access control but it does not address the other security properties such as: authentication, availability and confinement, confidentiality, integrity, non-repudiation, and secret stream.

3.3   The Adaptive Security Model for MAS

The adaptive security model [12] is an extension of the RBAC model [13]. This research proposed a meta-model of security in which the traditional role concept has been extended. The new concept incorporates the need of both security management as used by the access control based on roles (RBAC) and agent behavior in agent-oriented software engineering. In this model, the basic policy of access authorization has the following form:

Subject {(id, role, organization), Access Operation (op), Access Context (co), Resource (id, type)}

The meta-model was motivated by the requirements of the project "Health Agents" but it is generic and other application domains can use it. In this work, the RBAC is extended with permissions to assign to individuals and organizations. These permissions can be assigned to a set (or type) of resource or type of subjects with few exceptions. This is configured by a positive authorization policy for the entire collection and negative authorizations for individual exceptions.

Access Context is another extension proposed to give greater flexibility. The context of access includes a descriptive explanation of the access operation, where/when the requested data are provided, the duration of use of the data, the pre-condition and post-condition of the operation of access. In the interaction model, a role makes its behavior if and only if its authorization constraints are checked.

The adaptive security model is an agent-oriented language that focuses on access control and not considers other security properties (confidentiality, integrity, authentication, etc.).

3.4 The FAML Extensions

The FAML [14] (FAME Agent-oriented Modeling Language) is a generic meta-model to describe the characteristics of multi-agent systems. Two extensions of the meta-model are created to include security concepts. These concepts are modeled in two sets: the concepts of execution time "run-time" and the concepts of design time "design-time". Each set has two levels: system level and agent level.

This work defines the security requirements "SecurityRequirement" classifying them into specific security requirements to the system "SystemSecurityRequirement" and specific security requirements for agents' Agent-SpecificSecurityRequirement".

The proposed extension FAML also specifies security actions "Security ActionSpecification" which may be relocation actions "RelocateActionSpecification", recovery actions "RecoverActionSpecification", prevention actions «PreventAction Specification» or detection actions «DetectActionSpecification».

The authors proposed to control the access to resources by classifying them into private resources "PrivateResource" and public resources "PublicResource".

They also proposed to define elements for modeling security objectives "SecurityGoal", security constraints "SecurityConstraint", security tasks "SecurityTask" and knowledge of security "SecurityKnowledgeBase".

This work differentiates between security requirements that are modeled by software developers during the design phase and the security actions that are performed by the multi-agent system during run-time to satisfy the security properties.

The FAML is an agent-oriented language that not allows to model all the security requirements and there are other security concepts that are more complex and can be derived.

3.5 Discussion

All approaches previously described are useful for modeling security requirements in the design stage. However, some limits can be identified. In fact, the UMLSec and the Secure UML profiles allow only the design of security requirements of object (object-oriented approaches) and not address the design of security requirements of mobile agent. Also, the adaptive security model incorporate the security management based on role (role based access control) and the agent functional behavior but it does not deal directly with the security requirements of mobile agents. In the FAML extensions, the agent's modeling units added by these extensions are general and not sufficient to model all the security requirements of agents and mobile agents.

Thus, these presented works focus to integrate the security requirements in the design stage. However, they are essentially object-oriented languages and agent-oriented languages and not mobile agent-oriented language. Then, they not considered specific security requirements of mobile agents based systems, essentially the security of: place, resource, agents' communication acts, agent's migration, agent's cloning, and agent's running.

In the last years, some mobile agent-oriented languages have been developed to assist system designers in creating systems of mobile agents, such as MAM-UML profile [25, 26, 27], and [4]. These languages allow to model mobile agent based systems (entities, relationships, properties, methods). However, they so far have not considered the security requirements at the design stage, in order to build secure systems.

Indeed, we can say that in the current state of research, no mobile agent-oriented language yet exists to allow an adequate design of security requirements of mobile agent and then to prevent attacks described in Sect. 2.2.

To overcome this limitation, the aim of our research is to model the security requirement of mobile agent in order to implement more secure mobile agents based systems. I our previous work, we have proposed the MA-UML language [4], which offer a set of elements to model entities involved in systems of mobile agents (places, resources, mobile agent, stationary agent, region). However, this language hasn't considered the security of these entities.

Then, our proposal is to define new security properties into MA-UML language in order to allow it to design secure entities of mobile agents based systems. In this paper, we propose to define new security properties to secure places from malicious mobile agents. The proposed extensions are presented in the next section.

4   The Proposed Extensions

In our research work, we aim to provide a set of elements to model security requirements of mobile agent in the design stage of the development process. It is to be noticed that, in this paper, our work focuses on the modeling of security aspects of places, knowing that we are interested in the mobile agents system when there are only two kinds of entities: agents and static locations (places); and they are not well suited for mobile computing modeling (laptops, mobile phones, PDAs).

To contribute to secure places from malicious mobile agents, we propose to introduce new extensions to the MA-UML environment diagram.

In this section, we first present an overview of the MA-UML profile, and essentially the MA-UML environment diagram. Then we describe the new extensions to this diagram in order to allow it to design secure places.

4.1   MA-UML Environment Diagram

The MA-UML Profile [4] extends UML and AUML class diagrams and defines three new diagrams to model mobile agent static aspects, which are environment diagram, mobile agent diagram and itinerary diagram. Also the MA-UML proposed four diagrams to model mobile agent dynamic aspects, which are: lifecycle diagram, mobile agent activity diagram, mobile agent sequence diagram and navigation diagram.

The environment diagram is used to specify the environment's entities of the mobile agent (entities involved in an application based on mobile agents), their properties and structural relationships. This diagram contains stereotyped UML classes («place», «resource»), stereotyped AUML classes («mobile agent», «stationary agent»), stereotyped packages («region» , «m-agentsystem»), stereotyped associations («communicate» , «reside» , «manipulate» , «visitor» , «offer»), and new graphical notations (Fig. 1).

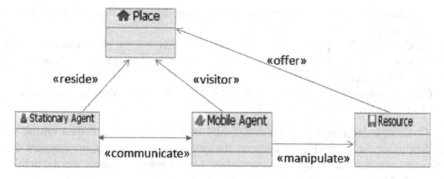

Fig. 1. Extract of MA-UML environment diagram

MA-UML environment diagram is suitable to model entities involved in a mobile agents system, but it is not considered the security of these entities. Thus, we judge that certain entities' security properties should be introduced into the MA-UML environment diagram to prevent attacks and which are necessary for each type of application.

In order to allow the MA-UML environment diagram to design a secure place entity in systems of mobile agents, we propose to extend it with new security properties. This extended diagram is presented in the next sub-section.

4.2 Extensions of MA-UML Environment Diagram

During their visit to different places, mobile agent can launch attacks to destination place. These attacks are: attack against the authentication, attack against the availability, attack against access control and attack against non-repudiation (these attacks are described in details in Sect. 2.3).

In order to protect places from malicious mobile agents, we propose to define four new extensions to prevent against these attacks (presented in the following sub-sections).

4.2.1 Extension to Prevent Availability Attack

During their visits to different places, mobile agents can launch denial of service attacks (availability attack) against a place by cloning indefinitely or migrating endlessly, in order to exploit system vulnerabilities, to disrupt the services offered by the place or to degrade its performance.

In order to specify a secure place and prevent the denial of service attacks, we propose to define new extension to the MA-UML environment diagram. We define a new stereotyped association-class, called «PlacePermission» between the stereotyped class «Place» and the stereotyped class «MobileAgent» . This association-class must contain a set of properties that sets the privileges assigned for each coming mobile agent in the destination place. As properties that must contain «PlacePermission» , we define:

- MaxNbClone: This property sets the maximum number of clones allowed to the coming mobile agent in the place. This property ensures that an agent does not attack a place by cloning indefinitely.

- CtrlCloneDuration: This property sets the duration for which the maximum number of clone (MaxNbClone) is defined.
- MaxNbVisit: This property sets the maximum number of visits allowed to the coming mobile agent to a place. This property ensures that an agent does not attack a place by migrating endlessly.
- CtrlVisitDuration: This property sets the duration for which the maximum number of visits (MaxNbVisit) is defined.

These new properties help prevent denial of service attack and then ensure the availability of the place. Figure 2 shows the extension made to the environment diagram to contribute to specify a secure place and to prevent against the availability attack of place.

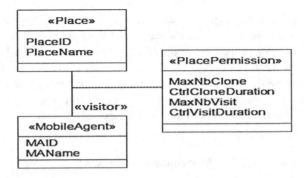

Fig. 2. Extension of environment diagram to prevent availability attack of a place

In the «PlacePermission» association-class, the designers of mobile agents based systems can define additional security properties in order to set other constraints imposed to mobile agents when it reaches a place.

4.2.2 Extension to Prevent Access Control Attack

Mobile agents need to migrate to places in order to access resources offered and to execute assigned tasks. However, a mobile agent can become a malicious agent and access the resource of a place without having the authorization and the right of access; this can affect the place. Also, mobile agents can consume resource more than authorized. Then we believe that it is necessary to protect a place's resource against malicious coming agents.

In order to specify a secure resource and prevent the unauthorized access attacks, we propose to define a new stereotyped association-class between the two stereotyped classes «MobileAgent» and «Resource» , called «ResourcePermission» . This association-class must contain a set of properties that sets the constraints imposed to mobile agent when it should to manipulate resource. Examples of these properties are:

- Right of access of mobile agent to the resource (read, write, update)
- Max time access: This property fixed the maximum time allowed to mobile agent to access to data of resource.

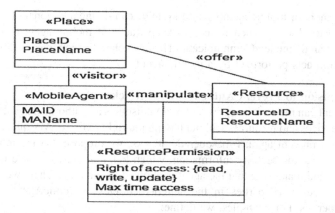

Fig. 3. Extension of environment diagram to prevent access control attack of a resource

These new properties help prevent access control attack and then ensure the security of the resource. Figure 3 shows the extensions made to the environment diagram to specify a secure resource and to contribute to prevent against the access control attack of a resource.

In the «ResourcePermission» association-class, the designers of mobile agents based systems can define additional security properties in order to set the constraints imposed to mobile agents when it should to manipulate a resource offered by a place.

4.2.3 Extension to Prevent Non-repudiation Attack

The repudiation occurs when a mobile agent can deny having performed an action in visited place, or migrate to destination place. For example, a mobile agent can deny visited a place and used its resources or execute actions. Then we believe it is necessary to keep traces of all actions made and established visits.

Then we propose to define new stereotyped classes to MA-UML environment diagram, which are: the «ActionHistory» class which keeps traces of the various actions made by mobile agents. Also we define the stereotyped class «VisitedPlace History» which keep traces of the different visits established. These two classes allow controlling actions and migrations of mobile agent and then preventing the non-repudiation attacks (Fig. 4).

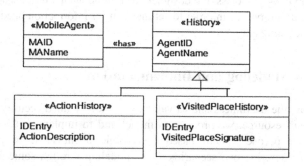

Fig. 4. Extension of environment diagram to prevent non-repudiation attack in visited place

The designers of mobile agents based systems can define additional classes inherit from the "History" class when it need to keep traces of mobile agent behavior. For example, we can define le «CommunicationHistory» class to keep traces of the different communication acts performed by a mobile agent.

4.2.4   Extension to Prevent Authentication Attacks

A mobile agent can masks its identity and present itself as an authorized agent in order to access the services and resources without having the right to do so (Masquerade attack).

In order to prevent against masquerade attacks, we propose that the mobile agent class must have some security information, which helps the visited place identify the mobile agent and make sure that the agent is allowed to run on it. Then, we propose to define new security properties in the stereotyped class «MobileAgent» with new security properties. For examples, we define:

- User Authentication Property: who is responsible for this mobile agent? Who is accountable for any of the charges it runs up?
- User Authorization Property: can this user execute this mobile agent? Which operations on which objects is this user allowed to invoke? What resources can this mobile agent consume?
- Mobile Agent Authentication Key Property (MA-authentication Key): is essentially for the authentication of mobile agent in the destination places.

Figure 5 shows the added mobile agent security properties in order to contribute to prevent against the authentication attack in the visited place.

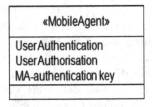

Fig. 5. Extension of environment diagram to prevent authentication attack in visited place

In the «MobileAgent» class, the designers of mobile agents based systems can add additional security properties in order to set the security information needed to identify an incoming mobile agent.

5   Scenarios Modeling and Implementation

In order to show the usefulness and to validate the new defined security properties to secure place and resource, we propose to model and to implement two scenarios of Healthcare Teleexpertise system based on mobile agent [15]. In the following sub-sections, we describe two scenarios, their modeling through some diagrams, and the description of the implementation.

5.1   System Description and Modeling

The Healthcare Teleexpertise system based on mobile agents [15] is composed of:

Requestor Center: represents the place of a user that confronts a difficult case and needs to take an advice of an expert.

Expert Center: represents the place of an expert that capable to provide answers to requests of expertise.

Patient Agent: is a mobile agent, which migrates from a place of requestor center to a place of expert center over the network in order to execute its request.

Security Agent: is a stationary agent that responsible to authenticate the visitor patient agent.

Database: represent a resource which provided by the expert center. The patient agent aims to manipulate this database in order to execute its mission.

Our objective in this system is to secure expert center (a place) and database (a resource) offered by expert center from malicious patient agents. For the modeling, we have used the MA-UML environment diagram and the new proposed security properties (Sects. 4.2.1 and 4.2.2). Figure 6 shows the extended environment diagram to model a secure mobile agent based Teleexpertise system.

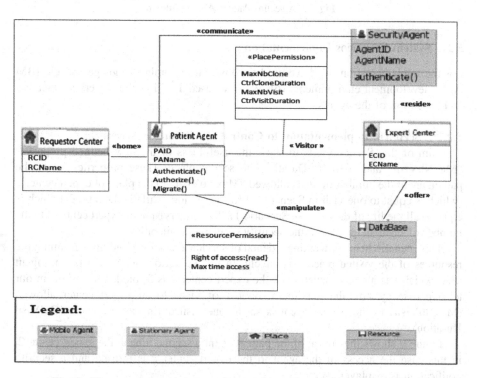

Fig. 6. The extended environment diagram for a secure Teleexpertise system

Figure 7 shows a secure specification of patient agent structure. For the modeling, we have used the MA-UML environment diagram and the too extensions proposed (Sects. 4.2.3 and 4.2.4).

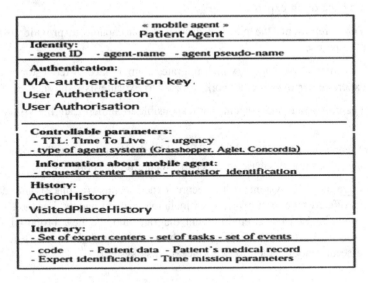

Fig. 7. A secure Patient Agent structure

5.2   System Scenarios Implementation

For the implementation, we have used the Java programming language and the IBM Aglet development environment [16]. We have used Tahiti as the servers for creation and execution of the agents.

5.2.1   Scenario Implementation to Control the Resource Access

The aim of this Scenario 1 is to show the usefulness of the new defined properties "MaxNbVisit" and "CtrlVisitDuration" to secure place. These properties set to the patient agent the number of visits allowed "MaxNbVisit" to the place of expert center 2 (which is equal to one visit in Scenario 1) for the period "CtrlVisitDuration" (which is equal to all the life of the agent in Scenario 1). The Supervision of expert center 2 to the number of visits helps ensure the security objective availability.

This scenario helps preventing a denial of service attack by avoiding consuming the resources of the visited place excessively. In this scenario (Fig. 8), the patient agent (PA) which has already visited once the expert center 2 is forbidden to revisit. In our teleexpertise system, the maximum number of visits to an expert center allowed (MaxNbVisit) to the patient agent is set to one visit during its life cycle (CtrlVisit Duration).

Figure 9 shows the arrival of the patient agent a second time at the expert center 2, in this case the access of the agent to the expert center 2 is refused and a security notification is displayed.

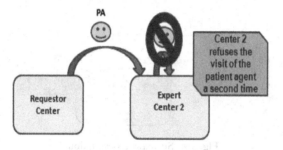

Fig. 8. Scenario 1 description

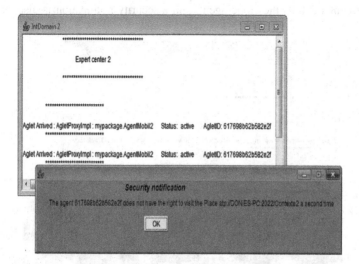

Fig. 9. Security notification indicating the prohibition of a second visit to place of expert center 2

5.2.2 Scenario Implementation to Control Cloning

The goal of this Scenario 2 is to show the usefulness of the new defined properties as "MaxNbClone" and "CtrlCloneDuration" to secure place. These properties set to the patient agent the number of clone allowed "MaxNbClone" (which is equal to 0 in Scenario 2) to the expert center 2 for the period "CtrlCloneDuration" (which is equal to all the life of the agent in Scenario 2). The supervision of the expert center 2 to the number of clone contributes to ensure the place security objective availability.

This Scenario 2 helps preventing a denial of service attack by avoiding cloning indefinitely. Clones indefinitely can have an effect on other agents because it can disrupt their access to the place or their use of resources.

In this scenario (Fig. 10), the expert center 2 prohibits the patient agent to clone itself because in our system the patient agent does not need to be cloned in the visited places (MaxNbClone equal to zero) during its life cycle (CtrlCloneDuration).

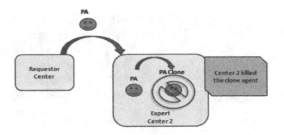

Fig. 10. Scenario 2 description

Figure 11 shows a case in which the patient agent performs a cloning action, then the expert center 2 kills the clone agent, and a security notification is displayed.

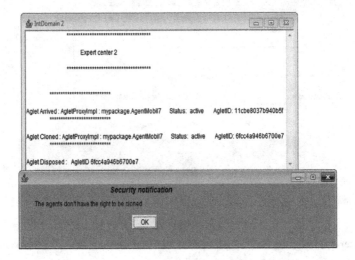

Fig. 11. Security notification indicating the prohibition of cloning

6   Conclusion

Security is perhaps the most critical problem in systems of mobile agents and its resolution is a real challenge. This challenge is explained by the importance of using mobile agents in distributed applications. Thus, in this paper, we have focused on issues related to security in systems of mobile agents. For that, we have proposed new security elements and properties to the MA-UML environment diagram to specify security of places. These new elements and properties contribute to the verification of security requirement relevant to mobile agents, which are: availability, authentication, access control, and non-repudiation. Finally, we have presented the modeling and the implementation of teleexpertise system scenarios in order to show usefulness of the new defined security properties to prevent availability attacks. This work opens several perspectives and future work can be considered. First, we propose to implement other teleexpertise system scenarios in order to show the usefulness of the rest of new defined security elements and properties to prevent the other attacks (authentication, access control, and non repudiation). Second, other extensions can be defined to MA-UML diagrams in order to taking into account other attacks: attack of the place to mobile agents, attack of an agent by another, and security between agents and external entities.

References

1. Weyns, D., Parunak, H.V.D., Michel, F., Holvoet, T., Ferber, J.: Environments for multiagent systems, state-of-the-art and research challenges. In: Proceedings of the first International Conference on Environments for Multi-Agent Systems, New York (2004)
2. Pham, V.A., Karmouch, A.: Mobile software agents: an overview. IEEE Commun. Mag. **36** (7), 26–37 (1998)
3. Mouratidis, H.: Modelling secure multiagent systems, pp. 859–866. University of Sheffield, New York, USA (2003)
4. Hachicha, H., Loukil, A., Ghedira, K.: MA-UML: a conceptual approach for mobile agents modelling. Int. J. Agent-Oriented Softw. Eng. (IJAOSE 2009) **3**(2/3), 277–305 (2009)
5. Alfalayleh, M., Brankovic, L.: An overview of security issues and techniques in mobile agents. In: Conference on Communications and Multimedia Security. University of Newcastle, Australia (2004)
6. Jansen, W.A.: Countermeasures for mobile agent security. In: Computer Communications Special Issue on Advances in Research and Application of Network Security, pp. 1667–1676. Elsevier (2000)
7. Loulou, M., Hadj-Kacem, A., Jmaiel, M., Mosbah, M.: A conceptual model for secure mobile agent systems. IEEE (CIS 06), Guangzhou, China, pp. 524–527, 2006. In: Proceedings of the IEEE International Conference on Computational Intelligence and Security (CIS 06), Guangzhou, China, pp. 524–527 (2006)
8. Ma, L., Tsai, J.P.: Formal modelling and analysis of a secure mobile-agent system. Piscataway, NJ, USA, pp. 180–196, 2008. IEEE Transactions on Systems, Man and Cybernetics, Piscataway, NJ, USA (2008)
9. Pankaj, M., Divya, B., Nripesh, K.: An efficient approach for mobile agent security (0975 – 8887). Int. J. Comput. Appl. **107**(6), 21–25 (2014)
10. Jurjens, J.: UMLsec: extending UML for secure systems developmen. In: UML 2002 - The Unified Modeling Language. Proceedings of 5th International Conference Model Engineering, Languages, Concepts, and Tools, Dresden, Germany, September/October (2002)
11. Lodderstedt, T., Basin, D., Doser, J.: SecureUML: A UML-based modelling language for model-driven security. In: The Proceedings of the 5th International Conference on the Unified Modeling Language (2002)
12. Xiao, L., Peet, A., Lewis, P., Dasmahapatra, S., Saez, C., Croitoru, M., Vicente, J., Gonzalez-Valez, H., Liuch i Ariet, M.: An adaptive security model for multi-agent systems and application to a clinical trials environment. In: Proceedings of the 31st IEEE Annual International Computer Software and Applications Conference (COMPSAC 2007) Volume II, IEEE Computer Society, pp. 261–268 (2007)
13. Sandhu, R.S., Coyne, E.J., Feinstein, H.L., Youman, C.E.: Role-based access control models. IEEE J. Mag. **29**(2), 38–47 (1996)
14. Beydoun, G., Gonzales-Perez, C., Low, G.C., Henderson-Sellers, B.: Towards method engineering for MAS: A preleminary validation of a generic MAS Metamodel. In: 17th Software Engineering and Knowledge Engineering Conference (2005b)

15. Loukil, A., Hachicha, H., Ghédira, K.: Using mobile agent technology for distributed health-care teleexpertise systems. In: The IFMBE Proceedings of the 3rd European Medical and Biological conference (EMBEC 2005), Prague, Czech Republic; November 20–25, vol. 11 (2005)
16. Lange, D.B., Mitsuru, O.: Programming and Deploying Java Mobile Agents Aglets. Addison-Wesley, Boston, MA, USA (1998)
17. Robert, S., Gray, L., David, K., George, C., Daniela, R.: D'Agents: Security in a multiple-language, mobile-agent system. In: A chapter in the book Mobile Agents and Security, pp. 154–187, edited by Giovanni Vigna
18. Rekik, M., Kallel, S., Loulou, M., Kacem, A.H.: Modeling secure mobile agent systems. In: Jezic, G., Kusek, M., Nguyen, N.-T., Howlett, R.J., Jain, L.C. (eds.) KES-AMSTA 2012. LNCS, vol. 7327, pp. 330–339. Springer, Heidelberg (2012)
19. Loulou, M., Jmaiel, M., Mosbah, M.: Dynamic Security framework for mobile agent systems: specification, verification and enforcement. IJICS 3, 321–336 (2009)
20. Jean, E., Jiao, Y., Hurson, A.R., Potok, T.E: SAS: a secure aglet server. In: Proceedings of Computer Security Conference (2007)
21. Todd McDonald, J., Yasinsac, A.: Security Models for Mobile Agent System. www.elsevier.com/locate/entcs
22. Nusrat, E., Ahmed, A.S., Rahman, G.M., Jamal, L.: SAGLET- secure agent communication model. In: Proceedings of 11th ICCIT 2008, pp. 371–375. IEEE (2008)
23. Mouratidis, H., Giorgini, P.: Secure Tropos: a security-oriented extension of the Tropos methodology". Int. J. Softw. Eng. 17, 285 (2007). doi:10.1142/S0218194007003240
24. Huget, M.P.: Nemo: An agent-oriented software engineering methodology. In: OOPSLA Workshop on Agent Oriented Methodologies Seattle (2002)
25. Belloni, E., Marcos, C.: Modeling of mobile-agent applications with UML. In: Proceedings of the Fourth Argentine Symposium on Software Engineering (ASSE 2003), 32 JAIIO (Jornadas Argentinas de Informática e Investigación Operativa), Buenos Aires, Argentina, September, ISSN: 1666–1141, vol. 32 (2003)
26. Kusek, M., Jezic, G.: Extending UML sequence diagrams to model agent mobility. In: Padgham, L., Zambonelli, F. (eds.) AOSE VII / AOSE 2006. LNCS, vol. 4405, pp. 51–63. Springer, Heidelberg (2007)
27. Kang, M., Taguchi, K.: Modeling mobile agent applications by extended UML activity diagram. In: Proceedings of the 6th International Conference on Enterprise Information Systems (ICEIS 2004), Porto, Portugal, April, pp. 519–522 (2004)

Innovative and Emerging
Applications of MAS

Dynamic Agent-based Scheduling of Treatments: Evidence from the Dutch Youth Health Care Sector

Erik Giesen[1]([✉]), Wolfgang Ketter[2], and Rob Zuidwijk[2]

[1] INITI8, Rotterdam, The Netherlands
giesen@initi8.nl
[2] Rotterdam School of Management, Rotterdam, The Netherlands
{wketter,rzuidwijk}@rsm.nl

Abstract. We use agent-based simulation to compare the performance of four scheduling policies in youth health care. The policies deploy push/pull and centralized/decentralized concepts. The simulation model represents an authentic business case and is parameterized with actual market data. The model incorporates, among other things, non-stationary Poisson arrival processes, reneging and return mechanisms, and care provider's client preferences. We have identified that performance measurement in youth health care should not be focused on queue lengths alone, which is presently the case, but should include a case difficulty parameter as well. The simulation results, together with contextual data obtained from stakeholder interviews, indicate that a push strategy with a centralized queue suits the sector best, which is different from the current real-world situation. This policy ensures a higher level of fairness in treatment provision because the care providers are compelled to take their share in treating the difficult and economically less attractive cases. The complexity of the case cannot be captured by current queuing theory methods. Our simulation approach incorporates these complexities, which turn out to be relevant for the scheduling policy decision. We validate the model and strategies using real market data and field expert discussions.

Keywords: Agent-based simulation · Resource allocation · Youth health care · Preference behavior · Policy scheduling

1 Introduction

The Dutch youth health care sector is providing care to youths under 19 and their families on a voluntary basis. The scheduling of care includes the allocation of clients to care providers and it features long waiting lists and long waiting times. As in many other countries, the issue is considered an urgent societal problem and has received a lot of media attention [21]. Earlier approaches that solely address the symptom of long waiting lists have proven to be ineffective. The government is funding the sector and it has instituted central bureaus in

© Springer International Publishing Switzerland 2015
J.P. Müller et al. (Eds.): MATES 2015, LNAI 9433, pp. 173–199, 2015.
DOI: 10.1007/978-3-319-27343-3_10

provinces and larger urban areas to manage youth care on a regional level.[1] Each
of these institutions operate without regional overlap and act as the gateway to
youth care for clients from the region that it serves. Clients in need of care enter
the system by visiting the institution for youth health care that diagnoses the
situation and provides the client with a diagnosis. This diagnosis can be seen as
a entitlement to health care. Typically the institution for youth health care also
selects the care provider expected to fit best to the problem and preferences of
the client, although it is at the clients' discretion to adhere to this allocation or
not. The care providers are compensated by the government for the care that is
provided corresponding with the diagnoses from the institution for youth health
care; see Fig. 1.

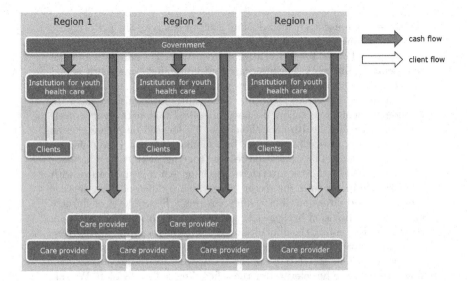

Fig. 1. Overview of the allocation mechanism in the Dutch youth health care system.

Parents, teachers, and other people involved with children have become
increasingly aware of potential problems and have also started to signal problems more often. While the question remains whether this can be seen as over-
signalling or not, it certainly results in an increase of the amount of clients
requesting help [2]. The institution of youth health care acts as a gateway more
than as a gatekeeper, as it is not equipped with the legal authority to dismiss a
case. As a result, there is not enough capacity at the care providers to deal with
the growing number of requests for care. In addition, the provision of care is on
a voluntary basis, so clients may renege, i.e. withdraw from the system at any
time while waiting for care. This further complicates the management of care

---

[1] This was the case until 1/1/2015 and reflects the data we used. Today however
municipalities are responsible for managing youth care among other types of care.

provision. Reneging may be caused by the fact that clients found other ways to be assisted with their problem, or that the issue at hand resolved itself without professional care. However, reneging may also occur in cases where youth health care should have been provided. This may leave youth health problems to remain unresolved or re-entering of the client in the system while the situation has persisted or even worsened. On the other hand, it has been argued that clients in genuine need of care are willing to wait longer for the requested care [12,13]. In such a manner, reneging would become a sort of natural way of balancing the system and filtering out cases not in genuine need for care.

As care providers are working with under-capacity, they effectively are able to select clients from the queues. In particular, more difficult cases are less attractive from a financial point of view. The selection process depends in an intricate way on a lot of factors such as the age or gender of the child, the type of problem, and the region in which the child lives. As a result, the selection process is not transparent and it allows the care providers to base their selections on financial incentives as well. In order to manage the youth health care system also in this respect, the performance of the system should be expressed both in terms of efficiency and social welfare, where the latter is based on indicators reflecting the actual treatment of difficult cases and waiting times. Such indicators may prevent difficult cases to be disadvantaged and help create a fair scheduling process. We elaborate on such indicators in Sect. 3.

To address the waiting line issues, this paper considers alternative solution directions that not only focus on the handling of contemporary waiting lists, but that may require structural changes in the scheduling of youth health care to clients. We elaborate on such structural changes by presenting an overview of multiple scheduling policies, based on a combination of push/pull and centralized/decentralized scheduling policies. The push and pull scheduling policies define the party which ultimately makes the actual allocation decision. Centralized and decentralized scheduling policies define the moment at which the actual allocation will take place.

Scheduling decision problems, as presented by the youth health care case, suit very well a multi-agent simulation approach for the following reasons. The behavior of stakeholders in the system has a decisive impact on scheduling decisions and therefore needs to be captured well in the decision model. The impact of how communication is organized between the different parties in the system needs to be incorporated as well. Furthermore, institutions and persons have their own objectives, are heterogeneous entities by nature, and the coordination thereof needs to be addressed explicitly. As a result, the actual client flow through the system is the result of a negotiation process between several parties in the supply chain. Indeed, a client scheduling procedure requires input from other parties in the sector on which the final decision can be based. A multi-agent simulation built of individual agents that pursue a specific personal goal can be used in this complex, dynamic setting to evaluate alternative scheduling policies.

To arrive at potentially structural changes that address the problems described above, a systematic approach is required. An analysis of what the various stakeholders expect from the system, what has presently been achieved, and what can be achieved, needs to encapsulate the rich problem context. The strategic objectives of the system and their target values need to be elicited, and they need to be expressed in terms of Key Performance Indicators (KPIs), which may vary among stakeholders. The actual performance of the system needs to be formalized as a baseline so that the performance gaps can be analyzed and so that performance improvements by alternative scheduling policies can be assessed. In this setting, one should anticipate that one size may not fit all, and that solution directions need to be specified for different contexts, e.g. for different geographical regions and for different care types in the youth care sector. To perform such an analysis in a complex, dynamic environment such as youth care, there is a need for a responsive design paradigm.

We contribute to the research in health care operations management, in particular resource scheduling, by providing a currently unused approach to counter queuing related issues. Simulation of the resource scheduling process helps to understand and test long term effects of a number of alternative scheduling policies and coordination decisions. Although operations research queuing models go a long way in incorporating behavior in queuing systems, such as customer impatience [3], we argue that these models fall short in capturing the behavior required to explain the system behavior in the youth health care sector. Indeed, our simulation approach addresses the complexities of the patient scheduling that were found in the real world case and incorporates, among others, a nonstationary Poisson arrival process, a reneging and return mechanism, and an algorithm to include the preference behavior of the care providers.

We further contribute to research in agent-based simulation, since our research proves the usability of an agent-based approach in a real world environment by not only matching the current decision making process but also by studying a number of alternatives. The model is loaded with an extensive amount of stochastic distributions based on actual market data and successfully matches the performance of the real world system.

Finally, we contribute to research in information systems by improving the human decision-making process. Our study on the different policies on the youth health care system decreases the information overload which increases the rate of fair child allocations. This will improve socially responsible welfare decision-making.

The paper is organized as follows. In Sect. 2 we review relevant literature. Section 3 describes the foundations and structure of our simulation model which is based on real world data. We present four scheduling policies, the first one serves as a benchmark and represents the current situation, and the other three are potential alternatives for future use. This section also describes the four care types, a balanced score card analysis which serves as a basis for our benchmark, and the four Key Performance Indicators (KPI's) we develop and use to evaluate the different policies. In Sect. 4 we present experimental results using our testbed. Finally, we conclude with directions for future research.

2 Related Literature

A common approach taken by governments to tackle waiting line problems is an ad-hoc supply of monetary resources. This provides only a short term solution to the youth health care sector, as available capacity and queue lengths reach a new equilibrium after a short while [22]. [26] identified five popular approaches to decrease waiting times: monitoring of procedures, using priority scoring tools, setting waiting time targets, using an external advisory body, and registering online. However, [23] argues that such methods do not work by themselves; better coordination and flow control are proposed to increase performance at the public sector. The approach in our paper adheres to this argument by comparing a number of scheduling policies.

Regarding the scope of our research, we emphasize that our discussion on client waiting time in an health care environment distinguishes itself from appointment systems as discussed in for example [20, 25]. In such settings, one distinguishes indirect waiting time, i.e. the time between request for treatment and appointment, and the direct waiting time beyond the appointed time at the health care facility, which usually is a result of the emphasis on the utilization of health care resources [15]. In our setting, the waiting time is equal to the time between diagnosis, which includes the identification of the appropriate health care package, and the moment an appointment can be made with a provider of the health care package. Therefore, both the direct and indirect waiting times related to an appointment system will be in effect only after the client has been allocated to the care provider.

Our empirical analysis has revealed that the Dutch youth health care system in which clients are waiting to be allocated to resources is subject to two behavioral patterns. First of all, the scheduling of clients may be subject to prioritization, based on certain client characteristics. Second, reneging is observed, i.e. some clients leave the system spontaneously without treatment after waiting for a certain amount of time. Both behavioral patterns have received some attention in the operations management literature. In the literature on priority classes and queueing models, the optimality of the so-called (generalized) "$c\mu$" priority rule has been established under various circumstances. This rule gives priority to customers with high marginal delay cost (c) and low expected treatment time ($1/\mu$) [27].

[3] explore the optimal capacity and cost of a queueing system in which arriving customers cannot observe their position in the queue and where they show a reneging rate linear in the queue length. However, reneging may be a more complex behavior. For example, several studies showed that the amount of time that a client is willing to wait for care is related to the urgency of the problem [12]. More urgent problems are difficult to treat elsewhere, while they genuinely require attention. These clients will accept longer waiting times. The converse holds for less urgent problems.

Most literature on waiting line management in health care is based on queuing theory and focuses mainly on resource utilization and determination of the minimum required amount of resources while maintaining a high service level [14].

[7] have emphasized the need for detailed data while analyzing queueing systems and have stated that traditional queuing theory does not capture, among other things, more complex customer reneging behavior, time-dependent parameters, and customer heterogeneity. [6] address the incongruence of behavior as modeled in the service operations management literature with the empirical findings from the behavioral literature. We have incorporated the aforementioned characteristics in our agent-based simulation model and we have calibrated the model with detailed, real-life data. Waiting line problems have also been studied using discrete event-based simulation, see for example [4,11,24]. While these studies do include more complex arrival and reneging processes, they still solely focus on utilization issues and capacity planning. For example, [11] use a generic discrete-event simulation model to investigate the feasibility of a particular national service waiting time target and present barriers, some of which related to capacity issues, to meet this target faced by the UK health care system.

Information systems in health care organizations become increasingly instrumental as they drive down the costs of services and support decision-making in complex environments. This is also high-lighted by the current debate of the digital transformation of health care [1]. As the authors point out, it is of paramount importance to learn all the significant institutional knowledge of the health care sector and therefore to collaborate with health care professionals. One of the authors of our team is a health care professional and we completely second their opinion. This has allowed us to gain deep insights into the health care sector, which would have been impossible otherwise. Furthermore, [10] show that investing in IT in the health care industry does lead to organizational profitability. Our research follows a design-oriented approach, as laid out by [16]. With the design and implementation of an agent-based [30] resource allocation decision support system we have created a valid artifact, which is relevant and necessary to solve existing problems in the health care IS domain, because it has the potential to address each of the desired features identified in this section. Agent-based approaches have successfully been applied to manufacturing supply-chain management scenarios, such as [8,9], but have not yet been used in health care systems.

Agent-based simulations, such as ours, TAC SCM [9], or Power TAC [19] along with many related computational tools are driving research into a range of interesting and complex domains that are both socially and economically important [5]. Since such experimental platforms allow market structures to be evaluated under a variety of real-world conditions and competitive pressures, they can also be used to effectively uncover potential hazards of proposed market designs in the face of strategic behaviors on the part of the participating agents. This can help policy makers in policy and regulation design.

3   The Simulation Model

In this section we describe our research framework, the different simulation model parameters and the overall model structure. Furthermore, we describe our scheduling policies, the care types, and list the different key performance indicators that we developed to evaluate our model.

3.1 Research Framework

The research framework aims at eliciting given characteristics of the decision context and the system design requirements at various decision levels (Fig. 2). The given characteristics are retrieved and validated based on real world data from the Dutch health care sector. The model is initiated with seven youth care institutions and eight care providers in particular regions. The design requirements at the various levels are elicited from interviews and workshops. Our approach comes down to the establishment of an active modeling paradigm for system redesign that evaluates alternative strategies in a risk-free test environment, while incorporating real-world data and expert interviews ("docking").

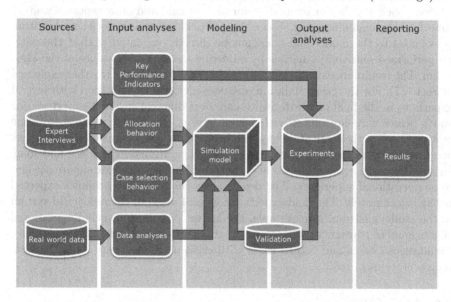

Fig. 2. Research framework.

The model is initiated as a non-terminating system since decisions and performance measures depend on long lasting developments. The model is pre-filled at start in a fully utilized state at the care providers while there are no waiting lists. This procedure will decrease the required warm-up time of the model. Warm-up time has been determined by the method of [28,29] to be 4 years simulation time. The replication length has been set to 20 years simulation time in total being 5 times the warm-up time.

The verification of the model is split in two types: First, the introduction of state-transition control and the implementation of numerous checks during the simulation which ensure a correct flow of cases through the system. Second, in-depth source review by others who didn't participate in the design of the model verified the correct coding of the model.

The validation process is split into three phases: First, the input analysis in which the input parameters of the model are calibrated with real world data. Second, two of the most important but less understood parameters of the model are analyzed for sensitivity. Third, a user validation by field experts is done. For the input analysis a comparison of stochastic variables with real world data is performed by analyzing the resulting distribution of values from the model. The theoretical and empirical distributions are visually compared. Analysis has been performed on direct parameters of the model like the arrival, age and difficulty distribution and indirect behavior of the model like reneging and return mechanisms which are partly set by parameters but are also a result of the operational behavior of the system as a whole. Table 1 lists the measures used for validation of the simulation model. At the core of the model lies the political influenced decision algorithm which makes the selection for the next to be treated case at the care provider. The algorithm chooses the case based on a trade-off between efficiency being a shorter estimated duration of care and an acceptable waiting time for the remaining cases. Since the political influenced decision algorithm is essential to the model and it cannot be directly validated against the data, we performed sensitivity analysis by adjusting the threshold values of the algorithm. The results showed moderate sensitivity on these values (further explained in Sect. 3.7). For the user validation phase we included consultation with several experts from the field of youth health care over different fields of expertise: one youth health care consultant with a high level of experience in the sector, one case manager at the institution of youth health care with operational experience, one financial director at a care provider with operational experience and some strategic experience, one director at a care provider with strategic experience and some operational experience. The results show that the model mimics expected behavior accurately. The field experts recognized much of the real world system in the model's output. For example, the arrival distribution including seasonal effects and the construction of treatment trajectories, in which a client can have simultaneous cases and return cases with crisis attribute, were found realistic representations of reality.

3.2 Model Parameters

The model takes as an input the given characteristics of the decision context, i.e. of the health care domain. These characteristics include client population characteristics such as demography and population density, the pattern of client arrivals into the system, which may include seasonal effects, the distribution of diagnostics and required medical care of the client population, and the characteristics of resources such as geographical location of the care providers and the medical expertise offered. The client arrival processes are generated during the time of the simulation by a non-stationary Poisson distribution to include a seasonal influenced arrival effect. Additional client attributes are specified such as age, home location, and case difficulty.

The non-uniform age distribution of the arriving clients is included in the simulation, as it is taken into account while allocating a client to a care provider.

Further, some cases are marked as a'crisis' and are allocated at once. These cases bypass the allocation strategy but do influence the usage of capacity in the model. A crisis denotes a case of extreme urgency and its level of difficulty can be of any kind. Each arriving child will be diagnosed with a varying amount of care needs. These needs can be indicated simultaneously at the first indication or re-indicated after reneging or a successful treatment. This also involves the analysis for reneging probabilities during the waiting phase and return probabilities after reneging or ending care. A return probability on reneging tends to be significantly higher than the probability for return after treatment. A return further involves a return interval since the child will not return immediately but after a varying amount of time. A case is provided with an identifier indicating the difficulty of the case, which is assumed to be uniformly distributed. The (expected) treatment time distributions depend on the difficulty identifier and the care provider. Table 1 lists the parameters and types of distributions as they are used in the model.

Validation of the parameters and model has been split up in three stages:

1. **Direct Validation:** Direct input parameters (like probabilities of multiple simultaneous care tracks, crisis distributions and geographical distributions) have been validated by extracting them back from the result set of the simulation. This stage ensures a correct working of the innermost basics of the model which in turn validates a correct outcome for the upcoming indirect measurements. The parameters were found to be behaving as expected.
2. **Indirect Validation:** Indirect output measures (like waiting times and lines, return rates and actual duration after being pitched on a cases' difficulty) have been validated by comparing these system measures against real world data. Specific waiting times and care durations were behaving significantly off in comparison to the real world data. The model is not capable of reflecting the same treatment and waiting trends as present in the real world. This is most likely a result of simplification of the system whereby the model smoothes results. While these measurements were off, the system as a whole functions as expected and generates comparable behavior as the real world system. The system was found to behave sufficient enough as expected.
3. **User Validation:** The model design and output measures have been validated by field experts who recognized and confirmed the behavior of the model, although the values in detail did not exactly match.

3.3 Structure of the Model

The structure of the model can be further explained while reflecting on design requirements at the strategic, tactical, and operational level. The design requirements at the operational level are supported by performance outcomes of an agent simulation model, in which behaviors have been specified that are established at the tactical level. The strategic decisions and requirements have been taken into account in the overall design and scenario analyses of the agent system, including sensitivity analyses. The scenario and sensitivity analyses ultimately serve as a tool to evaluate and compare the tactical and strategic decisions.

Table 1. Model parameters with type of distribution and short description

Parameter	Type of distribution	Description
Capacities	Absolute value	Maximum number of treatment positions available
Arrival distribution	Non-stationary Poisson distribution	Client arrivals including seasonal effects like the impact of summer holidays
Age distribution	Empirical distribution	The age of the child at arrival on which the birthdate is selected
Crises distribution	Probability (%)	The probability that a case is marked as crisis and will be allocated for immediate care
Parallel tracks	Probability (%)	The probability that there are multiple simultaneous types of care allocated at first arrival and the type of care they are
Difficulty	Uniform distribution	Classification of urgency, this is the base for all further comparisons between cases
Geographical distribution	Uniform distribution	The studied region is mapped to include distances between client and care provider, the clients are uniformly distributed over the map
Geographical range limitations	Probability (%)	The chance that a client is willing to travel mediate of high distances for his care
Care duration	Empirical distribution	Care duration per care type per care provider, the implementation in the model includes the difficulty factor (described above) to pitch the simulated durations towards the easiness or difficulty of a specific case
Reneging ratios	Calculated probability (%)	The chance that a case reneges during the waiting phase, the implementation in the model chooses the reneging date beforehand. If a case is still waiting at that date the case will be withdrawn from waiting
Return rate	Calculated probability (%)	The chance that a case will return for additional care (or care at all in case of withdrawal). In case of withdrawal the difficulty of the withdrawn case is considered relevant, the higher the difficulty the higher the chance on return. For an end of treatment the difficulty isn't considered relevant
Return interval	Uniform distribution	The interval between reneging or end of care and the return if applicable, the interval is chosen to be within the 0-180 days range

The *strategic level* decisions under consideration are push, pull and centralized, decentralized scheduling policies. The push, pull decision defines whether the care providers perform the allocation or that the decision is left to the discretion of the central youth health care bureau. The centralized, decentralized decision concerns the timing of the allocation which results in a queue only at the central youth health care bureau or at the care providers as well. The design requirements that constrain decisions at the strategic level concern the support of basic roles and responsibilities of the stakeholders involved and how they are related, and include requirements of the methods of communication and the scope of information sharing between actors in the system.

At the *tactical level*, the design of the health care system involves the establishment of policies of several stakeholders, given the queuing structure. The decisions of the client allocation system, i.e. the output of the decision process, need to be made considering the given domain characteristics mentioned above, and design requirements at the strategic, tactical and at the operational level. The design requirements at the tactical level constrain the behavior of the stakeholders (or agents). For example, the client preferences set allocation constraints based on geographical position or other relevant data. Client urgency is based on client diagnostics and other relevant data. The way that medical experts specify acceptance factors based on urgency and other relevant factors may be constrained as well.

At the *operational level*, a control mechanism is being specified that provides a work flow in which activities and decision moments are embedded, based on decision rules established at the tactical level. The work flow establishes paths through the system consisting of activities such as application, allocation, waiting, reneging, start of care and end of care. Table 2 summarizes the structure of the model as discussed above.

We now discuss some technical aspects of the model structure. The agent-based model is written on DSOL [17]. The model features three basic agent roles: a case manager agent, a care provider agent, and a child agent. The description of the agents involves the role they represent, and the types of data that they use. We first explain these types of data and then we describe the agent roles.

There are several types of data identified in the model. First, some data define fixed values like agent names, the theoretical distributions, and the geographical home location of an agent. These parameters are mined from real world health care data and health care expert interviews. Second, there are dynamic data stores which hold process information upon which an agent can make decisions. This type of data can be divided in two groups; the transactional data store and the decision data store. The transactional data store holds records of the overall process of an agent. For example, the agents that represent the institution for youth health maintain an internal care database holding all relevant client information. The data store holds factual information emulating historical record keeping. On the other hand, the decision data stores hold time specific data relevant to the execution of the allocation strategy. The value of this data in the decision process decays over time. For example, the decision on the most appropriate care location for a particular client, as determined by the institution for youth health, is based on available information at a particular point in time. Moreover, the agent-based model provides a communication platform enforcing straightforward message based communication between the agents. All inter-agent communication passes this platform such that only those pieces of information that are passed through becomes available to other agents.

Table 2. Structure of the model.

Decision level (stakeholders)	Design requirements Decisions (model structure)
Strategic level (policy makers)	*Policy maker preferences* Organizational roles and responsiveness (model scenarios: push, pull and centralized, decentralized)
Tactical level (care providers)	*Preference behavior of actors in the system* Care types offered Acceptance ratios (decision rules, either normative or descriptive)
Operational level (all actors in the system)	*Control mechanisms and interactions* - (multi-agent system structure)

We now describe the agent roles. The case manager agents act on behalf of the institution for youth health care and they maintain a shared transactional data store for record keeping and private data stores for allocation decisions. The care provider agents all operate on their own on behalf of a care provider. They use private transactional and decision data stores for record keeping and client selection. The client agents operate on behalf of individual clients and while they use both shared and private data stores, they merely initiate the process of care inquiry at the institution for youth health care. A client agent may choose to wait for care or may decide to renege after a certain amount of time.

The process of care provision is implemented on the case level rather than the client level. A single arriving client can be signed up for multiple types of care at the same time and for each of these types a new case is generated. Each of these cases can independently renege or get care and each of these cases are independently considered for returns after reneging or care provision. There is a strict activity path that is followed by all cases in the system as illustrated in Fig. 3. The activity path includes allocation, waiting phase, and treatment mechanisms. It includes client reneging during the waiting phase and client returns after treatment or reneging. An important step in the activity path is the client allocation process for treatment at the care providers which takes place during the waiting phase of a case. It is this specific point in the process were the different allocation scenarios in this research are focused on (see Sect. 3.5). When a care provider selects the next client for treatment, he will evaluate the clients in the queue based on certain characteristics in order to match the client with the available treatment location. While clients are to be selected on a first come, first serve basis, this is often violated by the care providers because they prefer clients that are easier to treat. Easier clients lead to higher throughput which increases profit.

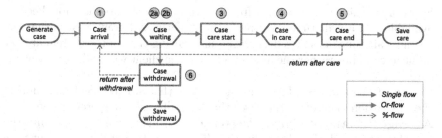

Fig. 3. Life cycle of a case with system measure points.

3.4   Model Measures

At the operational level, the model is about the cases and the events that take place to handle them, this is at the granularity level on which measurements take place. The case events are the base for measuring system performance. As Fig. 3 illustrates there is a strict path for each case implemented in the model. The figure also shows the measuring points of the system relative to the status of a case. There are two types of measures: (1) event counts; the amount of occurrences of a specific event and (2) time averages; the average amount of time spent in a specific state. We have the following system measures which are saved:

1. **Case Arrivals:** The amount of cases that are created during the replication. This includes the amount of cases created by the case generator, the amount of cases created due to returns after care and the amount of cases created due to returns after withdrawal without care. The case generator is identical for all scenarios which simulates the demand for care from the region throughout the replication and includes a correction for seasonal effects. The returns for both after care as well as withdrawal are implemented identical for all scenarios since the probability of return is related to the outcome of a case not the way the system is modeled. The outcome for the measure however can differ for both these returns since it depends on the amount of cases ending care or withdrawing. Note that a shift in the treatment portfolio from less to more difficult cases leads to higher average treatment times and therefore less treatment ends and probably more withdrawals due to capacity constraints. Simply put, one must choose to spend time on fewer difficult cases or more easier cases, while the available capacity stays the same. Returns after care are solely based on the probability of returning whilst the probability of returns after withdrawal also includes the difficulty factor which ensures that the more difficult cases tend to return more often than less difficult ones. In the end, the implementation of a scenario will have its effect on the outcome of case arrivals by influencing the returns as opposed to first arrivals.
2. **Average Waiting Time:** The average waiting time of a case until the next event, being either a start of care or a withdrawal during the replication. The measure has been split into two sub-measures to point out the difference

between a wait time resulting from waiting until a care position became available and a wait time resulting from an early withdrawal. Note that the second wait time doesn't reflect the actual waiting time of the system at that point in time but rather the amount of time the client was willing to wait for care.

3. **Starts of Treatment:** The amount of cases that started treatment during the replication. These are the cases that actually use the system resources.

4. **Average Treatment Time:** The average treatment time of a case until the end of treatment during the replication. The generation of the treatment time per case is implemented identical for all scenarios. The actual treatment time however is influenced by the difficulty factor. On average, a higher difficulty factor will yield higher treatment times and will therefore block the resource for a longer period than a lower difficulty factor would. The composition of cases that get treatment therefore influences the average treatment time and throughput on the resources.

5. **Ends of Treatment:** The amount of cases that ended treatment during the replication. Note that this measure will be equal to the starts of treatment with the absence of the cases that were still in treatment at replication end.

6. **Case Withdrawals:** The amount of cases that withdrew from waiting before a treatment position became available. Note that on average, a case with a higher difficulty factor will be willing to wait longer than a case with a lower difficulty factor. The selection behavior for who's getting the treatment of the model will therefore influence the composition of the withdrawals.

3.5 Scheduling Policies

The set of simulation experiments covers a number of variations of the model structure as exhibited in Table 2, i.e. push, pull and centralized, decentralized decision policies, the four care types, the stakeholder behavior expressed in terms of an acceptance ratio function, and sensitivity analyses.

We first consider the decision strategies.

1. **Decentralized Pushing:** Pushing cases to decentralized queues. As soon as a child has been diagnosed, the institution for youth health care pushes the case to one of the care providers. This strategy is currently implemented in the youth care sector. In this case, the care providers maintain and control their own queues. Workshops with professionals from the field revealed that the selection of children was biased by financial considerations, amongst other things. We have performed an analysis on real life selection data and have estimated a functional relationship between expected treatment time and selection likelihood (details are provided in Sect. 3.7). The institution for youth health care pushes a case to the applicable care provider with the shortest queue. This decision is based on incomplete information since the actual queue lengths at the care providers at runtime are unknown as updates are provided only periodically or upon a limited amount of requests during the allocation process.

2. **Centralized Pushing:** Pushing cases from a centralized queue. When a case has been diagnosed at the institution for youth health care, it is held in a centralized queue until capacity for the required treatment becomes available. The institution for youth health care maintains and controls the central queue while the care providers have no queue at all. The care provider announces its available capacity, and the institution of youth health care pushes the cases for treatment. Observe that any preference bias at the care providers has no impact on the allocation of cases, which is solely done by the institution for youth health care.

3. **Decentralized Pulling:** Pulling cases to decentralized queues. When a case is diagnosed at the institution for youth health care, it is published on a bulletin board in the model until it is selected by a care provider who commits future capacity to the case. The bulletin board is a passive intermediary whose sole function is to provide information to the involved agents to enable the allocation process. Both the institution for youth health care and the care providers hold queues in this strategy. In case a care provider wishes to select an easy case, it must also select all comparable cases in the queue that entered the system before the preferred case. Waiting for the preferred case to be first in line bears the risk of losing the case to another care provider. Therefore, the care providers need to balance the burden of accepting unfavorable cases against the risk of not utilizing their capacity to the full extent.

4. **Centralized Pulling:** Pulling cases from a centralized queue. When a case is diagnosed at the institution for youth health care, it is held in a centralized queue until it is pulled by a care provider which has available capacity. The institution for youth health care publishes the waiting list on a bulletin board for evaluation by the care providers. The care providers do not have queues themselves. The institution for youth health care monitors selection behavior and enforces a 'first come, first serve' policy among comparable cases. Care providers have some discretion to exercise their bias by selecting favorable cases at the expense of cases that are, strictly speaking, not comparable.

3.6 Care Types

The model facilitates four types of care present in the youth care system being ambulatory care (AH), day care (DH), foster care (PZ) and residential care (RH). First we'll discuss some of the main characteristics of these care types, followed by an overview of the main differences as the main reason to study them separately.

1. **Ambulatory Care:** A child is attended at home or at at the location of a care provider by a professional social worker. It includes a series of sessions between client (and parents when useful) and a professional from the care provider. Compared to the other care types the treatment time is on the low end. This is the most basic and cheapest type of care since it only involves little time of the professional. Since the client or the professional has to travel for each session it is preferred that treatment is provided locally. The capacity

is rather high compared to arrivals and clients do not have to wait very long for treatment, since this care type is provided by all care providers.

2. **Day Care:** A child stays at the care provider during the day so that a secure and stable setting can be provided to treat the client. Care is mainly provided to a group under close professional surveillance. Due to the relative lower costs of this type of care longer treatment times are possible. Capacity is sufficient, although waiting times are generally higher, since the care is provided locally and not all care provider provide this type of care.

3. **Foster Care:** A child is actively moved from his/her parental home into a stable and secure setting at a foster family. The care is provided by foster parents who are contracted by the care provider. This care is not provided locally; in certain cases it is even preferred to get clients away from their familiar region. Treatment times are on the high end compared to the other care types, and treatment is focused on longer term solutions in which it is necessary to separate clients from the home region. The care is cost friendly, capacity is sufficient, and waiting times are at the lower end.

4. **Residential Care:** A child is moved from his/her parental home into a stable and secure setting at a location of the care provider. Residential care is seen as the most drastic intervention since it acknowledges that the child requires additional attention from professionals above the basic need to get him/her away from the parental home. Treatment time can range up to months or even years. Due to the complex nature of the treatment it is the most expensive type of care making it important to limit treatments to only the cases who genuinely require it. In practice it often happens that a child receives a combination of several care types; many children who receive residential care are also supported with an ambulatory track, which sometimes even is used as a partial substitution for the more intensive type of care. Multiple care types may also be offered simultaneously in order to reduce the queue length. It is much easier to get a child into an ambulatory track than a residential one, and by doing so a child is already receiving basic care and is considered less an urgent problem than a child who isn't getting care at all. Capacity is sufficient and waiting times are at the lower end.

3.7   Acceptance Factors

The behavior of the health care providers is partly captured by their preferences for specific types of cases. Interviews with field experts revealed that care providers in addition show a preference behavior which is not consistent with a first come first serve principle. In fact, some cherry picking is taking place. In order to capture this behavior, a preference function is introduced in the simulation model. Equation (1) describes the actual preference order of cases which has been elicited by means of a balanced scorecard technique [18], based on interviews with field experts and the evaluation of real world data containing over 30,000 care trajectories. The parameter α_{bench} is called the acceptance factor. A case with a lower acceptance value factor is preferred by the care provider. The observed behavior is parameterized into the resulting equation which consists of two terms. The first term describes the impact of the waiting time t_{wait} of the case at the moment of evaluation and the second term describes the impact of the expected treatment time of the case t_{treat}. Equation (1) contains two fixed threshold values ϵ_{wait} and ϵ_{treat} which are estimated in such a way that the equation resembles the selection behavior as discovered during the interviews. Fine tuning has been done by visual inspection of the function' output. To illustrate the strategic behavior defined by Eq. (1), Fig. 4 shows an example of four potential cases [B,C,E,G] which is a subset of the actual waiting line [A-H] obtained by filtering on characteristics of both the clients and the open treatment position. The order of the clients in terms of waiting time (horizontal axis) differs from the preference order based on the acceptance values (right vertical axis). In Fig. 4, the order of decreasing waiting times is B-C-E-G, while the acceptance value increases along C-E-G-B. When solely looking at waiting time, client B would be selected, however the acceptance function describes a preference for client C.

$$\alpha_{bench} = \frac{\epsilon_{wait}}{t_{wait} + 1} + \frac{E(t_{treat})^2}{2\epsilon_{treat}^2} \tag{1}$$

The policies where studied with the same strategic decision making algorithm in place, given by Eq. (1). It was recognized that the algorithm would be ineffective in certain scenarios where the care providers are not able to exercise their preferences. Moreover, it can be assumed that a high level of control, exercised by the institution of youth health care in the "Centralized Pull" strategy, decreases the freedom to select clients at will. Nevertheless, the care providers will exercise this type of behavior when the design of the system permits them to do so and this phenomenon should therefore be studied accordingly. We perform a sensitivity analysis of this algorithm applied to the "Decentralized Push" allocation strategy by measuring the direct effects on waiting time. The approach is based on the continuum between a focus on the waiting time of clients, as promoted by the institution of youth health care and government, and a focus on the expected treatment time, which aligns with the economic incentives felt by the care providers. Indeed, governmental policies require that care is provided

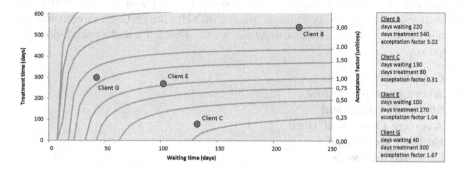

Fig. 4. Indifference curves of the strategic decision algorithm for specific acceptance factors including an example subset of clients ready for allocation.

first to the clients that have been waiting the longest. These policies are based on the recognition that clients cannot be distinguished based on urgency, so that waiting time serves as a proxy. The rationale represents a"first come-first serve" approach, which is in conflict with monetary incentives that favor clients that require the least treatment time. In our model, we study balances between acceptance rationales following governmental policies, i.e. which are based on waiting time, and acceptance rationales which are based on efficiency, i.e. treatment time. We analyze convex combinations of the two extreme rationales as described in Eq. (2). By increasing β step by step, we introduce unfairness between client selection by the care providers.

$$\alpha_{linear} = \frac{\beta \; \epsilon_{treat}}{E(t_{twait}) + 1} + (1 - \beta) \; t_{treat} \quad \text{for } \beta\epsilon[0, 1] \tag{2}$$

We also added a benchmark rationale in which the allocation is fully random as defined in Eq. (3).

$$\alpha_{random} = RAND \tag{3}$$

where RAND follows the homogeneous distribution on [0,1].

3.8   Key Performance Indicators (KPIs)

A number of Key Performance Indicators (KPIs) have surfaced while researching the interests of stakeholders in workshop discussions and desk research on professional publications, publications from the youth care sector and field data. First of all, the public health care system is bound by law to treat children in need within a reasonable amount of time, so waiting times are under scrutiny. On the other hand, it has also been recognized that reneging from queues, i.e. clients spontaneously leaving the queue after a certain period of time, may filter out those clients that are able to resolve issues by themselves. Children that need extensive care are likely not to belong to this category. However, beyond utilizing their capacity to the full extent, care providers have financial incentives to avoid the treatment of difficult cases, so there is a tendency to prioritize less difficult cases. To properly manage queues in YHC under these circumstances, we will study the system measures as discussed in Sect. 3.4 and shown below per scenario.

1. **Case arrivals**
2. **Average waiting time**
3. **Starts of treatment**
4. **Average treatment time**
5. **Ends of treatment**
6. **Case withdrawals**

KPIs 1 (less returns), 2 (less waiting time) and 6 (less withdrawals) can be seen as *social* indicators, since they relate strongly to the children who need care.

KPIs 3 (more starts of treatment), 4 (less treatment time) and 5 (more ends of treatment) can be seen as *efficiency* indicators, since they relate strongly to the overall efficiency and economic incentives of care providers.

Interviews with field experts indicated that a major shortcoming of the current system is the neglecting of difficult cases. However [2] argue that there are many cases which receive help via the institution for youth health care are not genuine cases requiring professional help. The authors indicate that these cases shouldn't enter the system because either the indication of a problem is falsely recognized or the problem is of such a low level that these are able to help themselves. The field experts support this conclusion. The discussions on these KPIs therefore includes a distinction of judgment on overall performance against a judgement based on a subdivision on the difficulty factor of cases.

4 Discussion of Results and Managerial Insights

The simulation is set to run 20 years of simulation time therefore including over 160,000 clients per replication on which a long running average waiting time is calculated. Each setting is run for 75 different seeds therefore making it possible to calculate reliable means with a 95 % confidence interval per setting.

4.1 Key Performance Indicators

In the Sect. 3.8, a number of KPI's have been studied to select the best scheduling policy. Most importantly we discussed that the difficulty of a case should be taken into account as well. As shown in Figs. 6, 7, 8 and 9, for each of the four scheduling policies, confidence intervals for means are presented for subsets of cases (left side) and all cases (right side). Please note that the scales differ among the figures to ensure comparability of values within a figure. The subsets of cases are created with bins of 10 % difficulty ranging from 0.0-0.1 (less difficult) to 0.9-1.0 (more difficult). The number of cases ending up in the bins is not equal since a bin is created on the difficulty factor itself rather than the resulting set of cases. I.e. the amount of treatment starts for bin 0.0-0.1 at day care in the push to central scenario (S1) with about 1200 treatments differs from the about 700 treatments for bin 0.9-1.0. Note that this also means that the waiting and treatment times are calculated on differently sized subsets. Vertically, the

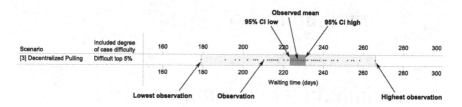

Fig. 5. Example of visualization method for result analysis.

confidence intervals for means are presented using five vertical lines indicating the 95 % confidence levels. See Fig. 5 for further guidance in reading the results.

4.2   Comparison of Scheduling Policies

Based on the KPI analyses as outlined in Figs. 6 to 9, we gain the following insights:

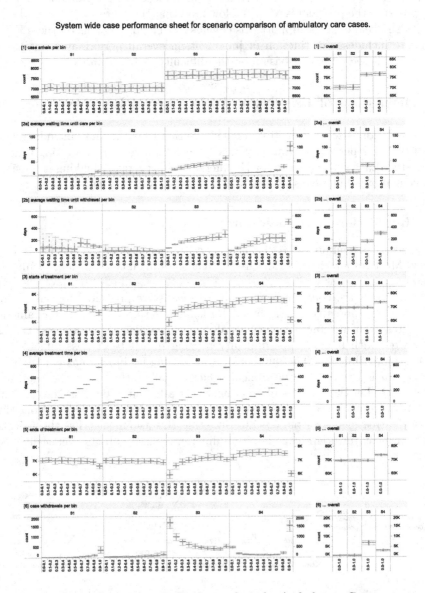

Fig. 6. Comparison 1: System analysis for Ambulatory Care.

System wide case performance sheet for scenario comparison of day care cases.

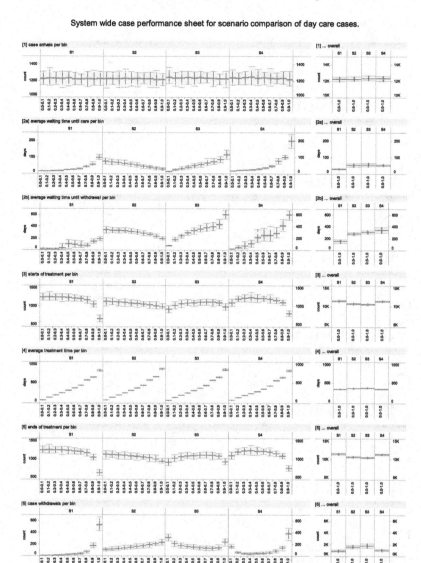

Fig. 7. Comparison 2: System analysis for Day Care.

Insights Ambulatory and Residential Care. For these two care types, the pull policies show a 10 % higher rate of arrivals due to returned withdrawals; this is especially true for the difficult cases. The central pull policy enables enforcement of "fairness", which can be inferred from the number of start events of the cases at the various difficulty levels. On the contrary, the decentralized pull policy generally neglects the most difficult cases, and the total throughput is the highest. Although the system is efficient, returned difficult cases create waiting lines and are not being treated.

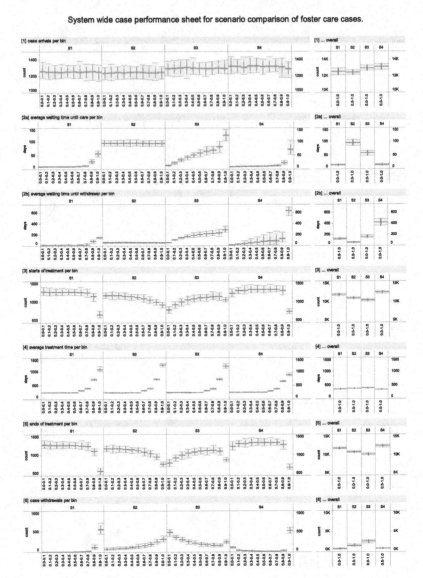

Fig. 8. Comparison 3: System analysis for Foster Care.

Insights Foster and Day Care. Arrivals pull and push policies are almost equal for these two care types, while for Ambulatory and Residential care types, pull and push policies show differences. Centralized policies maintain a certain degree in fairness. Due to increased waiting times, more easy cases withdraw. Therefore, we see that the difficult cases are more often treated than the easy cases. Decentralized policies tend to treat an equal amount of cases on all levels of difficulty, except the most difficult ones which are treated significantly less. Most of these effects are more pronounced for Day care.

Policy Comparison Over all Care Types. For push scenarios, withdrawal rates positively relate to case difficulty, while for pull scenarios, both easy and difficult cases show higher withdrawal rates.Since all systems demonstrate an increase of withdrawals when waiting times increase, there is less difference in performance

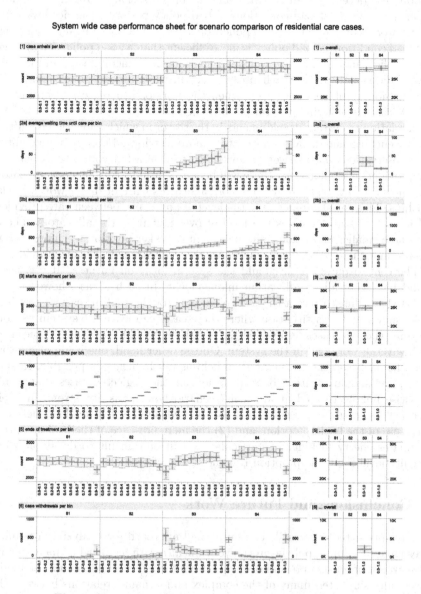

Fig. 9. Comparison 4: System analysis for Residential Care.

among the policies under such circumstances.While the decentralized policies have room to increase throughput by choosing easy cases over difficult cases, the centralized policies maintain fairness in the system, which comes at the cost of lower throughput.

Managerial Takeaways. One may argue that from a fairness viewpoint, push is good, pull is bad, and central is good, decentral is bad. Therefore, central push is good, and decentral pull is bad, while the mixed scenarios are in the middle. Under moderate workload conditions, a bad policy performs (service level) just slightly worse compared to a good policy, on average. On the contrary, under high workload conditions, a bad policy is more efficient than a good policy, on average. A bad policy under moderate workload neglects the difficult cases, and thereby creates additional workload when cases return, while a good policy handles all cases without problems. However, when the workload increases, accepting the difficult cases is affecting general performance.

In relation to current developments in the sector in which allocation is shifting from a central point (province level) to a more distributed point (municipality), these observations become very relevant. Instead of a few connections between care providers and allocators, there will be many. And instead of a few allocators who know each other, there will be more allocators without direct working relationships. This situation increases the level of ambiguity between care providers and allocators and decreases the level of oversight from the allocators. Therefore, these smaller allocation units will be in a weaker position to enforce a pull scenario and there will be more room for cherry picking at the care providers.

The central question is: should the system focus on fairness? If yes, there should be a centralized allocation management. In such a case, however, one needs to be willing to accept the costs of lower throughput of the easier cases. The model shows that in a situation where these cases can leave the system without returning (i.e., the cases resolve themselves), then it will have no noticeable effect on the overall workload of the system. On the other hand, one could argue that focus should be on the throughput to help as much clients as possible. In such a case, one should create a backup option for the neglected cases that would otherwise not be treated at all. This scenario however is not strong in itself, since (1) the case in question will have waited already for too long before it makes use of the backup option, and (2) the mere presence of the backup option legitimates cherry picking. In particular, it will be difficult to decide at what difficulty level the backup option becomes the preferred one.

5   Conclusions and Future Work

We have presented a versatile computational approach for analyzing a number of resource scheduling policies in the youth health care sector while including an extensive set of constraints and behaviors from the real world domain. The model successfully simulated many of the complex and dynamic relations between the involved parties in the healthcare sector. We demonstrated the ability of the model to incorporate different scheduling policies while maintaining an overall structure which deals with the common tasks outside the scheduling procedure. We discussed the differences between the scenarios and their impact on system performance. The introduction of a case's difficulty into performance measurement leads us to the advice of the push from a centralized scheduling policy for future resource scheduling in the youth health care sector. The postponement of the actual allocation in this policy ensures a higher level of fairness in treatment provision by the care providers because they cannot avoid the difficult cases anymore which increases overall social welfare.

Our approach shows the importance of agent-based modeling in complex, dynamic environments like the youth health care sector where much of the issues are related to coordination and communication between different heterogeneous parties. We contribute to research in service operations management by not only showing its usability in such a setting, but also showing the ability to study alternative scenarios which couldn't be studied otherwise with this level of complexity.

Generally, our findings show that a scheduling system which includes a reneging mechanism can handle a workload that is bigger than the available resources to the system while the system as a whole appears to be stable by using the reneging mechanism as a filter on arrivals. As we see in this health care case the measurement methods for performance (which can be translated as a key parameter for the rewarding structure) are out of balance with the social goals of the system and therefore the filtering effect is indirectly used to increase measured performance while social performance is neglected. When it is not possible to bring the measurement methods in line with the social goals, then it should be assured that there is no room for cherry picking. In this case it can be arranged by postponing the actual allocation towards the point that an independent party can make the final decision and ensure that this decision is in line with the social goals. Furthermore when the decision power is positioned at the party who has to perform upon this decision it becomes even more important that the performance indicators are in line with the social goals otherwise performance based preferences have an even stronger negative effect on the social performance.

The current model incorporates basic methods to emulate interdependencies between the available care types. In future, we plan to study the model in alternative configurations with varying settings for geographical distributions and number of agents in such that we are able to assist in strategic decision making.

References

1. Agarwal, R., Guodong (Gordon), G., DesRoches, C., Jha, A.K.: The digital transformation of healthcare: Current status and the road ahead. Inf. Syst. Res. **20**(4), 796–809 (2010)
2. Andriessen, S., Besseling, J.: Jongeren zijn steeds vaker niet normaal. Jeugd Beleid **2**(1), 87–95 (2008)
3. Armony, M., Plambeck, E., Seshadri, S.: Sensitivity of optimal capacity to customer impatience in an unobservable m/m/s queue (why you shouldnt shout at the dmv). Manufact. Serv. Oper. Manage. **11**(1), 19–32 (2009)

4. Bagust, A., Place, M., Posnett, J.W.: Dynamics of bed use on accommodating emergency admissions: Stochastic simulation model. Br. Med. J. **X**, 319 (1999)
5. Bichler, M., Gupta, A., Ketter, W.: Designing smart markets. Inf. Syst. Res. **21**(4), 688–699 (2010)
6. Britan, G.R., Ferrer, J.C., e Oliveira, P.R.: Managing customer experiences: Perspectives on the temporal aspects of service encounters. Manuf. Servi. Oper. Manage. **1**(1), 61–83 (2008)
7. Brown, L., Gans, N., Mandelbaum, A., Sakov, A., Shen, H., Zeltyn, S., Zhao, L.: Statistical analysis of a telephone call center. J. Am. Stat. Assoc. **100**(469), 36–50 (2005)
8. Collins, J., Ketter, W., Gini, M.: A multi-agent negotiation testbed for contracting tasks with temporal and precedence constraints. Int. J. Electron. Commer. **7**(1), 35–57 (2002)
9. Collins, J., Ketter, W., Sadeh, N.: Pushing the limits of rational agents: the trading agent competition for supply chain management. AI Mag. **31**(2), 63–80 (2010)
10. Devaraj, S., Kohli, R.: Information technology payoff in the health-care industry: a longitudinal study. J. Manage. Inform. Syst. **16**(4), 41–67 (2000)
11. Fletcher, A., Halsall, D., Huxham, S., Worthington, D.: The dh accident and emergency department model: A national generic model used locally. J. Oper. Res. Soc. **58**, 1554–1562 (2007)
12. Goldman, R.D., Macpherson, A., Schuh, S., Mulligan, C., Pirie, J.: Patients who leave the pediatric emergency department without being seen: case-control study. Can. Med. Assoc. J. **172**(1), 39–43 (2005)
13. Goodacre, S., Webster, A.: Who waits longest in the emergency department and who leaves without being seen? Emerg. Med. J. **22**(2), 93 (2005)
14. Gorunescu, F., McClean, S.I., Millard, P.H.: A queueing model for bed-occupancy management and planning of hospitals. J. Oper. Res. Soc. **53**, 19–24 (2002)
15. Gupta, D., Denton, B.: Appointment scheduling in health care: Challenges and opportunities. IIE Trans. **40**(9), 800–819 (2008)
16. Hevner, A.R., March, S.T., Park, J., Ram, S.: Design science in information systems research. Manage. Inf. Syst. Q. **28**(1), 75–106 (2004)
17. Jacobs, P.H.M., Lang, N.A., Verbraeck, A.: D-sol: A distributed java based discrete event simulation architecture. X, ed., In: Proceedings of the 2002 Winter Simulation Conference. San Diego, pp. 793–800. ISBN 0-7803-7614-5 (2002)
18. Kaplan, R.S., Norton, D.P.: The balanced scorecard: Measures that drive performance. Harvard Bus. Rev. **83**(7), 172–180 (2005)
19. Ketter, W., Collins, J., Reddy, P.: Power TAC: A competitive economic simulation of the smart grid. Energy Econ. **39**, 262–270 (2013)
20. Liu, N., Ziya, S., Kulkarni, V.G.: Dynamic scheduling of outpatient appointments under patient no-shows and cancellations. Manuf. Serv. Oper. Manag. **12**(2), 347–364 (2010)
21. Netherlands National News Agency, NANP. 2008. Millions of additional funding for youth care
22. Postl, B.D.: Final report of the federal advisor on wait times. Technical Report, Health Canada (2006)
23. Rachlis, M.: Public solutions to health care wait lists. Technical Report, Canadian Centre for Policy Alternatives (2005)
24. Ridge, J.C., Jones, S.K., Nielsen, M.S., Shahani, A.K.: Capacity planning for intensive care units. Eur. J. Oper. Res. **105**, 346–355 (1998)
25. Robinson, L.W., Chen, R.R.: Estimating the implied value of the customer's waiting time. Manuf. Serv. Oper. Manage. **13**(1), 53–57 (2011)

26. Saulnier, M., Shortt, S., Gruenwoldt, E.: The taming of the queue: Toward a cure for health care wait times. Technical Report, Canadian Medical Association (2004)
27. Van Mieghem, J.: Dynamic scheduling with convex delay costs. Ann. Appl. Probab. **5**(3), 809–833 (1995)
28. Welch, P.D.: On the problem of the initial transient in steady-state simulation. IBM Watson Research Center (1981)
29. Welch, P.D.: The statistical analysis of simulation results. The computer performance modeling handbook 268–328 (1983)
30. Wooldridge, M., Jennings, N.R.: Intelligent agents: Theory and practice. Knowl. Eng. Rev. **10**(2), 115–152 (1995)

Agent-Based Voting Architecture for Traffic Applications

Sophie L. Dennisen$^{(\boxtimes)}$ and Jörg P. Müller

Institute of Informatics, Clausthal University of Technology, Julius-Albert-Str. 4,
38678 Clausthal-Zellerfeld, Germany
{sophie.dennisen,joerg.mueller}@tu-clausthal.de

Abstract. We study voting rules as a promising option for collective decision making in traffic applications. The aim of our work is to compare the suitability of several voting rules for different traffic applications and to tackle problems which arise when applying voting rules in traffic management. Here, we propose a multi-agent based voting architecture for evaluation of the suitability of voting rules. The design of the voting architecture is informed by the requirements from two applications we intend to study. The J-MADeM architecture is adapted for the development of our architecture. We describe the voting theory model we intend to incorporate in the architecture, the initial applications we plan to investigate and the features of the voting architecture. Furthermore, we outline the first simulation we intend to conduct using the voting architecture, focusing on the aspect of iterative winner determination for the committee voting rules Minisum and Minimax Approval.

1 Introduction

Computational Social Choice (COMSOC) [9] investigates the design and formal analysis of methods for aggregating the preferences of multiple agents. So far, most research on COMSOC has focused on exploring mechanisms and their theoretical properties. There is relatively little published work focusing on the engineering of real-world applications using COMSOC methods and mechanisms for collective decision making, especially voting rules. In this paper, we propose the area of cooperative traffic management as an increasingly interesting area for applying voting rules, and we take first steps in investigating requirements for the architecture of a platform for engineering cooperative traffic applications incorporating voting rules.

Today, there is no strong interconnection between the decision making of individual traffic participants, e.g. in choice of routes and traffic modalities. Basically, each traffic participant follows her plans, restricted by some limitations like the given infrastructure, the traffic status and the information available. However, new technological trends are about to heavily affect traffic management systems, and are likely to change this picture: Vehicle-to-infrastructure (V2I) and vehicle-to-vehicle (V2V) communication (collectively referred to as V2X) enable

© Springer International Publishing Switzerland 2015
J.P. Müller et al. (Eds.): MATES 2015, LNAI 9433, pp. 200–217, 2015.
DOI: 10.1007/978-3-319-27343-3_11

real-time data exchange and coordination among vehicles and traffic infrastructure. Vehicles themselves become more and more autonomous through advanced assistance functions such as dynamic navigation and adaptive cruise control over speed, distance, and intersection assistants [2] as well as autonomous driving support [19].

As far as decision making in traffic networks is concerned, V2X communication will enable cooperation between individual traffic participants by exchanging their preferences or plans with the support of assistance systems. Knowing the others' preferences or plans, the traffic participants can adapt their original plans, give the other traffic participants feedback or agree on joint decisions. There are different collective decision mechanisms, for example auctions, negotiations and elections. We focus on elections as one specific kind of COMSOC mechanisms and plan to study voting as one promising option for collective decision making in traffic applications. To the best of our knowledge, there are no works systematically researching the use of common voting rules in traffic applications.

In our work, we tackle the following two research questions:

Are there voting rules which are more suitable for specific traffic applications than others? Which general challenges arise when applying voting rules in traffic management?

We aim to compare common voting rules in terms of their effect on quantities such as satisfaction of traffic participants, travel time and waiting time, using different forms of votes. We plan to study not only single winner elections but also committee elections.

Our objective is to evaluate different voting rules in the context of multi-agent based traffic simulations. To this end, we need an architecture which allows implementing and comparing various voting rules. The architecture must enable us to easily repeat a simulation for a specific scenario using several common voting rules to compare their effect on the quantities we want to study. We also request that it must be possible during a simulation to conduct parallel elections for several groups of traffic participants. As far as we know, there is no architecture which exactly meets our requirements.

Here, we propose using an adaptation of Jason Multimodal Agent Decision Making (J-MADeM), which we will call Jason Voting (J-Voting) in the following. J-MADeM is an architecture for using Multi Agent Resource Allocation (MARA) [10] as collective decision mechanism, developed by Grimaldo et al. [15,16]. J-Voting is designed with regard to two traffic applications of voting rules we plan to investigate, namely agreement on points of interest (POIs) to visit for share taxis and agreement on a speed value in platoons.

The article is structured as follows. In Sect. 2, we describe the J-MADeM architecture. In Sect. 3, we give the definitions for basic concepts in voting theory. In Sect. 4, we depict the share taxi scenario and the platooning scenario. In Sect. 5, we describe the requirements for a flexible architecture for application of voting rules in agent-based traffic simulations. Section 6 discusses related work. In Sect. 7, we describe the design of J-Voting. Section 8 concludes the paper and outlines research questions we will study using J-Voting.

2   J-MADeM

Grimaldo et al. propose an agent-based architecture implemented in Jason, J-MADeM, for multimodal decision making in the sense of first-price sealed-bid one-round auctions [15,16]. Grimaldo et al. [17] apply J-MADeM to develop a model for urban mobility simulation, following a market-based approach. They consider the social decisions made by each habitant of a city about how to get to work, e.g. by train, sharing a car etc. They compare different outcomes produced by societies of individualist and egalitarian agents, in terms of the average travel time, the use of the urban transportation and the air pollution.

Grimaldo et al. [15,16] describe J-MADeM as follows. J-MADeM is based on the Multi-Modal Agent Decision Making (MADeM) model proposed by Grimaldo et al. [14] which provides agents with a general mechanism to make socially acceptable decisions. In this kind of decisions, the members of an organization are required to express their preferences with regard to the different solutions for a specific decision problem. The model is based on the MARA theory, therefore, it represents each one of these solutions as a set of resource allocations. Note that they make some adaptations [14] to the original MARA definition.

Adapted MARA definition in the MADeM model

- A set of agents $A = \{a_1, ..., a_n\}$, where each a_i represents a particular agent involved in the decision. A vector of weights $w = (w_1, ..., w_n)$ is associated to each agent representing the internal attitude of the agent towards other individuals. This information is used to weigh the information received from other agents.
- A set of resources to be allocated by the agents $R = \{r_1, ..., r_m\}$.
- Instead of having only one utility function as in classical MARA problems, each agent in MADeM has a set of utility functions $\{U^1, ..., U^q\}$. These utility functions are used to evaluate the allocations from different points of view, so their model hardcodes a linear MAUT (multi-attribute utility function). Additionally, each agent has a vector of utility weights $w_u = (w_{u_1}, ..., w_{u_q})$ representing the importance given to each point of view in the multi-modal agent decision making.

MADeM can consider both tasks and objects as plausible resources to be allocated, which it generalizes under the term taskslots. Taskslots are considered as slots that need to be assigned in order to execute a task. When considering any kind of task, two main types of task slots are differentiated: agent slots, which correspond to agents that play different roles in the task execution, and object slots, that correspond to objects needed to perform the action. MADeM uses first-price sealed-bid one-round auctions as the allocation procedure and a multi-criteria winner determination problem to merge the different preferences being collected according to the kind of agent or society simulated. Figure 1 yields an overview and a detailed view of the J-MADeM Agent Architecture. In the following, the main components of the agent architecture are described.

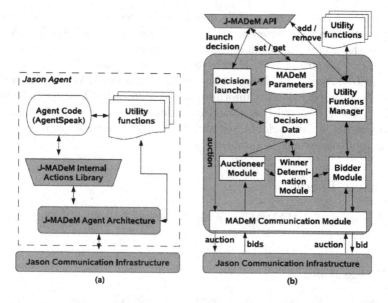

Fig. 1. (a) Overview and (b) detailed view of the J-MADeM Agent Architecture

- *MADeM Parameters*: This data storage contains the MADeM context currently defined for the agent. Essentially, it stores the personal weights, the utility weights, the collective utility function and the bid timeout to be used in future MADeM decisions.
- *Decision Launcher*: This module starts the MADeM process for a particular decision. Firstly, it stores the MADeM context for this decision into the *Decision Data* storage, thus allowing other decisions to be concurrently performed with different MADeM parameters. Secondly, it auctions each of the allocations being considered as solutions to the target agents.
- *Decision Data*: This data storage holds all the information related to the MADeM decisions still in process. Therefore, it contains their MADeM context, the considered allocations and the preferences received for each of them.
- *MADeM Communication Module*: This module extends the Jason agent communication module in order to deal with MADeM messages. When it receives a MADeM auction, it invokes the *Bidder Module* to get the agent's preferences over the considered allocations. On the other hand, when it receives a MADeM bid, it informs the *Auctioneer Module* about the received preferences.
- *Bidder Module*: This module manages the reception of a MADeM auction. It extracts the considered allocations and bids for them according to the agent's preferences. To express these preferences it relies on the utility values provided by the *Utility Functions Manager*
- *Utility Functions Manager*: This component acts as an interface between the built-in MADeM mechanism and the user defined *Utility Functions*. Thus, it is in charge of locating and invoking them in order to calculate the agents' utilities for the set of considered allocations.

- *Auctioneer Module*: This module manages the reception of MADeM bids. It extracts the sender's preferences and stores them into the *Decision Data*. As soon as the preferences from all the target agents have been received, it calls the *Winner Determination Module* to solve the decision.
- *Winner Determination Module*: This module solves the MADeM winner determination problem using the information stored into the *Decision Data* for the decision being resolved (i.e. considered allocations, agents' preferences, personal weights, utility weights, social welfare, ...) Once resolved, it notifies the agent about the winner solution.

3   Voting Theory

The adaptation of J-MADeM we propose here is based on Voting theory as defined in [23].

3.1   Voting Rules

An election or preference profile is defined as tuple (C, V) where

- $C = \{c_1, ..., c_m\}$ is the set of candidates.
- $V = \{v_1, ..., v_n\}$ is the list of votes over C. Each voter is represented via her vote which specifies her preferences over the candidates in C.

How the voters' preferences are represented depends on the voting rule used. Established types of votes are linear orders and approval votes, i.e. $\{0, 1\}^m$ vectors. Preferences can also be represented using trichotomous votes, i.e. $\{-1, 0, 1\}^m$ vectors.

A voting rule is a rule determining the winner(s) of a given election (C, V). Let $\mathcal{P}(C)$ denote the power set of C. Formally, a voting rule f defines a social choice correspondence

$$f : \{(C, V) | (C, V) \text{ is a preference profile}\} \rightarrow \mathcal{P}(C)$$

that assigns a set of winners to each given preference profile. Given a preference profile $P = (C, V)$, $f(P) \subseteq C$ is the set of winners which may be empty or may contain one or more than one winner. To determine a unique winner, it may be necessary to apply a tie-breaking rule.

Examples for Voting Rules. In the following, we give some examples for common voting rules.

- **Approval**: The Approval voting rule was introduced by Brams and Fishburn in [7]. For a fixed order of the candidates in C, an approval vector is a vector in $\{0, 1\}^m$ which has for $1 \leq i \leq m$ at the i-th position a "1", if the voter approves of candidate c_i, "0" if she disapproves of c_i. A candidate gets one point for each approval and the candidate with the highest score wins.

- **Borda**: The Borda voting rule proposed by Borda in [5] assumes as votes complete rankings over the candidates in C. With m candidates, each voter gives
  - $m - 1$ points to the candidate ranked at first position,
  - $m - 2$ points to the candidate ranked at second position,
  - ...
  - 0 points to the candidate ranked at last position.

  The candidate with the highest score wins.
- **Condorcet**: The Condorcet rule introduced in [12] assumes as votes complete rankings over the candidates in C. A candidate c is a Condorcet winner if she defeats every other candidate by a strict majority in pairwise elections.

3.2 Committee Elections

Similarly to the definitions in [23], one can define committee elections. If voters need to agree on a candidate set of fixed size, they need a committee voting rule. A committee voting rule assigns to each triple (C, V, k) with (C, V) preference profile and $k \le |C|$ nonnegative integer a set of winning committees of the form $K \subseteq C, |K| = k$.

Committee Voting Rules. We consider two examples for committee voting rules.

- **Minisum Approval**: Minisum Approval selects a committee with minimal sum of Hamming distance to all votes. For a fixed committee size k, this is a committee containing k candidates with highest Approval scores.
- **Minimax Approval**: Brams et al. proposed to use the minimax approach in [8]. Minimax Approval selects a committee for which the maximal Hamming distance to any voter is minimal.

3.3 Interaction Protocols for Voting

In the design of our architecture, we consider centralised voting as well as decentralised voting.

Centralised Voting. In Fig. 2, a simple interaction protocol for centralised elections is illustrated. The chair of the election asks the voters to submit their votes. After receiving all votes, the chair applies the given voting rule with the votes as input and transmits the outcome of the election to the voters.

Decentralised Voting. Figure 3 illustrates a simple interaction protocol for decentralised voting based on the two-phase commit protocol [22]. The user, who needs a collective decision, asks the voters to prepare their commit, i.e. to exchange their votes and to compute the outcome of the election. The "user" notion can for example be found in the article [18] by Hardekopf et al. who

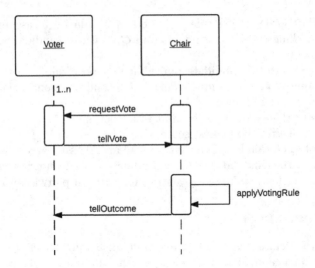

Fig. 2. Simple interaction protocol for centralised elections

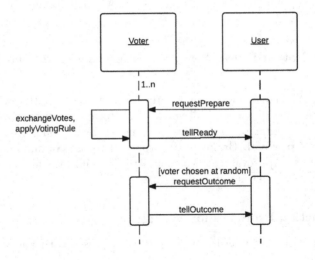

Fig. 3. Interaction protocol for decentralised elections

describe decentralised voting schemes. The voters independently apply the given voting rule to the exchanged votes and tell the user that they are ready for phase two. In phase two, the user chooses a voter at random for committing the outcome of the election.

4   Scenarios

As mentioned above, J-Voting is designed in view of two traffic scenarios which we plan to investigate.

4.1 Share-Taxi Scenario

In this scenario, we consider an intraurban area and assume that the city administration provides share taxis which collect travellers at predefined changing points and transport the travellers through the city, taking their preferences regarding the POIs into account. In our model, each group of travellers in a share taxi constitutes a voter group, i.e. they use a voting rule to aggregate their preferences to a joint decision. For our setting, we have the following assumptions and considerations.

- The passengers of a share taxi must agree on a POI set of fixed size.
- If several POI sets are "equally rated", the passengers need a rule to decide on an option.
- The scenario can include several share taxis.
- For the share-taxi scenario, the straightforward approach would be to use a centralised approach and to assign the chair role to the share-taxi agents.
- In the case of decentralised elections, one could consider the share-taxi agents as users, i.e. as agents who need to know the result of the collective decision(s).

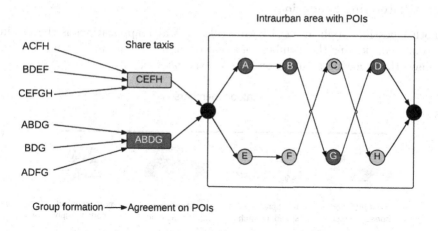

Fig. 4. Example for share-taxi scenario

Figure 4 provides an illustrating example with two share taxis, applying the committee voting rule Minisum Approval with committee size $k = 4$. The candidate set is a set of POIs, $\{A, B, C, D, E, F, G, H\}$. The first share taxi contains three travellers who want to visit the POIs ACFH, BDEF and CEFGH, represented by the approval vectors $(1, 0, 1, 0, 0, 1, 0, 1)$, $(0, 1, 0, 1, 1, 1, 0, 0)$ and $(0, 0, 1, 0, 1, 1, 1, 1)$. The approval scores are illustrated in Table 1. A winning committee in Minisum Approval contains k candidates with highest approval scores. Here, we have the unique winning committee $\{C, E, F, H\}$.

Table 1. Approval scores for first share taxi

A	B	C	D	E	F	G	H
1	1	2	1	2	3	1	2

The second share taxi contains three travellers who want to visit the POIs ABDG, BDG and ADFG, represented by the approval vectors $(1, 1, 0, 1, 0, 0, 1, 0)$, $(0, 1, 0, 1, 0, 0, 1, 0)$ and $(1, 0, 0, 1, 0, 1, 1, 0)$. The approval scores are illustrated in Table 2. Here, we have the unique winning committee $\{A, B, D, G\}$.

Table 2. Approval scores for second share taxi

A	B	C	D	E	F	G	H
2	2	0	3	0	1	3	0

4.2   Platooning Scenario

Another possible application of voting rules in traffic applications is the use in platoons, considering the members of a platoon as a voter group. For this setting, we have the following assumptions and considerations.

Platoon members

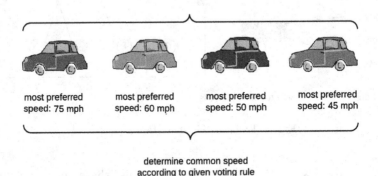

Fig. 5. Example for platoon scenario, car illustrations by Ariane Dehghan

- The platoon members need to agree on a speed value for all platoon members.
- If two speed values are "equally rated", the platoon members need a rule to decide on an option.
- All considered speed values in the joint decision of a platoon are feasible for all platoon members.

- The scenarios can include several platoons.
- There is initially no difference between the car agents which constitute a platoon.

An example for the platoon scenario is illustrated in Fig. 5. The four platoon members have different preferences regarding the platoon speed, the values for the most preferred speeds being 45 mph, 50 mph, 60 mph and 75 mph. A natural assumption would be that the preferences regarding the speed values are single peaked. The concept of single-peaked preferences was introduced by Black in [4]. Single-peakedness means that for each voter there is an "optimal" outcome, and the further an outcome is from this outcome, the less preferred it is by the voter. For the example, we assume single peaked approval vectors over the outcome space from 40 to 80 mph in steps of 5. Consider the approval vectors as illustrated in Table 3, with voters v_1, v_2 and v_4 approving of three and voter v_3 approving of four speed values. The unique winner of the election is the speed value 50 mph with approval score 3.

Table 3. Approval vectors and approval scores for platoon example

Speed value	40	45	50	55	60	65	70	75	80
v_1	1	1	1	0	0	0	0	0	0
v_2	0	1	1	1	0	0	0	0	0
v_3	0	0	1	1	1	1	1	0	0
v_4	0	0	0	0	0	0	1	1	1
Approval score	1	2	3	2	1	1	2	1	1

5 Functional Requirements

In the following, a range of requirements for the architecture needed to investigate the above depicted scenarios using several voting rules are described. Some requirements directly stem from the depiction of the scenarios, others are based on the objective to create an architecture which enables comparing several voting rules.

Requirements Based on Scenarios

Winner Determination

- Voting rules: If members of a platoon agree on a common speed, they need a voting rule to assign a set of possible winners to each preference profile. Thus the architecture must implement voting rules.

- Election of committees: If the passengers of a share taxi agree on a POI set of fixed size to visit, they need to apply a committee voting rule, thus the architecture must enable the election of committees.
- Tie-breaking rule for voting rules: The architecture must implement some sort of tie-breaking for voting rules. If members of a platoon want to agree on a common speed, they must be able to determine a unique speed value. If the voting rule yields several candidates, a tie-breaking rule is needed to determine a unique winner.
- Tie-breaking rule for committee voting rules: Analogously, the architecture must implement some sort of tie-breaking for committee voting rules. If the passengers of a share taxi agree on a POI set of fixed size to visit, they must be able to determine a unique POI set. If the committee voting rule yields several committees, a tie-breaking rule is needed to determine a unique winner committee.

Iteration Features

- Parallel elections: As the scenarios can include several share taxis or platoons, the architecture must enable the concurrent execution of several elections.

(De)centralised Voting

- Centralised Voting: As mentioned above, for the share-taxi scenario, the straightforward approach would be to assign the chair role to the share taxis. Thus, the architecture should enable centralised voting.
- Decentralised Voting: It would be advantageous to enable decentralised voting to avoid that a single agent gets too much influence (the chair).

Agent Roles

- Role switching: Considering the platooning scenario, there is initially no difference between the car agents, so all car agents should be able to choose between the voter role and the chair role (in the case of centralised elections) or between the voter role and the user role (in the case of decentralised elections).

Generic Requirements

Architecture extensibility

- Extensibility: The architecture should allow the implementation of any voting rule, in the sense that the voting rule is given as parameter for the simulation.

Preference handling

- Vote types: All established types of votes (approval vectors, complete rankings etc.) should be supported.
- Conversion: Since comparability of voting rules with different vote types is desired, we define the votes based on valuation functions, i.e. the valuation functions are converted into approval vectors, complete rankings etc.

6   Related Work

The most works in the COMSOC area researching voting rules are of rather theoretical nature and investigate voting rules regarding their theoretical properties. There are relatively few works researching practical applications of voting rules in specific domains, e.g. for designing recommender systems.

There are several works researching the application of collective decision mechanisms for multiagent systems and/or for traffic applications. We focus on such papers which research voting in multiagent systems and papers which investigate collective decision making mechanisms for traffic applications.

Ghosh et al. [13] propose a voting-based architecture for recommender systems. They do not design the architecture for usage of different voting rules but apply a specific voting rule, namely Black's voting rule.

Pitt et al. [20] propose a generic voting protocol designed to increase robustness in e-voting systems and describe two applications. They focus on providing a robust algorithm with a simple voting mechanism and do not compare several voting rules.

Aseere [1] implements a voting-based agent system for personalised e-learning in a course selection scenario. The agents are Java classes, implemented according to the JADE framework [3]. Aseere does not compare several voting rules but applies a specific voting rule, a newly proposed hybrid voting rule which combines features of the single-transferable vote rule and the cumulative voting rule.

Vasirani and Ossowski [25] propose auction-based procedures for intersection management. They do not apply voting rules.

Sanderson et al. use institutionalised Paxos for managing consensus formation in vehicular networks [24], naming agreement on a common speed as an example. Similarly to [20], they focus on providing a robust algorithm with a simple voting mechanism for dynamic situations and do not compare several voting rules.

None of these approaches fulfills the requirement that the application and comparison of several common voting rules and committee voting rules with different vote forms should be possible.

7   J-Voting Architecture and Design

7.1   Design

Grimaldo et al. [15,16] chose from the range of possible languages and interpreters the AgentSpeak language [21] and its open source interpreter Jason [6] because the language is based on the well known BDI approach and the interpreter can be easily customised.

7.2   Architecture Components

Figure 6 yields an overview and a detailed view of the components of the J-Voting Agent Architecture necessary for voting. In the following, we describe the main components of the J-Voting Agent Architecture.

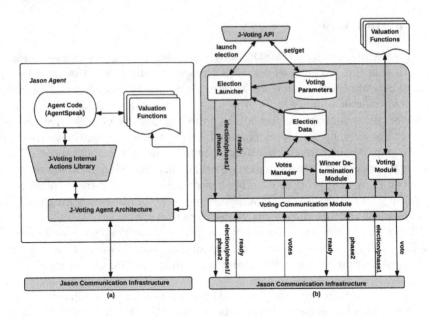

Fig. 6. (a) Overview and (b) detailed view of the J-Voting Agent Architecture

- *Voting Parameters*: This data storage contains the voting context currently defined for the agent.
- *Election launcher*: This module starts the voting process for a particular election. It stores the voting context for this election into the *Election Data* storage, allowing other elections to be concurrently performed with different parameters.
  In the case of centralised elections, it sends an "election" message to all voters. In the case of decentralised elections, it sends a "phase1" message to all voters. After receiving a "ready" message from all voters, it sends a "phase2" message.
- *Election Data*: This data storage holds all the information related to the elections still in process. Therefore, it contains their voting context, the considered candidates and the votes received, the respective (committee) voting rule, the committee size k in case of committee voting rules, the tie-breaking rule and a boolean variable which indicates if the election is decentralised or centralised.
- *Voting Communication Module*: This module extends the Jason agent communication module in order to deal with voting messages. When it receives an election, it invokes the *Voting Module* to get the agent's votes. On the other hand, when it receives a vote, it informs the *Votes Manager* about the received vote.
- *Voting Module*: This module manages the reception of an election. It votes for the considered candidates according to the agent's preferences.

– *Votes Manager*: This module manages the reception of votes. It extracts the sender's votes and stores them into the *Election Data*. As soon as the votes from all the target agents have been received, it calls the *Winner Determination Module* to solve the decision.

– *Winner Determination Module*: This module solves the winner determination problem using the information stored into the *Election Data* for the election being resolved (i.e. considered candidates, agents' votes, weights, (committee) voting rule and tie-breaking rule) Once resolved, it notifies the agent about the winner solution. In the case of decentralised elections, it sends a "ready" message to the user agent after the computation of the election result.

In our scenarios, agents can take three roles: chair role and voter role in centralised elections or user role and voter role in decentralised elections. Which modules are used by an agent depends on the type of election and on her role in the election.

In centralised elections, there will be exactly one agent who uses the votes manager module and calls the winner determination module, namely the chair agent. A centralised election is started as soon as the voter group is known, the chair knows about her role and as soon as she knows that an election is necessary. The chair determines according to some rule the agents taking part in the elections and the candidates available. That means that the chair agent calls the election launcher module with the necessary parameters as input.

In decentralised elections there is no designed chair - all voter agents use the votes manager module and call the winner determination module. A decentralised election is started as soon as the voter group is known, the user requesting the collective decision knows about her role and as soon as she knows that an election is necessary. That means that the user agent calls the election launcher.

7.3   Degree of Fulfillment

In this section, we argue how the requirements will be implemented in the architecture.

Winner Determination. The winner determination requirements can all be fulfilled by setting the corresponding parameters in the election launcher. The voting rule or committee voting rule is set as parameter in the module. The tie-breaking rule is also set in the module.

Iteration Features. As for parallel elections, the necessary parameters (candidates, votes, ...) are stored for each election into the election data storage, enabling other elections to be concurrently performed.

(De)centralised Voting. When setting the parameters for the election launcher, it is specified whether a decentralised election or a centralised election is conducted. The required modules are implemented in the Java class which defines the agent architecture.

Agent Roles. Role switching is realised as follows. Either the roles are assigned to the agents from beginning or the agents decide during runtime which role they take. If an agent takes the chair role, she initiates the voting process by sending an "election" message to all voters. If an agent takes the user role, she initiates the voting process by sending a "phase1" message to all voters.

Preference Handling. Which vote types can be used depends on the implementation of the voting module. The conversion of valuation functions into votes is conducted in the voting module.

Architecture Extensibility. The winner determination module will be implemented in such a way that it can use any voting rule.

7.4 Differences Between J-MADeM and J-Voting

Grimaldo et al. [16] aim at closing the gap between theory and actual implementation regarding the theory of multimodal social decisions by yielding an implementation of multimodal social decisions in Jason, where the multimodal social decisions are based on the MARA theory. In a similar vein, we aim to yield an implementation for common voting rules and committee voting rules in Jason.

In J-MADeM, the winner solution is determined based on a set of utility functions and the selected social welfare (Utilitarian, Egalitarian, Elitist or Nash). The winner solution in J-Voting is determined based on votes – which can take different forms – and the selected common voting rule or committee voting rule.

Note that J-MADeM considers allocations, which can be very simple but also more complex, depending on the considered situation. When considering elections in J-Voting, we assume that the agents simply agree on a candidate or a candidate set of fixed size.

Furthermore, J-Voting will allow the conduction of decentralised elections.

8   Conclusion and Outlook

In this paper, we have taken the first steps to designing a platform to support the application of voting (as a specific case of COMSOC mechanisms) in the engineering of next-generation cooperative traffic information and management systems. For the evaluation of different voting rules, we propose using a multi-agent based architecture enabling the conduction of parallel elections and the comparison of different voting rules. We propose using an adaptation of the J-MADeM architecture, J-Voting as solution approach. We contemplate implementing J-Voting as part of an extension of J-MADeM which allows modelling MADeM situations as well as elections.

J-Voting is based on the requirements for two initial scenarios, the first scenario being an example for the application of committee voting rules in traffic control. In this scenario, we consider the agreement on POI sets of fixed size for passengers of share taxis. The second scenario is an example for the application of voting rules in traffic control, where we consider the agreement on a speed value for the members of a platoon.

We will compare several voting rules and committee voting rules for the share-taxi and platoon scenarios with regard to the effects on quantities like travel time, waiting time and satisfaction of the traffic participants. To this end, we will create a library of common voting rules and combine the voting architecture with a suitable traffic simulator based on OSM data.

One aspect we plan to investigate with the help of J-Voting is the influence of allowing voters to leave the voter group if their dissatisfaction exceeds a fixed threshold. In the first simulation, we will consider the Minisum Approval rule and the Minimax Approval rule under the aspect of iterative winner determination. Both rules were investigated by Brams et al. [8] and measure the dissatisfaction for a single voter as Hamming distance between her vote and the (0,1)-vector representation of the resulting committee. The Minisum Approval rule selects a committee for which the sum of the voters' dissatisfaction values is minimal. In contrast, the Minimax Approval rule selects a committee for which the dissatisfaction of the most dissatisfied voter is minimal. If using Minisum Approval, it is possible that single voters are quite dissatisfied. If voters are allowed to leave the group if their dissatisfaction exceeds a certain threshold, this means that iterative winner determination is necessary. This can prolong the voting process. If Minimax Approval is used, fewer iterations for the winner determination should be necessary, but Minimax Approval is computationally more costly than Minisum Approval. A question which arises here is how to assign voters who leave their groups to new groups. We will consider the interdependency between voting and group formation for this situation and other situations. The environment for the first simulation will be rather simple, containing randomly created approval vectors. For the investigation of the effects on the traffic, we will combine the voting architecture with the traffic simulator.

An important aspect in the application of voting rules in traffic management is how to handle time effects. When you apply voting rules in dynamic situations, you have to ensure that the result of the election is computed in a reasonable period of time. Results in this direction could be transferred to other domains in which voting in dynamic situations is required.

We plan to consider how to extend the robust Paxos algorithm in [24] for enabling application and comparison of several voting rules and how to integrate the algorithm in J-Voting.

In the context of our research, we will also look into combinatorial voting as described in [11], i.e. voting when the set of alternatives has a combinatorial structure. In combinatorial voting, there are multiple issues and each alternative can be uniquely characterized by a vector of the values these issues take.

Furthermore, we aim to identify additional possible applications of voting rules in traffic management and to investigate the corresponding scenarios using J-Voting. A systematic analysis of the characteristics of possible scenarios and theoretical properties of voting rules will be selection criterions for further research. When considering voting rules, we will take the axiomatic method, the maximum-likelihood estimation approach and the distance rationalisability approach into account. Complexity of voting problems, i.e. winner determination, manipulation and control will also be considered.

Acknowledgement. This research has been supported by the German Research Foundation (DFG) through the Research Training Group SocialCars (GRK 1931). The focus of the SocialCars Research Training Group is on significantly improving the city's future road traffic, through cooperative approaches. This support is gratefully acknowledged.

References

1. Aseere, A.: A voting-based agent system to support personalised e-Learning in a course selection scenario. Ph.D. thesis, University of Southampton (2012)
2. Baskar, L., De Schutter, B., Hellendoorn, J., Papp, Z.: Traffic control and intelligent vehicle highway systems: a survey. IET Intell. Transport Syst. **5**(1), 38–52 (2011)
3. Bellifemine, F., Poggi, A., Rimassa, G.: JADE-A FIPA-compliant agent framework. In: Proceedings of PAAM, vol. 99, p. 33. London (1999)
4. Black, D.: On the rationale of group decision-making. J. Polit. Econ. **56**, 23–34 (1948)
5. Borda, J.C.: Mémoire sur les élections au scrutin. Histoire de L'Académie Royale des Sciences (1781)
6. Bordini, R.H., Hübner, J.F., Wooldridge, M.: Programming Multi-agent Systems in AgentSpeak using Jason, vol. 8. John Wiley & Sons, New York (2007)
7. Brams, S., Fishburn, P.C.: Approval Voting. Springer Science & Business Media, New York (2007)
8. Brams, S., Kilgour, D., Sanver, R.: A minimax procedure for negotiating multilateral treaties. In: M. Wiberg (ed.) Reasoned choices: Essays in Honor of Hannu Nurmi. Finnish Political Science Association (2004)
9. Brandt, F., Conitzer, V., Endriss, U.: Computational social choice. In: Weiss, G. (ed.) Multiagent Systems, 2nd edn, pp. 213–284. MIT Press, Cambridge (2013)
10. Chevaleyre, Y., Dunne, P.E., Endriss, U., Lang, J., Lemaitre, M., Maudet, N., Padget, J., Phelps, S., Rodriguez-Aguilar, J.A., Sousa, P.: Issues in multiagent resource allocation. Informatica (Slovenia) **30**(1), 3–31 (2006)
11. Chevaleyre, Y., Endriss, U., Lang, J., Maudet, N.: A short introduction to computational social choice. In: van Leeuwen, J., Italiano, G.F., van der Hoek, W., Meinel, C., Sack, H., Plášil, F. (eds.) SOFSEM 2007. LNCS, vol. 4362, pp. 51–69. Springer, Heidelberg (2007)
12. Condorcet, N.: Essai sur l'application de l'analyse à la probabilité des décisions redues à la pluralité des voix. Imprimerie Royale, Paris (1785)
13. Ghosh, S., Mundhe, M., Hernandez, K., Sen, S.: Voting for movies: the anatomy of a recommender system. In: Proceedings of the Third Annual Conference on Autonomous Agents, pp. 434–435. ACM (1999)
14. Grimaldo, F., Lozano, M., Barber, F.: MADeM: a multi-modal decision making for social MAS. In: Proceedings of the 7th International Joint Conference on Autonomous Agents and Multiagent Systems vol. 1, pp. 183–190. International Foundation for Autonomous Agents and Multiagent Systems (2008)
15. Grimaldo, F., Lozano, M., Barber, F.: J-MADeM, an open-source library for social decision-making. In: CCIA, pp. 207–214 (2009)

16. Grimaldo, F., Lozano, M., Barber, F., Guerra-Hernández, A.: J-MADeM v1.1: A full-fledge AgentSpeak(L) multimodal social decision library in Jason. In: The 8th European Workshop on Multi-Agent Systems (EUMAS 2010) (2010)

17. Grimaldo, F., Lozano, M., Barber, F., Guerra-Hernández, A.: Towards a model for urban mobility social simulation. Prog. Artif. Intell. **1**(2), 149–156 (2012)

18. Hardekopf, B., Kwiat, K., Upadhyaya, S.: A Decentralized Voting Algorithm for Increasing Dependability in Distributed Systems. In: 5th World Multi-Conference on Systemic, Cybernetics and Informatics (SCI2001) (2001)

19. Kang, J., Kim, W., Lee, J., Yi, K.: Design, implementation, and test of skid steering-based autonomous driving controller for a robotic vehicle with articulated suspension. J. Mech. Sci. Technol. **24**(3), 793–800 (2010)

20. Pitt, J., Kamara, L., Sergot, M., Artikis, A.: Voting in multi-agent systems. Comput. J. **49**(2), 156–170 (2006)

21. Rao, A.S.: AgentSpeak (L): BDI agents speak out in a logical computable language. In: Perram, J., Van de Velde, W. (eds.) MAAMAW 1996. LNCS, vol. 1038, pp. 42–55. Springer, Heidelberg (1996)

22. Reuter, G.J., Gray, J.: Transaction Processing: Concepts and Techniques. Morgan Kaufmann, San Mateo (1993)

23. Rothe, J., Baumeister, D., Lindner, C., Rothe, I.: Einführung in Computational Social Choice. Springer-Verlag, Heidelberg (2011)

24. Sanderson, D., Pitt, J.: Institutionalised Consensus in Vehicular Networks: Executable Specification and Empirical Validation. In: 2012 IEEE Sixth International Conference on Self-Adaptive and Self-Organizing Systems Workshops (SASOW), pp. 71–76. IEEE (2012)

25. Vasirani, M., Ossowski, S.: A market-inspired approach to reservation-based urban road traffic management. In: Proceedings of The 8th International Conference on Autonomous Agents and Multiagent Systems-vol. 1, pp. 617–624. International Foundation for Autonomous Agents and Multiagent Systems (2009)

Trading Strategies of a Champion Agent in a Multiagent Smart Grid Simulation Platform

Serkan Özdemir[✉] and Rainer Unland

DAWIS, Universität Duisburg-Essen, Schützenbahn 70, 45127 Essen, Germany
{serkan.oezdemir,rainer.unland}@icb.uni-due.de

Abstract. Local producers and storage units will play a major role in the future electricity grid along with the challenge of sustainability. For this reason, smart grid simulations are needed to forecast the challenges of two-way information and energy flow. The Power Trading Agent Competition (Power TAC) provides an open source simulation platform to enable and verify various smart grid studies from the perspective of sustainability. Besides, an annual competition is hosted in which autonomous agents trade in energy markets and make profits. AgentUDE won the Power TAC 2014 Final as a broker utilizing an adaptive agent. This paper details the trading strategies of AgentUDE and analyzes the tournament.

Keywords: Multiagent · Agent broker · Trading Agent · Smart grid · Simulation

1 Introduction

Smart grid has been turning into an exciting area for researchers and business entities as new power players, such as electric vehicles and power to gas units, involve in the electricity grid that make it possible to store electricity in a distributed way. On the other side, some of governments started to declare their energy transition policies such as Energiewende in Germany: Within Energiewende, 17 nuclear power plants will be permanently shut down by the end of 2022 [9]. Meanwhile, fossil fuel based electricity production is likely to be replaced with renewable energy production, which has a fitful energy production volume [5]. In the light of this energy transition policies, information and energy flow between these energy actors have to be simulated within a realistic smart grid simulation to identify future challenges and propose solutions. Power TAC provides an open source, smart grid simulation with the aim of addressing a solution to this challenge through making autonomous brokers trade in a smart grid environment. Alongside, it simulates the typical energy markets, such as wholesale, retail and balancing markets (details are explained in Sect. 3) [1].

This paper addresses the wholesale market, retail market and balancing activities of AgentUDE. In particular, the main focus of this paper is the aggressive tariff strategy and contributions of tariff fees where analyses showed that AgentUDE gained the serious portion of its cash balance through early withdrawal penalty (EWP) and bonus

© Springer International Publishing Switzerland 2015
J.P. Müller et al. (Eds.): MATES 2015, LNAI 9433, pp. 218–232, 2015.
DOI: 10.1007/978-3-319-27343-3_12

payment (BP). AgentUDE won the Power TAC 2014 Final games as the newest participant among seven brokers by earning the most profit. Behind AgentUDE, cwiBroker and CrocodileAgent took the second and third places, respectively [7, 8].

The structure of the paper is as follows. Specifics of Power TAC 2014 Final games are introduced in Sect. 2. Afterwards, related work is given in Sect. 3. Section 4 is dedicated to AgentUDE that details the retail, wholesale and balancing activities. Future work is identified in Sect. 5. Finally, the paper is concluded in Sect. 6 with an outlook to Power TAC 2015 Final games.

2   Power Trading Agent Competition and 2014 Final Games

The Power Trading Agent Competition (Power TAC) is an open source smart grid simulation platform which consists of a wholesale market, a tariff market, a distribution utility and a number of costumer and producer models. Autonomous brokers are also allowed to trade remotely in these markets. The wholesale market is a typical day-ahead market where the large generator companies, renewable production farms and brokers place their bids and asks for the future time slots. The retail market allows brokers to build their customer portfolio by means of offering multiple tariffs to local producers and consumers. In between retail and wholesale markets, the distribution utility keeps track of supply and demand, and charges brokers for their energy imbalances. Customers are simulated as independent consumer and producer models for goods including electric vehicles, households, storage units and solar panels. The interaction between customers and brokers takes place in the retail market through tariff subscriptions. Figure 1 illustrates the schematic landscape of the Power TAC environment.

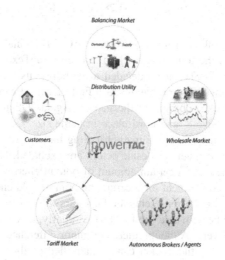

Fig. 1. Components of the Power TAC as well as autonomous brokers. Each component represents a different module.

Brokers represent the business entities in the simulation platform. They offer tariffs through the tariff market, and their goal is to increase the number of their subscribed customers. With this aim, they have to trade in the wholesale market, in order to match their total supply and demand for a particular future hour. Enabled future time slots are declared by the wholesale market in advance. At the beginning, each game starts under monopoly conditions, with a built-in broker called *default broker*. In order to create initial market environment, this broker trade in the markets before the login of autonomous brokers. This interval is called *bootstrap period*. Afterwards, the competing brokers are allowed to join in the game. Note that timing in the simulation platform is not continuous. Rather, the simulation time progresses in discrete time slots. Each time slot is equal to five seconds in the real world, and one hour in the simulation world [1].

In the Power TAC 2014 Final games, 72 games were played, and 7 brokers competed. Out of these, 16 games were 8-sized, 35 games were 5-sized and 21 games were 3-sized. As stated already, Power TAC has a built-in *default broker* which is always included in all game sizes. All the statistics and data that are included in the paper are collected through the extraction of game logs which are produced after each game by Power TAC server.

Table 1. Official results of Power TAC 2014 Final. Values represent the normalized total profits of brokers. Final ranking is formulized through summing all game sizes [10].

Broker	Game Size 3	Game Size 5	Game Size 8	Total
AgentUDE	0.279	1.499	1.976	3.754
cwiBroker	1.557	1.026	0.600	3.183
CrocodileAgent	0.952	-0.893	-0.560	-0.501
Maxon	-0.921	0.142	-0.643	-1.423
Mertacor	-0.945	-0.492	-0.865	-2.302
coldbroker	-0.922	-1.281	-0.509	-2.712

Table 1 shows the official results of Power TAC 2014 Final games [10]. In total, 7 brokers competed in the tournament. Unfortunately, TacTex is not included in the official result since the TacTex team decided to withdraw its broker from the tournament due to some connectivity problems. At a first glance, it can be clearly seen that AgentUDE and cwiBroker dominated the games. AgentUDE took the first place in game size 5 and game size 8, and third place in game size 3.

Figure 2 illustrates the wholesale market trading patterns of the brokers, in which generator companies and other wholesale actors are excluded. Here, a negative price indicates broker payment for a certain amount of bought energy. Similarly, a positive price refers to a received payment for a certain amount of sold energy. Colors indicate the time proximity. Red color represents the far future in the simulation time, at which contracted energy will be delivered (up to 24 h). Similarly, blue color indicates the near future for a sooner delivery. Although there are minor differences between game sizes, the main characteristics of the market can be identified easily: As seen on the graph above, the cheapest energy is usually available at the last enabled time slot. After the last enabled time slot, the most expensive interval starts: It means that wholesale energy is sold immediately whenever it is available.

Fig. 2. Cleared wholesale market prices of brokers.

The area to the right of the origin shows the selling activities of the brokers. It is not as active as the left side, since the priority of a broker is to match demand and supply. Very few brokers, such as Maxon, preferred to make brokerage in the market. Individual performances are detailed in Sect. 4.

Figure 3 presents the price trends of the brokers in the retail market. Apparently, brokers have their own individual price regimes, depending on their customer portfolio. What can be clearly seen here is that the hard competition takes place around 0.06 €/kWh. Further analysis can be found in the next section.

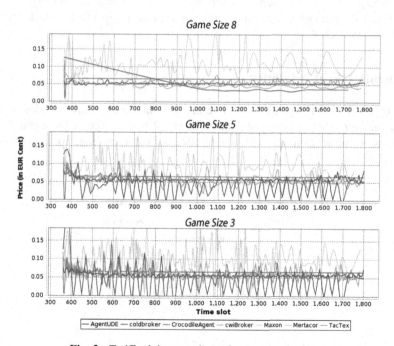

Fig. 3. Tariff minimum values of competing brokers.

3   Related Work

Power TAC publications can be classified into two groups: Reviews and broker descriptions. One of the broker papers has been published by the TacTex team to introduce their broker which won the Power TAC 2013 Final games. As explained in this paper [3], TacTex uses Markov Decision Processes to minimize the energy costs in the wholesale market. Besides, it optimizes the future demands, prices and predicted energy costs in order to pick an appropriate tariff among pre-created, fixed-rate candidate tariffs. Another broker publication by the AstonTAC team focuses on wholesale market trading, using Markov Decision Processes for price optimization and Non-Homogeneous Hidden Markov Models for future predictions [4]. The last broker paper is by the cwiBroker team, which was very successful in 2013 and 2014 Final games: They took the second places in both tournaments, utilizing a trading technique that uses the equilibrium in continuous markets [8]. The most comprehensive review paper to date has been published by Jurica Babic and Vedran Podobnik for the Power TAC 2014 Final games. In this paper, brokers are compared based on the pre-defined key performance indicators (KPI). Besides, retail and wholesale market activities, including market shares and proximities of the future time slots, are discussed in detail [7].

Compared to the broker approaches above, AgentUDE implements an adaptive method in the wholesale market. On the retailer side, it uses an empirical strategy, which is inspired by the German electricity retail market. Within this strategy, tariff fees are speculated along with aggressive tariff publication. These methods and strategies are detailed in Sect. 4.

4   AgentUDE at a Glance

The broker abilities of AgentUDE can be divided into three groups: wholesale, retail and balancing market activities. As shown in Fig. 4 below, AgentUDE evaluates and completes its basic facilities with a time slot. In the following, we address these activitiy groups.

Fig. 4. AgentUDE activities in a time slot.

The wholesale trading module of AgentUDE uses an adaptive method which tracks the past market data. Thanks to this method, the broker is able to catch the market trends regardless of weather conditions. However, statistics of the competition showed that wholesale market costs of brokers are very close to each other (See Table 2). Therefore retail activities are detailed more due to the diversity in tariff publication policies of the brokers. AgentUDE uses an aggressive tariff strategy by means of offering the cheapest tariff and speculating on tariff parameters (contract length, EWP and BP). There are two main goals in the retail strategy: To provoke other brokers to lower their tariffs and incentivate customers to change their tariffs. Eventually, this liquidity triggers the tariff penalties and results in profit. The results of this strategy are given in the next sub-sections.

Before turning to the wholesale market activities, an indicator used by AgentUDE has to be introduced here. It indicates the profit achievement acceleration of the broker, where a higher value means better profit performance. The idea behind it is to improve decisions in tariff creations and wholesale market activities. The following formula (1) evaluates the *rhythm value* at time slot t:

$$R_t = R_{t-1} + \omega * \left(\frac{\left(c_t - \sum_{n=0}^{5} \left(\frac{c_t - n}{5} \right) \right)}{c_t} \right) \tag{1}$$

Where R is the rhythm at given time slot, C is cash balance and ω is weight which is set experimentally. The formula above returns a value based on the cash positions. This rhythm is smoothed with a weight value to avoid bounces. The main impact of this parameter on the tariff publication cycle and profit margin given in Formula 3.

4.1   Wholesale Market Activities

Wholesale trading is a vital issue for all brokers to minimize their imbalanced energy. Additionally, brokers are challenged to buy the cheapest possible energy in order to be flexible against their competitors. In the end, customers would like to subscribe to the cheapest tariff available from their profitability perspective.

Price prediction takes place in two steps: The base price is a predicted utilizing past data. Afterwards, the final price is differentiated using the base price. Following formula (2) returns the base price at current time slot t for a future delivery at time slot T.

$$B_{t,T} = \left(B_{t-1,T} + C_{t-1,T} \right) * (1 - \omega) \\ + \left(F_{t,T} + max_t C(t,T) - min_t C(t,T) + R(t,T) \right) * \omega \tag{2}$$

Where B is a base price for the given current time slot t and future time slot T. C stands for the market equilibrium price for t and T. R is risk function that contributes to the price depending on time slot proximity. F indicates constants such as market mean and averages. The weight, ω is updated using the rhythm value which is given in Formula 1.

Fig. 5. Cleared bids and asks of AgentUDE.

Figure 5 illustrates the cleared bids and asks of AgentUDE. Overall, bidding density of AgentUDE is narrowed between 15 and 25 EUR/MWh. Consequently, the average buying price is realized at 22.7 EUR/MWh and selling price at 28.9 EUR/MWh (See Table 2). Surely, these cost prices make sense with imbalance activities. The cost can be easily decreased with a stingy bidding policy. However, this would eventually lead to poor imbalance performance.

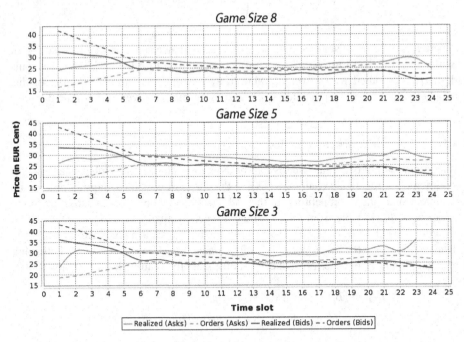

Fig. 6. Average cleared wholesale prices and trading performance of AgentUDE.

Figure 6 illustrates the prediction performance of AgentUDE in different game sizes. In 8-sized games, the success rate is higher than other game sizes since the market is more stable due to the large number of participants. Before fifth future time slot, selling prices are always less than buying prices. Therefore, this area is regarded as a risk area due to approaching delivery time and brokers may submit extraordinary prices in order to avoid imbalance penalties. These *panic orders* can clearly be seen in Fig. 2 as blue colored prices that are close to 100 EUR/MWh.

Table 2. Wholesale market averages of the brokers.

Broker	P_{bids} (€/MWh)	P_{asks} (€/MWh)
AgentUDE	22.70	28.90
cwiBroker	22.49	27.60
CrocodileAgent	43.11	13.08
Maxon	23.15	53.30
Mertacor	26.36	–
coldbroker	27.87	27.49
default broker	29.10	26.49
TacTex	22.94	19.81

Table 2 lists the wholesale bidding and selling costs of brokers. P_{bids} and P_{asks} indicate the average bidding and asking prices. AgentUDE has a market cost around 22.7 EUR/MWh and asking performance of 28.9 EUR/MWh, where the consumption share is 22.9 % of the total energy distribution. In this landscape, AgentUDE is the second best broker after cwiBroker in terms of the lowest market cost. However, these values are very close to each other and do not provide a serious contribution to the overall profits of the brokers. Instead, we take a closer look at retail activities in the next section, which makes AgentUDE stand out against the competition among other brokers.

4.2 Retail Market Activities

AgentUDE applied a new strategy on the retail side, which is not used by other brokers: Publishing aggressive tariffs with the lowest tariff values and customer binding tariff fees such as EWP and BP. Over the course of the competition, this strategy provoked other brokers to publish cheaper tariffs, which in turn triggered the EWP's of AgentUDE tariffs. As a whole, AgentUDE forced its customers to change their tariffs. In the end, this strategy contributed about 20 % to overall cash balance (See Fig. 7).

Table 3 shows the tariff statistics of the brokers. $N_{tariffs}$ is the total published tariffs. *Frequency* indicates the publication cycle in terms of time slot. M_{cons} is the mean price of consumption tariffs. Similarly, M_{prod} is the mean of production tariffs. S_{cons} is the average price of energy that is sold to customers. Likewise, S_{prod} refers to the price for bought energy. Finally, E_{cons} and E_{prod} are energy consumption and production shares of brokers, respectively.

As seen in Table 3, AgentUDE published most of the tariffs having a publication cycle of 27. After AgentUDE, Mertacor and TacTex have most of the tariffs. On the other hand, only AgentUDE, CrocodileAgent and the default broker published

Table 3. Tariff activities of the brokers in Power TAC 2014 Final.

Broker	$N_{tariffs}$	Freq.	M_{cons} (C/kWh)	M_{prod} (C/kWh)	S_{cons} (C/kWh)	S_{prod} (C/kWh)	E_{cons} (%)	E_{prod} (%)
AgentUDE	3791	27	6.0	1.52	6.3	1.52	22.9	30.9
cwiBroker	1071	97	7.8	–	7.8	–	21.5	–
Crocodile	1106	94	7.1	1.58	9.7	1.58	13.4	25.6
Maxon	1426	73	522	–	7.7	–	7.0	–
Mertacor	2732	38	7.3	–	6.7	–	4.4	–
coldbroker	607	171	5.3	–	5.4	–	8.2	–
default broker	144	725	50	1.50	50	1.50	0.2	43.5
TacTex	1670	62	7.3	–	5.6	–	22.4	–

production tariffs. However, the production tariff policy of AgentUDE is restricted with a simple rule. Only if the sum of minimum production tariff value and distribution fee is less than wholesale market cost, production tariffs are published. Otherwise, local producers are ignored.

All the games start with a number of uncertainties such as market status (production and consumption capacities) and the number of competitors. First of all, broker agents are not aware of their competitors' trading strategies. Therefore, initial tariffs have to be set carefully. Following piece of code states the initial publications of AgentUDE.

```
public void createInitialConsumerTariffs()
{
    tVal = MM + DF + PM + BC()
    FOR tNum = 1 to 5
        CALL publishTariff(tVal + tNum, EWP() - tNum)
    END FOR
}
```

Here, *MM* and *DF* are market mean price and distribution fee, respectively. These parameters are announced at the beginning of each game. Integer value of tariff number, *tNum* is included to "publishTariff" method in order to create different tariff variations. PM is profit margin, which is set heuristically. *BC* represents a function which takes the number of brokers into account: In case of high participation, tariff value, abbreviated as *tVal*, is decreased. According to the Power TAC specification [1], only the first five tariffs of each power type are visible to customers. Therefore five tariffs are initially published for the maximum exposure. Early withdrawal penalty is formulated as a function of *EWP* based on the number of brokers. Due to Inertia parameter described as $I_a = I * (1-2^{-n})$ and valued between 0 and 1, customers are highly sensitive to the new tariffs at the beginning of the games. Therefore, *EWP*'s are extremely useful fees to bind customers to the tariff. Eventually, customers' loyalty increases due to the *Inertia* parameter and they usually continue to stay within the tariff even if the tariff is not the cheapest one. As a part of retailer strategy, AgentUDE always set *EWP* if the tariff value, to be published, is the cheapest one in the market.

```
public void improveConsumerTariffs()
{
    CALL monopolyTest()
    CALL revokeUselessTariffs()
    IF isPublicationCycle() = True
      Return
    ELSE
      IF getSubscriptionRate() < getCriticalRate()
        IF getCompetitorsMinimum() < getCost()
          CALL publishTariff(getCost(), NULL)
        ELSE
          CALL publishTariff(getCompetitorsMinimum(), EWP())
        END IF
      END IF
    END IF
}
```

The simplified algorithm above describes the process how AgentUDE publishes new tariffs. Concisely, this method publishes two kind of consumer tariffs. If the offered price is the cheapest one among other tariffs, then it is published with a EWP fee. Otherwise, EWP is not set and tariff value is adjusted considering the market cost.

AgentUDE employs a number of controllers during the tariff publication process. One of these controllers is the "monopolyTest" method. This method is triggered if a price gap appears between AgentUDE and its closest competitor. Another controller is the "revokeUselessTariffs" method, which removes harmful tariffs. It is quite possible in a game that wholesale clearing prices increase due to high demand and weather conditions. In this case, some of the older tariffs might be outdated and harmful in terms of profitability. This method simply removes such tariffs.

Market cost is calculated by the "getCost" method and takes cleared wholesale market prices and distribution fee into account. Formula (3) shows the definition of the value computed by the method:

$$getCost_t = \frac{\left(\sum_{n=0}^{60} \sum_{m=1}^{24} P_{m,n}\right)}{\left(\sum_{n=0}^{60} \sum_{m=1}^{24} E_{m,n}\right)} + DF + PM \tag{3}$$

Where DF and PM represent the distribution fee and profit margin, respectively. P and E refers to total money and energy transactions and the formula above runs up to the most recent 60 h and 24 enabled future auctions of the wholesale market. Consequently, the fraction yields an average cost price by means of dividing the total payment to the total energy. Another controller is the "getCompetitorsMinimum" method, which scans the tariff repository and identifies the competitors' minimum tariff with a small margin. Other controllers are "getCriticalRate" and "getSubscriptionRate"; they represent the goal and current situation, respectively. The critical rate is the minimum percentage of total customers that AgentUDE has to reach; the subscription rate refers to the percentage of currently subscribed customers.

The subscription rate and critical rate shape EWP fees. The number of subscribed customers is proportional to EWP fees, based on the Formula (4). All together, the calculation of early withdrawal penalty fee can be formulated as follows:

$$EWP_t = (getCriticalRate() * T) * \varphi - S * \omega \qquad (4)$$

Where T is the number of total customers in the competition environment, and S is the number of subscribed customers. The weights, φ and ω differ based on the power type.

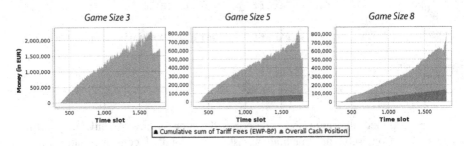

Fig. 7. Total cash position and cumulative sum of EWP and BP.

Figure 7 shows the overall cash balance and collected money from tariff fees as a result of the strategy. In the same figure, red area shows the cumulative sum of tariff fees which is the approximately 25 % of the overall cash position. This rate increases in 8-sized games due to stiff competition. In other words, high number of tariffs means higher liquidity in terms of customer subscriptions and withdrawals (see Fig. 9).

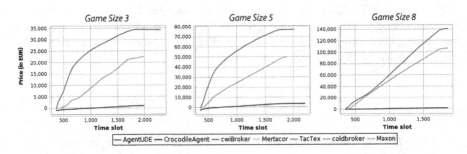

Fig. 8. Average cumulative profits that are collected from EWP and BP.

Figure 8 compares the tariff fee performances of all the brokers. Surprisingly, only AgentUDE and TacTex benefitted from tariff fees. Here, maximum profit achieved from 8-sized games.

In order to earn more profit from this strategy, some requirements have to be met: Active customers and a stiff competition. First, customers have to see some profitable tariffs on the desk before leaving their current retailer. If not, customers tend to ignore the available tariffs and stick to their tariff. In this case, the strategy offered by

AgentUDE does not work well. Second, a broker has to offer competitive tariffs, so that customers can see them and change their tariffs if it is really profitable for them. To illustrate this analysis, competitive and non-competitive brokers are tested in 3-sized games below.

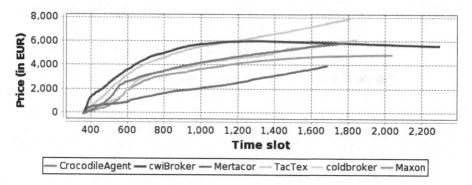

Fig. 9. Cumulative tariff fee earnings of AgentUDE that are collected through 3-sized games.

Figure 9 draws the tariff fee earnings of AgentUDE as a result of 3-sized games between AgentUDE and the respected broker. Apparently, TacTex, CrocodileAgent and cwiBroker provided the most profit to AgentUDE while Mertacor, Maxon and coldbroker did less. In the same fashion, this symbiotic relationship is proportional to the official results given in previous sections. Another result is that TacTex, cwiBroker and AgentUDE offer the most profitable tariffs to the customers and convince them to change their tariffs.

4.3   Balancing Activities

Brokers have to meet their demand and supply. If not, they may lose the largest portion of their profits by paying huge imbalance fees. The most challenging issue is to predict future consumptions. AgentUDE uses the consumption data of customers to make predictions. However, this method does not always give the best result due to changing conditions, including weather. Balancing market sends signals to brokers regarding their imbalance status. Accordingly, needed energy is calculated as the sum of predicted consumption and imbalance signal. The final amount of needed energy is smoothed and submitted to the market.

Figure 10 illustrates the cumulative imbalance volumes. In this figure, negative and positive volumes are regarded as absolute values and they are summed regardless of their signs. Apparently, 3-sized games give the best result for AgentUDE. Since the figure illustrates the volumes, increasing number of participants makes it difficult for AgentUDE to adjust its imbalance due to changing demand. Besides, customers have more tariff options in game size 8 in comparison to game size 3. Therefore, withdrawal or sign-up activities of customers eventually result in last-minute imbalances.

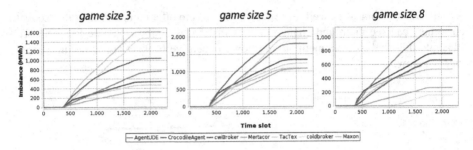

Fig. 10. Cumulative volume of negative and positive imbalances.

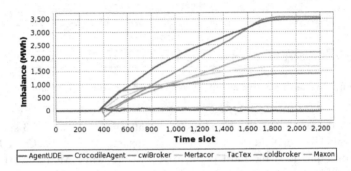

Fig. 11. Cumulative sum of positive and negative imbalances (all game sizes).

Figure 11 shows the average imbalances where negative and positive values are summed. AgentUDE draws a flat line due to wave-style imbalance activity. In other words, positive and negative values are almost same. Figure 12 illustrates the overall imbalance payments from brokers to the distribution utility. AgentUDE is the second best broker in terms of paying the least money to the distribution utility. However this payment only consists of imbalance penalties since the total imbalance energy is close to the zero line.

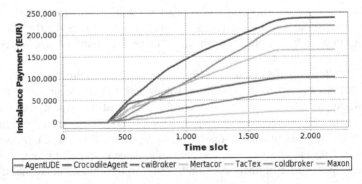

Fig. 12. Total imbalance payments from brokers to distribution utility (all game sizes).

For a typical negative imbalance, brokers have to pay the sum of penalty fee and price of imbalanced energy. TacTex and cwiBroker paid 100 k EUR for their 1700 MWh and 1450 MWh imbalanced energy, respectively. If a comparison is needed at 70 k EUR, where the imbalanced energy of AgentUDE is almost zero, TacTex and cwiBroker paid 70 k EUR plus 17.6 EUR/MWh and 20.6 EUR/MWh, respectively for their negative imbalance. With respect to the wholesale market costs shown in Table 2, TacTex and cwiBroker had a good deal on the balancing market over AgentUDE.

5   Future Work

AgentUDE seems to be a promising broker. However, there are issues to be improved upon. Following points are the most important topics that are expected to be solved for the upcoming Power TAC 2015 games.

One of the most important issues is efficiency in wholesale trading. AgentUDE still loses sizeable amounts of money through its relatively inefficient bids and asks. Therefore, price predictions in the wholesale market ought to take weather forecasts into consideration, in order to catch such future trends.

A second improvement regards the utilization of unused power figures. In the Power TAC environment, there are many new generation power actors, such as storage units, controllable customers. However, most of the brokers do not use them. No doubt, utilizing these components improves the efficiency of the broker.

Another issue is capability of surviving in a longer game period: As asked for the future competitions, AgentUDE has to be compatible for longer games.

6   Conclusion

This paper covers the basic strategies of AgentUDE and results of the competition from the business perspective, as a winning agent in Power TAC 2014 Final. However, success is a relative term, especially on such a dynamic and progressive platform. The participating teams get stronger year by year, and change their strategies. As a result, the competitiveness of the game is raised aggressively. For this reason, comparisons are valid only for the specific releases of participating brokers.

As has been noted in the wholesale market section, the gaps between the market performances of brokers are very close to each other. It is clearly seen that all the brokers have a decent market performance based on their customer profiles and risk levels. What placed AgentUDE one step ahead are its competitive and aggressive tariff strategies. In addition, the results showed that AgentUDE earned the serious portion of its profit through tariff fee speculation. This strategy was never used before by another broker and turned AgentUDE into a more competitive and flexible competitor. Lastly, the Power TAC 2014 Final showed that it has an enormous benchmark potential for smart grid studies. Therefore, we kindly invite new teams to take part in this competition.

References

1. Ketter, W., Collins, J., Reddy, P., Weerdt, M.: The 2014 Power Trading Agent Competition. ERIM Report Series (2014)
2. Ketter, W., Collins, J., Reddy, P.: Power TAC: A competitive economic simulation of the smart grid. Energ. Econ. **39**, 262–270 (2013)
3. Urieli, D., Stone, P.: TacTex'13: a champion adaptive power trading agent. In: Proceedings of the Twenty-Eighth AAAI Conference on Artificial Intelligence, pp. 465–471 (2014)
4. Kuate, R.T., He, M., Chli, M., Wang, H.H.: An intelligent broker agent for energy trading: an MDP approach. In: Proceedings of the Twenty-Third International Joint Conference on Artificial Intelligence, pp. 234–240 (2014)
5. Federal Environmental Agency (FEA). Energieziel 2050: 100 % Strom aus erneuerbaren Quellen. http://www.umweltbundesamt.de/publikationen/energieziel-2050. Accessed 4 November 2014
6. Somani, A., Tesfatsion, L.: An agent based test bed study of wholesale power market performance measures. IEEE Comput. Intell. Mag. **3**, 56–72 (2008)
7. Babic, J., Podobnik, V.: An analysis of power trading agent competition 2014. In: Ceppi, S., David, E., Podobnik, V., Robu, V., Shehory, O., Stein, S., Vetsikas, I.A. (eds.) AMEC/TADA 2013 and 2014. LNBIP, vol. 187, pp. 1–15. Springer, Heidelberg (2014)
8. Liefers, B., Hoogland, J., Poutré, H.L.: A successful broker agent for power TAC. In: Ceppi, S., David, E., Podobnik, V., Robu, V., Shehory, O., Stein, S., Vetsikas, I.A. (eds.) AMEC/TADA 2013 and 2014. LNBIP, vol. 187, pp. 99–113. Springer, Heidelberg (2014)
9. Morris, C., Pehnt, M.: Energy Transition: The German Energiewende. Heinrich Böll Stiftung (2014)
10. Power Trading Agent Competition, http://www.powertac.org. Accessed 2 December 2015

Agent-Based Decision Support for Allocating Caregiving Resources in a Dementia Scenario

Tobias Widmer[✉] and Marc Premm

Information Systems 2, University of Hohenheim, Stuttgart, Germany
{tobias.widmer,marc.premm}@uni-hohenheim.de

Abstract. Due to the increasing number of Dementia patients, the overall costs for caregiving has grown by 32 % between 2002 and 2008. The efficient use of smart decision support systems for managing ambulant care and mobile nursing services that provide professional care for Dementia patients is an important challenge to reduce cost and increase service quality. The optimal allocation of caregiving resources from different mobile nursing service firms to a growing number of Dementia patients, however, is a difficult problem in the healthcare domain. We approach this problem from a multiagent systems perspective by designing and implementing a distributed decision support system that utilizes an auction-based protocol for allocating caregiving resources subject to Dementia-specific service attributes. We demonstrate the usefulness of the proposed protocol by an early stage prototype implementation presenting the system's proof-of-concept.

Keywords: Decision support · Multiagent systems · Auctions

1 Introduction

The increasing number of Dementia patients has caused the overall costs for caregiving to grow by 32 % between 2002 and 2008. The World Alzheimer Report [1] unveils that in year 2010, a total of US$ 239 Billion were spent for caregiving services in Dementia. More than 80 % of all caregivers for Dementia patients state that they frequently experience high levels of stress and almost half report that they suffer from depression [2].

Agent-based software solutions offer a potential base for supporting both Dementia patients and professional caregivers in a wide range of applications. For example, the optimization of the visiting schedules and the provisioning of medical assistance for Dementia patients in geriatric residences have been realized by designing decision support systems by means of multiagent systems. These agents facilitate the caregivers' and physicians' work by providing updated information about patients and emergencies, as well as historical data [3]. In addition, caregiving resources can be represented by means of nursing care service models to design language extensions in high-level decision support systems [4].

The optimal allocation of caregiving resources among a growing number of Dementia patients is a difficult problem in the healthcare sector. Patients with differing disease stages require caregiving services from professional caregivers at different competency levels. More advanced stages of the Dementia disease, for example,

© Springer International Publishing Switzerland 2015
J.P. Müller et al. (Eds.): MATES 2015, LNAI 9433, pp. 233–248, 2015.
DOI: 10.1007/978-3-319-27343-3_13

demands family members to bear the full caregiving burden– often at the cost of their own health condition. On the other hand, caregiving professionals employed by different mobile nursing service firms are subject to highly varying working environments and scheduling conflicts. In addition, changing personnel of professional caregiving network institutions require access to sensitive patient health data which often leads to nonprofessional handling of health-related information subject to strict privacy. Hence, multiple caregivers from different mobile nursing services offer their services to a range of Dementia patients at varying disease stages, subject to heterogeneous service attributes.

We address this problem by designing an agent-based decision support system that implements an auction-based communication protocol for efficient caregiving resource allocation subject to a set of Dementia-specific service attributes. Resource allocation is a well-established field in multiagent systems research [5]. Hence, we propose a software system in which each individual actor is represented by an intelligent software agent that acts on behalf of its user (patient respectively caregiver). The emerging multiagent system captures two distinct features. First, it respects privacy-aware information sharing. Second, the allocation process is based on a double-sided auction which achieves a socially optimal allocation of caregiving resources across multiple patients and professional caregivers from different mobile nursing service firms. A generic overview of the described setting is presented in Fig. 1.

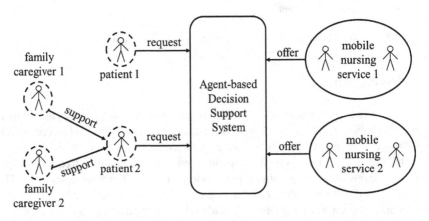

Fig. 1. Agent-based decision support system for allocating caregiving resources.

This research is conducted in accordance to the design science paradigm [6]. The objectives are to: (1) develop and implement an auction-based protocol for allocating Dementia caregiving resources in multiagent systems (method artifact) and (2) evaluate this artifact in a Dementia scenario with multiple patients and caregivers (scenario-based evaluation). The contribution of this research is the design and the initial prototype implementation of an agent-based decision support system for supporting the caregiving allocation among Dementia patients and their caregivers.

The remainder of this paper is structured as follows: In Sect. 2, we review the extant literature related to our research. In Sect. 3, we present the multi-attribute double auction protocol for allocating caregiving resources. In Sect. 4, we report the scenario-based evaluation of the protocol within the initial prototype implementation. Section 5 concludes the paper and gives an outlook of future work.

2 Literature Review

We discuss extant literature on decision support in eHealth and auction-based resource allocation approaches and examine the allocation of caregiving resources from a multiagent system perspective.

2.1 Decision Support in eHealth

The support of patients suffering from Dementia with the help of electronic devices has been analyzed and developed since the emergence of modern IT. There is a lot of work in literature that tries to support the family caregiver or directly the patient itself with computer supported guidance. In one of the first approaches, Brennan et al. developed the electronic support ComputerLink and showed in field experiment that the use of computer decision support for home caregivers could reduce isolation and enhance decision making skills [7, 8]. However, the individual intensity of system usage significantly varied between different end-users. Also, the static implementation has been replaced by the use of adaptive and intelligent systems in the healthcare section [23]. The multiagent systems paradigm suits well for designing improved decision support systems that are able to represent the interest of each individual actor. Schuele et al. present a method that enables end users represented by software agents to cooperate in the decision making process still ensuring data security and privacy for the participants [9]. A similar approach has been presented by Corchado et al. with the stronger focus on the monitoring aspect. The "Alzheimer Multi-Agent System" enables nurses to optimize and dynamically adapt the working time and guarantees that each patient assigned to a nurse receives the right care [3]. However, multi-attribute patient-nurse allocation with multiple participants is not considered. With an optimizing approach from Operations Research, Lanzarone and Matta [10] study the problem of assigning the right caregiver to each patient by an analytical approach to provide decision support of healthcare management with a focus on hospitals. Aktas et al. presented a similar approach [11]. From the perspective of one professional caregiving provider all information relevant for the problem optimization is available. However, this precondition is not available in scenarios with multiple parties that have conflicting interests like on a market for caregiving resources.

While the previously discussed approaches support only the work of the family or the professional caregiver, the correlation between both also has to be considered for an optimal system performance. For instance, at more severe stages of the disease family members have to be replaced by professional caregivers because the caregiving burden exceeds the family caregiver's capacity. This requires an efficient resource allocation that includes the interest of all parties involved. Couch et al. present a model that involves time and money for the allocation of caregiving resources [12]. The authors examined different household types with family caregivers and their response on the circumstances of the dementia patient. The study shows that the response is strongly influenced by economic considerations and states that future demand for professional caregivers that may help family caregivers will increase. Bargaining approaches for family caregivers' resources in intergenerational household formations have been examined by Pezzin and Schone [13]. The theoretical framework includes one single elderly parent's well-being as well as the daughter's time used to serve in caregiving and in labor market participation.

Bearing in mind the monetary aspects of Dementia worldwide, one may not lose sight of the disease itself. In any case, high-priority tasks such as assistance at meals must be performed and cannot be shifted or even ignored by any allocation process. One method that copes with the issue of prioritizing tasks in home caring scenarios is presented by Hirdes et al. The method for assigning priority levels (MAPLe) is used to categorize the need for caregiving activities of a patient [14]. The priorities are set on a discrete scale from "low" to "very high" and were evaluated in numerous countries. MAPLe furnishes an algorithm to set the appropriate priorities and can be connected with an agent-based approach to ensure data security and privacy issues. Together with a resource allocation approach that involves additional factors like time, money, or caregiving skills, the overall efficiency of the caregiving system is significantly improved. Since one major problem of the task aligning family and professional caregivers is the absence of a central instance that holds all necessary information, the method needed has to deal with the distributed nature of this problem.

2.2   Auction-Based Approaches in Resource Allocation

There are few approaches available that incorporate the previously stated requirements. One prevalent possibility that is commonly used in resource allocation problems is the design of an auction. Auctions support the distributed nature of the problem with various groups and participants following different goals and, thus, inherent different utility functions. New mechanisms even support the coincident usage of multiple attributes [15] and, hence, include multiple attributes such as time, money, priority and caregiving skills.

In multiagent systems research, auctions have become a popular means to efficiently allocate resources among software agents [5]. Auction-based approaches promise a significant increase in efficiency when allocating resources in agent-based systems. Such agent-based decision support systems allow for increasing the efficiency in the context of allocating caregiving resources to patients. Therefore, what is still missing is an auction-based approach that uses multiagent technology to cope with the efficient allocation of caregiving resources of multiple caregiver or caregiving facilities to numerous patients. For this setup, double auctions have been proven to outperform other mechanisms and are also well-suited for the use with a multiagent system representing real world actors [16].

Paulussen et al. take a game-theoretic perspective to analyze an intra-unit scheduling problem in hospitals [20–22]. In their work, patients and hospital resources (e.g., physicians, medical devices) are represented by self-interested software agents who coordinate with each other to resolve each individual's goal conflicts. Multiple competing market participants on both sides of the market, however, are not considered in their work.

3   Multi-attribute Double Auction Protocol

This section introduces the protocol used by the multiagent system for allocating caregiving resources among participating agents. We start by laying out the overall software architecture of the decision support system, followed by an analysis of the Dementia-specific requirements to the allocation of caregiving resources. Then, we present the formal model of the underlying double auction and describe the high-level communication protocol of the multiagent system.

3.1   Software Architecture

The overall software architecture of the multiagent system implementation is presented in Fig. 2. Dementia patients and caregiving professionals interact via individualized portals accessible through an Internet browser or a mobile application. External interfaces allow for communication and interaction with the actual multiagent subsystem which constitutes the core of the prototype implementation. Within the multiagent subsystem, each actor (i.e., patients and caregivers) is represented as a software agent in the proposed approach. These agents are able to perform autonomous actions in order to pursue its individual objectives [17].

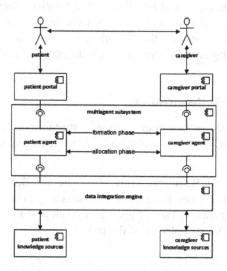

Fig. 2. Software architecture of the multiagent system implementation.

The multiagent subsystem enables individual agents to communicate and negotiate with each other through an agent communication language. A standard language for agent communication is the Contract Net protocol which is a high-level protocol for achieving efficient cooperation through task sharing in networks of communicating problem solvers [17].

The proposed communication and interaction scheme consists of two distinct phases. In the first phase, the formation phase, patient agents and caregiving agents exchange data that is necessary for the allocation process. Due to the high sensibility of health-related patient data, the formation phase is characterized by distributed, privacy-aware knowledge sharing among the agents. Schuele et al. have identified software design considerations that enable shared decision making in patient-health professional relationships within the scope of a decision support system in eHealth [9]. This concept is applied to the current proposal to enable privacy-aware patient-caregiver interaction.

In the second phase, the allocation phase, the agents use the data exchanged in the first phase to perform the actual caregiving resource allocation. The protocol implementation internalizes an auction-based allocation approach for the optimal distribution of caregiving resources among the agents. Optimality in this mechanism design approach refers to maximizing the utilitarian social welfare, which is a common performance measure in multiagent resource allocation [5]. Due to the double-sided nature of the problem (patients and caregivers), the concept of a double auction [18] is applied to guarantee the best possible outcome of the resource allocation. In a double auction, both sides of the market submit bids to an auctioneer which then dictates the optimal allocation of caregiving resources and determines the appropriate market-clearing price.

The multiagent subsystem exposes interfaces to the data integration engine. The data integration engine is a semantic-based knowledge management system that integrates heterogeneous knowledge sources and provides access to these sources through semantic reasoning processes. For example, this component is capable of representing knowledge contained in a personal health record of a patient. Similarly, a professional caregiver's availability calendar can be accessed via the data integration engine.

In the following, we focus on the domain-specific requirements of the allocation phase within the multiagent subsystem implementation.

3.2   Dementia-Specific Requirements

Caregiving resources and services require specific attributes that must be considered to meet the needs in the Dementia scenario. These requirements are listed in the following.

Caregiving Service and Required Time. The care for Dementia patients can be divided into individual services. Each service requires a specified time to be completed by the caregiving professional. Table 1 gives an overview of selected services with the average time required for completion of the task.

Table 1. Caregiving services (tasks) and required time for patient care.

Task	Required Time
Complete personal hygiene	20-25 min
Partially personal hygiene	8-10 min
Shave	5-10 min
Dental hygiene	5 min
Full bath/shower	20-30 min
Urination and defecation	5 min
Assistance at meals	15-20 min
Cooking of meals	20 min
Room cleaning	30 min
Shopping service	60 min
Mobility service	30-45 min
Relief service	20 min
Activation (Walking, ...)	60-90 min
Activation (Mental training, ...)	30-45 min
Wound care	10 min
Medication assistance	5 min

Service Quality. A patient must be able to specify a particular service quality when requesting for a caregiving service. Examples of quality attributes include the competency level of caregiving professional as well as the popularity level of caregiving professional that is implemented by a rating system. In the following, we focus on the competency level of caregiving professionals.

Patient Day Care. The daily routine of a Dementia patient is divided into five time slots in which caring tasks should be completed. Each time slot has a duration of two hours for a task to be completed. Tasks can be shorter than two hours, but cannot exceed it. Figure 3 illustrates the individual time slots of the daily routine of a Dementia patient (left hand side) and an example setting for possible caregiving services during these time slots (right hand side).

Full day	Early morning	7:00 to 9:00	Full day	Early morning	• Complete personal hygiene • Assistance at meals
	Late morning	9:00 to 11:00		Late morning	• Full bath/shower • Activation (Walking, ...) • Mobility service
	Noon	11:00 to 13:00		Noon	• Cooking of meals • Assistance at meals
	Afternoon	13:00 to 17:00		Afternoon	• Activation (Mental training) • Relief service
	Evening	17:00 to 20:00		Evening	• Partially personal hygiene

Fig. 3. Time slots of a patient day routine (left hand side) and an example setting for possible caregiving services during these time slots (right hand side).

Caregiving Availability. Different professional caregivers from mobile nursing services are typically available at different times for different durations. Within the five time slots described above, caregivers may specify several durations in which they are available. An example of a caregiver's availability is illustrated in Fig. 4.

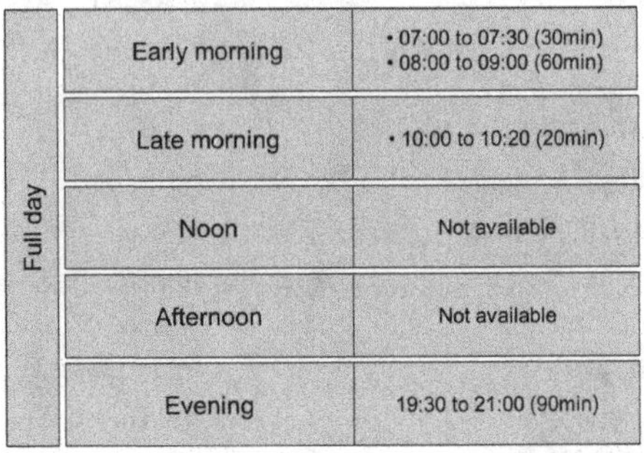

Full day	Early morning	• 07:00 to 07:30 (30min) • 08:00 to 09:00 (60min)
	Late morning	• 10:00 to 10:20 (20min)
	Noon	Not available
	Afternoon	Not available
	Evening	19:30 to 21:00 (90min)

Fig. 4. Time slots of a caregiver's availability requirements during a full day.

Priority Services. A service which is requested by a patient receives a priority attribute. For example, the services "assistance at meals" and "complete personal hygiene" receive a high priority, while "activation (walking etc.)" obtains a lower priority. In this way the services can be provided depending on the priority.

Valuation of Patients and Cost of Caregivers. When specifying its demand, the patient agent expresses its valuation for the requested service. Similarly, the caregiving professional agent specifies its cost to provide the requested service to a patient agent. Valuation and cost can be seen as bids in an auction and are represented by monetary units. The underlying auction mechanism is then responsible for finding the best match between patient and caregiving professional.

3.3   Auction Model

The agents' participation in the auction requires service requests and bids. Requests are submitted by patient agents and include the requirements specified in the previous section and must be considered in the underlying allocation process. Requests of patient agents and offers by caregivers are assumed to be standardized so that they can be matched together. In this work it is assumed that the number of requests and offers is large enough to ensure appropriate matches. For instance, caregiving networks such as the German organization "Pflegenetz Heilbronn" [19] manage an increasing number of patients and caregivers (e.g., individuals and caregiving institutions). Such organizations guarantee that the market on both sides is large enough.

Request. Let i denote the index of a patient. Then each patient agent's request is given by the tuple

$$R_i = (r_1, r_2, \ldots, r_k), \tag{1}$$

where each individual request r_k for $k \in \{1, \ldots, K\}$ is given by

$$r_k = (s, q, t, p, v). \tag{2}$$

In the tuple r_k, the quantity s denotes the required service including the average time required to fulfill the task, q is the requested service quality (i.e., the requested competency level), t is the time slot in which the service is needed, p is the priority of the service, and v is the valuation the patient agent assigns to the requested service. In this notation, parameter s contains the service description as well as the average time needed to complete the service (see Table 1). The valuation of a patient may correspond to a certain caregiving level assigned by the patient's health insurance. Depending on a patient's health condition, an insurance will be willing to reimburse a certain amount of money for a caregiving service. Hence, the valuation of a patient may depend on the severity of her health condition. An example request of patient agent $i = 1$ may be

$$r_1 = (\text{``dentalhygiene''}, \text{``medium''}, \text{``earlymorning''}, \text{``high''} \text{``20''}), \tag{3}$$

$$r_2 = (\text{``roomcleaning''}, \text{``medium''}, \text{``latemorning''}, \text{``low''}, \text{``15''}) \tag{4}$$

$$R_1 = (r_1, r_2), \tag{5}$$

Patient agent $i = 1$ therefore requests for two services in two different time slots. First, the service "dental hygiene" at service quality "medium" within the predefined time slot "early morning" at a high priority. The valuation the patient agent assigns to this multi-attribute service request in this example is given by the monetary unit "20". Second, the patient agent requests for the service "room cleaning" with similar attributes. In this way, patients have the ability to plan out a full caregiving day routine.

Offer. Let j denote the index of a caregiver agent in the system. Each caregiving agent's offer is given by the tuple

$$O_j = (o_1, o_2, \ldots, o_L), \tag{6}$$

where each individual offer o_l for $l \in \{1, \ldots, L\}$ is given by

$$o_l = (q, t, d, c) \tag{7}$$

In the tuple o_l, the quantity q denotes the service quality (i.e., the competency level), t is the time slot in which the caregiver is available for d minutes (the duration for which the caregiver is available in this particular time slot), and c is the cost accruing to the caregiver agent for completing the requested service. An example offer may be

$$o_1 = (\text{"medium"}, \text{"early morning"}, \text{"15 minutes"}, \text{"18"}) \tag{8}$$

$$o_2 = (\text{"high"}, \text{"late morning"}, \text{"10 minutes"}, \text{"20"}) \tag{9}$$

$$O_1 = (o_1, o_2). \tag{10}$$

Caregiving agent $j = 1$ therefore offers two distinct availability bids to provide any service (notice that a caregiver is not bound to a specific service). First, the caregiver is available within the predefined time slot "early morning" for a duration of 15 min within this time slot. The cost accruing to the caregiving agent to provide this multi-attribute service is given by the monetary unit "18". Similar attributes are given for the second offer. Collusion formation among caregiving agents is out of scope in this work.

Auctioneer. Let the number of patient agents in the system be $I \in \mathbb{N}$ and the number of caregiving agents be $J \in \mathbb{N}$. The auctioneer agent collects all patient requests $\{R_1, R_2, \ldots, R_I\}$ and caregiver offers $\{O_1, O_2, \ldots, O_J\}$ from all agents, sorts these bids into time slot and duration categories, and determines the optimal allocation of caregiving resources to patients by considering the required attributes. For calculating the optimal allocation within one category, the auctioneer agent employs the concept of a *double auction*. This process is described in the following section in detail.

3.4   Auction Protocol

The auction protocol for allocation caregiving resources among the agents involves two phases. In the first phase, the auctioneer agent sorts all received requests and offers into appropriate categories for one whole day. Tasks of high priority are assigned immediately before the actual action begins in order to ensure that these tasks are always executed. Further, a category contains services of the same quality as well as the same time slot and duration. In the second phase, the auctioneer performs a double auction within each category and determines the optimal match between caregiver and patient for that day. The auction protocol comprises the following steps:

- All patient agents submit their requests $\{R_1, R_2, \ldots, R_I\}$ to the auctioneer agent, each of which specifies a full day routine of necessary services.
- All caregiving agents submit their offers $\{O_1, O_2, \ldots, O_J\}$ to the auctioneer agent, each of which specifies a full day routine of offered services.
- The auctioneer agent sorts all requests and offers by matching the specified attributes together. In particular, requested time slots by patients are matched to the offered time slots by caregivers for one whole caregiving day. At this point all requests and offers are sorted into distinct categories.
- For each category, the auctioneer agent performs a double auction by taking the valuations and costs into account. In particular, the double auction performs the following. Given a total of n requests with valuations $\{v_1, v_2, \ldots, v_I\}$ within a category, sort the valuations in *descending* order such that

$$v_1 \geq v_2 \geq \ldots \geq v_n \tag{11}$$

Further, given a total number of m offers with costs $\{c_1, c_2, \ldots, c_m\}$ within a category, sort these costs in *ascending* order such that

$$c_1 \leq c_2 \leq \ldots \leq c_m. \tag{12}$$

Next, the auctioneer ranks both sequences against each other and matches the highest valuation with the lowest cost, the second highest valuation with the second lowest cost, and so on, as long as the valuation is strictly greater than the cost. The remaining services that cannot be matched in the current round of the auction are postponed to the next round if their assigned priority is low. High priority tasks will always be executed and are not subject to the postponing process. Then, the auctioneer determines the market-clearing price for each category via

$$price = \frac{v_k + c_k}{2}, \tag{13}$$

where k is the largest index such that $v_k \geq c_k$. This market-clearing price is calculated once per category. For subsequent categories a new price is determined which is independent of the price of the previous category.

- The protocol is repeated until one full day for each patient's care is allocated.

Hence, this communication protocol captures three distinct features. In a first step, matching time slots and matching service durations are grouped together. In the second step, within each group a double auction is performed and caregiving resources are allocated to patients. In the final step, all remaining requests and offers are moved to the next protocol iteration to be considered in the subsequent double auction for the next day. Therefore, this iterated protocol allocates all caregiving resources for the current full day and moves the unmatched service requests and offers to the next day. In this way, no service request is ignored and high priority tasks are completed immediately.

4   Evaluation

We present a scenario-based evaluation [6] that applies the auction-based caregiving resources approach within the scope of a software prototype implementation. Apart from an initial proof-of-concept, we provide an early version of the implementation. We first describe the scenario setup and then discuss the findings.

4.1   Description

The scenario includes a set of Dementia patients who request for caregiving services from a set of caregivers. Through the respective portals, both patients and caregivers submit their bids to the auctioneer. Figure 5 illustrates an example for an auction market with two caregivers and two patients, each bidding their offers respectively requests to the auctioneer.

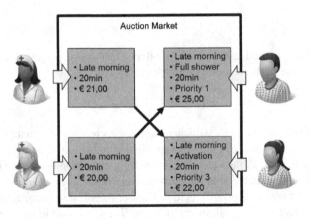

Fig. 5. An auction market with two caregivers and two patients.

As specified by the interaction protocol of the multiagent system, all bids are sorted with respect to the submitted attributes. For example, all bids for resources requested for the "late morning" shift including the appropriate duration for service completion are grouped together. Second, the concept of a double auction is applied to allocate the caregiving resources in an optimal way.

The agent-based prototype implementation exposes a set of graphical user interfaces (GUI) that can be used by the individual portals of the system. Once a patient agent submitted all bids requesting for caregiving resources for a full-day routine, these bids are visible via the GUI of the patient portal as shown in Fig. 6. Notice that the column "Caregiver" is empty in this stage as the auction has not been launched yet. Therefore, the status of the allocation is set to PROPOSED in the "Status" column of the submitted bid list. The column "Bid/Price" contains the submitted valuation of the patient agent to receive the respective service. Once the allocation protocol terminates, this column contains the calculated market-clearing price which the patient agents pays the allocated caregiver for service provisioning.

Date	Description	Daytime	Duration	Competence	Bid/Pri.	Patient	Caregiver	Status	Priority
2014-01-29	Partial personal hygiene	Morning (7:00-9:00)	20	2	3.0	johann.doe@patient.de		PROPOSED	2
2014-01-29	Assistance at meals	Morning (7:00-9:00)	30	1	4.0	johann.doe@patient.de		PROPOSED	1
2014-01-29	Medication assistance	Morning (7:00-9:00)	10	3	3.0	johann.doe@patient.de		PROPOSED	1
2014-01-29	Activation (Walking, ...)	Forenoon (9:00-11:00)	60	1	6.0	johann.doe@patient.de		PROPOSED	6
2014-01-29	Cooking of meals	Noon (11:00-13:00)	60	1	4.0	johann.doe@patient.de		PROPOSED	1

Fig. 6. GUI of patient portal displaying the submitted bids.

Similarly, a caregiver agent submits its bids for a full day specifying the availability of the caregiving professional. The bids submitted by a caregiving professional are collected and displayed via the GUI of the caregiving portal as shown in Fig. 7. Here, the column "Patient" is empty because no resource has been allocated at this point in time. Similar to above, the "Status" column is set to PROPOSED. Again, the column "Bid/Price" contains the submitted costs that accrue to the caregiving agent to provide

Date	Descripti...	Daytime	Duration	Competence	Bid/Price	Caregiver	Patient	Status
2014-01-29		Morning (7:00-9:00)	10	1	1.5	max.holmes@care.net		PROPOSED
2014-01-29		Morning (7:00-9:00)	10	1	1.5	max.holmes@care.net		PROPOSED
2014-01-29		Morning (7:00-9:00)	10	1	1.5	max.holmes@care.net		PROPOSED
2014-01-29		Morning (7:00-9:00)	10	1	1.5	max.holmes@care.net		PROPOSED
2014-01-29		Morning (7:00-9:00)	10	1	1.5	max.holmes@care.net		PROPOSED
2014-01-29		Morning (7:00-9:00)	30	1	4.0	max.holmes@care.net		PROPOSED

Fig. 7. GUI of caregiving portal displaying the submitted bids.

a service. Upon termination of the auction, this column contains the calculated market-clearing price which the caregiving agents receives from the patient receiving the service.

Once all bids are submitted by all patients and caregivers, the auctioneer agent collects all these bids and starts the auction. The GUI of the auctioneer is presented in Fig. 8. The upper part of the GUI shows a list of caregiving offers that could not be matched to any patient request on that particular day. Reasons for unmatched requests and offers include too high costs of caregivers or low valuations of patients.

The lower part of the GUI is the result page of successful matches. It displays a list of patient requests that has been moved to the next day. Since "room cleaning" has a rather low priority, it is moved to the next day's allocation process where it will be auctioned off automatically.

Auction | **Result**

Choose date for auction: 2014-01-29

Start Auction

Reset

Provider supplies:

Date	Daytime	Duration	Competence	Bid/Price	Caregiver	Status
2014-01-28	Morning (7:00-9:00)	10	1	1.5	vera.care@clinic.net	DEPRECATED
2014-01-28	Morning (7:00-9:00)	30	1	4.0	vera.care@clinic.net	DEPRECATED
2014-01-28	Forenoon (9:00-11:00)	10	1	1.5	max.holmes@care.net	DEPRECATED
2014-01-28	Afternoon (13:00-17:00)	45	1	1.0	max.holmes@care.net	DEPRECATED
2014-01-28	Evening (17:00-20:00)	10	1	1.5	max.holmes@care.net	DEPRECATED
2014-01-28	Evening (17:00-20:00)	20	2	3.0	max.holmes@care.net	DEPRECATED
2014-01-28	Forenoon (9:00-11:00)	30	1	4.0	frank.miller@nurse.net	DEPRECATED
2014-01-28	Forenoon (9:00-11:00)	30	1	4.0	frank.miller@nurse.net	DEPRECATED

Customer demands:

Date	Description	Daytime	Duration	Competence	Bid/Price	Patient	Status
2014-01-29	Room cleaning	Morning (7:00-9:00)	60	1	4.0	michael.schuele@patient.de	IN AUCTION

Fig. 8. GUI of auctioneer portal displaying the failed matches (above) and the patient requests moved to the next day (below).

Figure 9 shows the GUI of the auctioneer portal containing a list of all successful allocations for the current day. In particular, it shows the market-clearing price that was calculated by the double auction ("Price" column).

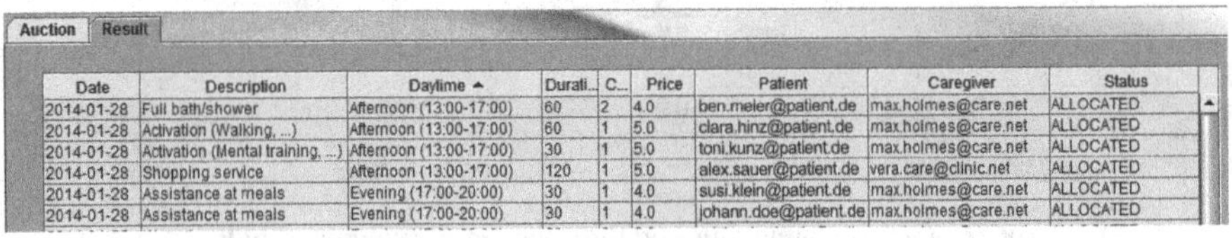

Date	Description	Daytime ▲	Durati...	C...	Price	Patient	Caregiver	Status
2014-01-28	Full bath/shower	Afternoon (13:00-17:00)	60	2	4.0	ben.meier@patient.de	max.holmes@care.net	ALLOCATED
2014-01-28	Activation (Walking, ...)	Afternoon (13:00-17:00)	60	1	5.0	clara.hinz@patient.de	max.holmes@care.net	ALLOCATED
2014-01-28	Activation (Mental training, ...)	Afternoon (13:00-17:00)	30	1	5.0	toni.kunz@patient.de	max.holmes@care.net	ALLOCATED
2014-01-28	Shopping service	Afternoon (13:00-17:00)	120	1	5.0	alex.sauer@patient.de	vera.care@clinic.net	ALLOCATED
2014-01-28	Assistance at meals	Evening (17:00-20:00)	30	1	4.0	susi.klein@patient.de	max.holmes@care.net	ALLOCATED
2014-01-28	Assistance at meals	Evening (17:00-20:00)	30	1	4.0	johann.doe@patient.de	max.holmes@care.net	ALLOCATED

Fig. 9. GUI of auctioneer portal displaying the results of the successful resource allocation.

4.2 Discussion

With the proposed approach we provide an agent-based prototype implementation that enables caregiving resource allocation in a shared patient-caregiver context considering multiple Dementia-specific service attributes. The usability of the system is a very important issue in order to not fail because of low technology acceptance of the users. The multiagent system paradigm enables users to delegate their individual objectives to an autonomous software agent while preserving privacy-related requirements with regards to sensitive patient health data.

We aim to achieve the following benefits for the different participants. Caregivers of Dementia patients are often family members of that patient undergoing severe caregiving burdens depending on the stage of the disease. Hence, our approach provides an IT-based decision support system providing individual support for handling the patient's care. Family caregivers can specify the individualized needs of the Dementia patient via an easy-to-use portal and thus obtain customized support from professional caregivers working for mobile nursing services. Due to the high competition involving many patients and caregivers, the auction-based allocation process guarantees an affordable market price for the caregiving service. Therefore, the proposed software system can finally reduce the caregivers' burdens and improve their quality of life. At the same time, costs can be managed more efficiently allowing for a more flexible caregiving service model.

Professional caregivers have the opportunity to plan their caregiving day routine in a more efficient way. Mobile nursing services can submit service offers that cover all times of the day and consider the specific competency levels of their employees. The underlying auction-based allocation process allows for a more flexible payment scheme that can be applied to the employees of the nursing service. At the same time, the daily time management of professional caregiving personnel can be improved by allowing for a flexible bidding language incorporating multiple service attributes. Hence, the full time and service schedule of multiple competing mobile services is determined by a double auction process that guarantees optimal caregiving allocations as well as market usual prices.

The allocation outcome achieved by a double auction has a number of desirable economic properties [18] which are listed briefly in the following. First, the resulting allocation maximizes the social welfare. Second, all agents are sure to be better off in terms of utility after they participated in the auction. Third, no third party must subsidize the auctioneer, i.e., the auction is able to finance itself. At last, for a growing number of agents, the allocation process is incentive compatible for all participating agents.

5 Conclusion

This work presents an agent-based decision support system for modelling caregiving resource allocation in a Dementia scenario and proposes a communication protocol that implements a double auction considering multiple attributes specific to the Dementia use case. Patients and professional caregivers are represented as software agents that autonomously negotiate service provisioning based on a set of different Dementia-related service attributes. We evaluate this protocol in a scenario-based evaluation in which multiple patients and caregivers submit bids to the auctioneer agent. Within the scope of the evaluation, we present an initial prototype implementation of the proposed multiagent system that exposes a set of graphical user interfaces for each actor. The current protocol implementation is limited to two specific agent types, namely patient agents and caregiving agents. Furthermore, collusion formation among caregiving agents is not considered in this work. The formation of cartels or bidding rings among the agents potentially entails severe efficiency losses in terms of the auction's economic properties [24]. However, the protocol developed by [25] as a special case of general collusion in double auctions maintains a set of these crucial properties even if bidders can submit false-name bids. In our future work, we plan to extend the current decision support system to include further types of agents such as physician agents and facility agents, each of which having their domain-specific service attributes.

Acknowledgement. This work has been supported by the eHealthMonitor project (http://www.ehealthmonitor.eu) and has been partly funded by the European Commission under contract FP7-287509.

References

1. Alzheimer's Disease International: The World Alzheimer Report 2010. www.alz.co.uk (2010). Accessed 21 August 2014
2. Etters, L., Goodall, D., Harrison, B.E.: Caregiver burden among dementia patient caregivers: A review of the literature. J. Am. Acad. Nurse Pract. **20**, 423–428 (2008)
3. Corachado, J.M., Bajo, J., de Paz, Y., Tapia, D.I.: Intelligent environment for monitoring Alzheimer patients, agent technology for health care. Decis. Support Syst. **44**(2), 382–396 (2008)
4. Hess, M., Meis, J.: Entwurf ausgewählter Spracherweiterungen zur Ressourcenmodellierung in Pflegedienstleistungsmodellen. In: Wirtschaftsinformatik Proceedings 2011, paper 109 (2011)
5. Chevaleyre, Y., Dunne, P.E., Endriss, U., Lang, J., Lemaitre, M., Maudet, N., Padget, J., Phelps, S., Rodriguez-Aguilar, J.A., Sousa, P.: Issues in multiagent resource allocation. Informatica **30**, 3–31 (2006)
6. Hevner, A.R., March, S.T., Park, J., Ram, S.: Design Science in Information Systems Research. MIS Q. **28**(1), 75–105 (2004)
7. Brennan, P.F., Moore, S.M., Smyth, K.A.: Computerlink: electronic support for the home caregiver. Adv. Nurs. Sci. **13**(4), 14–27 (1991)
8. Brennan, P.F., Moore, S.M., Smyth, K.A.: The effects of a special computer network on caregivers of persons with alzheimer's disease. Nurs. Res. **44**(3), 166–172 (1995)

9. Schuele, M., Widmer, T., Premm, M., Criegee-Rieck, M., Wickramasinghe, N.: Improving knowledge provision for shared decision making in patient-physician relationships– a multiagent organizational approach. In: Proceedings of the 47th Annual Hawaii International Conference on System Science (HICCS), pp. 646–655 (2014)

10. Lanzarone, E., Matta, A.: Robust nurse-to-patient assignment in home care services to minimize overtimes under continuity of care. Oper. Res. Health Care **3**, 48–58 (2014)

11. Aktas, E., Ülengin, F., Sahin, S.Ö.: A decision support system to improve the efficiency of resource allocation in healthcare management. Socio-Econ. Plann. Sci. **41**, 130–146 (2007)

12. Couch, K.A., Daly, M.C., Wolf, D.A.: Time? money? both? the allocation of resources to older parents. Demography **36**(2), 219–232 (1999)

13. Pezzin, L.E., Schone, B.S.: Intergenerational household formation, female labor supply and informal caregiving– a bargaining approach. J. Hum. Resour. **34**(3), 475–503 (1995)

14. Hirdes, J.P., Poss, J.W., Curtin-Telegdi, N.: The method for assigning priority levels (MAPLe): a new decision-support system for allocating home care resources. BMC Med. 6 (9) (2008)

15. Bichler, M.: An experimental analysis of multi-attribute auctions. Decis. Support Syst. **29**, 249–268 (2000)

16. Das, R., Hanson, J.E., Kephart, J.O., Tesauro, G.: Agent-human interactions in the continuous double auction. In: Proceedings of the International Joint Conferences on Artificial Intelligence (IJCAI), pp. 1169–1176 (2004)

17. Wooldridge, M.: An Introduction to MultiAgent Systems, 2nd edn. Wiley, Chichester (2009)

18. Wilson, R.: Incentive efficiency of double auctions. Econometrica **53**, 1101–1115 (1985)

19. Pflegenetz Heilbronn e.V. http://www.pflegenetz-heilbronn.de. Accessed 26 June 2015

20. Paulussen, T.O., Zöller, A., Rothlauf, F., Heinzl, A., Braubach, L., Pokahr, A., et al.: Agent-based patient scheduling in hospitals. In: Kirn, S., Herzog, O., Lockemann, P., Spaniol, O. (eds.) Multiagent Engineering - Theory and Applications in Enterprises, pp. 255–275. Springer, Berlin (2006)

21. Paulussen, T., Jennings, N.R., Decker, K.S., Heinzl, A.: Distributed patient scheduling in hospitals. In: Proceedings of the Eighteenth International Joint Conference on Artificial Intelligence (IJCAI 2003). Morgan Kaufmann (2003)

22. Paulussen, T., Pokahr, A., Braubach, L., Zöller, A., Lamersdorf, W., Heinzl, A.: Dynamic patient scheduling in hospitals. In: Mulitkonferenz Wirtschaftsinformatik, Agent Technology in Business Applications, Essen (2004)

23. Tan, J., Wen, H.J., Awad, N.: Health care and services delivery systems as complex adaptive systems. Commun. ACM **48**(5), 36–44 (2005)

24. McAfee, R.P., McMillan, J.: Bidding rings. Am. Econ. Rev. **82**(3), 579–599 (1992)

25. Yokoo, M., Sakurai, Y., Matsubara, S.: Robust double auction protocol against false-name bids. Decis. Support Syst. **39**(2), 214–252 (2005)

A Comparison of Agent-Based Coordination Architecture Variants for Automotive Product Change Management

Janek Bender, Stefan Kehl[(✉)], and Jörg P. Müller

Department of Informatics, Clausthal University of Technology,
Clausthal-zellerfeld, Germany
{janek.bender,stefan.kehl,joerg.mueller}@tu-clausthal.de

Abstract. Automotive companies tend to apply modular approaches in their product development processes in order to save costs and meet increasingly diversified customer demands. In largely decentralized environments with cross-branded development projects over multiple departments in different sites this modular approach leads to very complex and large data structures. Maintaining consistency and transparency, as well as coordinating information flows in such an environment is a major task which is often accomplished manually. Based on a real world case study, this paper analyzes a key development process: the connection of geometric (geometries) and logistical data (parts). During this time consuming process information carriers (geometries and parts) with independent lifecycles that are maintained by different stakeholders (designer and purchaser) of different departments (and in this scenario even within multiple brands) are linked as these carriers themselves are mutually dependent. This paper then proceeds to model five agent-based architecture variants to support this process. In addition, an algorithm to map geometric and logistical data which aims to relieve the actors involved (regarding the organizational overhead) is outlined. The paper concludes with a comparison of the different agent architecture variants and emphasizes the most promising variants to partly automate the connection of geometric and logistical data.

1 Introduction

Rising competitive pressure in the automotive industry forces manufacturers into extensive cost saving measures. International markets constantly demand more variety in shorter time periods. While in the 1990 s the product portfolio of most car manufactures covered about eight different models, today's industry offers a steadily increasing amount of different products (e.g. the portfolio of the Audi Group covers about 50 different products) in various configurations in order to meet as many customer demands as possible [13,14]. This way of manufacturing cars specifically suited to customer needs in mass production is known as *mass customization* [11]. In order to achieve customized products at a cost level near mass production some manufacturers pursue approaches to increase the degree of

© Springer International Publishing Switzerland 2015
J.P. Müller et al. (Eds.): MATES 2015, LNAI 9433, pp. 249–267, 2015.
DOI: 10.1007/978-3-319-27343-3_14

commonality. One approach to achieve this goal is the modularization of products so that components are combined into interchangeable modules [2,5]. Ideally, a complete product can be configured using the modular design principle. However, this approach is not entirely applicable for complex products (such as vehicles), because of the large amount of connections between those modules which have to be considered [10]. Changes of such components may have a major impact on other components [3]. Furthermore, a modularization beyond an optimum range would lead to higher product costs [1].

In addition to the need for mass customization, international corporations often operate in a decentralized fashion, with several brands, different business units, and multiple departments and teams, all in geographically dispersed locations. Thus, efficient communication and coordination between sites is mandatory [12].

This work is based on three real world use cases derived from case studies at a major automotive OEM. Based on these use cases, Sect. 2 highlights certain problems in the current development process of connecting geometric and logistical data sets from different entities in a decentralized environment. Following the Virtual Product Model (VPM) proposed by Kehl et al. in [6] five architecture variants for an agent-based approach to automate this key development process are modeled in Sect. 3. Section 4 discusses the pros and cons of these architecture variants as well as their applicability to fulfill the requirements defined in Sect. 3. Section 5 compares the architecture variants; Sect. 6 concludes this paper and gives an outlook on future work.

2   Background

In previous work [6], we performed an analysis of challenges in managing development processes of complex products in the automotive industry. We proposed the concept of a *Virtual Product Model (VPM)* to manage such complex and cross-branded development processes. In practice a product data is organized in different hierarchical and static structures [4]. Each of these manually maintained structures represents a domain specific view on the product (e.g. a Bill of Material (BOM) for purchasers or an Engineering BOM for designers) which are linked to or transformed into one another [16]. In contrast, the VPM described in [6] offers a more flexible and component-based view on a product, because each domain specific structure is considered as a view on the overall product which is built dynamically, based on the information it carries and the connections between them (VPM-C). The concept of a VPM aims to fulfill three crucial requirements in a product development process:

Reusability. One VPM-C can be assigned to multiple products, yet there is an element that holds context-specific information.

Patency. From the early stages to the end of a product's development the information flow should not be interrupted. Data has to be kept consistent between all involved entities.

Transparency. It is mandatory to establish traceability of changes on components and connections between them throughout the entire development process.

Each *Virtual Component (VPM-C).* can be divided into four elements:

Part. A part represents a logistical data set describing a real world vehicle part. It contains information such as the supplier, color, count or material. In practice parts are organized in a BOM.

Geometry. A geometry is a 3D-CAD file which holds data such as the size, shape, or position of a part. Furthermore, a part may be realized by a geometry.

Feature. A feature may be a technical description or a certain functionality of the component.

Process. The production process(es) the component is assigned to. This element might contain information about different production sites.

This paper builds on the VPM concept, yet some of its elements are rendered out of scope for the problem at hand. The elements considered in this paper are *parts* and *geometries*. Also, contrary to the original VPM proposal this work limits itself (for the sake of clarity) to only two different roles involved in the mentioned use cases:

Engineer. The engineer constructs and combines vehicle parts by using CAD software. His work is based on geometries (3D-CAD files), containing information like size, shape, or position of a component.

Purchaser. The counterpart in logistics is the purchaser whose main responsibilities are the procurement of parts and materials and managing supply chains. He views product models from a logistic perspective and works based on parts (logistical data sets) containing information such as the supplier, color, count, material, among others.

2.1   Use Cases

As part of this work, three use cases, totaling six distinct workflows, have been derived from case studies from the automotive industry. These use cases show the underlying problem this paper aims to tackle and are used to conceptualize possible solutions. An overview about the three major use cases is given below.

Use Case 1: New Construction of a VPM-C. A new component is developed based on a given specification. First, the engineer designs the new geometry with his CAD software. He will then proceed to position the newly constructed geometry within a 3D environment, relative to other previously constructed geometries. Lastly, the engineer assigns the geometry to one or multiple vehicle contexts.

Use Case 2: Reuse of a VPM-C. An existing geometry is assigned to a new context. It may have to be re-positioned within the 3D environment in order to fit the new context.

Use Case 3: Further Development of a VPM-C. Contrary to use case 1, an existing geometry is developed further within its context and may have to be re-positioned within the 3D environment.

In each of the above use cases, geometric data must be connected with logistical data. Steps to achieve this connection might vary depending on the use case.

2.2 An Exemplary Workflow of a New Construction

To illustrate the problem and the solution statement a small example shall be given at this point. Assuming that a new vehicle generation should receive a door hinge constructed from scratch, the engineer would first have to design a 3D geometry using a CAD software. He would then position the new geometry in relation to close-by components, like the door frame, wiring, or the window lift, making sure the new geometry does not cut other geometries within the 3D space. The engineer would thereafter proceed to assign the new geometry to the respective vehicle context of the new vehicle generation. After the engineering is completed the data is sent to the purchaser who requests a new distinct part number. Using the part number, the purchaser will create a new branch within the Bill of Material (BOM) data structure. Finally, the geometric data and the logistical data are connected within the data structure. In the following, the establishment of this connection is referred to as *Part-Geometry-Mapping*.

The first problem in the previously described process is the decentralized generation and administration of data in multiple brands and departments. This data must be kept consistent throughout all entities involved in the vehicle construction process. Furthermore, there is little transparency on which parts belong to which geometries and vice versa. The same geometry might realize multiple parts in different vehicles and different markets. Especially when a certain part in one vehicle has shown so far unforseen problems after the product launch, it becomes crucial to quickly identify all other vehicles using this very part. Right now, it is only possible to achieve the needed transparency by devoting a lot of manual efforts to the cause. Also, by connecting and maintaining logistical and geometric data within the same data structure the used BOMs exceed a healthy size and develop redundancies at some point. Both engineers and purchasers find themselves confronted with data irrelevant to their own tasks. For instance, engineers need geometries to do their work while purchasers rely on logistical data, yet it is stored in the very same structure.

3 An Agent-Based Approach to Part-Geometry-Mapping

The problems shown in the example above arise from largely decentralized processes. Information is created and maintained in different brands with multiple departments and teams at geographically dispersed locations. Managing changes on VPM-Cs and maintaining consistency throughout all involved parties is a major task. However, there is no single entity overseeing the whole development and all its changes. Furthermore (as described in Sect. 2.2), in practice, the Part-Geometry-Mapping is a manual process. Due to the decentralized problem and the distributed stakeholders (purchasers and designers from different brands), an agent-based solution is proposed in this paper, as mentioned in our previous work [6]. The basic idea builds on so called *active components* representing certain entities in the process. An *active component* is controlled by an agent which is considered "a software system that is situated in some environment, and that is capable of autonomous action in this environment in order to meet its delegated objectives" [8]. Furthermore, Wagner [15] has already deployed an agent-based approach into a similar environment with success. In order to investigate whether an agent-based approach is feasible and offers real advantages over the manual mapping of parts and geometries, five possible agent architecture variants have been developed. These architecture variants model structural and behavioral aspects of *active components* and may be realized through real software agents in future research. This section is structured as follows: Sect. 3.1 describes the underlying problem in detail and in the Sects. 3.2 to 3.6 the five architecture variants are illustrated.

3.1 Part-Geometry-Mapping

Before discussing the different agent architecture variants in detail, the understanding of the elements and their relations should be clarified. Figure 1 gives an overview.

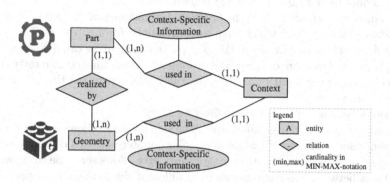

Fig. 1. Elements of the mapping process

As already mentioned *parts* are realized by *geometries*. A part or geometry can be *used* in several *contexts* (platforms or vehicles). The *usage* of a part or geometry comes with certain *context-specific information*, for example the position of a geometry in a specific context.

Thus the main requirements are:

- Contribute to establishing transparency and traceability of changes in order to be able to quickly answer the two questions:
  1. Which revisions of a given component are used in which platforms, or vehicles?
  2. Which components in which revisions are used in a given context?
- By (partially) automating the part-geometry-mapping in order to get a hold of the complex and decentralized information generation and maintenance. Make key information available where it is needed and keep it consistent throughout all involved entities.

To simplify the modeling of possible solutions both geometries and parts are abstracted into the generic term *component*. The necessary properties of the component are described below:

- Parts and geometries are elements of a VPM-C as they are both offering different views on the same real world counterpart.
- Over the iterative course of development a component forms *multiple revisions*. Each change on the component causes a new revision which can be *assigned to a context* (vehicle or platform). As an example, revision #1 might be a *development build* only used as placeholder or prototype during the development. Revision #2, a fully developed version of the component, goes into production and is thereby part of the manufactured vehicle. Now the vehicle series receives a facelift and the component needs to be adapted leading to revision #3.
- Since multiple revisions of a component may be assigned to the same context (in the above case revisions #1 and #2), each revision has a *validity* property and is only used within a specified start and end date.
- A component can offer a certain *function*. For instance, a rim allows someone to attach tires to a car which then are part of the *feature* "driving".
- Based on an idea by Wagner in [15], the participating roles can define *rules* for components. These are either *configuration rules* describing certain restrictions of the component itself or *connection rules* which regulate the relations to other components.
- A component belongs to a *pre-defined category*.
- A component is from a specified *side*. The side property allows for the division of components and identification of possible counterparts of a component from another side. In extension, the category property allows someone to draw connections between two components from different sides. Thus, both properties are mandatory and play a vital role in the *mapping process*.

For example, a new rim is developed from scratch. The component of the geometry is on side 0 and the matching component of the part information on side 1. However, both belong to the same category "Wheels". There is no mapping between these two thus far, but this information alone is sufficient to specify that these two *components* are *possible counterparts* for each other. Figure 2 illustrates the *component* term.

In the following, the five proposed architecture variants for an agent-based approach are discussed.

3.2   Architecture Variant I - Dedicated Element Agents

This architecture variant covers the most basic and intuitive approach in modeling a MAS capable of autonomously conducting part-geometry-mappings within given contexts, or even more abstract: component-mappings. Figure 3 shows an overview of proposed agent classes, marked by boxes. "Dedicated Element Agents" refers to the fact that each element involved in the process (namely

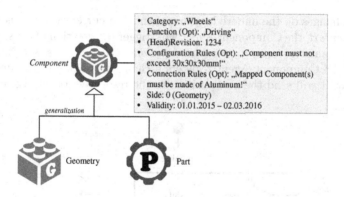

Fig. 2. The component

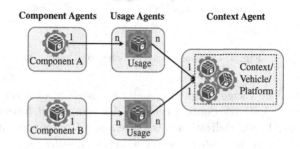

Fig. 3. Architecture Variant I - Dedicated Element Agents

geometries, parts, their respective usages / revisions, and contexts) is represented by a single agent with specified tasks and goals.

Three basic agent classes are explained below. It should be noted that both geometries and parts are considered components and thus be represented by a *Component Agent*.

Component Agent. The Component Agent represents a component within the system. It initializes once a component is first created and destroys when the underlying component is disabled. Its main purpose is to maintain static information about the component such as *category* or *ID*. Furthermore the Component Agent knows all revisions of a component and retains data about its different usages. A Component Agent will remain passive most of the time, monitoring the engineers' actions within the CAD-Program and tracking changes on the component.

Figure 4 shows a behavioral view of the Component Agent. Upon initialization a new Component Agent receives parameterized information regarding *category, component, function, rules,* and *side*. It will then idle in its main loop until either the underlying component is disabled, which results in the destruction of the Component Agent, or it receives new information. The latter happens if another agent sends new information to the Component Agent or the engineer performs changes on the underlying component. If a current revision is assigned to a *new context*, the Component Agent will trigger the creation of a *Usage Agent* with the parameters *category, context, function, revision, rules, side*, and *validity*. Once the Component Agent registers a changed position of the underlying component, it will send the new position to the respective Usage Agent.

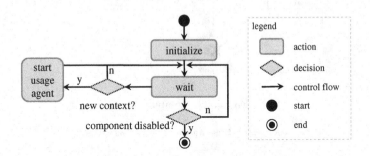

Fig. 4. Component agent behavioral view

Usage Agent. The Usage Agent represents the revision of a component in a specific context. It initializes once a revision of a component has been assigned to a new context. The initialization is triggered by a Component Agent. Passed parameters are *category, context, function, revision, rules, side*, and *validity*. A Usage Agent's main task is to map his own component on another component within the context. It therefore actively looks for mappable components of the *same category* but *different side* and contacts them in order to find one or more matches. A Usage Agent's component can have *multiple mappings* and the Usage Agent is only active as long as its component has zero mappings. After a Usage Agent has been successfully mapped it will still react to mapping requests of other agents but discontinue to actively look for mappings. If the component of the respective Component Agent is being disabled or the given validity of the revision runs out, the Usage Agent will be destroyed.

Figure 5 shows a behavioral view of the Usage Agent. The mapping process itself is described in detail in Sect. 4. Upon initialization the Usage Agent receives the parameters *category, context, function, revision, rules, side*, and *validity*. As part of the initialization the Usage Agent will contact the Context Agent to register itself. The Usage Agent remains in its main idle loop until it receives new information from another agent or becomes active by looking for mappable components or responding to incoming mapping requests from other Usage Agents. If a Usage Agent does not have any mappings yet, its top priority is to find a matching component from the same category but another side. Therefore, it contacts the respective Context Agent in order to request a list of mappable components based on category and side. It will then iterate through the returned list and contact each component's Usage Agent to take on mapping negotiations. If a negotiation ends with a negative result the respective component is removed from the list and the Usage Agent will approach the next in line. If the list has been emptied and a successful mapping has not been found, the Usage Agent returns to idle state and will request a new list in the next cycle. A positive negotiation ending results in a successful preliminary mapping which is then communicated to both the respective Context and Component Agents. The Usage Agent will then return to the idle state and become reactive to incoming mapping requests and new information.

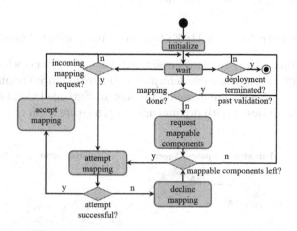

Fig. 5. Usage agent behavioral view

Context Agent. The Context Agent overlooks a specific context. It holds data concerning active Usage Agents within the context, assists in the mapping process and knows all of the successful mappings. Once a new context is being created the Context Agent initializes with the *context* parameter. It then remains in the idle state until it receives new information or requests from other agents.

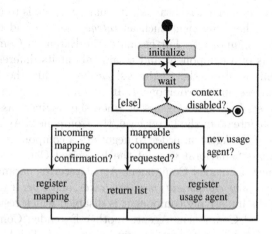

Fig. 6. Context agent behavioral view

The Context Agent's main tasks are to register new Usage Agents and successful mappings and to compile and return lists of mappable components to Usage Agents. With the termination of the context, the Context Agent is destroyed.

Figure 6 shows a behavioral view of the Context Agent. After initialization, it will remain idle until it receives new information or requests from other agents. If a Usage Agent requests a list of mappable components, the Context Agent may run a simple query on its own database.

3.3   Architecture Variant II: Extended Component Agent

This second proposed architecture variant features one agent class less. Instead of heaving dedicated agents for each element like in Architecture Variant I the Component and Usage Agents are merged into one: an Extended Component Agent. It takes over the duties of both original agents, rendering them obsolete (Fig. 7).

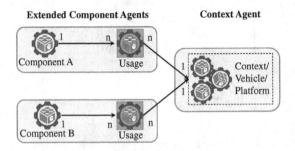

Fig. 7. Architecture Variant II - Extended Component Agent

Extended Component Agent. The Extended Component Agent represents a component and all its usages. It initializes once a component is first created and destroys when the component is disabled. Its main purpose is to maintain static information about the component such as *category* or *ID* and to conduct the mappings on other components. Furthermore, the Extended Component Agent knows all revisions of a component and retains about its different usages. The Component Agent monitors the Engineers' actions within the CAD-Program and tracking changes on the component. It becomes reactive upon incoming information requests from other agents or when the Engineer assigns a current revision to a new context. In the latter case, the Component Agent will contact the respective Context Agent in order to negotiate a component mapping.

Figure 8 shows a behavioral view of the Extended Component Agent. On initialization, a new Extended Component Agent receives parameterized information such as *category, component, function, rules,* and *side.* It idles in its main loop until either the underlying component is disabled which results in destruction of the Extended Component Agent, another Extended Component Agent sends a mapping request or it receives new information. The latter happens if another agent sends new information to the Extended Component Agent or the

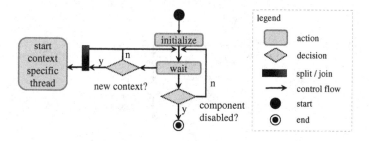

Fig. 8. Extended component agent behavioral view

Engineer performs changes on the underlying component. If a current revision is assigned to a new context, the Extended Component Agent will contact the Context Agent with the parameters *context*, *revision*, *validation*, and *category*. It opens a new thread in its behavior, dedicated to handle all context specific matters, i.e. the matters that in Architecture Variant I have been covered by the Usage Agent.

Context Agent. The Context Agent in Architecture Variant II has not changed compared to Architecture Variant I. Both its tasks and behavior can be modeled exactly the same way.

3.4 Architecture Variant III: Vertically Extended Usage Agent

Architecture Variant III models the idea of having a vertical approach at the Usage Agent. Matching components from two different sides may be represented by a single agent within a specific context. Figure 9 shows an overview of proposed agent classes, marked by boxes.

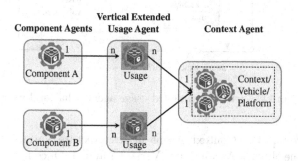

Fig. 9. Architecture variant III - vertically extended usage agent

Component Agent. This agent's tasks and behavior stay the same, aside from a small detail as shown in Fig. 10. Instead of triggering the initialization of a Vertically Extended Usage Agent, the Component Agent notifies the respective

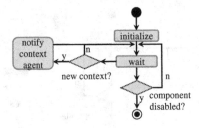

Fig. 10. Component agent behavioral view

Context Agent which will then proceed to ensure the mapping is processed. As soon as a component within a context has a Vertically Extended Usage Agent assigned, the respective Component Agents can update the information base of that Usage Agent.

Vertically Extended Usage Agent. The Vertically Extended Usage Agent functions similar to the regular Usage Agent known from Architecture Variant I. However, it will not try to achieve a mapping on its own. Instead, it remains passive until contacted by the Context Agent. Figure 11 shows the behavior in detail.

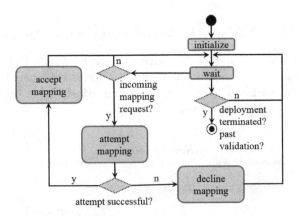

Fig. 11. Vertically extended usage agent behavioral view

Context Agent. The Context Agent in Architecture Variant III assumes a more active role than in Architecture Variant I and II. Once it receives a notification from a Component Agent about a new Component within its context, it tries to convey it to all existing Vertically Extended Usage Agents. If that fails, the new component is considered not mappable in this cycle and a new Usage Agent is deployed, representing the component. In the next cycle another new component may join the context and is shown to all existing Vertically Extended Usage Agents in order to find a match. Figure 12 shows the behavior in detail.

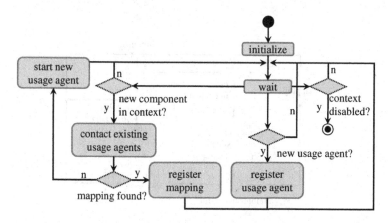

Fig. 12. Context agent behavioral view

3.5 Architecture Variant IV: Extended Context Agent

This architecture variant is based on the idea of having Component Agents directly communicating with an Extended Context Agent, which is processing all context related matters, including the mapping. Figure 13 shows an overview of proposed agent classes, marked by boxes.

Component Agent. This agent's tasks and behavior remain unchanged, aside from a small detail as already shown in Fig. 10. Instead of triggering the initialization of a Usage Agent, the Component Agent notifies the respective Context Agent which will then proceed to ensure the mapping is processed.

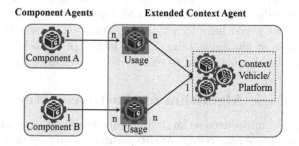

Fig. 13. Architecture Variant IV - Extended Context Agent

Extended Context Agent. As already stated, the Extended Context Agent takes over all tasks of both the regular Context Agent as well as the Usage Agent. The Extended Context Agent holds context-specific data, especially about the mappings. When a new component enters the context, the Extended Context Agent will try to map this component on an already existing component within

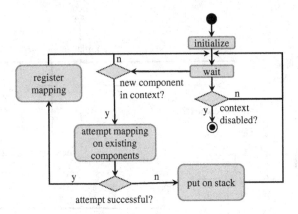

Fig. 14. Extended Context Agent behavioral view

the context. If there are no mappable components in the context or no mapping was found, the component is moved on a stack for later. As soon as new context-specific information comes up or another new component joins the context, the Extended Context Agent again tries to map the components. Figure 14 shows the behavior in detail.

3.6 Architecture Variant V: Vertically Extended Component Agent

Lastly, an agent architecture could be modeled with a Vertically Extended Component Agent which vertically connects components from two different sides.

However, we consider this architectural variant not applicable to our case for several reasons. Firstly, actual mappings can only exist between two revisions of a component and are thus not directly applicable on underlying components. Secondly, because of the decentralized nature of the problem and the generation of data throughout different brands and departments, Vertically Extended Component Agents would have to act across sites, i.e. they would have to exist in multiple spaces at the same time. Unlike in the prior architecture variants where context-related agents used to exist within a context only.

4   Sketch of the Algorithm for Part-Geometry Mapping

To apply the model introduced so far, finding an efficient and automatable way of mapping components is mandatory. At this point, an outline of such an algorithm is given. An actual implementation is planned for future work. To recapture, the agent architecture variants from Sect. 3 introduced the component term which, when set into a *context*, comes with properties relevant for the mapping process. Namely these properties are *category*, *function*[1], *rules*, *side*, and *validity*. Where

---

[1] It should be noted that the function property is optional as not every component fulfills a specific function. For example, a simple screw that is used a few hundred times across different locations within a vehicle. It does to some extend contribute to several functions but cannot be connected to one specific function.

rules are divided into *configuration rules* and *connection rules*, as proposed by Wagner in [15]. Configuration rules can be considered as *internal*, meaning they specify certain regulations when creating or changing the component. For example, a part needs to have a material specified. Connection rules on the other hand can be considered *external*, as they regulate connections between components. These rules may *force* or *forbid* a certain matter. For example, a geometry of a rim has a connection rule in place that dictates a mapped part must be made of aluminum.

In preparation of this paper, known consensus algorithms have been reviewed. Primary subjects of investigation were the Paxos protocol [7] and Raft [9]. However, these algorithms have not been found suitable for the task at hand as their main purpose is to coordinate client-server systems with a (fail safe) redundant server architecture. An alternative approach which we studied is based on matching algorithms known from the field of Operations Research / Graph Theory. These methods were also rendered not suitable as reviewed matching algorithms implicitly assume that matching compatibilities are a known fact. Thus, a new, special algorithm to solve the mapping problem is needed. The idea of which is outlined below.

In a first step the *respective agent*[2] tries to find a *proper subset of other components* that could fit his own. That means it compiles a subset of components in which every has *exactly not the same side* as the own component but *exactly the same category*. In extension, the respective agent rules out components with *validity data* that does not exactly fit or include its own validity.

That leaves the respective agent with a proper subset of all components within the context. It proceeds to contact these components' respective agents in order to *attempt a mapping*, i.e. enter mapping negotiations.[3] Therefore, both agents send each other *information sets* with data about the *underlying component, positional information,* and its *function*. Both agents proceed to check each others' information set against their own data and connection rules. If no force or forbid connection rules fail, and function and position parameters approximately map, an agent sends an accept to the other agent. If the other agent returns an accept a *preliminary mapping* is established. Both agents proceed to save the preliminary mapping and contact their *respective users*[4] for *confirmation*. An accept by the user results in a *confirmed mapping* while a decline revokes the preliminary mapping. More so, the respective agents will blacklist declined mappings and refrain from attempting a mapping with these components in the future again to prevent infite looping. Algorithm 1 summarizes this behaviour in pseudo code.

---

[2] Depending on the architecture variant this could be the Extended Component, Extended Context or (Extended) Usage Agent.

[3] It should be noted that the whole communication part does not apply to Architecture Variant IV because there is only one agent (the Extended Context Agent) which handles the mapping negotiations internally.

[4] Engineers and Purchasers.

Algorithm 1. Part-Geometry-Mapping

```
procedure MAPCOMPONENTS(List<Components> mappableComps)
    for all Components c: mappableComps do
        Agent a = c.getAgent()                          ▷ Identify the comp's agent
        Set inInfo = a.attemptMapping(outInfo)          ▷ Contact the comp's agent
        bool positionMapped = tryPosMapping(inInfo)       ▷ Check incoming data
        bool ruleCheck = checkRules(inInfo)              ▷ Check connection rules
        bool outResp = positionMapped & ruleCheck
        bool inResp = a.sendResponse(outResp)        ▷ Send and retreive responses
        if outResp & inResp then             ▷ If both agents agree on mapping
            savePreliminaryMapping()
            requestConfirmation()              ▷ Contact user for confirmation
    return mappedComponents
```

As shown, an agent-based approach might not be able to completely automate the mapping process. However, intelligent agents are able to cut down the number of possible mappings at least, saving the users time, and assisting the goal of establishing transparency.

5 Comparison

This section discusses the five agent architecture variants shown in Sect. 3 and their stance on the mapping algorithm outlined in Sect. 4.

Architecture Variant I - Dedicated Element Agents. Covers the most intuitive approach in which every element within the development process is reprentend by a single, autonomous agent. It could be argued that this approach is a variant of a peer-to-peer architecture as there are no real leading agents or agents overseeing the bigger picture. It certainly fits the idea of a decentralized, intelligent multi-agent system quite well and offers a lot of of room for extensions. The downside is the massive amount of communication needed between agents and possibly redundant data storage which needs to be kept consistent and made easily accessible to the users. The only agent class where intelligence is really needed is the Usage Agent as it is responsible for the negotiation of preliminary mappings. All other agents could be modeled as reactive sub-systems which follow a strict behavioural pattern and mainly serve as data storages or communication arrays between Usage Agents and users.

Architecture Variant II - Extended Component Agent. Merges the Component Agent and its Usage Agents into one. This reduces the communication needed but adds to the complexity of the Extended Component Agent which now has to manage all its contexts. As a revision is basically just an extension of its component, it might be more logical to represent both elements in one agent. Queries about what revisions are assigned to which contexts could be answered faster than in Architecture Variant I as it is not necessary anymore to contact the Usage Agents in order to acquire this context-specific information. The intelligence is moved into the Extended Component Agent rendering the Context Agent as sole data storage and administration system. Fewer agent classes might make future extensions more difficult and change the system to be less flexible.

Architecture Variant III - Vertically Extended Usage Agent. Tries to realize a comprehensive approach where revisions from different sides are represented by a single agent. This approach causes less communication efforts during the mapping process as it is all handeled internally by the Vertically Extended Usage Agent, which in extend plays the only intelligent role again. If no match is found on the first try, the component's revision exists within the context but lacks an agent to represent it until a mapping has been found. Furthermore, once two revisions from different sides have been succesfully mapped, the Vertically Extended Usage Agent needs to act across dispersed locations and departments. Thus, Architecture Variant III might be feasible but probably not optimal.

Architecture Variant IV - Extended Context Agent. Leads the system's intelligence away from the components and towards the context. It is by that more centralized but less communication efforts are needed. Contrary to the peer-to-peer approach from Architecture Variant I, this architecture variant establishes a hirarchy, in which the Extended Context Agent is overseeing the whole context and all its matters. Component Agents merely act as registers and entry points for users who wish to find out where the revisions of a component are used in. All context-specific information is stored within the Extended Context Agent and by that leaves most likely the fewest redundancies of all architecture variants. However, implementing future extensions might be harder.

Solely based on the requirements established in Sect. 3 Architecture Variants I-IV deliver satisfying concepts. Architecture Variants II and IV seem to be the ones with the fewest drawbacks while Architecture Variant I offers the most flexibility and should be easy to extend with more functionality. Future implementations or more desired functionalities might lead to a clearer result or alter the architecture in ways which could not be covered in this paper.

Table 1 summarizes the prior comparison:

Table 1. Comparison of Feasible Agent Architecture Variants

	Architecture Variant I	AV II	AV III	AV IV
Communication	high	medium	medium	low
Complexity	low	medium	medium	high
Redundancy	high	low	medium	low
Flexibility	high	medium	medium	low
Location of Possible Intelligence	Usage Agent	Extended Component Agent	Vertically Extended Agent	Extended Context Agent

6   Conclusion

In this concept paper, an agent-based approach on automating a key development process in the automotive industry, the connection of geometric data (*geometries*) and logistical data (*parts*), within a decentralized environment has been modeled. Based on the concept of a *Virtual Product Model (Component)* by Kehl et al. in [6], which was applied on three use cases derived from case studies in the automotive industry, five agent architecture variants have been developed. Four of these five architecture variants have been rendered feasible in order to support both the given requirement to (partly) automate the *part-geometry-mapping* as well as contributing to a *more transparent system* with *changes made traceable*. The four feasible agent architecture variants have been discussed in detail, especially regarding their expected incurring communication, data redundancy, and extendability. In addition, an algorithm functioning in each of the agent architecture variants for the mapping process itself has been outlined which, based on given data, is not able to determine mappings fully on its own but is at least capable of significantly curtailing the amount of possible mappings.

Future work will include a prototyped implementation of the agent architecture variants. On a more conceptual level, additional requirements could be determined and the architecture variants could be extended and enriched with more functionality.

References

1. Cheng, H., Chu, X.: A network-based assessment approach for change impacts on complex product. J. Intell. Manuf. **23**(4), 1419–1431 (2012). http://dx.doi.org/10.1007/s10845-010-0454-8
2. Clarkson, J.P., Simons, C., Eckert, C.: Predicting change propagation in complex design. In: ASME 2001 Design Engineering Technical Conferences and Computers and Information in Engineering Conference. Pittsburgh, Pennsylvania (2001)
3. Fricke, E., Gebhard, B., Negele, H., Igenbergs, E.: Coping with changes: Causes, findings, and strategies. Syst. Eng. **3**(4), 169–179 (2000)
4. Glauche, M., Rebel, M., Müller, J.P.: Produktstrukturierung als Erfolgsfaktor: Systematisierung und Analyse von Einflussfaktoren der Produktstrukturierung. ZWF - Zeitschrift für wirtschaftlichen Fabrikbetrieb **11**, 878–881 (2013)
5. Jarratt, T., Eckert, C.M., Caldwell, N., Clarkson, P.J.: Engineering change: an overview and perspective on the literature. Res. Eng. Des. **22**(2), 103–124 (2011). http://dx.doi.org/10.1007/s00163-010-0097-y
6. Kehl, S., Stiefel, P., Müller, J.P.: Changes on changes: Towards an agent-based approach for managing complexity in decentralized product development. In: International Conference on Engineering Design (ICED 15). vol. 3, pp. 220–228. Milan, Italy (2015)
7. Lamport, L.: The part-time parliament. ACM Trans. Comput. Syst. **16**(2), 133–169 (1998)
8. Michael Wooldridge: An Introduction to MultiAgent Systems. John Wiley & Sons, 2 edn (2009)

9. Ongaro, D., Ousterhout, J.: In search of an understandable consensus algorithm. In: Proceedings of the 2014 USENIX Conference on USENIX Annual Technical Conference. pp. 305–320. USENIX ATC 2014, USENIX Association, Berkeley, CA, USA (2014). http://dl.acm.org/citation.cfm?id=2643634.2643666
10. Simon, H.A.: The sciences of the artificial, vol. 3. MIT Press, Cambridge (1996)
11. Tseng, M.M., Jiao, J.: Mass customization: 25. In: Handbook of Industrial Engineering, pp. 684–709. John Wiley & Sons, Inc (2007). http://dx.doi.org/10.1002/9780470172339.ch25
12. Verband der Automobilindustrie (VDA): Auto 2008 - jahresbericht. online (July 2008).www.vda.de/de/services/Publikationen/Publikation.489.html
13. Verband der Automobilindustrie (VDA): Jahresbericht 2012. online (July 2012). https://www.vda.de/de/services/Publikationen/jahresbericht-2012.html
14. Verband der Automobilindustrie (VDA): Jahresbericht 2013. online (August 2013). https://www.vda.de/de/services/Publikationen/jahresbericht-2013.html
15. Wagner, T.: Agentenunterstütztes engineering von automatisierungsanlagen. atp-online Automatisierungstechnische. Praxis **50**(4), 68–75 (2008)
16. Xu, H.C., Xu, X.F., He, T.: Research on transformation engineering bom into manufacturing bom based on bop. Appl. Mech. Mater. **10–12**, 99–103 (2008)

Selected Extended Abstracts of Doctoral Papers

Electric Vehicles: An Agent-Based Approach to Sustainability

Micha Kahlen$^{(\boxtimes)}$ and Wolfgang Ketter

Erasmus University Rotterdam, Burgemeester Oudlaan 50,
3062 Rotterdam, PA, The Netherlands
{kahlen,wketter}@rsm.nl

Abstract. Renewable energy sources such as wind and solar are difficult to balance for the grid because they are weather dependent. We study how the storage of electric vehicles can balance a grid with an increasing intermittent renewable energy content in the short term and contribute to a more efficient and sustainable smart grid. In the Power Trading Agent Competition, a mulitagent platform, we represent fleets of electric vehicles to make a tradeoff between the conflicting interests of storing intermittent energy in the electric vehicles and driving them. The richness of this platform allows us to draw conclusions for the future of a sustainable grid with electric vehicles.

Keywords: Electricity broker agents · Electric vehicles · Smart grid · Virtual power plants

1 Introduction

With rising greenhouse gas emissions we are faced with the global challenge of climate change. A large share of these emissions come from electricity production and transportation [3]. Increasingly, renewable energy sources, that work in parallel with conventional energy sources, and electric vehicles come into operation to reduce greenhouse gas emission. However, renewable energy sources are extremely weather dependent causing a change towards a more supply driven (instead of demand) driven energy supply chain. Because of this high volatility and uncertainty we will need tools that facilitate decision making in these fast changing markets [1]. Our solution to that is energy broker agents. Traditionally the grid has back up capacity to deal with variations in demand and supply of electricity in the short term (seconds to minutes). However, as the number of both renewable energy sources and electric vehicles increases, there is insufficient back up power available. If energy demand and supply are not in balance at all times, blackouts can occur endangering human lives and causing large economic damage. The energy broker agents are able to (partially) shift consumption to times when renewable energy is abundantly available. In particular, in our project we study how intelligent agents can facilitate the charging and discharging process of electric vehicles in coordination with energy supply (in the short term especially driven by renewable energy sources).

© Springer International Publishing Switzerland 2015
J.P. Müller et al. (Eds.): MATES 2015, LNAI 9433, pp. 271–274, 2015.
DOI: 10.1007/978-3-319-27343-3_15

Charging electric vehicles in coordination with the energy supply, especially volatile renewable energy sources, is a paradigm shift in the energy sector. This shift is related to the decentralization of energy, where no longer large power plants dominate the energy landscape, but mostly distributed energy sources [2]. In addition, electric vehicles are distributed and can both be a source of energy and consume energy. In this case the management of electric vehicles becomes a challenging task. When they should charge and provide electricity to the grid is difficult to determine centrally because of the sheer number of electric vehicles in the future. We take battery cost into account, the depreciation cost are relatively high, but the short term balancing markets offer relatively high prices to compensate for that. Therefore we create agents that guide the electric vehicle charging based on pricing signals and preferences of owners to incentivize them to charge at times when renewable energy sources are producing. Multiagent systems are particularly suited to model this charging an discharging behavior, as they are able to represent several autonomous interests of these people and see their aggregate effects on the electricity system.

2   Research Design

We model the highly complex energy supply chain with the help of the Power Trading Agent Competition (Power TAC, [6]). It is a state-of-the-art smart grid simulation that includes consumers of electricity such as households and industrial customers, but also conventional electricity generation and decentralized energy sources such as wind and solar. It has been validated in previous studies [5,8]. Energy is bought and sold by self-interested autonomous energy broker agents that offer retail tariffs to energy consumers. These agents have to be in balance, i.e. they have to purchase or produce as much electricity as their subscribed customers consume. We build on Power TAC as a testbed to introduce electric vehicles. Fleets of electric vehicles are represented by agents that serve their energy need, but also sell the flexibility of when to charge the car as power options to agents that need to balance their power supply.

Previous research has contributed to the understanding of the role of batteries in the grid [7,9]. We focus more on the driving aspect, which makes the problem more complex because there is uncertainty involved about the availability of vehicles - people cannot always predict when they will use their cars. Yet the agent needs to make an autonomous decision when to charge the electric vehicle and make a trade off between selling flexibility to other agents, and having the electric vehicle available for driving at all times. Our agent draws on real world carsharing data to make an accurate allocation and pricing decision. We use carsharing data where cars are rented on a minute or hour basis because it allows us to make a monetary tradeoff between the availability of electric vehicles and the benefit it has for the energy balancing market. On the one hand it learns when and where electric vehicles have a high probability to be rented out and on the other hand it learns from other agents how much it can earn from selling flexibility. Selling flexibility means that the electric vehicles are charged or discharged as usual, but the timing of the charging is flexible and coordinated with renewable energy sources, which is valuable for the grid operator. It turns out that this decision has asymmetric payoffs. Selling flexibility proves much less profitable than renting; the agent has to be very certain that an electric vehicle will not get rented out to make profits from selling flexibility. We use machine learning algorithms which are able to incorporate and predict these asymmetric payoffs and customer behavior as to maximize profits for the electric vehicle fleet agent.

3   Contribution

Our goals are to enable a sustainable energy system that will provide stable electricity output despite a high content of weather dependent renewable energy sources. With a smart coordination of electric vehicle charging and discharging this is possible, but is too tedious to be done manually because it needs to be done around the clock. Intelligent software agents that control the charging prove to be a reliable solution to do so. These are our preliminary conclusions from a simulation study using the large scale smart grid simulation Power TAC. Even though the agents that we have designed maximize their profits, the market in Power TAC is designed and optimized to simultaneously maximize the welfare for people, and the planet. We therefore use the triple bottom line account-ing method to account for the impact on people, planet, and profit. We are already able to demonstrate significant improvements for the grid and benefits for carsharing fleet owners in all three areas [4]. If our agents participate in the simulation people pay lower energy prices, there are fewer carbon emissions, and the agents in charge of electric vehicle fleets make a profit. Furthermore we have derived sustainable new revenue streams for electric vehicle rental companies without compromising their rental business (customer inconvenience). Besides, we are studying the limitations to profitability. We consider critical values for the prices that the market is willing to pay for flexibility on short term balanc-ing markets, how to account for battery degradation and the costs of replacing them, and how the infrastructure needs to develop in order to make this possi-ble in the first place. One limitation of is that we focus on carhsaring electric vehicles only. However, the rising popularity of carsharing and the tendency to move towards mobility rather than owning cars lead us to this design decision, as we are interested in future developments.

For future research we are interested in the impact of autonomous driving on the possibility of providing flexibility to the electrical grid with electric vehicles. Specifically, how one can reroute electric vehicles to different neighbourhoods and coordinating their operation with the charging process. Next, we are also interested in training agents not only to treat driving patterns as necessary, but to incentivize people to drive at times when the electric vehicles are needed for flexibility and to give them incentives to return electric vehicles to charging stations where they are most needed.

References

1. Bichler, M., Gupta, A., Ketter, W.: Designing smart markets. Inf. Syst. Res. **21**(4), 688–699 (2010)
2. Collins, J., Ketter, W.: Smart grid challenges for electricity retailers. KI-künstliche Intelligenz **21**(3), 191–198 (2014)
3. International Energy Agency: CO2 Emissions From Fuel Combustion Highlights 2014, OECD/IEA, Paris, France (2014)
4. Kahlen, M., Ketter, W.: Aggregating electric cars to sustainable virtual power plants: the value of flexibility in future electricity markets. In: Proceedings of the Association for the Advancement of Artificial Intelligence (AAAI) Conference, Austin, TX, pp. 665–671 (2015)
5. Ketter, W., Peters, M., Collins, J.: Autonomous agents in future energy markets: the 2012 power trading agent competition. In: Proceedings of the Association for the Advancement of Artificial Intelligence (AAAI) Conference, Bellevue, WA, pp. 1298–1304 (2013)
6. Ketter, W., Collins, J., Reddy, P., de Weerdt, M.: The 2015 Power Trading Agent Competition. Technical report, ERS-2015-001-LIS, RSM Erasmus University (2015)
7. Ramchurn, S., Vytelingum, P., Rogers, A., Jennings, N.: Agent-based control for decentralised demand side management in the smart grid. In: International Conference on Autonomous Agents and Multiagent Systems (AAMAS), Taipei, Taiwan, pp. 5–12 (2011)
8. Urieli, D., Stone, P.: TacTex13: A champion adaptive power trading agent. In: Proceedings of the Association for the Advancement of Artificial Intelligence (AAAI) Conference, Quebec, Canada, pp. 1447–1448 (2014)
9. Vytelingum, P., Voice, T., Ramchurn, S., Rogers, A., Jennings, N.: Theoretical and practical foundations of large-scale agent-based micro-storage in the smart grid. J. Artif. Intell. Res. **42**, 765–813 (2011)

Towards A Formal Model of Opportunism Based on Situation Calculus

Jieting Luo[⊠], Frank Dignum, and John-Jules Meyer

Utrecht University, PO Box 80089, 3508 TB Utrecht, The Netherlands
{J.Luo,F.P.M.Dignum,J.J.C.Meyer}@uu.nl

1 Introduction

Opportunism is a social behavior that achieves own gains at the expense of others. In this study, we propose a formal model of opportunism, which consists of the properties knowledge asymmetry, value opposition and intention, based on situation calculus.

Consider a common social interaction. A seller sells a cup to a buyer. It is known only by the seller beforehand that the cup is actually broken. The buyer buys the cup for its good appearance, but of course gets disappointed when he uses it. In this example, the seller earns money from the buyer by exploiting the opportunity of knowledge asymmetry about the cup. Such a social behavior intentionally performed by the seller is named by economist Williamson as opportunism [1]. Opportunistic behavior commonly exists in business transactions and other types of social interactions in various forms such as deceit, lying and betraying. Viewing individuals as agents, we may have similar problems in multi-agent system research. Interacting agents were modeled to behave in a human-like way with characteristics of autonomy, local views and decentralization [2]. When such agents possess different amounts of relevant information and try to maximize their benefits, they may probably behave opportunistically to others, which is against others' benefits or the norms of the system.

In order to explore this problem, we first need to have a formal specification of opportunism so that we can understand more clearly the elements in the definition and how they constitute this social behavior. More importantly, we can derive interesting properties that are useful for our future research such as better understanding where and when opportunism arises, automatically detecting opportunism in (computer-based) human interactions, or designing agents that are (or are not) opportunistic. Therefore, in this extended abstract we present a basic formal definition of opportunism with the notion of value, which outlines the elements knowledge asymmetry, value opposition and intention that should be represented in the model, thus introducing the first step towards building a formal model of opportunism.

2 Defining Opportunism with Value

The classical definition of opportunism is offered by Williamson [1] as "self-interest seeking with guile". While this definition has been used in a large amount

© Springer International Publishing Switzerland 2015
J.P. Müller et al. (Eds.): MATES 2015, LNAI 9433, pp. 275–279, 2015.
DOI: 10.1007/978-3-319-27343-3_16

of research, it only makes two attributes, self-interest and guile, explicit, leaving other attributes for researchers to interpret from different perspectives. In this study, based on the definition of Williamson, we redefine this social behavior in a more explicit way:

Opportunism is a behavior that is motivated by self-interest and takes advantage of relevant knowledge asymmetry[1] to achieve gains, regardless of the principles.

From this informal definition, it is clear that opportunistic behavior is performed with self-interest motivation in the precondition knowledge asymmetry, ignoring the results to others. Furthermore, although we did not explicitly declare the effect of such behavior, it must result in gains at the expense of others.

Value is something that we think is important, and various types of values together with their orderings form a value system. By integrating the notion of value into our model, the result of performing opportunistic behavior is represented as the promotion of opportunistic individuals' value and the demotion of others' value. Furthermore, even though a value system is relatively stable for individuals, it may differ across different individuals and societies. For societies, each has its own value system as part of the social context and it serves as the basis for any judgment within the society. In this sense, some behaviors which are regarded as opportunistic in one society may not be considered as opportunistic in another society, if the two societies do not share the same value system. Given the value system of the society, opportunistic behavior promotes the self-interest which is in opposition with others' value.

3   Formalizing Opportunism

Our formalization of opportunism is based on situation calculus, a formal language for representing and reasoning about dynamical domains based on first-order logic [3–5]. There are three sorts: actions A that can be performed by agents, situations S representing a history of action occurrences and objects for everything else. Situation S_0 represents the initial situation that no action can result in. The special predicate $do(a, s)$ denotes the unique situation that results from the performing of action a in situation s. Symbol $Poss(a, s)$ represents the set of preconditions to perform action a in situation s. The properties of situations are specified through relational and functional fluents taking a situation term as their last argument, which means their truth value may vary from situation to situation. With situation calculus, we can reason about how the world changes by actions. After John McCarthy's introduction of this theory, people made extensions capable of representing knowledge, belief, intention and obligation in order to better reason about actions and their effects on the world [6–9].

---

[1] Many papers in social science use information asymmetry to represent the situation where one party in a transaction knows more compared to another. We argue that once the information is stored in our mind and can be used appropriately it becomes our knowledge. For this reason, we would rather revise the term as knowledge asymmetry in this paper, which is also consistent with our technical framework.

We will introduce and adopt those modalities $Know$ and $Intend$ as appropriate. Since in situation calculus the last argument is always a situation, we will follow this convention for any definition of fluents and predicates.

Relevant knowledge asymmetry provides the chance to individuals to be opportunistic. Opportunistic individuals may break the contracts or the relational norms using the relevant knowledge that others don't have. We first adopt the epistemic fluent $Know(\phi, s)$ from [7],

$$Know(i, \phi, s) \stackrel{def}{=} (\forall s')K_i(s', s) \rightarrow \phi[s']$$

where $K(s', s)$ is a binary relation reading as situation s' is epistemically accessible from situation s. This definition shows that an agent has knowledge about ϕ if and only if ϕ holds in all the epistemic possible situations of the agent. Then we can have the definition of knowledge asymmetry:

$$KnowAsym(i, j, \phi, s) \stackrel{def}{=} Know_i(\phi, s) \wedge \neg Know_j(\phi, s) \wedge Know_i(\neg Know_j(\phi, s), s)$$

It is a fluent expressing in situation s where agent i has knowledge about ϕ while j does not have.

Using the notion of value, the effect of performing opportunistic behavior can be represented as: agent i's value gets promoted, while agent j's value gets demoted, as they evaluate the state transition by the behavior from their own perspectives. This property of a state transition is named value opposition in this study. In order to represent it, we first define a symbol $\mathcal{V}$ to denote agents' value, and then a functional fluent $Eval : \mathcal{A} \times \mathcal{V} \times \mathcal{S} \rightarrow \mathfrak{R}$ which returns a real number that represents an agent's evaluation over his value about a specific situation. Based on it, we define value opposition for a state transition:

$$ValueOppo(i, j, v, s, s') \stackrel{def}{=} Eval(i, v, s) < Eval(i, v, s') \wedge Eval(j, v, s) > Eval(j, v, s')$$

This is a property of state transitions where a state transition from s to s' promotes value v from the perspective of agent i but demotes value v from the perspective of agent j.

As our informal definition suggests, opportunistic behavior is performed by intent rather than by accident. We adopt the definition of intention from [8],

$$Intend(i, a, \phi, s) \stackrel{def}{=} (\forall s')I_i(s', s) \rightarrow done(a, s') \wedge \phi[s, s']$$

where $I(s', s)$ is the intentional accessibility relation, and $done(a, s')$ is true when action a is finished in situation s', and ϕ is true for the state transition from s to s'. Based on it, we have instances for value promotion $pro(j, v) = Eval(j, v, s) < Eval(j, v, s')$ and value demotion $de(j, v) = Eval(j, v, s) > Eval(j, v, s')$ by action a:

$$Intend(i, a, pro(j, v), s) \stackrel{def}{=} (\forall s')I_i(s', s) \rightarrow done(a, s') \wedge Eval(j, v, s) < Eval(j, v, s')$$

$$Intend(i, a, de(j, v), s) \stackrel{def}{=} (\forall s')I_i(s', s) \rightarrow done(a, s') \wedge Eval(j, v, s) > Eval(j, v, s')$$

$Intend(i, a, pro(j, v), s)$ denotes that agent i intends to promote the value of agent j by action a in situation s. Similar for $Intend(i, a, de(j, v), s)$. When $i = j$, agent i intends to promote or demote his own value by action a.

The above definitions are pivotal elements that we need for having the formal model of opportunism: knowledge asymmetry as the precondition, value opposition as the effect, and intention as the mental state. Besides, based on the informal definition we gave in Sect. 2, there are two more aspects that should be suggested in the definition. Firstly, the asymmetric knowledge should be relevant to the state transition. Secondly, opportunistic agents are aware of the result caused by the behavior beforehand but still ignores it. Opportunism is defined as follows:

$$Opportunism(i, j, a, s) \overset{def}{=} (\exists v \in V)(Poss(i, j, a, s) \equiv KnowAsym(i, j, \phi, s)) \wedge$$
$$Intend(i, a, pro(i, v), s) \wedge \phi$$
$$where\ \phi = ValueOppo(i, j, v, s, do(a, s)).$$

This formula defines a predicate $Opportunism$ where action a is performed by agent i in the situation s. The precondition of action a is knowledge asymmetry about the state transition from s to $do(a, s)$, and action a is performed by intent and results in value opposition.

One observation from the model is about the subjectivity of opportunism. We can see through the functional fluent $Eval$ that agents always evaluate the situations and consequently the state transition from their own perspectives. If the value systems upon which they have evaluation change to another, the property value opposition may be false. Our formalization also captures an interesting property. Given an opportunistic behavior a performed by agent i to agent j in situation s, it is not the intention, but the knowledge, of agent i to cause harm to agent j. This is characterized by:

$$\vDash Opportunism(i, j, a, s) \rightarrow Know_i(de(j, v), s)$$
$$\nvDash Opportunism(i, j, a, s) \rightarrow Intend(i, a, de(j, v), s)$$

The core of the proof lies in the distinct relations of knowledge and intention. Certainly more interesting properties exist, but lie beyond the scope of this extended abstract.

4   Conclusion

This extended abstract took the initiative to propose a formal model of opportunism based on the extended informal definition from Williamson and situation calculus. Through the model, we showed the subjectivity of opportunistic behavior and an interesting property that the asymmetric knowledge owned by agents is the knowledge about the state transition, rather than the intention of opportunism. It is important to keep in mind that this is the first step of our investigation about opportunism and we try to present a fundamental approach that can be later extended to many contexts and scenarios. We plan to elaborate the formalization and build a formal system based on it.

References

1. Williamson, O.E.: Markets and Hierarchies, Analysis and Antitrust Implications: A Study in the Economics of Internal Organization. New York (1975)
2. Wooldridge, M.: An Introduction to Multiagent Systems. Wiley, New York (2009)
3. McCarthy, J., Hayes, P.J.: Some philosophical problems from the standpoint of artificial intelligence. In: Readings in Artificial Intelligence, pp. 431–450 (1969)
4. Reiter, R.: The frame problem in the situation calculus: A simple solution (sometimes) and a completeness result for goal regression. In: Artificial Intelligence and Mathematical Theory of Computation: Papers in Honor of John McCarthy, vol. 27, pp. 359–380 (1991)
5. Levesque, H., Pirri, F., Reiter, R.: Foundations for the situation calculus. In: Linkping Electronic Articles in Computer and Information Science, vol. 3, Issue 18 (1998)
6. Shapiro, S., Pagnucco, M., Lesprance, Y., Levesque, H.J.: Iterated belief change in the situation calculus. Artif. Intell. 175(1), 165–192 (2011)
7. Scherl, R.B., Levesque, H.J.: Knowledge, action, and the frame problem. Artif. Intell. 144(1), 1–39 (2003)
8. Parra, P.P., Nayak, A.C., Demolombe, R.: Theories of intentions in the framework of situation calculus. In: Leite, J., Omicini, A., Torroni, P., Yolum, I. (eds.) DALT 2004. LNCS (LNAI), vol. 3476, pp. 19–34. Springer, Heidelberg (2005)
9. Demolombe, R., Parra, P.P.: Integrating state constraints and obligations in situation calculus. Inteligencia Artif. Rev. Iberoamericana de Inteligencia Artif. 13(41), 54–63 (2009)

Adaptive Services Reconfiguration in Manufacturing Environments Using a Multi-agent System Approach

Nelson Rodrigues[1,2(✉)], Paulo Leitão[1,2], and Eugénio Oliveira[2,3]

[1] Polytechnic Institute of Bragança, Campus Sta Apolonia,
Apartado 1134, 5301-857 Bragança, Portugal
{nrodrigues,pleitao}@ipb.pt
[2] Artificial Intelligence and Computer Science Laboratory,
Porto, Portugal
eco@fe.up.pt
[3] Faculty of Engineering, University of Porto,
Rua Dr. Roberto Frias s/n, 4200-465 Porto, Portugal

Abstract. The era of mass customization of goods forces manufacturing systems to promote agility, flexibility and responsiveness, leading to complex and unpredictable systems. Such challenges have an impact in terms of the system responsiveness and adaptation, production costs, product quality, etc. In order to improve those aspects, some flexible control manufacturing paradigms were proposed offering elasticity to change available skills and provide new services. However, the understanding of when and how to (self-) reconfigure the system aiming to perform a fast changeover, is a crucial issue. This work proposes a self-organizing multi-agent system approach for an efficient and on the fly reconfiguration of services in the manufacturing domain. Besides self-organizing techniques, other dimensions, e.g., "social-based" trust and QoS metrics, are used to ensure a constant QoS in an agile production system. The insertion of intelligent agents facilitates the improvement of strategies that perform the service reconfiguration, and in addition, permits to understand when and how self-reconfiguration takes place in order to allow a continuous improvement of the system performance. Additionally, this work addresses solutions for real industrial applications, being aligned with some characteristics of the Industrie 4.0 initiative, namely the distributed intelligence and self-* methods, e.g. self-adaptation, self-organization and self-configuration.

1 Introduction

Nowadays, due to the growing interest of customized products/services, companies are forced to deliver high quality products facing the clients' requirements at short time. These complex and dynamic environments are usually favourable to perturbations, such as broken machines, performance deviations and new product/service demand, which requires adaptive and responsive systems. Given this fact, several researchers suggest tackling this problem by considering new manufacturing paradigms that provide more flexibility, robustness and re-configurability, e.g. Flexible Manufacturing

© Springer International Publishing Switzerland 2015
J.P. Müller et al. (Eds.): MATES 2015, LNAI 9433, pp. 280–284, 2015.
DOI: 10.1007/978-3-319-27343-3_17

Systems (FMS) [1], Reconfigurable Manufacturing Systems (RMS) [2] and Evolvable Manufacturing Systems (EPS) [3]. Typically, the implementation of such paradigms mitigates the performance deviations that will delay the product delivery. To tackle this sort of dynamic environments, mechanisms for service reconfiguration were analysed. The adaptation performed on the demand and the provided services, transforms the way the system works. There are already some projects addressing the service reconfiguration in manufacturing, namely IMC-AESOP (www.imc-aesop.eu) that addresses continuous monitoring and self-adaptation functions and FP6-SOCRADES (www.socrades.eu) that is oriented to smart embedded devices with enterprise applications [4]. More recently, the PRIME project (www.prime-eu.com) relies on a plug and produce architecture for assembly systems, where automatic reconfiguration is mainly performed at the design phase. The proposed approach takes a step forward by evaluating potential possibilities in advance, having the capability to self-reconfigure the multi-agent system by performing run-time adaptation in the agents' behaviours without the need to stop or re-program, reducing the perturbation impact and decreasing the need of external intervention. The analysis of the state of the art shows that it is worth studying *"when should the system evolve"*, and *"how should the system be reconfigured in order to adapt and becoming more profitable"*, without compromising the quality of the product agreed. Thereby, intelligent agents are designed to manage the device functionalities, which are encapsulated as services and are offered to other agents that can invoke them according to their needs. The agents can improve their functionalities and publish them across the network of agents as new services, permitting new service compositions that allow to meet the desired quality. This approach is not the solution for all reconfiguration problems, but it offers a continuous and intelligent adjustment of triggers for the reconfiguration process, supported by the inclusion of the following main capabilities:

(i)   Learning mechanisms to assist the identification of opportunities to perform the reconfiguration.
(ii) Self-organization principles to support the adaptation and evolution of the service composition in a dynamic and automatic manner.
(iii) Quality of service (QoS) provides metrics to quantitatively measure the quality of the generated service compositions. The QoS metrics join several non-functional attributes, such as execution time, cost and availability as well as trust evaluation for the judgment of the dynamic behaviours.

By using the previous capabilities, the system becomes more efficient, adaptive and responsive, and consequently promoting a competitive advantage by offering re-configurability benefits [3, 5].

2   Proposal

Traditional solutions, which rely on centralized decisions, provide good optimization results under static operational conditions but fail to respond promptly to dynamic plan disruption, unexpected disturbances or production changeovers. We propose a dynamic approach consisting in the reconfiguration of services provided and performed by intelligent and autonomous agents. In a simple manner, each agent drives the continuous self-adaptive reconfiguration process based on the potential improvement of the system efficiency. Based on [6], two types of adaptation were selected to drive the system into a more beneficial state, namely (i) changing its functionalities to provide better services (behavioural adaptation), and (ii) changing the selection of service providers to provide a better composed service (structural adaptation). The strategies about when and how to execute the self-reconfiguration require concepts well known from Service-oriented Architectures (SOA), namely service discovery, service monitoring, service composition and service orchestration. These concepts are logically set up in the behaviour of the agents to support the expected reconfiguration (see Fig. 1).

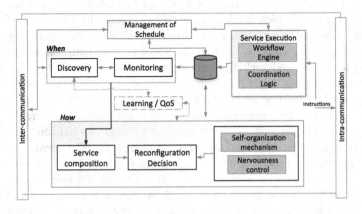

Fig. 1. Architecture for a generic agent

The reconfiguration process can be reached by different triggers from different agent's roles for example: (i) when the agent is performing the role of a service provider, i.e. providing atomic or composite services and (ii) when the agent is performing the role of service consumer, i.e. requesting composite services or atomic services as well. Despite the type of role played, it is vital to recognize when the adaptation should be performed. Four situations were identified:

1. Promote new composite services periodically, triggering the division of the composite services into atomic components allowing to test new combinations of service compositions with different levels of granularity.
2. Discover new services (discovery behaviour), allowing to perceive modification on available services and recognize new service providers, by searching in the service repository or announcing to the other agent's network the intention to discover a specific service.
3. Detect the degradation of the service's efficiency (monitoring behaviour), which needs data analytic methods that are running continuously.
4. Recognize a new service demand (discovery behaviour), which realizes the need to adapt the provided services to meet a new service reconfiguration.

To cope with the "how to make the composition" question, concepts of service composition using top-down approaches with template-based or bottom-up approaches using Artificial Intelligence methods were analysed together with self-organization mechanisms. This inspiration on self-organization techniques allows to regulate the service composition in environments where it is difficult to predict the global behaviour (e.g. the overall production plan). Looking from a high-level perspective, the structural adaptation works at the system level with a strong dependency on the physical layer. The addition or removal of physical components in the system, is another responsibility of the structural adaptation. This type of adaptation also has a larger impact on the behavioural system adaptation that works at the operational level by adjusting the provided services (e.g. add/remove/modify services).

In order to permit the module "when" to recognize unexpected events and react appropriately to them, it was considered a learning mechanism. Basically, due to the impossibility and uncertainty to model the entire world together with the self-organization mechanism, a reinforcement learning algorithm was adopted, in particular the Q-learning for modelling the feedbacks of the service performance. The feedback values results into a set of non-functional criteria, e.g., service response time, throughput and availability. Additionally, different kind of input values, like trust and reputation associated to the provided services, can also be considered by the Q-learning algorithm. The adopted trust model holds the historical knowledge about the services executed in specific contexts, e.g. process plans, set of involved machines, different configurations, etc. The outcome of the learning algorithm allows to select an accurate reconfiguration trigger. In parallel, the same result also represents a context awareness reconfiguration, which is an important characteristic to tune the nervousness module, and allows to decide if continuing using the old settings or to explore potential new solutions. The intra-/inter-communication modules permit the interaction with other agents and physical devices, and lastly the service execution is responsible to execute the requested service.

All these modules are independently designed, creating a generic architecture capable to offer a solution for the dynamic reorganization of the manufacturing system based on the adaptation and reconfiguration of services provided by intelligence of agents. Particularly, a real flexible manufacturing cell [7] has been considered for the evaluation of our proposal, for example, in terms of the downtime impact caused by production variations [8]. Briefly, each machine is controlled by an agent that provides a given set of services that are necessary for the production process; agents are responsible to verify the need for service reconfiguration, adapting their skills and behaviour accordingly and efficiently.

3 Conclusions and Future Work

The described research work explores the automatic service reconfiguration applied to a flexible manufacturing system to cope with the challenges that arises from disturbances or production changeovers. For this purpose, multi-agent systems and service-oriented principles are combined to properly solve the dynamic reconfiguration of services. It is also promoted on the agents, the need for service adaptation in order to meet given requirements in the presence of uncertainty. This implies not only the identification of opportunities when the agents should reconfigure their services, but also how to maintain the desired quality of products and at the same time become more valuable by providing different services. In this sense, the agents adapt and work together as a global behaviour, after recognizing opportunities or after the plug-in or plug-out of hardware components. Such continuous cooperation among the agents reinforce the system towards a better state. As future work, a further specification of the architecture will be conducted as well as its implementation and validation into different case studies.

References

1. El Maraghy, H.A.: Flexible and reconfigurable manufacturing systems paradigms. Flex. Serv. Manuf. J. **17**, 261–276 (2006)
2. Koren, Y., Heisel, U., Jovane, F., Moriwaki, T., Pritschow, G., Ulsoy, G., Van Brussel, H.: Reconfigurable manufacturing systems. CIRP Ann. Manuf. Technol. **48**, 527–540 (1999)
3. Ribeiro, L., Barata, J., Colombo, A.: MAS and SOA: a case study exploring principles and technologies to support self-properties in assembly systems. In: Self-Adaptive and Self-Organizing Systems Workshops, 2008. (SASOW 2008), pp. 192–197 (2008)
4. Cannata, A., Gerosa, M., Taisch, M.: SOCRADES: a framework for developing intelligent systems in manufacturing. In: Industrial Engineering and Engineering Management, 2008. IEEM 2008, pp. 1904–1908 (2008)
5. Leitao, P., Marik, V., Vrba, P.: Past, present, and future of industrial agent applications. IEEE Trans. Industr. Inf. pp. 1–11 (2012)
6. Dignum, V., Dignum, F., Sonenberg, L.: Towards dynamic reorganization of agent societies. In: Proceedings of Workshop on Coordination in Emergent Agent Societies 2004, pp. 22–27 (2004)
7. Trentesaux, D., Pach, C., Bekrar, A., Sallez, Y., Berger, T., Bonte, T., Leitão, P., Barbosa, J.: Benchmarking flexible job-shop scheduling and control systems. Control Eng. Pract. **21**(9), 1204–1225 (2013)
8. Rodrigues, N., Leitão, P., Oliveira, E.: Self-interested service-oriented agents based on trust and QoS for dynamic reconfiguration. In: Service Orientation in Holonic and Multi-Agent Manufacturing (SOHOMA 2014), Nice, France (2014)

Hydrogen: A Fuel Option to Future Transportation as a Part of Smart Grid

Serkan Özdemir[✉] and Rainer Unland

DAWIS, University of Duisburg-Essen,
Schützenbahn 70, 45127 Essen, Germany
{serkan.oezdemir, rainer.unland}@icb.uni-due.de

Abstract. Fossil based liquid fuels, primarily used in transportation systems, are likely to be replaced with renewable resources thanks to energy transition policies. However, shifting from stable energy production (using coal, natural gas) to highly volatile renewable production will bring a number of problems as well. On the other side, tremendous developments in solar and wind power technologies encourage energy investors to maximize their contributions over the electricity grid. This highly volatile energy resources bring a strong research question to the attention: How to benefit from excess energy? Power-to-gas seems to be a strong candidate to store excess energy. Besides, power-to-hydrogen is seen as a liquid fuel for fuel cell vehicles. This work aims to analyze hydrogen as a future fuel option. Additionally, the role of energy markets, on-site production, renewable penetrations, investment and optimization problems will be also covered under this research. This research will reveal the feasibility of hydrogen as a fuel option in future smart grid.

Keywords: Hydrogen · Transportation · Multi-agent · Simulation · Power to gas

1 Introduction

Due to energy transition policies of governments and recent developments in renewable energy technologies, fossil and nuclear based power plants tend to be replaced with renewable resources. Recent developments show that the number of installed capacity will dramatically increase in the near future. Solar siding and roof-top panel technologies are rapidly growing since they have a large footprint compared to other renewable resources. This work assumes that energy transition will shift towards renewables as already planned by many countries.

In case of high renewable penetration, future smart grid will face with a number of challenges, such as meeting the supply and demand in balance. Since the renewable energy production is highly weather-depended, a distributed energy storage is needed at off-peak hours or days to benefit from excess energy. Among other storage options, power-to-gas has the most storage capacity over other technologies [1, 9, 15]. The first step product of power-to-gas, obtained through electrolysis process, can be used as fuel in fuel cell vehicles. This way is more efficient than methane in terms of energy loss. Hydrogen is also nature friendly fuel and the output of fuel cell vehicles is only water.

© Springer International Publishing Switzerland 2015
J.P. Müller et al. (Eds.): MATES 2015, LNAI 9433, pp. 285–289, 2015.
DOI: 10.1007/978-3-319-27343-3_18

However hydrogen cannot be delivered to far away due to high pressure problems. For this reason, on-site production is proposed for hydrogen [8, 9, 11].

Fuel cell vehicles are not competitors of battery electric vehicles. Because fuel cells are also a battery electric vehicles. In addition to battery electric vehicles, they have high pressure hydrogen tank and fuel cell stack which converts hydrogen into electricity. For this reason, fuel cell can be solution to charging, efficiency and driving-range problems of battery electric vehicles (BEV) [12, 13].

This works aims to analyze hydrogen production through electrolysis process on the city level. Power Trading Agent Competition (Power TAC) is selected to simulate future smart grid conditions [16, 17]. A hydrogen station is designed as a server module in which a number of fuel cell and conventional vehicles are simulated. Refilling station consists of an electrolysis unit, high pressure storage unit, dispensers and on-site renewable resources. The station is an active participant of a local wholesale market. The wholesale market is a typical hour-ahead market which allows participants to submit orders 24 h prior to delivery. Technical details and methodology are explained in Sect. 3.

2 State of the Art

Both power-to-hydrogen (PtH$_2$) and fuel cells are quite old concepts. Basically, the electrolysis extracts water into oxygen and hydrogen ($H_2O \rightarrow H_2 + O$). Among different electrolysis approaches, alkaline electrolysis is the most common one in use. Conversion efficiency rate depends on the load, but the typical rate is 60-70 % at full load. Hydrogen can be also injected into natural gas grid [14]. In a typical PtH$_2$ power plant, investment and operation-management costs have severe roles on the profitability of the plant. Following table shows the basic inputs and outputs of a PtH$_2$ power plant (Table 1).

Table 1. Inputs and Outputs of a PtH2 power plant and fuel station.

	Today	2030
Investment (electrolysis) (IC$_e$) [8]	1750 EUR/kW$_{input}$	700 EUR/kW$_{input}$
Investment (refueling st. + storage) (IC$_{rs}$) [3]	16 % of IC$_e$	8 % of IC$_e$
Operational costs [10]	3 % of IC$_e$ + IC$_{rs}$	
Water consumption	0.2 l/kW$_{input}$	
Hydrogen production	1 kg/48 kW	-0.492
Oxygen output	6 kg/48 kW	-1.281
Useful heat	11 % of input.	
Wholesale market fees	15000-25000 EUR/year [7, 8]	
Recurring market and grid fees, taxes	0.1-0.2 EUR/MWh	Possible incentives.

Besides the advantages of CO2 emission level and driving range, fuel cells also performs a promising well-to-wheel performance for the future transportation. Following table compares roughly the well-to-wheel performances of fuel cell vehicles, battery electric vehicles and diesel vehicles (Table 2).

Table 2. Comparison of different fuel types. Reference vehicles are B segment economy cars of Mercedes, Toyota and Hyundai.

	Fuel Cell Vehicle	Battery Electric vehicle	Diesel Vehicle
Range (100 km)	1 kg H_2 (48 kWh el. input)	18 kWh	5 liter
Well-to-wheel wholesale[a]	1.2 EUR	0.62 EUR	2.9 EUR [2]
Well-to-wheel retail	9 EUR [4]	4.68 EUR [5]	5.75 EUR [6]

[a] The row indicates wholesale costs without taxes, profits and service fees.

There are a number of possible incentives that are subject to PtH_2 plants. However, on the legal side, some are not matured due to uncertainties on the future fuel options. But the good news is, there are many ongoing acts regarding to hydrogen fuel utilizing renewable electricity. Currently, many companies, such as OMV, Hydrogenics, Toyota and e-on are active in the hydrogen business by producing fuel cell cars, power plants and refilling stations.

On the other side, energy markets have the vital role on power-to-gas power plants and will be more important in the future due to high fluctuations. In the current situation, electric vehicles are exposed to retailer prices since it is not possible for each electric vehicle to trade in wholesale markets. Unlike electric vehicles, power-to-gas power plants and their refilling stations are able to trade in energy markets. For this reason, fuel cell transportation is seen as one of the strongest candidates for the future transportation system.

3 Methodology

In order to analyze hydrogen as a fuel option, a Power TAC server module is created. This module simulates a hydrogen refilling station and on-site hydrogen production. Local wholesale market and on-site renewables are electricity resources of hydrogen production. Note that Power TAC is simulated on the city level with a population of about 50 thousand residents, which fits to on-site PtH_2 power plant scenario since the long-haul distribution of hydrogen is not possible [14].

The proposed refilling station simulates the following components:

- Electrolysis Unit: Converts input power to hydrogen having an efficiency rate which depends on the size of electrolysis unit and input power.
- Hydrogen Storage Unit: This unit stores the produced hydrogen thorough electrolysis process. It also supplies hydrogen to dispensers.
- Dispensers: Final end-point where refilling hydrogen to simulated fuel cell vehicles takes place.
- A number of fuel cell and traditional vehicles.
- On-site solar panels and wind mills which supply electricity to electrolysis unit.
- Trader module: Trades in the wholesale market and optimize the costs considering various variables and on-site production.

Trading in the wholesale market is the most significant part of the research since the motivation of the research is to benefit from the excess energy. Unlike electricity retailers, hydrogen trader unit can make flexible decisions and watch cheap prices at future hours thanks to its hydrogen storage unit. Storage unit can easily tolerate several time slots to let trader unit find cheaper energy in an hour-ahead market. To coordinate these facilities, two methods are proposed. One of them is "Markov Decision Process" with Q-learning. In this approach, all hours are represented as 24 individual processes. Each process has 25 states which represent the time slot proximity as well as "success" state. Other method is "Fuzzy Cognitive Maps" to take multiple variables into account. Weather forecasts, production and consumption volumes are the examples of entities in a cognitive map.

Proposed design above enables various studies from different perspectives. First, a legal landscape (taxation, incentives and transition policies) and a future projection will be covered under this research. Second, renewables have to be taken into account deeply since they are the main drivers of the future energy production. Within this scope, all of penetration levels will be simulated with the proposed trading methods. Third, size of refilling station, such size of electrolysis unit, storage unit, dispensers and so on, will be subject to an optimization problem considering investment and operational costs.

This work aims to control a number of variables.

- Size of electrolysis unit (MW). An electrolysis unit is the most efficient at 25 % electricity input.
- Size of hydrogen storage (kg). A bigger size of storage unit can put trader unit into a more flexible position.
- Share of vehicle groups. Percentages of fuel cells, battery electric vehicles and traditional vehicles among all passenger vehicles (cars, buses, vans).
- Production volume (including local producers). Various production rates will be subject to experiments.
- Distribution fee. This fee is paid if the bought energy is originated from wholesale market. Incentives can waive this fee.
- Trading approaches. These approaches will be defined in Markov processes later on.
- Number of retailer/broker companies.

All of these variables are controlled to optimize the cost and investment problems as well as further possible analysis. Existing works in the literature are usually based on the static data or estimations. Power-to-gas is usually considered as a profitability problem or balancing approach which are far away from transportation perspective.

In summary, the smart grid will bring a lot of benefits such as excess energy. On the other side, fuel cells have all the functionalities of a battery electric vehicle in addition to hydrogen storage and fuel cell stack. This capability provides opportunity to drive with hydrogen or electricity no matter which one is available in the vehicle. Obviously, both ways are nature friendly and do not replace each other.

References

1. Hall, P., Bain, P.: Energy-storage technologies and electricity generation. Elsevier, Oxford (2008)
2. Mineralölwirtschaftsverbande. V. Statistiken–Preise, 03 December 2014. http://www.mwv. de/index.php/daten/statistikenpreise/?loc=1
3. Pure Energy Centre. Hydrogen refueling station, 05 December 2014. http://pureenergycentre. com/hydrogen-fueling-station/
4. Kurier. Erste Wasserstoff-Tankstelle: Künftig tanken wir Kilos, 12 December 2014. http:// kurier.at/wirtschaft/1-wasserstoff-tankstelle-kuenftig-tanken-wir-kilos/824.355
5. Verivox. Direktvergleich, 24 November 2014. http://www.verivox.de/strompreisvergleich
6. Clever Tanken. Aktuelle Diesel, Benzinpreise, 11 December 2014. http://www.clever-tanken.de
7. Nord Pool Spot. Nordic and Baltic Trading Fees, 11 December 2014. http://www. nordpoolspot.com/TAS/Fees/Nordic-Baltic/
8. EPEX Spot. Price List, 14 December 2014. http://static.epexspot.com/document/29089/ EPEXSPOT_Price_List_January_2015.pdf
9. Federal Ministry of Transport and Digital Infrastructure (BMVI). Power-to-Gas (PtG) in transport: Status quo and perspectives for development. Berlin (2014)
10. National Renewable Energy Laboratory. Hydrogen Station Compression, Storage, and Dispensing Technical Status and Costs (2014)
11. Zero Regio. The future cost and competitiveness of hydrogen as a transport fuel in Europe (2010)
12. Lizbeth, C.G.M.: Assessment of usage of hydrogen as alternative fuel into NETPLAN (Ph. D. dissertation). Iowa State University (2013)
13. Fuel Cell Today. Water Electrolysis & Renewable Energy Systems (2013)
14. Sterner, M.: Power-to-Gas: Perspektiven einer jungen Technologie (2013)
15. Reichert, F., Brian, V.M.: Wind-to-Gas-to-Money? Economics and Perspectives of the Power-to-Gas Technology (master thesis). Aalborg University (2012)
16. Ketter, W., Collins, J., Reddy, P.P., Weerdt, M.D.: The 2015 Power Trading Agent Competition. ERIM Report Series Reference No. ERS-2015-001-LIS (2015)
17. Ketter, W., Collins, J., Reddy, P.: Power TAC: A competitive economic simulation of the smart grid. Energy Econ. **39**, 262–270 (2013)

Author Index

Printed in the United States
By Bookmasters